THE COMPLETE IDIOT'S GUIDE® TO

# Lean Six Sigma

by Breakthrough Management Group
with Neil DeCarlo

ALPHA

A member of Penguin Group (USA) Inc.

*To Jeannie, who was there with me every step of the way while writing, editing, and assembling this book.*
*Neil DeCarlo*

*Dedicated to my grandmother, Helen Albert, who recently passed away, just four months after her 100th birthday. She is one of my heroes, and her memory always will bring a smile to my face. Tom Jones*

*Thanks to my wife, Anita, for supporting my career decisions landing me in Six Sigma, and to my daughter Holly and son Adam, who confirmed that 10-year-olds can apply these techniques better than some engineers. A special mention goes to Doug Rausch for proving that breakthroughs can happen in a week using these tools. Don Wilson*

*Written only with the loving support and patience of my wife Chihiro, daughter Reina, and son Rio.*
*Chris Hodges*

## ALPHA BOOKS

Published by the Penguin Group

Penguin Group (USA) Inc., 375 Hudson Street, New York, New York 10014, USA

Penguin Group (Canada), 90 Eglinton Avenue East, Suite 700, Toronto, Ontario M4P 2Y3, Canada (a division of Pearson Penguin Canada Inc.)

Penguin Books Ltd., 80 Strand, London WC2R 0RL, England

Penguin Ireland, 25 St. Stephen's Green, Dublin 2, Ireland (a division of Penguin Books Ltd.)

Penguin Group (Australia), 250 Camberwell Road, Camberwell, Victoria 3124, Australia (a division of Pearson Australia Group Pty. Ltd.)

Penguin Books India Pvt. Ltd., 11 Community Centre, Panchsheel Park, New Delhi—110 017, India

Penguin Group (NZ), 67 Apollo Drive, Rosedale, North Shore, Auckland 1311, New Zealand (a division of Pearson New Zealand Ltd.)

Penguin Books (South Africa) (Pty.) Ltd., 24 Sturdee Avenue, Rosebank, Johannesburg 2196, South Africa

Penguin Books Ltd., Registered Offices: 80 Strand, London WC2R 0RL, England

## Copyright © 2007 by Breakthrough Management Group

International Standard Book Number: 978-1-59257-594-7
Library of Congress Catalog Card Number: 2006936695

15          15   14

Interpretation of the printing code: The rightmost number of the first series of numbers is the year of the book's printing; the rightmost number of the second series of numbers is the number of the book's printing. For example, a printing code of 07-1 shows that the first printing occurred in 2007.

*Printed in the United States of America*

**Note:** This publication contains the opinions and ideas of its author. It is intended to provide helpful and informative material on the subject matter covered. It is sold with the understanding that the author and publisher are not engaged in rendering professional services in the book. If the reader requires personal assistance or advice, a competent professional should be consulted.

The author and publisher specifically disclaim any responsibility for any liability, loss, or risk, personal or otherwise, which is incurred as a consequence, directly or indirectly, of the use and application of any of the contents of this book.

Most Alpha books are available at special quantity discounts for bulk purchases for sales promotions, premiums, fund-raising, or educational use. Special books, or book excerpts, can also be created to fit specific needs.

For details, write: Special Markets, Alpha Books, 375 Hudson Street, New York, NY 10014.

**Publisher:** *Marie Butler-Knight*
**Editorial Director/Acquiring Editor:** *Mike Sanders*
**Managing Editor:** *Billy Fields*
**Development Editor:** *Nancy D. Lewis*
**Senior Production Editor:** *Janette Lynn*
**Copy Editor:** *Amy Borrelli*

**Cartoonist:** *Shannon Wheeler*
**Book Designer:** *Trina Wurst*
**Cover Designer:** *Kurt Owens*
**Indexer:** *Brad Herriman*
**Layout:** *Ayanna Lacey*
**Proofreader:** *John Etchison*

# Contents at a Glance

**Part 1:** **Understanding Lean Six Sigma**     1

1   What Is Lean?     3
*See how Henry Ford and a guy named Taiichi Ohno set the stage for a productivity revolution.*

2   The Basics of Lean     11
*Lean makes your processes flow like a river, with no resistance or waste.*

3   What Is Six Sigma?     23
*Hint: Six Sigma has something to do with statistics and the reduction of variation.*

4   The Basics of Six Sigma     35
*To be world-class, your processes will have to produce no more than 3.4 defects or errors per million opportunities.*

5   What Is Lean Six Sigma?     47
*Making your organization better and faster. Improving productivity and quality at the same time.*

**Part 2:** **Defining and Measuring Performance**     61

6   Develop Project Opportunities     63
*Discover the fountain of projects and how to qualify those worth pursuing.*

7   Clarify the Problem     77
*What does your process look like? Who are your customers and suppliers? What exactly is the problem you need to solve?*

8   Set the Goal     89
*Knowing just how good you need to be is a good thing. But first you have to know how good you are now, and how far you have to go.*

9   Finalize the Plan     101
*Getting to your destination entails getting the right people on the bus. It also involves anticipating barriers and having a plan to overcome them.*

10   Measure the Process                                                          113
*Ask everyone involved to say how things get done, and see
the confusion for yourself.*

11   Validate Measurement Systems                                                 127
*Find out how you can make your measurements real.*

12   Characterize the Process                                                     139
*Your process has an inherent capability to perform, just
like you do in certain areas of life. Knowing that capability
makes all the difference in the world.*

Part 3:    **Analyzing, Improving, and Controlling Processes**                    151

13   Identify Potential Causes                                                    153
*Every cause has an effect, and every effect has a cause.
Begin to find out what's causing your performance to fall
short of your expectations.*

14   Conduct Efficiency Analysis                                                  165
*Finding out why your process is not as productive as possible
will lead you to making it better.*

15   Find Significant $x$s                                                        179
*If you knew why you have a performance problem, you
wouldn't have a performance problem. So you're going to
have to dig.*

16   Solve the Problem                                                           193
*You have to question and dig even deeper now, by torturing
your data.*

17   Create the Future State                                                     207
*Start by envisioning what your process will look like once
it's improved. Then make it happen.*

18   Generate and Evaluate Solutions                                             219
*When your performance problem is complex, it's not that
easy to solve, even when you know what's causing it. So
make the effort to come up with some viable solutions.*

19   Implement the Solution                                                      231
*Pick your very best solution with diligence. Anticipate what
could go wrong. Make a foolproof plan for change.*

20   Develop the Control Plan                                                    241
*A new process is only as good as it's faithfully practiced.
Make it impossible for your process to go back to its old self.*

21 Use Control Charts 253
*If you know how to use Control Charts, your organizational life will never be the same.*

22 Lock In the Gains 263
*You're not done until you're done. And you'll want to leave your legacy. Close your project and celebrate!*

**Part 4: Leading Lean Six Sigma Initiatives 275**

23 Lean Six Sigma Deployment 277
*Believe it or not, Lean Six Sigma is not the answer to everything. But it does have a very important place in the big picture of business transformation.*

24 Prepare the Path 289
*You can't deploy a Lean Six Sigma initiative if you don't know why. Believe it; many try to do this, to their demise.*

25 Design Your Destiny 303
*The best plans can be ruined with improper action. But no good action can come without a plan.*

26 Enable Everyone Involved 317
*People always make the difference. But you have to give them what they need to do what they have to do.*

27 Make It Happen 327
*Implementing your plan for transformation is one thing. Renewing your effort year after year is quite another. Doing both is your ticket to the sky.*

**Appendixes**

A Glossary 339

B Road Maps and Blueprint 353

C Sigma Conversion Chart 355

D Resources 359

Index 363

# Contents

**Part 1:  Understanding Lean Six Sigma**                                     1

**1  What Is Lean?**                                                           3

It's All About Value ..................................................................3

Lean Is One Big Waste-Removal Machine..............................4

Where Did Lean Come From? ...............................................5

*Henry Ford's Big Problem*...............................................6

*Taiichi Ohno's Revelations*............................................6

*The Machine That Changed the World* ........................8

What Is a Kaizen Event? ......................................................9

**2  The Basics of Lean**                                                     11

*Muda, Muda, Muda* (The Eight Types of Waste).....................11

*The Waste of Waiting*...................................................12

*The Waste of Overproduction* .....................................13

*The Waste of Rework* ..................................................13

*The Waste of Motion* ...................................................14

*The Waste of Transportation* .......................................14

*The Waste of Processing* ...............................................15

*The Waste of Inventory*................................................16

*The Waste of Intellect* ..................................................16

You Know More About Lean Than You Think.....................17

*Practice Rapid Changeover*...........................................17

*Keep the Flow* ..............................................................18

*Pull What You Need* .....................................................19

*Balance the Workload* ..................................................20

*Develop Cellular Layouts* .............................................20

*Embody the Five Ss*......................................................21

*Make Mistakes Impossible* ...........................................21

*Standardize Work and Processes* ...................................22

**3  What Is Six Sigma?**                                                     23

Many Things to Many People.............................................24

Can You See Your Hidden Process? .....................................25

Where Did Six Sigma Come From? .....................................27

*Quality Beginning*........................................................27

*Quality Crazy* ..............................................................27

*Quality Business*..........................................................28

You Know More About Six Sigma Than You Think .................. 29

*Y = f(x)* ........................................................................ *30*

*Measure, Measure, Measure* .......................................... *31*

*Claim Your Entitlement* ................................................ *32*

The Six Sigma DMAIC Methodology ................................. 33

**4   The Basics of Six Sigma                                             35**

It's All Greek to Me ........................................................... 36

*Basic Statistical Terms* ................................................... *36*

*What Is a CT?* ................................................................ *37*

*What Are Specifications?* ................................................ *37*

*What Is a Statistical Population?* ................................... *37*

*What Is a Standard Deviation?* ...................................... *38*

What Does Six Sigma Look Like? ....................................... 38

It's All About Variation ....................................................... 40

How Capable Is Your Process? ............................................ 41

*Mind Your CTs* .............................................................. *41*

*Multiply Your Yields* ..................................................... *42*

Beware of Shift and Drift ................................................... 43

**5   What Is Lean Six Sigma?                                             47**

Lean Six Sigma Is Faster, Better, and Cheaper ..................... 47

*The Business Focus* ......................................................... *49*

*The Statistical Focus* ...................................................... *50*

*Better Isn't Always Better* ............................................... *51*

The Job of Business Is Value Creation ................................. 53

The Lineage of Lean Six Sigma .......................................... 54

Evolution Cannot Be Stopped ............................................ 56

Ode to the Pioneers ........................................................... 57

*AlliedSignal* ................................................................... *57*

*Maytag* .......................................................................... *58*

DMAIC, or Kaizen Event? ................................................. 59

**Part 2:   Defining and Measuring Performance                           61**

**6   Develop Project Opportunities                                        63**

Figure Out What's Critical ................................................. 64

*The Customer View* ........................................................ *64*

*The Business Owner's View* ............................................ *65*

Brainstorming Project Possibilities ..................................... 66

More Idea Sources.................................................................67
    *The Balanced Scorecard*...............................................*68*
    *Voice of the Customer*...................................................*68*
    *Value Stream Mapping*..................................................*70*
    *The Bigger Picture*........................................................*71*
Separate Wheat from Chaff.................................................72
What's Most Important?......................................................74
The Prioritization Matrix....................................................75

**7 Clarify the Problem** **77**

Introducing Define ............................................................78
Write Problem Statement...................................................78
Define the High-Level Process ..........................................80
    *It All Comes Down to Processes* .................................*80*
    *The SIPOC Map*.........................................................*81*
    *Document the Process*..................................................*82*
    *Value-Added, Non-Value-Added*..................................*83*
    *Spaghetti You Don't Eat* .............................................*84*
Collect the Voice of the Customer .....................................85
    *The Kano Model* .........................................................*86*
    *Focus on What Must Be*...............................................*87*

**8 Set the Goal** **89**

A Note About Scope ..........................................................90
Define Project Metrics.......................................................91
    *One Project, One Y*.....................................................*91*
    *Primary, Secondary, Consequential* .............................*92*
Verify Alignment to Business Metrics ................................92
Establish Baseline and Entitlement ....................................94
    *Calculate Your Standard Deviation* .............................*95*
    *Don't Forget to Benchmark*.........................................*96*
Develop an Objective Statement ........................................96
Estimate Financial Benefits................................................97
    *Savings, Cost Avoidance, and Revenue* ........................*98*

**9 Finalize the Plan** **101**

Identify Project Team.......................................................102
Identify Stakeholders.......................................................103
    *Stakeholder Analysis* ................................................*103*
    *Power Influence Map* ................................................*104*
    *Stakeholder Action Plan*...........................................*105*

Identify Project Risks .................................................................105
Establish Project Timeline........................................................107
Create Project Charter...............................................................107
Choosing Your Methodology....................................................109
Communicate, Communicate, Communicate.........................111
Conduct Tollgate Review..........................................................111

**10  Measure the Process                                            113**

Introducing Measure.................................................................114
Knowing What to Improve........................................................114
  *Not as Easy as You Think*........................................................*115*
  *Four Things to Do*...................................................................*116*
Primary Metric Defects or Time? ............................................117
  *Flow the Process Flow* .............................................................*117*
  *Swimming in Lanes*.................................................................*118*
  *The 8.5-by-11 Syndrome* .........................................................*120*
  *Significant Other Test*.............................................................*120*
  *Value Stream Maps*.................................................................*121*
Expose Simplification Opportunities.......................................124
  *Executing Quick-Hit Opportunities*.......................................*125*
  *Where Do I Go From Here?*.....................................................*126*

**11  Validate Measurement Systems                                   127**

Identify Existing Measurement System....................................128
Analyze the Measurement System ...........................................128
  *Attribute MSA*........................................................................*129*
  *Variable MSA* .........................................................................*131*
Improve the Measurement System ...........................................134
Validate Customer Requirements.............................................136
  *Defect-Based Requirements* .....................................................*136*
  *Time-Based Requirements*........................................................*137*

**12  Characterize the Process                                       139**

Collect Data ..............................................................................140
  *Make a Plan*............................................................................*140*
  *Sampling*..................................................................................*141*
Examine Process Stability ........................................................143
  *Run, Run Chart, Run*..............................................................*143*
  *Control Chart*..........................................................................*144*
  *Histograms*...............................................................................*145*

Perform Capability Analysis ................................................. 146
   *Why Sigma Score?*......................................................... *147*
   *Process Capability and Time*.......................................... *148*
Conduct Tollgate Review.................................................. 149

**Part 3:** **Analyzing, Improving, and Controlling Processes** **151**

**13** **Identify Potential Causes** **153**
Introducing Analyze ....................................................... 154
Focus on the *x*s................................................................ 154
   *Wayne and Fred* ............................................................. *155*
   *Extracting Causes from Process Mapping* ..................... *156*
   *Brainstorming Techniques*............................................. *156*
   *Affinity Diagrams* ........................................................ *156*
   *Fishbone Diagrams* ....................................................... *157*
   *Ask Why Five Times* ..................................................... *159*
Failure Mode and Effects Analysis .................................... 159
Narrow the Potential Causes............................................. 161
   *Multivoting*.................................................................. *162*
   *Cause-and-Effect Matrix* ............................................. *162*
Pick Your Analyze Tool Set............................................... 163

**14** **Conduct Efficiency Analysis** **165**
Name That Waste........................................................... 166
Value Analysis................................................................ 167
Examining Inventory Levels ............................................. 168
   *Queueing Theory*........................................................... *168*
   *Little's Law* ................................................................. *169*
   *Takt Time Analysis* ..................................................... *170*
   *Do You Kanban?*.......................................................... *171*
Analysis of Resource Usage .............................................. 172
   *Ideal Manning*............................................................. *173*
   *Workload Balance* ........................................................ *173*
   *Analyzing Standard Work Combinations* ..................... *174*
   *Spaghetti Diagrams*...................................................... *174*
Overall Equipment Effectiveness....................................... 175
   *Quick Changeover Opportunities*................................... *176*
   *Total Productive Maintenance (TPM)*........................... *177*
Identifying Bottlenecks in the Process .............................. 177

**15  Find Significant *xs***                                                                           **179**

Collect Data on the *x*s.................................................................180
  *Computer Databases* ...............................................................*180*
  *Logs (Logbooks and Log Sheets)*..............................................*181*
  *Data Collection Forms* ...........................................................*181*
  *Check Sheets* ..........................................................................*182*
  *Control Charts*.........................................................................*182*
  *Observation of Processes*..........................................................*182*
Special Studies ...........................................................................183
Sample Size Calculations ...........................................................184
  *Comparing Averages*................................................................*185*
  *Comparing Percentages (Proportions)* ....................................*186*
Graphical Analysis......................................................................186
Conduct Statistical Analysis ......................................................189
p-Values and Hypothesis Testing................................................189
Statistical Analysis Methods......................................................190
  *Tests for Averages* ...................................................................*191*
  *Tests for Proportions*...............................................................*192*

**16  Solve the Problem**                                                                              **193**

Prioritize the *x*s .......................................................................194
  *Focus on the Primary Metric*....................................................*194*
  *Revisit the Cause-and-Effect Matrix*.........................................*195*
Evaluate the Impact on *Y*..........................................................*195*
  *Design of Experiments* .............................................................*197*
  *Analysis of Variance* ...............................................................*199*
  *Simulation*...............................................................................*200*
State the $Y = f(x)$ Equation.......................................................201
Conduct Tollgate Review ...........................................................205

**17  Create the Future State**                                                                        **207**

Introducing Improve  .................................................................208
Your Future State .......................................................................209
  *What Needs to Change?*............................................................*209*
  *Which Path to Take?* ................................................................*209*
The Five Ss..................................................................................210
  *Sort (Seiri)*..............................................................................*210*
  *Store (Seiton)* ..........................................................................*211*
  *Shine (Seiso)*............................................................................*211*
  *Standardize (Seiketsu)* .............................................................*211*
  *Sustain (Shitsuke)*....................................................................*212*

Standard Work ..................................................................212
   *Managing Standard Work*.......................................213
   *Multiple Skills Matrix*..........................................214
Cellular Layout.................................................................215
   *Rebalance Equipment*...........................................215
   *Quick Changeover* .................................................216
   *Implementing TPM*................................................216
Kaizen Events ..................................................................217

**18 Generate and Evaluate Solutions**     **219**

Generate Solutions ...........................................................220
   *Still Need Solutions?* .............................................220
   *Brainstorming* .......................................................220
   *Structured Innovation*...........................................221
   *Applying Lean Concepts* ........................................222
   *Process Thinking*....................................................222
Evaluate Potential Solutions.............................................222
   *Find Affinities and Consolidate* .............................223
   *Potential Solutions Matrix* ....................................223
Conduct Experimental Trials............................................224
   *Simulations* ...........................................................224
   *Mathematical Models*............................................224
State the $Y = f(x)$ .............................................................226
   *Contour Plots*........................................................227
   *Optimization* .........................................................227
   *Monte Carlo Simulation* .......................................228
   *DOE Methods for Multiple Solutions* .....................229

**19 Implement the Solution**     **231**

Select the Solution ...........................................................232
   *Ease, Permanence, Impact, and Cost*.......................232
   *Selecting Competing Solutions* ...............................233
Pilot the Solution ............................................................234
Evaluate Pilot Performance ..............................................234
Identify Risks and Countermeasures .................................236
Develop Implementation Plan...........................................237
   *Update Stakeholder Analysis* .................................238
   *The Training Plan*.................................................238
   *Systems and Supports*.............................................238
   *Communicate*.........................................................239
Conduct Tollgate Review..................................................239

**20 Develop the Control Plan** **241**

Introducing Control.................................................................242
Control *x*, Monitor *Y*............................................................242
   *An Ounce of Prevention*....................................................243
   *Update Your Process Flow*.................................................246
   *Update Your FMEA*...........................................................247
Be Consistent and Standardize...............................................247
Plan for Control......................................................................249

**21 Use Control Charts** **253**

What Are Control Charts?.......................................................254
Constructing Control Charts...................................................255
   *Individuals Control Chart*..................................................256
   *Other Control Charts*.........................................................257
Interpreting a Control Chart...................................................258
   *Special Causes*...................................................................259
   *Common Causes*.................................................................261
Acting on the Interpretation...................................................261

**22 Lock In the Gains** **263**

Show Me the Money.................................................................264
Make It Known ......................................................................265
   *Project Storyboard*.............................................................266
   *The Final Report*................................................................266
Herding Cats ..........................................................................267
Opportunities and Obstacles...................................................269
   *Opportunities*.....................................................................269
   *Obstacles*...........................................................................270
Pass the Baton ........................................................................270
Conduct Tollgate Review .........................................................272
Let's Celebrate........................................................................273

**Part 4: Leading Lean Six Sigma Initiatives** **275**

**23 Lean Six Sigma Deployment** **277**

How Does a Business Excel? .....................................................278
Product/Service Life Cycle.......................................................279
   *Innovation and Growth*.......................................................279
   *Design and Development* .....................................................280
   *Operations and Support* ......................................................281

Total Performance Excellence ............................................. 282
Deployment Phases ............................................................ 283
   *Assess Performance* ..................................................... 283
   *Plan Improvements* ..................................................... 283
   *Enable Execution* ....................................................... 284
   *Execute Projects and Events* ......................................... 284
   *Sustain Improvements* .................................................. 285
Critical Success Factors ..................................................... 285

**24  Prepare the Path**                                              **289**

Assess Road Map ............................................................... 290
Assess Organizational Readiness ......................................... 290
   *Conduct Needs Assessment* ........................................... 290
   *Establish Cultural Readiness* ........................................ 291
   *Conduct Stakeholder Assessment* ................................... 291
Evaluate the Organizational Situation ................................. 293
   *Review Organizational Strategy* .................................... 293
   *Review Competitive Position* ........................................ 293
   *Customer Value Proposition* ......................................... 294
   *People Matter* ........................................................... 294
Conduct Opportunity Assessment ...................................... 295
   *Establish Approach* ..................................................... 295
   *Educate and Engage Personnel* ..................................... 296
   *Project Identification* .................................................. 297
   *Prioritize Projects* ..................................................... 300
   *Assign Methodology* .................................................... 300
   *Complete Project Charters* ........................................... 300
   *Project Tracking Software* ............................................ 300

**25  Design Your Destiny**                                           **303**

Design Road Map .............................................................. 304
Establish Deployment Objectives ........................................ 304
   *Design Overall Objectives* ............................................ 304
   *Current-Year Priorities* ............................................... 305
   *Design the Organization* .............................................. 306
Engage Leadership Support ................................................ 306
   *Secure Executive Sponsorship* ...................................... 306
   *Demystify the Approach* .............................................. 307
   *Engage Deployment Champions* .................................... 307
   *Champions and Process Owners* ..................................... 308
Install Deployment Infrastructure ...................................... 308

*Human Resources*.................................................................*309*
*Finance*.............................................................................*309*
*Information Technology*.......................................................*310*
*Project Management*...........................................................*310*
*Training*............................................................................*311*
*Communication* .................................................................*312*
Design Governance Model ................................................*312*
*Design Governance Metrics*................................................*312*
*Long-Term Practitioner Strategies*....................................*313*
*Establish Practitioner Selection Process* ............................*314*
*Identify Practitioners*.........................................................*314*
*Align Projects and People* ..................................................*315*
*Set Performance Objectives*...............................................*316*

**26   Enable Everyone Involved                                    317**

Enable Road Map..............................................................318
Adapt Approaches and Intellectual Property ............................318
*Evaluate and Adapt Methodology*.......................................*318*
*Adapt Curriculum* .............................................................*319*
*Integrate with Other Initiatives* .........................................*319*
Management Awareness and Education ......................................320
*Deployment Champion Education*.......................................*320*
*Project Champion Training*................................................*321*
*Process Owner Training*......................................................*321*
*Functional Champion Training*...........................................*322*
Black Belts, Green Belts, and Facilitators ................................322
*Welcome to Your New Career*..............................................*323*
*Training and Project Work* .................................................*324*
*Coaching and Mentoring* ...................................................*326*

**27   Make It Happen                                              327**

Execute and Sustain Road Map ................................................328
Execute and Review Progress ...................................................328
*The Implementation Plan* ..................................................*328*
*Execute and Review Projects*...............................................*329*
*Champion Review* .............................................................*330*
*Steering Committee Review*.................................................*331*
*Executive Team Review*.......................................................*331*
Sustain the Initiative................................................................332

Master Development.................................................332
   *Role Definition and Selection*.............................*332*
   *Train and Certify Masters* .................................*333*
Adapt and Customize Deployment.......................333
   *Mine for Gold in Your Own Backyard*.................*334*
   *Manage and Disseminate Knowledge*...................*334*
Health Check and Dashboard Review.....................335
   *Deployment Health Check*....................................*335*
   *Doctor, Doctor, Give Me the News*......................*336*
Re-energize the Program...........................................337
   *Deployment Objective Review*..............................*337*
   *Evaluate Performance and Resources*....................*337*
   *Establish Focus for Next Year*.............................*338*

## Appendixes

**A   Glossary**                                                    **339**

**B   Road Maps and Blueprint**                                     **353**

**C   Sigma Conversion Chart**                                      **355**

**D   Resources**                                                   **359**

   **Index**                                         **363**

# Introduction

You may have picked up this book because your company is adopting Lean Six Sigma and you want to get a leg up. Great! You're ambitious and on the ball. Or you might be considering a career path as a Lean Six Sigma leader or practitioner. All the better. Maybe you've already been trained as a Lean Six Sigma Black Belt or Champion and want to keep a simple reference on hand.

You've come to the right place. Yes, you, too, the small business owner with 12 employees. Use this book to get them all proficient in Lean Six Sigma thinking. Apply some of the principles and tools in your own way to benefit your customers and your business.

Lean Six Sigma is a systematic approach to making your organization better—right where it counts, in your day-to-day work and processes. If you don't buy into this, and instead prefer the chaos of shooting from the hip, read no further. But if you want to discover the difference between average and world-class organizations, this book will go a long way to help.

First, we give you the concepts and principles of Lean Six Sigma. We believe those who plan and execute change initiatives need to be intelligent about what they're doing. It's not enough to just do things. You're best off when you know why you're doing what you're doing, and what purposes are driving you.

Second, we give you road maps, because road maps provide grounding and structure. If you are executing a Lean Six Sigma project, or deploying a Lean Six Sigma initiative throughout your organization, this book shows you the process to follow. (Of course, you can adjust and make detours if necessary.)

Third, we give you tools. The directions won't mean anything if you don't have the skills and tools you need to get there. So within the structure of a road map for doing Lean Six Sigma, we give you the most common tools (and only the most common) you'll need.

View the principles of Lean Six Sigma as your best friend. Look at the road maps as guides, not gospel. Know that the tools are only the most commonly used ones. With this in mind, we hope you'll experience the value of this book as a clear, concise primer and reference. Nothing more and nothing less.

## How This Book Is Organized

This book is presented in four sections:

**Part 1, "Understanding Lean Six Sigma,"** is a general overview of the methodology. While not a suspense novel, it's pretty interesting to know the history of Lean and Six Sigma and how they found each other in matrimony. Aside from that, we take the complexities of Lean Six Sigma and spell them out for you. What specifically is waste and inefficiency? Where does it hide in organizations? How can you root it out? Why do you have to perform at a Six Sigma level of no more than 3.4 defects, or errors, per million opportunities? That sounds crazy. Can't you just be good 99 percent of the time instead of 99.9997? No matter who you are or what your role is in an organization, read this part to get your brain set in the right place.

**Part 2, "Defining and Measuring Performance,"** is the first of two parts covering the Define-Measure-Analyze-Improve-Control (DMAIC) project execution road map. What is your process and what's wrong with it? What exactly needs to improve and by how much? How can you translate that need into a project charter? You get all the details here, and tools you can use. Primarily for the Lean Six Sigma practitioner, and secondarily for the Lean Six Sigma leader, this part gives you the skinny on defining projects and measuring performance (first two phases of DMAIC). If you have a good background in statistics and industrial engineering, or are one heck of a smarty, you can use this part as a guide to completing the Define and Measure phases. But don't be surprised if you need more resources or training, especially if your process is more technical or complex.

**Part 3, "Analyzing, Improving, and Controlling Processes,"** covers the latter three phases of the Lean Six Sigma project execution road map (DMAIC). What process factors (methods, people, machines, etc.) are responsible for your poor performance or excess process variation? How do you know what's wrong and what, exactly, you need to change? These seem like simple questions, but they're not, especially in organizational environments. This part of the book, like the last, is also for the practitioner first and the leader second. It brings you into the deep end of the statistics pool. Maybe you can't touch the bottom, but at least you have the courage to get in there. With the help of Lean Six Sigma analytics, you'll end up with the very best improvement to your process. Then you'll be delighted to do what wise people do: ensure that your new and improved process stays the same, for a long time.

**Part 4, "Leading Lean Six Sigma Initiatives,"** is about organizational change, in step-by-step fashion, but not to the extent of a detailed cookbook. No, you can't turn off your mind and lead Lean Six Sigma. But you can take heed and learn about what's worked before. When do you implement Lean Six Sigma, and when do you pursue some other approach? On what business metrics do you focus? Who is responsible for meeting financial targets for the initiative? Try rolling Lean Six Sigma out to six different countries speaking three different languages, and operating at more than 600 locations worldwide. If that proposition doesn't sound interesting to you, skip this part. If it does, then you were born for leadership. So by all means, build your infrastructure for change, drive it, empower it, and enjoy the satisfaction that only widespread change can bring.

## Things to Help You Out Along the Way

Throughout this book you'll encounter sidebar messages with interesting, concentrated content. Read these to get the Lean Six Sigma edge. They will definitely make you smarter and keep you from making unwanted mistakes.

### Lean Six Sigma Lingo

To be proficient, you need to speak the language. We've highlighted all the Lean Six Sigma terms you need to know. Go ahead and impress your co-workers and bosses by learning the Lean Six Sigma lingo!

### Lean Six Sigma Wisdom

You're sure to find some valuable tidbits here for making the Lean Six Sigma journey easier. Look for helpful tips from the people who've been living and breathing Lean Six Sigma for a long time.

### Real-Life Story

It helps to know someone somewhere has actually done Lean Six Sigma, and has successfully applied its many tools. Find out who has done this and what they did by looking here.

### Technically Speaking

Maybe you're interested in technical details, and maybe you're not. If you are, pay attention to these little side conversations. All are welcome—not just statisticians and math mongers!

**Performance Pitfall**

Lessons learned the hard way. These are mistakes made by those who don't apply Lean Six Sigma right the first time. Learn from them, and don't make the same mistakes yourself!

 **Quotable Quote**

How many times have you heard words worth remembering? Probably not that often! But when you do, it pays to remember them. So don't miss these quotes of inspiration.

## Acknowledgments

This book is what it is because of many talented people at the Breakthrough Management Group. Brian Watson was irreplaceable in helping develop the book's outline, providing project execution road maps, and reviewing chapters. Wes Waldo kept the manuscript on track when it was diverging from its true purpose of Lean Six Sigma integration.

Our hats are also off to Colin Moore, our graphic artist who meticulously and beautifully created the book's more than 150 charts, graphs, tables, and other visual material. Colin is a talented artist who worked with pride, commitment, and professionalism. Thank you, Colin! Several others provided chapter reviews when needed under demanding circumstances and tight deadlines. These are BMG's consultants, trainers, statisticians, and deployment leaders. On the statistical and technical side, Russ Kiehl was there when we needed him, after long days of teaching. George Rommal was there, too, reviewing technical matters that needed his refined statistical acumen. Thanks, guys. And thanks also to Michele Quinn and Michael Gebhardt, who reviewed chapters in Part 4.

No, we're not done, because the contributions of Ethan Schaerer, Perry Giles, Luis Ramirez, and Jessica Schneider merit mention. These great colleagues and friends came through to provide the right input and material at the right time when it was needed. Once again, and as always, you all showed what it means to exceed expectations.

## Trademarks

# Part 1

# Understanding Lean Six Sigma

Lean Six Sigma is not a simple subject, and you can get lost in the details pretty fast. That's why this part summarizes the key points and principles of Lean Six Sigma. What is Lean Six Sigma? From where did it come? What are its main objectives? You'll do well to answer these questions before jumping into the details of project execution and Lean Six Sigma leadership. Therefore, use this first part to educate yourself, and to pick up some great fodder for explaining Lean Six Sigma to your boss, co-workers, spouse, friends, or anyone else who will listen!

# What Is Lean?

## In This Chapter

- The definition of Lean
- The benefits of Lean
- The history of Lean
- Kaizen Events

This chapter will give you a straight-out definition of Lean. We'll also tell you where Lean came from and why it exists. (Preview: to eliminate waste and improve efficiency!) Finally, we'll give you the basic scoop on Kaizen Events, the vehicles for making rapid Lean improvements.

## It's All About Value

Lean is a body of knowledge and tools organizations use to remove all non-value-added time and activity (or waste) from their processes. Whether you work for a government agency, small business, large corporation, hospital, school, or any other organization, your company exists to provide value to customers. You should recognize that schools call customers "students," health-care professionals call them "patients," government agencies call them "citizens," and so on.

For some, Lean is a set of methods and tools for improving a process. For others, Lean is an improvement system, like the Toyota Production System, that sets the framework for how the whole enterprise operates. As much as Lean is a tool used to improve processes, it's also a philosophy and system by which to run an organization or company.

**Lean Six Sigma Wisdom**

The benefits of Lean are as follows: removes non-value-added activity, reduces waste, cuts lead times, slashes inventories, lowers cycle times, improves cash flow, minimizes downtime, reduces defects and errors, improves productivity, fool-proofs processes, and increases customer satisfaction.

While all organizations are different, they are all the same in that they exist to fulfill some human or societal need. In fulfilling that need, all organizations take a certain set of inputs and transform them into certain outputs, called "products," "services," "transactions," etc. A school, for example, takes curriculum and course materials and, through the functions of teaching and administration, injects this knowledge into students' heads. At least that's what's supposed to happen, with the students' help!

# Lean Is One Big Waste-Removal Machine

All along the pathways of what organizations do, there is ample opportunity for wasted time, people, equipment, space, steps. There are many, many chances to make mistakes, which then require you to incur unnecessary costs in fixing them.

As you know, there is one best way to do anything. If you pride yourself in being good at something, then you know there's always a better way to do that something. Ask any fly fisherman, basketball player, seamstress, or parent if there are good ways of performing, and if there are also not-so-good ways.

Now imagine an organization the size of the U.S. Postal Service with 700,000 employees, 170,000 vehicles, and nearly 40,000 separate locations. Can you even imagine the work involved in delivering more than 700 million pieces of mail each day, excluding Sundays and holidays? That's about 213 billion pieces of mail each year!

Further, can you imagine the waste and lost dollars caused by just one simple inefficiency that gets replicated throughout the entire system? Or the savings implications of making one replicable part of the system run a little better? You're talking millions and millions of dollars sitting on the table, if not billions.

Even small organizations have plenty of chances to incur waste as they serve clients day by day. Waste and inefficiency are everywhere. Poor quality is everywhere.

Because of this, everything you do is constantly subjected to the law of improvement: No matter how well or fast you do something today, you can improve the way you do it tomorrow.

And by the way, improvement isn't optional: it's necessary for survival. In Lean terms, this is called "striving for perfection," and it's at the heart of Lean Six Sigma.

The key point in defining Lean is that its heritage and techniques are grounded in the drive to make business operate faster. Any time you can do this, you'll also probably experience fewer defect and quality problems (which Six Sigma fixes). Similarly, Six Sigma exists primarily to reduce defects, but in doing so usually enables organizations to operate faster (see Chapter 5).

**Lean Six Sigma Wisdom**

Lean uses time as the primary metric of interest. The cycle time it takes to do a task, lead time it takes from order to delivery, time a person waits, etc. It was Benjamin Franklin who coined the phrase, "Time is money." He may not have invented the tools of Lean, but he certainly got the metrics right.

# Where Did Lean Come From?

We trace the roots of Lean back to the early days of mass production (1910) and Henry Ford, who enacted the groundbreaking work of Fredrick Taylor (scientific management), Frank Gilbreth (father of industrial engineering), and such others as Henry Gantt (inventor of the Gantt Chart). Like all industrialists, Ford wanted to make as many units as possible in the shortest possible time.

Gilbreth pioneered the study of "time and motion" with a moving-picture camera to dissect how certain industrial tasks were performed, and how long they took. By focusing first in the construction industry, he noted that different bricklayers enacted different actions in doing their jobs.

He then used this data to standardize the one best way to lay bricks and perform other tasks. By doing this, and by developing a scaffold, he reduced the number of actions required to lay a brick from 18 to 4.5! This is the spirit and practice of Lean embodied by someone who lived a long time ago. Today this spirit lives on in the countless people and companies that constantly strive to do more in less time.

# Henry Ford's Big Problem

There's certainly a lot we could say about Henry Ford and his contribution to business. But when it comes to Lean, the hallmark of his contribution was the design of his River Rouge factory and its continuously moving assembly line. Still, as marvelous as Ford's company was and is today, it had one big problem back then. There was only one model in one color! (The black Model T.)

"They can have any color they want, as long as it's black," said Henry Ford. A true industrialist, Ford understood the huge challenges and downtime involved in changing from one mode of production to another. Automaking in the 1950s required sheets of steel to be stamped by large presses into fenders and other parts, and each part required a unique die in the stamping press.

The die on a press could be changed, but it took a team of special mechanics an entire day to do so. The positioning of the die was critical, and startups on a new die were often fraught with misalignment and high scrap rates. Given the expense of these die changes, the wisdom of the day was to make large batches, going for months at a time between changeovers.

In industry, you can always produce mass quantities of identical items in short periods of time with few defects. All you have to do is perfect one thing, one process, one way, and you are there. But the reality of demand is that many consumers want many products and services in many different ways. Just ask your local bartender or pizza maker about the varied needs of customers.

Ford's dilemma had to be solved because customers began demanding cars in different colors, and eventually demanded different models. The whole world in general would become a place where many different kinds of people would want many different kinds of things. Change was inevitable and mass production could only lead to one place eventually: mass customization.

**Real-Life Story**

Toyota is consistently and by far the most profitable automaker in the world, although it's only the third largest behind GM and Ford.

# Taiichi Ohno's Revelations

Lean greatly matured when Taiichi Ohno developed much of the thinking and practices that later became the Toyota Production System (TPS). Ohno was a forward-thinking assembly manager at Toyota in the 1940s and 1950s, when the company was on the verge of bankruptcy and couldn't afford to invest in new equipment or large inventories.

At the same time, the world was moving from mass production to more flexible, shorter, varied batch runs. People not only wanted the same car in different colors, but they wanted different cars with different features. All fine and good, but delivering on this would require enormous change for Toyota and every other carmaker in the world.

As the mother of invention, necessity did her job at Toyota, with Ohno's help. As always, common wisdom and belief had to fly out the window, giving way to a new world order. Ohno, Toyota, and the TPS would redefine the imperative of business: to solve the paradox of assembly line efficiency and marketplace variety.

To do this, Toyota had to solve the problem of changing from one production mode to another, so it could provide variety, not just one automobile, one way. Therefore, Ohno collaborated with Shigeo Shingo, the main purveyor of a technique called the *Single Minute Exchange of Die (SMED)*, or, as it is known by many today, *Rapid (or Quick) Changeover.*

Shingo was inspired by Ohno, who in turn was inspired during a trip to America where he watched the Indy 500. Watching race cars in the pit stop get refueled and serviced, Ohno saw the light. Why couldn't die changes be made in a minute, not in a day? Streamlined, simplified, and Mistake Proofed, new changeover techniques were developed and quickly mastered by stamping press operators.

But that's not all Ohno saw during his trip to the United States. He also noticed that when inventory at American grocery stores became thin, this triggered a replenishment signal to suppliers. In other words, why order materials in large batches regardless of production demands when you can order them only as they are needed?

If you visit a Toyota assembly line today, you see cars move down the line at 57-second intervals. It's fast-paced, just like Ford's River Rouge plant, but with the added feature of mass customization.

> ### Lean Six Sigma Lingo
>
> The Lean practice of changing over from one mode of production to another, like switching from making black cars to making red ones, is called **Rapid (or Quick) Changeover**, or **Single Minute Exchange of Die (SMED)**, and is based on the work of Shigeo Shingo.

> ### Real-Life Story
>
> Because of its innovative use of Lean techniques, Toyota lowered its new product development process for related vehicles down to about 12 months. This is half the time it takes most competitors to do the same.

Among other differences, you see a mix of colors coming down the line: perhaps three white cars, then one tan, one blue, two green, one red, two black, and then the sequence repeats. The mix is changed as the customer orders change, but the concept remains: make what the customer is buying. Not just black for everyone!

## The Machine That Changed the World

Who are you when you get your B.A. in political science from the University of Chicago, a Master's from Harvard in transportation systems, and a Ph.D. in political science from MIT? You guessed it: James Womack, the one who coined the term "Lean Manufacturing" with co-author Daniel Jones in their landmark book, *The Machine That Changed the World* (1990).

While Womack's education is in political science, his doctoral dissertation and subsequent work was focused on comparative industrial policy in the United States, Germany, and Japan. That's how he developed his extensive knowledge and relationships for writing his 1990 book and his follow-up book, *Lean Thinking*, in 1996.

Womack's Lean Principles are as follows:

1. **Value**—Act on what's important to the customer of the process.

2. **Value stream**—Understand which steps in the process add value and which don't.

3. **Flow**—Keep the work moving at all times and eliminate waste that creates delay.

4. **Pull**—Avoid making more or ordering more inputs for customer demand you don't have.

5. **Strive for perfection**—There is no optimum level of performance; just continually pursue improvements.

While Ohno and Toyota built the house of Lean brick by brick, and while many other companies have adopted TPS principles and practices, Womack brought it all together into a thinkable and deployable system. Womack's work has also gone a long way in migrating Lean practices into the heart and soul of the entire enterprise, not just the manufacturing functions.

Consequently, similar to the path of quality and Six Sigma, the business world has fully awoken to the undeniable fact that Lean is for banks and hospitals and service companies as much as it is for manufacturers.

A bank used Lean to reduce loan-approval processing time from 21 days to 1 day. A hospital reduced the average emergency room patient wait time from 100 minutes to 10 minutes without adding any staff. Southwest Airlines applied Rapid Changeover to achieve best-in-class gate turnaround times.

If you have a process (and who doesn't?), the principles of Lean apply. And who can we thank or acknowledge for this? Even more than the big names like Ford, Ohno, and Womack, we can thank the thousands of companies that stamped Lean's imprint into their organizations. They are the true testament to Lean's universal applicability.

So if you understand the principles and aims of Lean, how do you enact them? Typically, you implement Lean changes in your organization through a series of activities called Kaizen Events.

# What Is a Kaizen Event?

A Kaizen Event is a planned and structured process-improvement effort that enables a small group of people to improve some aspect of their business in a quick, focused manner. Kaizen is the tool used in Lean transformations to break down the "project mentality" and create a "bias towards action" in a war-room-like environment.

There are several different names and generic types of Kaizen Events, which, by the way, are also known as Rapid Improvement Events. A *Flow Kaizen* looks at improving the entire Value Stream and is typically led by a senior manager. A *Point Kaizen* (sometimes called *Genba Kaizen*) works to improve a specific point in the Value Stream and is led by a front-line associate.

Further, sometimes Kaizen Events are referred to as Sigma Kaizens when they are enacted to move rapidly through the five phases of the Six Sigma breakthrough strategy—Define-Measure-Analyze-Improve-Control (DMAIC). Others call the Kaizen Event a Lean Sigma Event, when it incorporates the philosophy and tools of both Lean and Six Sigma.

This can sometimes lead to confusion, with people believing there are a great number of different Kaizen Event types. But in reality the process of planning and executing a Kaizen is almost the same regardless of the objectives or tools used. Here are some general guidelines:

◆ **Successful Kaizen Events require *thoroughness*.** The devil is always in the details. Kaizen Events are fast-paced, and there is no time for major adjustments once they are underway. Therefore, do your homework and preparation up front, and consider all of the variables, people, and interactions prior to the event kickoff.

- **Successful Kaizen Events require *training*.** This includes training and knowledge of many Lean tools and techniques; you can't expect people to make Lean improvements if they don't know how to think in a Lean way or apply Lean techniques.

- **Successful Kaizen Events require *change management*.** While some people are born leaders, you can learn and teach people how to manage change. Aside from the technical and mechanical knowledge required, your ability to lead and motivate people—and keep them on track—is the determining factor in your success.

- **Successful Kaizen Events require *participative management*.** During a Kaizen Event, managers are concerned with getting everyone's participation, not in telling people what to do. And workers are much more involved in creating solutions than they are in the rote aspects of their jobs. Everyone comes together, especially those closest to the process, to examine how the work really gets done and what needs to improve.

## The Least You Need to Know

- Any and every organization can use Lean and its tools to remove non-value-added time and activity (or waste) from its processes.

- Lean helps you to cut lead times, slash inventories, lower cycle times, improve cash flow, minimize downtime, and "foolproof" processes.

- The roots of Lean go back to the industrial revolution, Henry Ford, and the Toyota Production System, which is the benchmark for Lean.

- James Womack and Daniel Jones popularized Lean with their 1990 publication of *The Machine That Changed the World.*

- A Kaizen Event is a planned and structured process-improvement effort that enables a small group of people to improve some aspect of their business in a quick, focused manner.

# Chapter 2

# The Basics of Lean

## In This Chapter

- ◆ Waste is produced in many forms
- ◆ Rapid changeover is key
- ◆ Keep your operations flowing
- ◆ Make it impossible to fail

In this chapter, we'll summarize the eight types of waste because they are the targets of your Lean arsenal. You really should know what you're shooting at before you start shooting!

Also in this chapter, we'll briefly introduce the main ways you'll want to attack waste in your organization. Call them techniques for taking out the garbage. This is where you'll be introduced to many of Lean's family members: the siblings of Pull, Flow, Mistake Proofing, and others. Trust us … if you know these, you know how to keep your operational house clean.

## Muda, Muda, Muda (The Eight Types of Waste)

The Japanese word *muda* means "waste" in English. "So just what is this waste we seek to destroy?" asked one eager Lean trainee. "Many types, my friend, many types," said the Lean Master. "Seven to be exact, at least as originally defined by Taiichi Ohno. But later one more form of waste, intellect, was added to Ohno's original list, so really there are eight."

The harsh reality is that waste exists in all processes in all organizations. Knowing this is a truism about you and your organization, wouldn't you want to know more about it? Wouldn't you want to know as much about waste as possible so you could find it and throw it in the garbage? Learn each of the following types of waste and see where your garbage is hiding:

- Waiting
- Overproduction
- Rework
- Motion
- Transportation
- Processing
- Inventory
- Intellect

## The Waste of Waiting

How much time have you wasted standing in line, waiting your turn? There's no question that you would consider that waste. Another example of waiting is taking your car into a service garage for routine maintenance. It takes less than 10 minutes to change the oil in your car. Yet you sit in the waiting room for more than an hour. That's waste.

**Performance Pitfall**

Don't fret when a problem seems to fit into more than one category of waste. They often do. The objective is to identify the opportunity and do something about it, not to create a perfect categorization scheme.

Now imagine you're a computer under assembly on a manufacturing line. The workers are all there, the equipment is ready, and then production on you comes to screeching halt. The workers are waiting for a missing part. That's waste.

The waste of waiting applies to all processes, not just production. Imagine you're a document that's routed around for approval. Each time you go into that in-box, you're waiting. No action is underway. When no action is underway, no value is added. No action = waste.

## The Waste of Overproduction

Imagine a steel mill where the slab-making manager gets a bonus based on how much product his operation makes. Since the finishing process that rolls these slabs into finished sheets of steel has its schedule tied to the customer orders, what happens to the unneeded slabs? The mill runs out of storage space and has to store them outside where they rust and are scrapped. Producing more than you need is waste.

 **Real-Life Story**

Did you know a bank is required to publish a quarterly financial statement? Do you care? We do, because now we can tell you about an overly ambitious bank officer we know who insists on submitting 50-page statements, even though the requirement is 10 pages. Not only is this a wasteful use of the bank officer's time (overproduction), but the customer of the report (FDIC) is not happy because they spend more time reading it. This adds processing time and is unnecessary.

Overproduction sounds like it can only happen in manufacturing, doesn't it? Not so. What about a book writer who produces three words for every one that ends up in the manuscript. Is this waste? Yes, it's the waste of overproduction, and don't doubt it for one second: it is rampant in most information-intensive businesses and business functions.

## The Waste of Rework

Scraping the burnt crust off of toast that has been heated too long is necessary to salvage the toast, but, still, it is waste. It's so much better to get the toast right the first time. Better tasting, faster, and less effort.

In manufacturing plants, the need for rework is usually easy to spot. Quality attributes are measured, defects are tagged, and the item is set aside for rework. Manufacturing operations have a leg up on many of their nonmanufacturing brethren, because the act of reworking is more visible.

On the other hand, rework is largely invisible in nonmanufacturing environments. That's why it's called the "hidden factory." In fact, sometimes rework is built right into the process as a "necessary" step, called "editing" or "correction" or "revision." As in manufacturing, the goal of any service process should be to do it right one time only, the first time.

**Lean Six Sigma Wisdom**

Keep in mind that some waste, such as inspection and rework, is actually expected and unavoidable until you redesign the process that creates the defects.

Usually rework isn't even measured and tracked in transactional and service environments. How well do you think office workers would fare if their communication errors were counted? Let's see, all those memos and e-mails, all those meetings … plenty of opportunity for errors, don't ya think?

What about rework due to management decision error? We won't even go there, even though it might be fun. Just know that decision error has huge implications on the performance of an organization. One bad decision can cause a decade or more of rework. Just ask IBM, which had to rework its strategy after deciding that there was no market for personal computers.

## The Waste of Motion

Any extra movement by people that does not add value is waste. Walking throughout the house, lifting sofa cushions, looking for those misplaced car keys is a waste of motion.

Picture the packing station at a fruit plant where the packers had to walk 60 feet each time they needed a new empty box. By revising the storage area layout and adding a simple roller conveyor for the empties, the workers now had the boxes coming to them. The motion waste of those 60 steps was totally eliminated.

As another example, a hospital blood-testing lab diagrammed the path a technician takes to complete a test procedure. Because of poor placement of the test equipment and the computer terminal, the technician was covering 800 feet for each test procedure run. By just rearranging the workplace, the distance was reduced to 400 feet, reducing the waste of motion for that position.

## The Waste of Transportation

Ever notice that restaurant dining rooms are located next to kitchens? It's to minimize the transportation time of food so it gets to the customer faster, and in its best possible eating state. Placing the dining room farther away only increases waste; any unnecessary movement of product or information is the waste of transportation.

A manufacturer of paper had two processing steps, making and finishing. Space was at a premium, so the work-in-process inventory (large rolls of paper weighing 3,000 pounds) were stored in a warehouse about 4 miles away.

The rolls were moved from the making area to the truck-loading dock by fork truck, where they were loaded onto a semitruck. The truck took a load of rolls to the warehouse, where they were unloaded by another fork truck and put into storage. When needed, a fork truck was used to load the rolls back onto the truck. They were transported back to the loading dock, unloaded, and moved to the finishing area by fork truck. The truck, fork trucks, drivers, and dock were all components of the waste of transportation.

What's the difference between the waste of motion and transportation, you ask? Great question!

Some say motion pertains to the distance covered or actions made by a person or machine fixed in one location—like the sequence a technician would follow in turning on and off five water valves lined up left to right. And the waste of transportation is when anything, including a person, has to be moved from one place to another to get a job done—like flying parts from one factory to another to complete a final assembly.

Others, however, think of motion as relating only to the workers in the process, while transportation refers only to the movement of product or material through the process, not a person. Remember, there are no hard, fast rules about where one type of waste starts and another begins.

## The Waste of Processing

Do you know someone who washes the dishes before putting them in the dishwasher? That's called "double processing," and it is wasteful. ("Double processing" is *not* a Lean term; we just thought it sounded kind of cool). In any case, effort that adds no value to the service or product is waste.

An aircraft manufacturer found that it took an average of 123 days to process a change to an engineering drawing. The process was diagrammed in detail and found to have 144 steps, many of which were non-value-added, redundant reviews. Eliminating these enabled the process to clip along with only 25 steps at a rate of 10 days average. All those extra reviews were overprocessing.

How about all those e-mails? How many do you get that really don't matter to you? We're not talking about spam here, but about all the work-related e-mails people get that they don't need. Yes, the time involved in copying people and routing messages around that are not essential does fall into the category of processing waste. But much more so is the time people waste reading the unnecessary e-mails.

**Lean Six Sigma Wisdom** _____

You're pretty smart if you're asking how the waste of processing is different from the waste of rework or overproduction. Well, they are all similar in nature. While rework generally has to do with fixing a product because it wasn't right the first time, processing waste is doing more work than needed to complete a task or unit.

Overproduction, on the other hand, is the result of making more units than you need—like a student who writes and submits 10 case studies instead of the 8 for which the instructor asked. Essentially, the wastes of rework, overprocessing, overproduction—and even motion and transportation—all come down to performing more steps and actions than are required to get a job done.

## The Waste of Inventory

A friend who plays tennis got a great deal on tennis balls and bought eight cases of them—a four-year supply! "10 cents a ball," he would brag around the court. Unfortunately, the cases took up so much room in his garage, he had to park his car outside. Sadly, after one year, the remaining balls had gone flat and weren't playable.

As another example, a hospital ordered four years' worth of a patient information booklet. Less than six months later they changed some of their policies and the hospital was left with three and a half years of obsolete booklets. Many insurance companies process claims in batches, and the claim work has to move between, say, four different work areas. Claims accumulate, then they are moved to the next step when they reach a certain number. Meanwhile, they sit idle. One company reported that it spent only one hour actually processing claims, even though the time in to the time out was at least five days. Remember, value cannot be added to an item in inventory.

Having more material, parts, or information than you need at any time is waste. While too much inventory is waste, not enough inventory is waste, too. How come? Because then the process has to stop and wait. Remember the waste of waiting?

## The Waste of Intellect

Have you ever worked at a job where your ideas weren't welcome? Where your boss said, "Just shut up and do what you're told"? That's a waste of your intellect, and great companies will always do their best to tap into your brain, experience, talent, creativity, and ideas.

A copper-smelting plant had 400 employees, 340 of whom were shift workers performing the operations. When management selected project teams to increase production, not one of the 340 shift workers was chosen. Meanwhile, most of them had years of experience and, undoubtedly, valuable insights and ideas. It's too late now … the plant missed its production targets and was shut down. How things might have been different if the intellects of the people who knew the most were not wasted.

A hospital recognized the latent talent in its staff and selected eight nurses to be part of their first class of Lean Six Sigma *Black Belts*, which received training and got time to work on improvement projects. Their work was so successful that the hospital continues to select at least one third of each Black Belt class from its nonmanagement ranks. The hospital is reducing the waste of intellect and reaping the benefits.

 **Lean Six Sigma Lingo**

> A **Black Belt** is an expert problem solver who is trained in Six Sigma methods and statistical tools. A Master Black Belt teaches Black Belts (and Green Belts) to become proficient in executing Six Sigma projects. A Champion is a manager or business leader who spearheads the selection and implementation of Six Sigma projects.

# You Know More About Lean Than You Think

Now that you know about all the ways waste can happen, what are you going to do about it? Future chapters give you all the tools for identifying, measuring, and removing waste in your organization. Here, you can keep learning before jumping into the details of actually doing a Lean Six Sigma project.

And before you do, anyway, it might be very helpful to know that certain techniques underlie Lean and the application of its tools. These techniques follow, so know them well because they'll put you in the right mind-set for Lean success.

## Practice Rapid Changeover

Do you know how much money it costs an airplane to "wait" at the gate for passengers? It's about $100 per minute of delay, or about $6,000 an hour. That's why companies like Southwest Airlines have used Rapid Changeover principles to minimize the amount of time its planes are sitting at gates. Makes a whole lot of sense, and it keeps airfares down.

 **Lean Six Sigma Wisdom**

> The key to Rapid Changeover is to study the change process and each of its steps. Steps that are not adding value are eliminated. Certain other necessary steps are performed in parallel so there is less idle wait time.

While your time may not be worth $100 a minute, you do a changeover every day—when you wake up in the morning and take a shower before work! You are changing yourself over, getting ready for a new day, just like an airplane has to get ready for its next load of passengers. The question is: how long do you take to shower, and what could you gain by shortening that time? Saving 6 minutes a day would give you an extra 1.3 days a year of time.

## Keep the Flow

Do you get upset with long lines at a grocery store? You're not alone. It takes less than 3 minutes to scan and bag your items, yet you stand in line waiting for 15 minutes. What's up with that? Wait time is not adding value to you as the customer, and you are not flowing unfettered through the process. Don't they know how important you are?

The focus of Lean Flow is to keep you moving through the process, or to keep parts moving through a process, or to keep information processing on a computer at all times. Can you see how good flow helps you attack the waste of waiting, processing, and inventory? How about making sure knowledge workers have good mental flow rates? That's an interesting one to ponder.

The value proposition for any process includes quality, price, and timeliness. If two grocery stores offer the same inventory at the same price, which will you frequent—the one with the shorter or the longer lines? If you have two ways to go to work, and one is a little longer but you get to work faster because of your flow rate, which route will you take? (These are not trick questions.)

You've heard the phrase "go with the flow." Well, that doesn't apply in the world of Lean—not for manufacturing or for service- and transaction-based businesses or functions. If you want to be lean and mean, you have to measure your Flow and determine what your "Flow Time Efficiency" is. This is the beginning of the change process: coming to terms with how good or not good you really are.

Therefore, the Lean metric of your Flow Time Efficiency is calculated like this:

$$\text{Flow Time Efficiency} = \frac{\text{Theoretical Flow Time}}{\text{Average Flow Time}}$$

This equation takes into account where theoretical Flow Time is the actual amount of time it takes to perform the process steps with no waiting or rework, and where average Flow Time is the actual amount of time it takes to complete the steps, including waiting and rework.

Here are some typical Flow Time efficiency statistics in some white-collar environments:

## Flow Time Efficiency Examples

| Industry | Process | Average Flow Time | Theoretical Flow Time | Flow Time Efficiency |
|---|---|---|---|---|
| Life insurance | New policy application | 72 hours | 7 minutes | .16% |
| Commercial bank | Consumer loan | 24 hours | 34 minutes | 2.4% |
| Hospital | Patient billing | 10 days | 3 hours | 3.8% |
| Auto Manufacturer | Financial closing | 11 days | 5 hours | 5.6% |

Source: Blackburn, J.D. "Time Based Competition: White-Collar Activities," Business Horizons, 35 (4): 96-101 (1992).

## Pull What You Need

The Lean principle of Pull says that you allow the actual use of a resource, or input, to dictate when it is restocked or replenished. A good example of this is a vending machine, which in many cases creates a visual signal to the supplier that it is time to restock. The signal is visual, easily understood, and easy to administer.

Lean Pull systems are called "Kanban" systems in Japanese. Loosely translated, Kanban means "card" or "sign." If you've never seen a live manufacturing or assembly plant using visual Kanban systems, you might want to plan a field trip. It will be well worth your while to see the system of pull cards working in real life. Used at some stock point, the Kanban pull system orders new material batches from suppliers only when the previous batch is withdrawn from the system.

Nursing-station supply cabinets function as pull systems when they are set up like vending machines. Such items as gloves have designated slots, and vendors restock the machines regularly with the needed, or missing, quantities. This eliminates the problem of not having a needed item in stock while also preventing the waste of oversupply.

**Lean Six Sigma Wisdom** _____

Kanban pull systems are often used as pieces of an overall "Just in Time" approach to inventory management. Just in Time systems are designed to keep materials out of inventory, such that they are delivered directly from the supplier to the workplace when they are needed to make or assemble a product. Information, too, can be Just in Time, such as when you receive Lean Six Sigma training right as you are implementing your first Lean Six Sigma project.

## Balance the Workload

Have you noticed that many fast-food restaurants have two windows? You give your money at the first window while you get your food at the second. Both windows are staffed during peak times, but only one window is staffed during low-demand times, when the same person handles all money collection and food disbursement. In the meantime, the person who was staffing the other window during the peak time is off of work, or performing some other needed task.

Some smart people soak their dishes in the sink before washing them. If you do this, you are balancing your workload. After Thanksgiving dinner, it's peak washing time, baby! The dishwasher is full and there are more dishes to do. If you let the dishes soak in water, that will loosen the grime and make your washing job easier, or, shall we say, "more level."

## Develop Cellular Layouts

Anyone who's ever remodeled a kitchen knows about the design principle of the triangle. Good kitchen layouts use the triangle layout of sink, stove, and refrigerator to reduce the waste of travel time between work spaces.

Sometimes the triangle is made with the range in the middle, as an island. This is the place where the cooking work gets done, and ideally it's quickly accessible from the refrigerator and/or the pantry. Also, it's good when the sink is near the cooking island, too, as used pots and pans have to be placed into the next step in the process.

In manufacturing environments, Cellular Layouts enable customization work, as well as a cross-trained, cross-functional team approach to assembly. In offices, Cellular Layouts also encourage effective teamwork, as various contributing functions have access to each other along the Value Stream. Imagine a think tank in one room versus five people sitting in their own separate cubes trying to solve the same problem.

The hallmarks of Cellular Layout are flexibility, speed, real-time coordination, small batches, customization, and high-quality work. Can you see how Cellular Layout might address one or more forms of the eight types of waste?

## Embody the Five Ss

Have you admired the kitchen, garage, or closet of a friend where everything is neatly organized and uncluttered? That friend is applying the 5 Ss of Lean: **S**ort out what's not needed, neatly **S**tore what is needed, clean and **S**hine the area, **S**tandardize the layout, and **S**ustain the effort. You feel better working in such a space and waste less time looking for things.

The Five Ss apply to working environments of all types, everywhere. Have you ever heard the axiom "cleanliness is next to godliness"? Well, we don't really know how true this is, do we? Some very good people are very messy, and some very clean people are not so nice. In any case, no matter where you work or what you do, keeping an orderly working environment leaves less opportunity for mistakes, inefficiencies, and mishaps.

## Make Mistakes Impossible

The Japanese term "poke-yoke" means "inadvertent mistake" (poke) and "prevent" (yoke). Therefore, if you poke-yoke a system, you are making it very difficult for people to make an inadvertent mistake.

Before the term poke-yoke, the Japanese phrase used was translated as "idiot proof." In other words, a system designed to resist inadvertent mistakes is an idiot-proof system. But this was not politically correct. In fact, people make mistakes in general, regardless of their intelligence or level in the organization. Nevertheless, we hope you can see the humor of calling a process or action step "idiot proof."

Have you noticed that some paper application forms highlight the required fields? This has proven to reduce the occurrence of incomplete applications. In this digital age, electronic forms go a step further and Mistake Proof the application process by not accepting it until all the required fields are completed.

Did you know a desktop computer is idiot-proof? Well, it must be if you're using it! (Ha ha, if you can't take this joke you shouldn't have bought an *Idiot's Guide* in the first place!) Your computer has all the plug-in ports for your printer, mouse, power, Ethernet, and so on. You couldn't plug the wrong cable into the wrong place if you tried.

Which form(s) of waste do you think Mistake Proofing addresses? Go ahead and look at the previous section and figure it out yourself. We do know you're far from an idiot, and won't have any problem mapping all these Lean principles and practices back to the eight types of waste.

## Standardize Work and Processes

Otherwise known as the infamous standard operating procedure, Standardized Work is the key to sustaining your Lean gains. How good would your grades be, for instance, if you had no set way of studying for exams? And what kind of a student would you be if you didn't standardize the way that works best for you?

What if you had no set way of mowing the lawn and just erratically zigzagged your way through it differently every time? Do you have a set place for your car keys and, if not, how much time do you spend searching for them on a regular basis? What if a surgeon sometimes washed his hands before surgery and sometimes not? Chaos. That's what would happen, and sometimes even the harm of human life.

The fathers of scientific management taught us the value of work standardization a long time ago and, in regard to this, nothing has changed since then. True, sometimes you have to build flexibility and spontaneity into an otherwise hardwired process, and you have to do this more these days than ever before. But the need to standardize certain work functions will probably never go away.

## The Least You Need to Know

- Lean defines eight types of waste you need to attack: waiting, overproduction, rework, motion, transportation, processing, inventory, intellect.

- The eight types of waste intersect each other, so when one type exists that makes it more likely that other types will exist as well.

- There are many Lean techniques for attacking waste, such as Rapid Changeover, Flow, Pull systems, Workload Balancing, Cellular Layout, Five Ss, Mistake Proofing, and Standardized Work.

- The Lean techniques underlie the application of the many Lean Six Sigma tools. They are the main categories into which you can organize these tools in your mind.

# Chapter 3

# What Is Six Sigma?

## In This Chapter

- ◆ Improving processes and organizations
- ◆ You can't see it but it's there
- ◆ Six Sigma's roots are deep
- ◆ Underlying concepts are critical
- ◆ The Six Sigma breakthrough strategy

This chapter will give you a straight-out definition of Six Sigma, and will elaborate on that definition just enough to make you dangerous. We'll also tell you where Six Sigma came from and why it exists. (Preview: to eliminate defects!) We'll summarize the Six Sigma problem-solving methodology known around the world as DMAIC (for Define-Measure-Analyze-Improve-Control).

Also in this chapter, we'll briefly introduce the key principles that underlie Six Sigma. You may have heard the phrase "$Y$ is a function of $x$." This is the central principle of Six Sigma: that every observed effect $(Y)$—be it desired or undesired—is attributable to one or more "root causes" $(x)$. How you get from the $Y$ to the $x$ is the essence of Six Sigma.

# Many Things to Many People

In its fullest form, Six Sigma is a world-class management system for driving, achieving, and sustaining breakthrough improvements in every part of an organization. Through structured planning and systematic project execution, an organization leverages Six Sigma to achieve its most important business objectives.

Essentially, Six Sigma is about improving processes, or the way work gets done in an organization. This is where the rubber of performance improvement meets the road. If you operate your processes at Six Sigma quality, then you commit no more than 3.4 defects per million opportunities for defects. This means you have to operate your processes correctly the first time 99.9997 percent of the time!

If that sounds too stringent, consider the table that follows. It gives you the counterintuitive truth about how good you have to be. In today's business world and organizational climate, 99 percent good is simply not good enough. To stay in business and be competitive, you have to be Six Sigma good.

## The Difference Between Good and Great

| 99 percent good (3.8 sigma) | 99.99966 percent good (six sigma) |
|---|---|
| 20k lost articles of mail per hour | Seven articles lost per hour |
| Unsafe drinking water for almost 15 minutes each day | One unsafe minute every 7 months |
| 5,000 incorrect surgical procedures per week | 1.7 incorrect operations per week |
| Two short or long landings at major airports each day | One short or long landing every 5 years |
| 200,000 wrong drug prescriptions each year | 68 wrong prescriptions each year |
| No electricity for almost 7 hours each month | 1 hour without power every 34 years |

In its totality, Six Sigma is a vision, a philosophy, a management system, a scientific methodology, and a performance-improvement toolbox.

- The **vision** of Six Sigma is to delight customers by delivering world-class products and services through achieving the highest levels of performance in everything you do.

◆ The **philosophy** of Six Sigma is to apply a structured, systematic approach to achieve operational excellence across all areas of your business, understanding that defect-free processes result in performance breakthrough.

◆ The **management system** of Six Sigma is a structured approach to setting important business objectives, then coordinating and deploying the knowledge, skills, people, and projects required to meet those objectives.

◆ The **scientific methodology** of Six Sigma is Define-Measure-Analyze-Improve-Control (DMAIC), and it is the approach that everyone follows in solving specific performance problems and making specific performance improvements.

◆ The **toolbox** of Six Sigma is the many templates, statistical tests, process analysis techniques, and deployment aids used to implement DMAIC projects and lead performance-improvement initiatives.

**Lean Six Sigma Wisdom**

The benefits of Six Sigma are as follows: Defect Reduction, predictable product and service performance, lower costs, increased operating margins, higher customer satisfaction, shorter cycle times, improved processes capability, increased capacity, and increased revenue.

# Can You See Your Hidden Process?

The point of Six Sigma is to operate nearly flawless processes such that all the work performed is right the first time. Here's the disturbing reality of how most organizations operate: they have far more defects and errors than they think. The reason is because they think their scrap rate might be, say, just 1 percent as shown by the simple Flow diagram that follows.

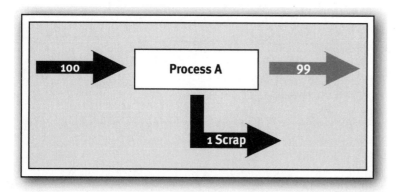

*If you only look at scrap, you might see a process that yields 99 percent.*

100 → **Process A** → 99

1 Scrap

Proud managers look at numbers like this and say, "We're not doing too badly; only 1 out of every 100 products or transactions we make is defective." What they aren't examining as closely is the cost, time, and resources involved in achieving the 99 percent yield.

Typically, organizations engage in huge amounts of rework to achieve the yield they claim. A part is the wrong size, so the final product has to be reassembled with the right part. A track house has to be painted over again because the wrong color was applied at first. A creditor needs to reapply a payment that was wrongly applied to another customer's account.

In the end everything looks fine, but in the process you commit a cardinal business sin: you engage in rework to make it right when you could have done it right the first time. Therefore, in reality, your 99 percent yield might look like the following diagram.

In this example, you see that 20 items (or outputs) were not completed right the first time, so they had to be put through the rework process. While yield looks like 99 percent, *first-time* yield is only 80 percent. And the expense to the organization is enormous. Therefore, it's all about how you get there; if you arrive at your destination through rework, you are losing money along the way. If you do it right the first time, you keep your money in your pocket where it belongs.

*If you uncover your hidden factory, you see that the same process yielding "99 percent" really yields only 80 percent the first time, before all the rework happens.*

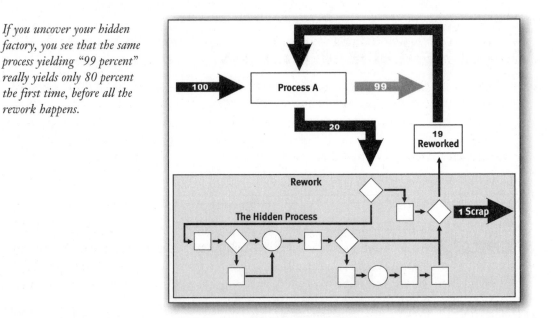

# Where Did Six Sigma Come From?

As with Lean, we can trace the roots of Six Sigma to the nineteenth-century crafts-man, whose challenges as an individual a long time ago mirror the challenges of orga-nizations today. The craftsman had to minimize wasted time, actions, and materials; he also had to make every product or service to a high standard of quality the first time, each time, every time.

## Quality Beginning

The roots of what would later become Six Sigma were planted in 1908, when W. S. Gosset developed statistical tests to help analyze quality data obtained at Guinness Brewery. About the same time, A. K. Erlang studied telephone traffic problems for the Copenhagen Telephone Company in an effort to increase the reliability of service in an industry known for its inherent randomness. It's likely that Erlang was the first mathematician to apply probability theory in an industrial setting, an effort that led to modern queuing and reliability theory.

With these underpinnings, Walter Shewhart worked with Western Electric (a fore-runner of AT&T) in the 1930s to develop the theoretical concepts of quality control. Lean-like industrial engineering techniques did not solve quality and variation-related problems; more statistical intelligence was needed to get to their root causes. Shewhart is also known as the originator of the Plan-Do-Check-Act cycle, which is sometimes ascribed to Dr. Edwards Deming, Shewhart's understudy.

As the story goes, Deming made the connection between quality and cost. If you find a way to prevent defects, and do everything right the first time, you won't have any need to perform rework. Therefore, as quality goes up, the cost of doing business goes down. Deming's words were echoed in the late 1970s by a guy named Philip Crosby, who popularized the notion that "quality is free."

## Quality Crazy

War and devastation bring us to Japan, where Deming did most of his initial quality proselytizing with another American, Dr. Joseph Juran. Both helped Japan rebuild its economy after World War II, consulting with numerous Japanese companies in the development of statistical quality control techniques, which later spread into the sys-tem known as Total Quality Control (TQC).

As the global economy grew, organizations grew in size and complexity. Many administrative, management, and enabling functions grew around the core function of a company to make this or that product. The thinking of efficiency and quality, therefore, began to spread from the manufacturing function to virtually all functions—procurement, billing, customer service, shipping, and so on. Quality is not just one person's or one department's job. Rather, quality is everyone's job!

This is when quality circles and suggestion programs abounded in Japanese companies: no mind should be wasted, and everyone's ideas are necessary. Furthermore, everyone should continuously engage in finding better ways to create value and improve performance. By necessity, quality became everyone's job, not just the job of a few … especially in Japan, at a time when there was precious little money to invest in new equipment and technology.

The rest of the story might be familiar if you're old enough to remember. By the late 1970s, America had lost its quality edge in cars, TVs, and other electronics—and they were suffering significant market share losses. Japanese plants were far more productive and superior to American plants, according to a 1980 NBC television program, *If Japan Can Why Can't We?*

In response to all this, American companies took up the quality cause. They made Deming and Juran heroes, and institutionalized the Japanese-flavored TQC into its American counterpart, Total Quality Management (TQM). They developed a special government award, the Baldrige Award, to give companies that best embodied the ideal practice of TQM. They organized all the many elements and tools of quality improvement into a teachable, learnable, and doable system—and a booming field of quality professionals was born.

## Quality Business

The co-founder of Six Sigma, Dr. Mikel Harry, has often said that Six Sigma shifts the focus from the business of quality to the quality of business. What he means is that for many years the practices of quality improvement floated loosely around a company, driven by the quality department. And as much as the experts said that quality improvement has to be driven and supported by top executives, it generally wasn't.

Enter Jack Welch, the iconic CEO who led General Electric through 2 decades of incredible growth and consistent returns for shareholders. In the late 1980s, Welch had a discussion with former AlliedSignal CEO Larry Bossidy, who said that Six Sigma could transform not only a process or product, but a company. In other words, GE could use Six Sigma as AlliedSignal was already doing: to improve the financial health and viability of the corporation through real and lasting operational improvements.

Welch took note and hired Mikel Harry to train hundreds of his managers and specialists to become Six Sigma Black Belts, Master Black Belts, and Champions. Welch installed a deployment infrastructure so he could fan the Six Sigma methodology out as widely as possible across GE's many departments and functions. In short, Welch elevated the idea and practice of quality from the engineering hallways of the corporation into the boardroom.

Lest we not be clear, the first practical application of Six Sigma on a pervasive basis occurred at Motorola, where Dr. Harry and the co-inventor of Six Sigma, Bill Smith, worked as engineers. Bob Galvin, then CEO of Motorola, paved the way for Bossidy and Welch in that he proved how powerful Six Sigma was in solving difficult performance problems. He also used Six Sigma at Motorola to achieve unprecedented quality levels for key products. One such product was the Motorola Bandit pager, which failed so rarely that Motorola simply replaced rather than repaired them when they did fail.

**Real-Life Story**

Twenty years after its inception, Six Sigma has saved an estimated $427 billion for Fortune 500 companies alone.

*Sources: iSixSigma (www.isixsigma. com) and iSixSigma Magazine (www.isixsigma-magazine.com)*

In Six Sigma, then, we find the most mature system for ensuring quality at the organizational level, the operational level, the process level, and the individual product level. This is what gives Six Sigma its status as a world-class approach to quality improvement: its scientific validity, its focus on the execution of many different projects in all functions, its requirement to achieve financial return, and its robust nature as a management system.

# You Know More About Six Sigma Than You Think

We hope what you've read so far in this chapter doesn't seem like Greek to you, even though sigma is a Greek letter! Statistics really aren't as intimidating as they seem, and it's not as hard as you might think to become astute about Six Sigma. Of course,

Parts 2 and 3 of this book will take you a little deeper into some of Six Sigma's methods as they are integrated with those of Lean.

Here in this section, you can keep having fun just learning about Six Sigma without the hard work of actually doing a Six Sigma or Lean Six Sigma project. And before you do, anyway, it might be very helpful to understand some of the Six Sigma concepts that underlie the application of its tools. These concepts follow, so know them well because they'll put you in the right mind-set for success.

# $Y = f(x)$

In your travels around your company, you may hear the phrase "$Y$ is a function of $x$" coming from Black Belts, Green Belts, and others. If you only memorize one Six Sigma equation, memorize this one. It will not only change your view of business, but it will change your view of life.

$Y$ is the outcome you desire. The $x$s are the causal factors, or inputs, that are critical to producing the outcome. The $f$ is the function performed on the inputs to produce the outputs. $Y$ is a function of $x$.

A good cup of coffee ($Y$) is a function ($f$) of properly managing the quality and interaction of several critical $x$s: beans, coffeemaker, water. A low golf score is a function of the golfer's swing, strategy, mood, course conditions, weather, caddy, and so on.

The most important thing to know about $Y = f(x)$ is that few rather than many $x$s carry leverage in producing the desired outcome. This is true for any product or system, no matter how complex. Of the thousands of variables affecting any system, only a few really matter.

Say you are applying for a job but you can't get an interview. Or you get interviews but never get offered a job. What is the issue? $Y$ is a function of $x$. You might conveniently make yourself think "they just don't see how good I am." So they are the cause, the $x$.

Upon deeper introspection, maybe your resumé has errors, or maybe you talk loudly and come across a little "rough." Maybe your expectations are too high and you are applying for jobs that really require more education or experience. In any case, you better figure out what the real connections are between your $Y$s and $x$s or you'll never get what you want.

The other part of thinking in terms of $Y = f(x)$ is that it drives you down the chain of causation as far as possible, to the place where the real leverage resides. Say you want money. How do you get money? You need a good job; you need an entrepreneurial business. How do you get these? You need some education or some experience, some training; you need a mentor. Which training or mentor do you choose and why?

Go all the way back. Ask why five times. Do not settle for surface-level thinking. Go back to the bottom-most source of leverage and work there. In this sense $Y = f(x)$ is much like the paradox of the self: the more you focus on a problem, or on fixing a problem, the worse it can get.

Sometimes you have to take your eye off the goal and focus on the process—the necessary $x$s that will naturally produce the goal like it is ripe fruit falling off a tree. This is the root cause. If you want money, you might want to start improving your personality, because then more people will like you. Then you might want to get to know as many people as possible—to increase your odds of becoming favored by someone who can give you a great job, or connect you to one.

If you're already a people person, the best thing for you might be to hit the books for a while. Whatever you do, if you want something, or your organization needs to do something better, it is advisable to meditate on $Y = f(x)$. The more thought you put into it, the more likely you are to discover the leverage you need to make your dream come true.

## Measure, Measure, Measure

This is the very concept that grounds Six Sigma to reality. It's all too easy for any business executive or even a design engineer to make decisions based on "experience" or "gut feel" because they're just so darn good at what they do. Six Sigma is not biased toward this type of thinking. Six Sigma says that if you don't have the data, you don't have squat.

And by the way, if you do have data, it better be valid. So your random sample better be taken with adherence to proper statistical standards; your measurement gauges better be accurate (remember root cause?) If your data is inaccurate because it was produced by faulty measurement gauges, then your analysis of that data will yield conclusions that are useless. All your effort will still not stop that stubborn defect from recurring over and over again.

If operational excellence is your goal, then you have to embrace data like it's your best friend. Your very best friend. That means you'll certainly know it well enough to know where it is, what it represents, and what it means. And you'll certainly know if and when it is lying to you!

Dr. Harry has often said, "You only measure what you value; if you don't measure it, you really don't value it." How true this is. When is the last time you checked the balance in your checkbook or bank account, and how often do you do so? The answer will tell you exactly how much you value money or not.

Numbers really do tell all, especially when it comes to businesses and organizations. Even if you are the United Way, you want to demonstrate how many children you help with the donor's dollars. While United Way does not exist to make money, it still measures what it values. Without a strong competence in measurement, no organization can survive.

Six Sigma simply takes this undeniable fact to a deeper level. It has great value when performance problems are complex, or when smart people and common sense simply fall short of solving problems. If you take this seriously, you will experience the same discovery thousands have discovered.

You will find that data, when gathered, analyzed, and interpreted correctly, will often teach you something you didn't know. Think of data and an obsession with measurement as your way of checking up on yourself. You don't build a bridge without the numbers; and you don't run a process without the numbers, either. If you do, you will crash and burn.

## Claim Your Entitlement

No, we don't mean this in the same sense of someone getting something they don't deserve. You may feel entitled to your job, but you always have to justify your suitability for it. In other words, you are only entitled to the very best you can possibly do. Or the very best you deserve.

Companies, too, can only expect to do their very best with what they have. Yet by no means does this mean an organization can just "try hard" and leave the rest to fate. To operate at *Entitlement* means that your process is producing its best possible output levels. All the conditions and possible errors or interruptions are held at bay.

**Lean Six Sigma Lingo**

**Entitlement** is the best your process can perform according to its design, and disregarding the many forms of variation you can't control.

Some rightly describe the idea of Entitlement as the best you can possibly operate without redesigning your process. So if one day you put 18 widgets through the process, while usually you make 15 or 16, then you've taught yourself something about what is possible. You've taught yourself that you are entitled to make 18 units a day, no less, and maybe even more.

A car has an Entitlement performance that can be achieved, depending on how the owner uses it. The car is entitled to a certain miles per gallon, tire life, top speed, life span. Your yard is entitled to be free of weeds at all times, only requiring certain functions to be performed as scheduled with no error.

But not all things operate at their Entitlement at all times, because the function varies, or, more specifically, the way the work gets performed isn't always the same. Therefore, your goal should be to reduce the variation in your processes. Always change your oil every 3,000 miles. Every six months, give your yard a weed pre-emergent treatment, cutting them off at the source before they grow. And so on.

Entitlement is where Six Sigma can take your process the way it's currently designed. A hacksaw, for example, is made to cut through certain metals with certain properties. You surely can't use it to chop down a big tree—not in a timely manner, anyway.

Say you use that hacksaw to cut through a 2×4. With no interruptions or unnecessary problems, you can cut through the 2×4 in 12 minutes with zero errors. That is your Entitlement, and you know because you've studied and optimized the functions (using data) of using the hacksaw for cutting 2×4s.

If you change your technology and use a handsaw with a large blade, your 2×4 cutting Entitlement changes. Now you are entitled to cut through your wood in 1 minute, not 12—with no errors, of course. This is the role of Design for Six Sigma (DFSS): the application of Six Sigma tools to *build in* better quality and to prevent defects (time or quality related) from occurring in the first place.

Some say that the typical level of Entitlement for the typical process is around four sigma (99.379 percent good); if you want to reach six sigma (99.9997 percent good) performance, you usually have to redesign the process using DFSS or some other tool. In any case, you should always strive to operate your processes at their Entitlement level, all the time.

# The Six Sigma DMAIC Methodology

We would miss the mark of informing you about Six Sigma if we didn't tell you about the DMAIC methodology. That's the Define-Measure-Analyze-Improve-Control cycle, which is also known as the Six Sigma breakthrough strategy. This is the structured process by which you move through the stages of solving your performance problem, or making a performance improvement.

Another way of thinking about DMAIC is in terms of the scientific method, which requires data and measurement—and repeated confirmation—as the basis of knowledge.

In the world of process improvement, DMAIC is like the scientific method: its structure requires that you have the data and confirmation you need to proceed with improving your processes.

Say you have to go to the doctor:

♦ You first Define your problem (I don't feel well).

♦ Then you Measure your problem (take temperature; it's 103).

♦ You Analyze to find the root cause (have medical assessments performed to test your hypotheses of what you think could be wrong).

♦ Next you Improve your situation (doctor prescribes antibiotics, you take them, drink fluids).

♦ Finally, you Control your gains (temperature is monitored and healthy habits are established).

## The Least You Need to Know

♦ Six Sigma is a vision, philosophy, management system, scientific methodology, and set of performance-improvement tools for achieving breakthrough improvements in every part of an organization.

♦ Six Sigma had its foundations laid by Walter Shewhart (1930s), and later evolved with Dr. Edwards Deming (1950s), then with the Baldrige Award and Total Quality Management (1980s).

♦ The term Six Sigma and its use originated in the late 1980s at Motorola. Then AlliedSignal and General Electric deployed Six Sigma pervasively, establishing it as a strategy for corporate improvement.

♦ Key Six Sigma concepts include the hidden factory, $Y = f(x)$, Measurement, and Entitlement.

♦ The breakthrough strategy is the scientific method applied to the goal of performance improvement. The breakthrough strategy is known as DMAIC, for Define-Measure-Analyze-Improve-Control.

# Chapter 4

# The Basics of Six Sigma

## In This Chapter

- ◆ Specifications and standard deviations
- ◆ Understanding the hidden factory
- ◆ The different types of variation
- ◆ All about performance characteristics
- ◆ The reality of Rolled Throughput Yield
- ◆ The shift-and-drift phenomenon

In this chapter, you'll learn about some of the more technical aspects of Six Sigma. Still, we'll only scratch the surface of what there is to know about data, process, and product metrics, and using the many Six Sigma tools to uncover the root cause of complex performance problems.

You'll learn that variation is the key cause of defects—whether they're related to products, transactions like a stock purchase, or services like airline baggage handling or prescription filling. By reading this chapter, you'll also understand more about why Six Sigma is such a strict performance target.

# It's All Greek to Me

The 18th letter in the Greek alphabet is sigma (σ), and in the world of statistics it describes the *standard deviation*, or variation, of a population. But don't confuse sigma level (sometimes called *sigma value, sigma score,* or just *sigma*) with standard deviation. While the Greek letter sigma is used to describe the standard deviation in statistics, the word sigma in the context of Six Sigma is used to define what statisticians call the *Z-score*.

 **Lean Six Sigma Lingo**

A **Z-score** is a statistical measure that quantifies the distance a data point is from the mean (in standard deviation units). If a test had a mean score of 75 and a standard deviation of 5, then a score of 80 would be equivalent to a Z-score of 1. If the raw score were 70, then the Z-score would be -1. If the raw score were 90, then the Z-score would be 3. (The negative sign simply tells you the test score is to the left of the mean.)

Here is the essence of Six Sigma: how many standard deviations can you fit between your average (mean) performance and your *specification* limits for any given *Critical-To* characteristic? If you can fit three standard deviations, then you operate at three sigma performance; if you can fit 4.4, then you operate at 4.4 sigma, and so on.

Before you can understand what we mean by "fitting" three, four, five, six, or however many standard deviations between your mean and your specification limits for any given performance characteristic, you have to have some background in statistics. If you do, then skip over the next couple of pages and go right to the section titled "What Does Six Sigma Look Like?" If you don't, you'll want to read on.

## Basic Statistical Terms

The statistical **mean** is a measure of central tendency that is determined by adding all the data points in a population, then dividing the total by the number of points. The resulting number is the mean—or the typical value of the population, otherwise known as the *average*.

**Variation** is the range of difference between the statistical mean and all the data points that are used to calculate the mean. Or the extent to which performance varies around the average. In the context of Lean Six Sigma, you always want to minimize variation as much as you can.

A **defect** is any output of any process or business task that does not meet its intended performance target. For example, serving cold food at a restaurant (when it's supposed to be hot) is a defect. Showing up 20 minutes late to a meeting is a defect (or "error," as many like to say in nonmanufacturing environments). Of course, when you take your new computer out of the box and it doesn't work, that's a defect, too.

## What Is a CT?

A Critical-To characteristic (CT) is any feature of a product or process that is important to the customer. A tire has a color, a weight, an exact shape so it fits on a rim. All these characteristics have to perform to specification, or the final product will not perform as intended. Therefore, Six Sigma focuses as *upstream* as possible in the value chain—toward the ultimate root causes of performance shortfalls.

Some people call CTs CTQs, for "critical to quality." Others call them CTXs, because a trait can be critical to quality, cost, delivery, time, or some other important aspect of performance. Generically speaking, every performance characteristic is critical to quality, but if you want to be more exact you can say critical to cost or delivery, and so on. If you want to be more generic in your communication, you can use the terms CTs or CTXs.

> **Lean Six Sigma Lingo**
>
> Referring to activities and steps in a process as **upstream** means they are closer to the beginning of the process. Naturally, steps and activities closer to the end of a process are referred to as downstream.

## What Are Specifications?

Specifications are the exacting requirements for CTs expressed mathematically so they can be constantly measured and monitored. In manufacturing, for instance, a specification for a piece of metal might be 3.2 to 3.4 millimeters. Any produced metal piece that falls outside these limits is considered defective. In a service environment, like a hospital, you might have a specification of changing the dressing on a wound no more than once every eight hours.

## What Is a Statistical Population?

A statistical population is a distribution of data points around a mean, or average. Often you will hear the words "normal distribution" to depict data that form the bell-shaped curve that is so prevalent in nature.

For example, if we plotted the height of all men, we would see a bell-shaped population whereby the majority are between about 5'8" and 6' tall. Fewer men would be shorter than 5' or taller than 6'. Fewer still would be shorter than 5'8" and taller than 6'. It's the same with IQ, college entrance exam scores, weight of people, etc.

Sometimes populations are not normal and are described as "skewed," meaning they're biased toward one end of the measurement spectrum or another. Sometimes, too, populations can have double (bimodal) or multiple (multimodal) peaks—which means that data are clustered around certain values throughout the measurement scale.

## What Is a Standard Deviation?

The standard deviation ($\sigma$) is a measure of how spread out the values in a data set (population) are. The standard deviation of a data set is a measure of dispersion of the data points around their arithmetic mean. If all the data points are close to the mean, then $\sigma$ will be closer to zero. If the data points are spread out farther away from the mean, then $\Sigma$ will be bigger.

Calculating the standard deviation from a sample of data entails taking the square root of the sum of the squared differences of each data point from the mean, divided by the number of data points minus one. (See Chapter 8 for a Standard Deviation formula and sample calculation.)

# What Does Six Sigma Look Like?

What follows is a performance characteristic, or Critical-To characteristic, with one standard deviation identified. We also show a performance characteristic with lower and upper specification limits, and it shows that its capability is three sigma. This translates into 66,807 defects per million opportunities for defects, or a process yield of 93.32 percent.

**Technically Speaking**

Some quality and Six Sigma professionals make a distinction between a defect and an error. While all defects are the result of errors, not all errors result in defects. For instance, failing to signal is an error that doesn't always lead to the defect of a car wreck.

Now if we make this same CT perform at a six sigma level, we see a distribution that looks like the next graph. Note that there are six standard deviations falling within the upper specification limit—which means that the process is operating at no more than 3.4 defects per million opportunities. It's really as simple as that. No mystery, no magic. If you can design and operate your processes in a way that yields six sigma performance, you will be world-class in what you do.

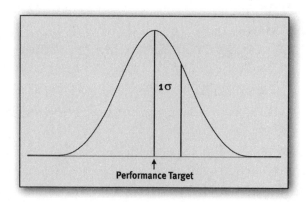

*The distance between the mean (μ) and the inflection point is the standard deviation (σ).*

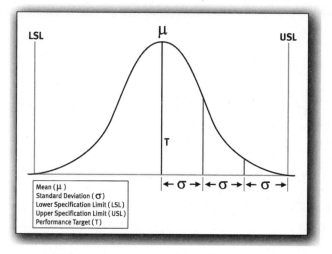

*In this depiction, the performance of the CT is three sigma, because you can fit three standard deviations between the mean and the upper specification limit.*

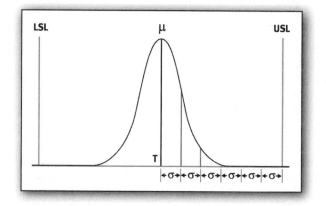

*In this depiction, the performance of the CT is six sigma, because you can fit six standard deviations between the mean and the upper specification limit.*

# It's All About Variation

Did you know that no two coins are exactly the same width? How about those grains of sand on the beach, or on all beaches in the entire world? Did you know that no two people are the same size or weight? Hard to believe, but true. That's right, no two grains of sand anywhere are the same size or weight—or diameter or circumference, for that matter.

Six Sigma statisticians will tell you how important it is to measure variation in any process, product, part, system, and so on—and they are right, because variation can kill a business, especially uncontrollable variation. This is key: some variation is controllable, and some variation is uncontrollable. Six Sigma helps you perform to standard all the time regardless of the variation you can't control; at the same time, Six Sigma ensures that you prevent the kind of variation you can control.

In Six Sigma terminology, most variation in the performance of any quality characteristic falls under the designation of *Common Cause variation*. This is the variation you get by virtue of nature, or by virtue of the way you design your product or process. Every time you get a cup of cappuccino at a coffee shop, for example, it's a different temperature, even though in general it's "hot."

*Special Cause variation*, on the other hand, is when the coffee shop serves you a cold cup of cappuccino. Obviously a defect like this is "special." Something went unusually wrong with the process, and it produced a faulty output—the root cause of which can be determined and rectified. Maybe the guy who makes the coffee forgot to steam the milk in the cappuccino, or maybe the milk steamer is not working properly.

 **Lean Six Sigma Wisdom** _____

Design for Six Sigma (DFSS) is the branch of Six Sigma that enables you to prevent defects from occurring in the first place through superior design. One of the hallmarks of DFSS is that it enables you to make your products, services, and transactions "robust" to Common Cause variation. Therefore, you use DFSS to "vaccinate" yourself against the variation in nature that you can't control. You also use DFSS to prevent the occurrence of Special Cause variation, or the kind of variation you can control.

Both Special and Common Cause variation can wreak havoc on businesses and organizations—since reliability and consistency are critical to the success. How long would you keep your exterminator if he showed up for only half of his scheduled appointments? How many jet engines do you think Boeing would buy from

Honeywell if they worked most of the time but sometimes failed? When it comes to transporting humans, variation, especially the kind that leads to error, is intolerable.

# How Capable Is Your Process?

One of the key activities of Six Sigma practitioners is measuring and characterizing the behavior of a process, or a Critical-To characteristic. This is what people mean when they talk about performance capability, and it's at the root of Six Sigma. If your CT is the weight of a product, or its color, or the timeliness of a service, then how often does that product or service perform as intended?

This is the capability of your process: the percentage of time it performs within its intended specifications.

Let's use a car wash as an example—a process that results in a flawlessly clean vehicle. To do this, you have to perform several functions in a consistent way over time. You have to shoot water at the car at a certain pressure for a certain amount of time. You have to release the right amount of soap at the right time, and guide the car through the wash via some foolproof system.

In addition to machines, some car washes have personnel who perform a series of actions on the car—before it goes through and after it comes out of the automated part of the process. People on the front end determine what kind of wash you want, and often try to sell you the kind you don't want. They tag your car and vacuum it before it gets washed. They dry it when it comes out and shine your tires (if you paid for that option).

All these major steps are critical to achieving the outcome of a flawlessly clean car each and every time. Sure, it's easy on average to turn out pretty clean cars; but it's not easy to turn out superiorly clean cars each time, every time. To do that you have to define and control all your many quality characteristics; if you want your final outcome to be perfect, then you have to be nearly perfect at each and every step in the process.

## Mind Your CTs

We're afraid there's more you'll have to know about process capability if you want to be Six Sigma proficient. It's not enough to just understand that every process has a number of steps to be managed and controlled. Each step itself is a world of quality characteristics unto its own! That means the steps of washing and rinsing your car have their own quality characteristics, which in turn have theirs, and so on.

Obviously, the more complex a system, the more CTs there are because they keep getting nested and nested. A large jet has three million parts that come together in a complex assembly of systems and subsystems, all coordinated together to make it fly you and about 250 other people around the world.

A car wash is simpler, but all of its parts and CTs have to work together just the same. So the automated washing system has various functions it performs by virtue of a power system, hydraulics, water flow, water removal, signaling devices for the customer, and so on.

The key point about Six Sigma is that it Defines, Measures, Analyzes, Improves, and Controls (DMAIC) the functionality of all CTs in a system. If you want your process to function properly, then all your CTs have to function properly as well. The way to ensure this is to apply Six Sigma (or Lean Six Sigma) to your processes, which we show you how to do in Part 2.

## Multiply Your Yields

You may already know that the numerical definition of Six Sigma is *no more than 3.4 defects per million opportunities for defects.* But what does this mean? Does this mean if you're a Six Sigma trial lawyer, you'll only lose 3.4 cases for every million you try? It could, if that's your target and definition of success.

Certain industries have certain performance expectations. For example, the airline industry operates well above Six Sigma performance when it comes to transporting passengers. Far fewer than 3.4 per million end up not reaching their destinations due to crashes.

Your luggage, on the other hand, has a much worse chance than you of getting where it's supposed to go. That process classically yields only around four sigma performance—which means about 6,200 pieces of luggage for every million don't make it where they're supposed to go.

But here's where it gets a little tricky. Let's say you want your car wash to operate at a "Six Sigma" level. What do you mean? Do you mean that no more than 3.4 cars per million washed will display any defects causing a customer complaint? If this is the case, how well would each step in the process have to operate, and each part of each step?

Remember the jet airplane discussed in the previous section? The car wash, too, has many CTs that all need to be defect-free if the final product is to be defect-free. Not three million parts like the jet, but probably more than you might imagine.

The key for you to know is that each CT has a probability of failing—of not meeting its designed specification. So the rinse cycle might run without the required volume of water; or the vacuuming people at the front end might leave some area undone; or the guy who washes your windows could leave a smudgy fingerprint.

Rolled Throughput Yield (RTY) is a key concept that tells half the story of why Six Sigma is such a stringent performance target. The reason is because each CT in a system has its own probability of success or failure—of meeting or falling short of its specification(s). Yet if any one CT fails, that puts the final product in jeopardy of meeting its performance target (or customer expectation).

In other words, the probability of failure tends to propagate throughout a system as a function of multiplying the yields of each CT in the system. So let's say the intake guy at the car wash has a 90 percent chance (yield) of doing his job right, and the vacuum people have a 90 percent chance of doing their jobs right, and the washing machine has the same chance, as does the tire shining, drying, and window washing functions.

Therefore:

$$.90 \times .90 \times .90 \times .90 \times .90 \times .90 = .53$$

That's the probability of failure for:

$$CT1 \times CT2 \times CT3 \times CT4 \times CT5 \times CT6 = \text{Rolled Throughput Yield}$$

Therefore, given this oversimplified example, your car has only a 53 percent chance of meeting the performance target of "perfectly clean car," as defined of course by the detailed completion checklist used religiously by the managers of the car wash.

Imagine the Rolled Throughput Yield calculations required for the building of that jet with three million parts. A 747 ain't no car wash! And the implications are different when it fails. This is the reality of Rolled Throughput Yield, and why you should take Six Sigma seriously.

# Beware of Shift and Drift

The other half of the Six Sigma story (from a statistical perspective) is that the behavior of a process tends to "shift and drift" over time. Take the car wash personnel, for example. Their behavior will fluctuate over time, and there is nothing the car wash manager can do to prevent this. As a population, the car wash workers will perform within some limit of short-term variability, as well as some limit of long-term variability.

Therefore, if you measure your process performance on any given day, or within any given short period of time, you will get some distribution of variability around your process mean. This is true for the final output of a process as well as any of its steps or CTs.

*Short-term variation around a process mean.*

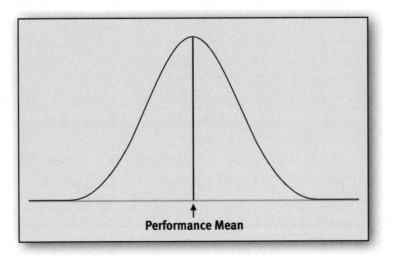

*Any instances of performance that fall outside the specification limits are considered defects.*

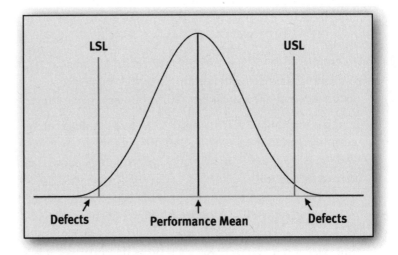

This is not a book about Six Sigma, so you're not going to get a lot of the statistics. We just want you to take note that, over time, your sampled performance distributions will vary, as shown in the chart that follows. Just like samples you take of your hair length will vary from sample to sample over time. Just like any samples the car wash manager takes of his staff's performance—they, too, will vary from sample to sample.

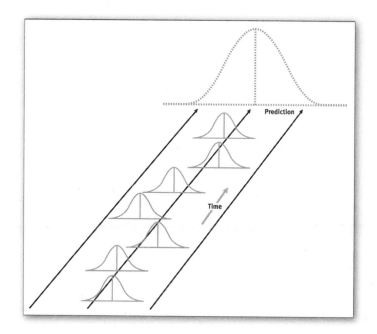

*Every process "wiggles" back and forth over time. This is known as "the 1.5 sigma shift."*

We mentioned before that every CT has to perform within certain specifications, or performance limits. When it doesn't, you have a defect, and this creates problems and rework. The following chart shows the statistical representation of a defect in terms of a performance distribution.

You know those self-serve car washes where you spray your car with water from a wand? To be effective, and not cause defects, the water has to come out at a certain pressure. But we know there is variation in everything, so it is unrealistic to expect that the pressure can remain constant. Therefore we set some lower specification limit (LSL) and some upper specification limit (USL).

When the pressure coming out of the hose falls below the lower limit, we can say a defect has occurred. Similarly, when the pressure exceeds the upper limit, a defect occurs. If this happens 66,807 times per million opportunities, then the water jet is a three sigma activity. If this happens 6,210 times, then it is a four sigma activity. If defects occur 233 times out of a million, we have a process that operates at five sigma, and so on.

But here's the rub, a process that displays Six Sigma performance in the short term might operate at 4.5 sigma in the long term. (Thus the "1.5 sigma shift.") This is true for a car wash, a jet engine maker, a bank, a particular machine in a particular factory, lawnmowers made by XYZ company, the fitting of the wheels on the mower, the level of satisfaction customers have with a hotel—anything and everything that holds leverage in bringing about the desired outcome of a process.

That means to achieve Six Sigma performance (3.4 defects per million opportunities) over the long haul, you have to display no more than *one defect per billion* opportunities in the short term!

We're hoping now you have the full picture of why Six Sigma is such a strict performance target. Not only do you have to account for the propagating nature of error (Rolled Throughput Yield), but you also have to make sure you operate at a full 1.5 sigma level higher in the short term than you want to operate in the long term.

## The Least You Need to Know

- ◆ Six Sigma is focused on defect reduction through the minimization of performance variation around the statistical mean.

- ◆ Six Sigma performance is when an organization commits no more than 3.4 defects per million opportunities for defects at the quality characteristic level.

- ◆ Most companies will not even approach Six Sigma performance, but by attempting to do so will dramatically improve their operational and financial performance.

- ◆ The more Critical-To (CT) characteristics there are in a system, the better you have to perform, due to the phenomenon of Rolled Throughput Yield.

- ◆ Process performance tends to "shift and drift" over time as much or more than 1.5 sigma. Therefore, if you measure 233 defects in the short run (five sigma), you are likely to have about 22,700 defects (3.5 sigma) in the long run.

# Chapter 5

# What Is Lean Six Sigma?

## In This Chapter

- ◆ A world-class improvement method
- ◆ Better, faster, and cheaper
- ◆ Why Lean Six Sigma was inevitable
- ◆ The history and lineage of Lean Six Sigma
- ◆ Lean Six Sigma as a means for creating additional value

Lean Six Sigma is the combination of two world-class approaches to organizational performance improvement. This chapter will give you more details about why and how the two methods of Lean and Six Sigma became blended into one. We also show you which companies have led the way in this important integration. Finally, we'll focus on the concept of value, or Value Creation, which is the overriding principle of Lean Six Sigma.

## Lean Six Sigma Is Faster, Better, and Cheaper

Think of business as a constant drive to accomplish the mission of the organization better, faster, and cheaper. To make products better, faster, and cheaper. To deliver services better, faster, and cheaper. And to operate processes better, faster, and cheaper. As an organization evolves, it improves the synergy between these three elements of success.

However, sometimes these elements of business success work at odds. Making the process better means slowing it down; speeding the process up through technology makes it more expensive, at least in the shorter run. Cutting costs results in a reduction of quality and sometimes speed. The key is to leverage Lean Six Sigma in a way that enables you to get better, faster, and cheaper all at the same time, as shown in the diagram that follows.

*The basic idea behind Lean Six Sigma is to blend the two root methodologies into one approach that optimizes the quality, speed, and cost of doing business.*

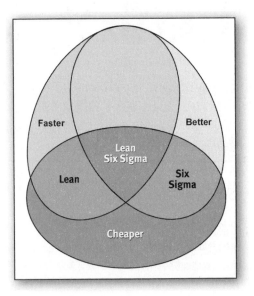

### Performance Pitfall

Don't pigeonhole Lean or Six Sigma. Be careful not to say Lean is good for one thing (like waste removal and cycle time reduction), and Six Sigma is good for another (like defect and cost reduction). Doing this will take your mind off of thinking "Lean Six Sigma"—thinking of every performance challenge in terms of what both approaches can do together.

Really, the connected goals of better, faster, and cheaper all exist to overcome some shortfall preventing optimum operation, like any shortfall that exists in the human body. Everyone has some areas of compromised functioning in their bodies—some part of the spine, some aspect of the organs, some system that is not functioning optimally.

Organizations are no different, as they do not function in an optimal manner. In fact, organizations tend to get more complex, disorganized, and inefficient over time. The only reason they don't, and instead get more efficient over time, is because those who run them are constantly improving what they do and how they do it.

# The Business Focus

Notice the diagram that follows, which brings the aspects of doing business faster and better more closely together under one roof. This is the essence of Lean Six Sigma: understanding the different approaches of Lean and Six Sigma, and knowing how to apply them to make processes faster and better.

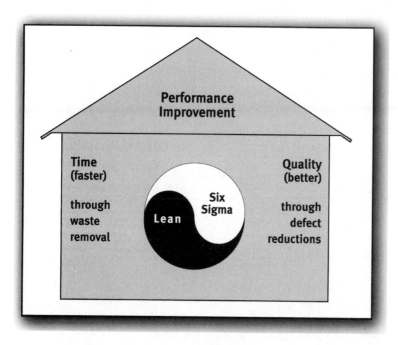

*You should not view Lean and Six Sigma as separate methodologies achieving different objectives—although, generally speaking, Lean is time-driven, and Six Sigma is quality-driven. Picture the wheel of Lean and Six Sigma spinning so fast that the two methods become blurred into one approach.*

Generally speaking, Six Sigma has been used to reduce defects and errors, thereby making processes function better. But in the process, Six Sigma also removes waste and streamlines processes. Same with Lean. While it is used primarily to decrease waste, it often reduces defects, too. In fact, one of the eight types of waste (mentioned in Chapter 2) in Lean is rework. And you can't reduce rework without reducing defects.

Therefore, the most sensible way to view the twin methodologies of Lean and Six Sigma is to make them one approach. The goal of such a marriage is, of course, to derive more value together than apart. With an integrated Lean Six Sigma approach, the focus is always on optimizing process performance (better and faster) to satisfy the needs of customers, and to generate the best possible returns for the organization.

# The Statistical Focus

We just examined how you can view Lean Six Sigma from a business perspective. Yet all of business ultimately comes down to the efficiency with which you transform inputs into outputs. At the process level, you have to transform your inputs into your outputs very fast and, in the best case, flawlessly. To do this, it helps to also have a *statistical* understanding of business performance, and of Lean Six Sigma.

From this standpoint, Lean Six Sigma combines the drive to *move the mean* of performance with the need to *reduce variation* around the mean. Historically, especially when it comes to time-related metrics, Lean is employed for making mean-related improvements, while Six Sigma is employed to make variation-related improvements. Using the two methods as one enables you to accomplish both statistical agendas simultaneously.

*This is Lean Six Sigma: an integrated approach for improving your performance averages, while also reducing your performance variation around those averages. Picture the wheel of Lean and Six Sigma spinning so fast that the two methods become blurred into one approach.*

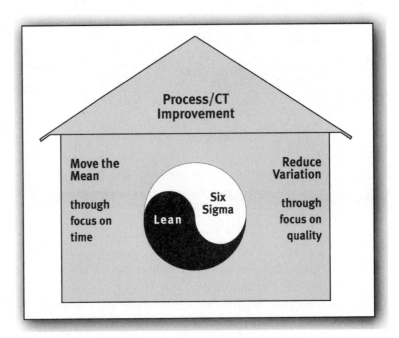

But we have to be equally careful here to not form the impression that Lean is for one thing (move the mean), and Six Sigma is for another (variation reduction around the mean). While some think loosely in these terms, the key is to be fully conscious of both performance dimensions as you surgically operate on your processes and CTs. In other words, Lean Six Sigma enables you to improve the velocity of your process while also improving its accuracy and precision.

Therefore, a tire company might use the thinking and practices of Lean to increase its daily production rate, but then it might incorporate Six Sigma practices to keep that rate steady. But it might also, or instead of Six Sigma, use Lean Flow practices to minimize variation, or Pull practices, or Mistake Proofing for that matter. Further, it might use Six Sigma to ensure that virtually all the tires are free of defects.

Ideally, you integrate Lean and Six Sigma thinking together in everything you do.

**Performance Pitfall**

There are scenarios in which using Lean to reduce mean performance can significantly increase variation, which you don't want. And sometimes, if you're not careful, you can reduce variation around a poor performance standard, and this isn't good, either. Pay attention to your performance mean and your variation.

## Better Isn't Always Better

Let's take a look at a mortgage application process where the critical metric is how long it takes from application receipt to approval/rejection by the lender. That loan-approval time has been averaging 24 hours, with 90 percent of the loans processed within 48 hours (as shown in the figure that follows). Since the lender promises a decision within 48 hours in their advertising, the 10 percent that take longer are considered defects.

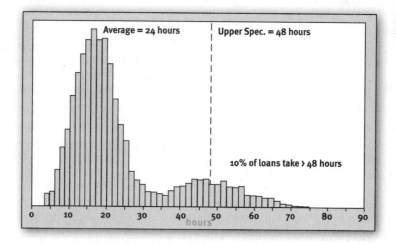

The process is not meeting the promise of "within 48 hours" for 10 percent of the customers. A traditional approach to solving this problem of late decisions is to reduce the average time it takes. We can be wildly successful and cut the average in half, from 24 hours to 12 hours. Problem solved, right? Not so fast—we need to look at variation as well. Even though the average has been drastically reduced, we still have the same percentage of late decisions, as shown in the next figure. Overall time was reduced, but we still have the same number of customers unhappy due to defects—and we still don't know why.

*Even though the average processing time was cut in half, the process still falls short of expectation for 10 percent of customers.*

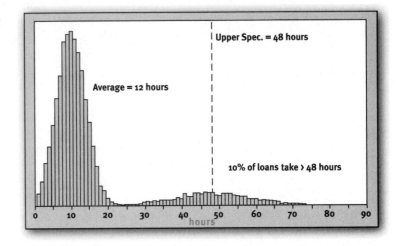

Lean Six Sigma gives us the tools to measure, analyze, and improve both the average and the variation. Both are usually important, and neither should be ignored. The next figure shows the progress you can make with Lean Six Sigma. The reduction in variation has eliminated the "late decisions" and, with that, average time dropped to 18 hours from 24 hours, well within the specification limit.

This is the preferred solution, given the company's promise of "48 hours" to its customers. Of course, there's always room for more improvement. With more work, the process average and variation could be lowered to "all applications within 24 hours." If that's of strategic advantage to the lender, Lean Six Sigma provides the means to make the needed process changes (refer to the next figure).

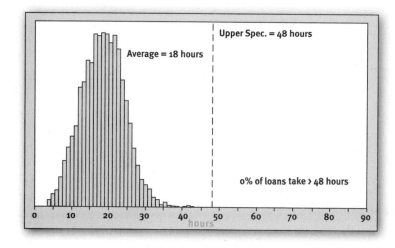

Average = 18 hours

Upper Spec. = 48 hours

0% of loans take > 48 hours

*This is the best solution: a lowered average processing time to 18 hours with zero loan applications taking longer than the promised 48 hours.*

# The Job of Business Is Value Creation

There are many principles, practices, and tools in the Lean Six Sigma toolbox. We have the big concept of waste reduction, which has its roots in Lean. We have Pull, Flow, Workload Balancing, Rapid Changeover, and other Lean concepts and practices. On the Six Sigma side, we have the all-important practices of Defect Reduction, Problem Solving, CT Flow Up/Down, Entitlement, and variation—to name a few. We also have a full smorgasbord of tools, many dozens, in the Lean Six Sigma repertoire.

Still, if you need a simple way of understanding the core of Lean Six Sigma, or you have to explain its essence to your co-workers, bosses, or subordinates, you might want to use the concept of Value Creation. In a nutshell, Value Creation is the act of transforming a set of inputs into a set of outputs that bring in revenue greater than the costs incurred.

For instance, a hospital surgical team performs a function using various instruments, people, procedures, raw material, and so on. A guy needs his kidney removed to save his life, so all the many inputs are brought together in a certain way to perform the operation. For this, the patient (and hopefully his insurance company) is willing to pay a price.

**Lean Six Sigma Wisdom**

All relationships, not just business relationships, are based on the *mutual exchange of value*. When one or both sides of the exchange are not happy with the value derived, the relationship is at risk. Lean Six Sigma is your tool, your ace in the hole, for safeguarding your relationships with customers.

*All of business hinges on the ability to transform inputs into outputs for which consumers are willing to pay. Lean Six Sigma is focused on optimizing the process by which the inputs are transformed into outputs.*

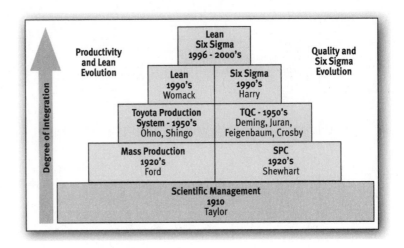

Therefore, if the patient's life is saved, and the hospital makes money doing it, then the conditions for business existence have been satisfied. After all, business is nothing more than the mutual exchange of value. I provide you with a shirt you need; you give me $20 for that shirt; you are happy because you feel you got your money's worth; I am happy because I have made a profit rather than a loss.

Classically, the goal of Lean and all its tools is often summed up as "striving for perfection," while Six Sigma's goal of no more than 3.4 defects per million opportunities is a mature extension of the drive for "never-ending improvement." Of course the two phrases are virtually synonymous. When you break them down into their most common denominator, you realize that Value is the underlying cord that ties them together.

So maybe your Lean Six Sigma elevator speech is this: Lean Six Sigma is the best-known and proven set of skills we have today for continually improving the way we transform the inputs of a process (or business as a whole) into the outputs customers want. And since all business relationships between a company and its customers are based on the mutual exchange of value, we use Lean Six Sigma to ensure that we derive the most possible value from everything we do.

# The Lineage of Lean Six Sigma

You can trace the life path of both methodologies back to their roots in scientific management—the basic premise of which was to quantify and optimize the way an organization creates value, or does what it does. It's interesting that certain key developments on the Lean (or productivity) side of that history happened in parallel with certain key developments on the Six Sigma (or quality) side.

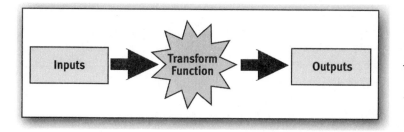

*The concepts, tools, and processes of Lean and Six Sigma have evolved along two different lines, yet they have been related in theory and practice, with scientific management at their base and in their cores.*

In the 1920s, Henry Ford and others were mechanizing the parts and parcels of production. They were measuring time and motion, and were dividing and sequencing labor in a way that enabled them to produce more products in less time at a lower cost. This was the industrial engineering framework that guided the work of these early pioneers.

Meanwhile, Walter Shewhart was devising the concepts and practices of statistical quality control (SQC) at Western Electric and Bell Labs. After all, what good is it to produce 100 cars a day if 10 or 20 of them are defective? Through Shewhart's SQC techniques, an assembly line could make a certain number of products per unit of time not just consistently, but consistently well. Just ask Ford how important this was; at the time, he was providing a repair toolbox with every purchase of a Model T.

Earlier in this chapter, we discussed the focus of Lean on time (making business faster) and the focus of Six Sigma on defects (making business better). We also looked at the statistical purpose of Lean to move the mean of performance, while Six Sigma's main purpose is to reduce variation around the mean.

Well, this is where it all got started—while Ford was frantically making all of his identical black cars, and while Shewhart was figuring out how to install systems for measuring, characterizing, and ensuring the quality of what was made. Since then, for nearly 100 years, the twin sciences of productivity and quality improvement developed mostly along separate lines, although all world-class companies are competent in both skill sets.

Through the lineage of the Toyota Production System (TPS), through the work of Edwards Deming and the global quality movement, the two improvement thrusts came that much closer together. As we fast-forward to the present day, we have passed through the point at which the best thinking and tools of productivity have become widely known and practiced as Lean. Similarly, the best practices of quality improvement have become known, packaged, and applied under the moniker of Six Sigma.

The logic and reality is simple. Lean Six Sigma puts all the best approaches to increasing productivity and improving quality into one system. Lean is the best method for reducing waste, decreasing cycle times, and, in general, improving productivity; Six Sigma is the best method for preventing defects, reducing variation, and generally improving quality. And there you have it: whether it's called Lean Six Sigma or something else, it was inevitable that some methodology would become established as the best one for simultaneously improving productivity and quality.

# Evolution Cannot Be Stopped

Among futurists and technologists there is an evolutionary principle called *hybridization*, which basically says that certain functions of products and systems become melded together over time. For instance, once the pencil and the eraser existed and functioned as separate instruments. Then some brilliant person at the right time found a way to blend the functions together into one instrument.

You know the principle of hybridization has played itself out when you see a new product and think to yourself, Oh yeah, I could have thought of that. Invention always seems obvious after it happens!

While Lean Six Sigma is not a hybridized *product* like a cell phone with a camera or a checking account in which you can also trade stocks, it is a hybridized *solution*. And it is a hybridized solution that has come of age, meaning it is applied in companies that formerly would have applied each of its core elements (Lean and Six Sigma) separately.

There are now enough people in organizations who are proficient in both skill sets (Lean and Six Sigma). At the same time, consulting and training firms (or solution providers) have integrated the road maps and tools of each method, designed Lean Six Sigma curricula, and perfected the processes and supports required to deploy it throughout large, global companies.

 **Performance Pitfall**

There are risks involved with hybridization, which at first entail increased complexity. With more working parts, you have a greater risk of malfunction—like a television with an embedded DVD player, it's the same with Lean Six Sigma. It has more functionality but it can be more complex, and therefore takes greater expertise to deploy and implement.

In other words, implementing Lean Six Sigma is not like bringing your cell phone and notebook computer with you on a business trip so you can enjoy the benefits of both. Lean Six Sigma is like bringing along your handheld device so you can achieve the objectives of a phone and a computer with one integrated product.

Like all true hybrids, the functionality of the whole always exceeds the sum of its parts, and Lean Six Sigma fits this description. Additionally, because the demand is present and the availability is there, Lean Six Sigma can be deployed and executed in a cost-effective manner. This is why it has become commercialized as a world-class methodology for achieving business improvement.

# Ode to the Pioneers

We'd probably be remiss if we didn't highlight some of the companies that pioneered the integration of Lean and Six Sigma, so we want to do this here. While we focus primarily on Maytag and AlliedSignal, there are many other pioneering Lean Six Sigma companies.

Therefore, this section is not a complete history of Lean Six Sigma. It's a way of sharing the thinking and approach of two important companies that 1) were among the very first to integrate Lean and Six Sigma, and 2) did so for the same reasons.

The reason these and other companies have integrated Lean and Six Sigma into one overall approach is the same as what we have said in other chapters and sections of this book:

- ◆ All businesses face a host of ongoing operational challenges. Some are related to quality (low yield, high defects, high variation), while others are related to time (slow lead times, long cycle times, lack of flexibility).

- ◆ A performance-improvement expert must have the ability to solve any kind of operational problem; rid any operation of waste; streamline any process; fix the source of defects for any product, transaction, or service; and so on.

## AlliedSignal

Around 1994, AlliedSignal adopted Six Sigma as a corporate initiative and enjoyed great financial benefit for doing so. Still, within a year the company realized it needed to improve process speed and accelerate lead times. Therefore, Allied introduced Lean in certain business units, and the initiative was soon adopted companywide under the banner "Lean Enterprise."

At first, Six Sigma and Lean at Allied were deployed as separate initiatives, but later they were rolled together under one corporate VP reporting directly to then-CEO Larry Bossidy. The thinking was clear: the opportunity of deploying the two methods together, and achieving synergies, was too compelling to ignore.

To achieve Lean Six Sigma integration at the practitioner level, Allied added one week of Lean training to its Six Sigma Black Belt training. Similarly, the company added one week of Six Sigma training to its Lean Expert training. Both groups adopted the Six Sigma training and initial project approach of taking one week of training, then applying what they learned in the workplace to make real improvements.

In years following, it was not unusual to see various parts or areas of Allied running multiple Lean and Six Sigma improvements at the same time, coordinating both in tight concert. As well, the company rolled out a Lean Six Sigma "Green Belt" training program that contained equal elements from both methodologies. This powerful, integrated Green Belt approach allowed Allied to capitalize on many "quick-hit" opportunities with minimal investment and effort.

## Maytag

Did you know that the term "Lean Sigma" is a service mark of Whirlpool? Well, if you didn't, now you do. So if someone ever asks you, "Hey, how come we don't just call it Lean Sigma?" you can tell them, "Because Whirlpool owns the service mark on that; therefore we use the term Lean Six Sigma."

Actually it's not even that simple. Whirlpool bought Maytag in 2006, and it's really Maytag that first used the term Lean Sigma on a pervasive basis. Actively on the path of Lean Sigma since 1998, Maytag introduced Lean Sigma Black Belts who are proficient in both methods.

Maytag also leveraged the Kaizen Event approach to create Lean Sigma Events. You guessed it … a Lean Sigma Event entails moving through the five phases of Six Sigma (DMAIC) in a compressed time frame of days and weeks rather than months, or for doing a more classic Kaizen Event made stronger with Six Sigma tools.

**Quotable Quote** _____

The cooking plant was one of our first Lean Sigma events. Initially, they wanted to spend $30 million to improve material handling through the use of more conveyors, forklifts, returnable packaging, etc. The Lean Sigma process allowed us to recognize that the answer was to move work stations closer to where they needed to be in order to improve demand flow. So, instead of spending $30 million, we spent $5 million and effectively reorganized the entire Cleveland, Tenn., plant.

—Arthur B. Learmonth, vice president of manufacturing and engineering of Maytag Appliances (Source: www.appliancedesign.com/CDA/Archives)

In just one quarter, Maytag is known for having completed about 800 Kaizen Events, resulting in as much as 20 to 30 percent cost reductions. That's a lot of Lean Six Sigma, and a lot of money saved. By using Lean (Six) Sigma to reorganize workflow in one plant alone, Maytag cut production costs by 55 percent and saved more than $25 million.

# DMAIC, or Kaizen Event?

As a Lean Six Sigma practitioner or leader, you'll constantly solve performance problems and improve processes. In previous chapters, we pointed out that the methodology for Six Sigma is DMAIC, while the approach for Lean is the Kaizen Event. Historically, DMAIC is more sophisticated and takes longer to implement (four to six months), due mostly to its insistence on having good data. The DMAIC process also takes longer because it is employed when performance problems are complex, and their root causes are not known.

On the other hand, you employ a Kaizen Event when the root cause of a problem is known, or when cycle time reduction is your primary objective (as opposed to defect reduction). Also known as a *Kaizen Blitz*, the idea behind this approach is to gather in a war-room-like environment for a full week to plan and implement a series of changes very quickly. Because you don't need as much measurement and analysis, you can run a Kaizen Event in a much shorter period of time than you can complete a full-blown DMAIC project.

By their different natures, there are advantages and disadvantages to each approach. DMAIC projects sometimes take longer than they need to, and Kaizen Events sometimes don't bring the rigor of data-driven measurement and analysis to their solutions.

Therefore, the key is to use the right methodology for the right type of performance-improvement opportunity. And in true Lean Six Sigma fashion, you can integrate aspects of Kaizen Events into DMAIC projects, thereby accelerating them. Likewise, you can incorporate elements of DMAIC into your Kaizen Events, thereby increasing the scientific rigor by which you make decisions and implement your solutions.

*Essentially, the Six Sigma problem-solving method of DMAIC follows the same progression as a Kaizen Event—in this case powered by a method called SCORE. Each methodology has its unique strengths, depending on your improvement objectives.*

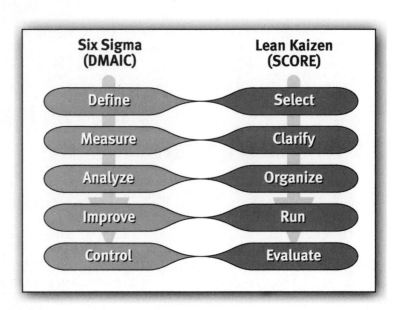

## The Least You Need to Know

◆ Lean Six Sigma enables you to simultaneously do business faster (time reduction) and better (defect reduction). When you do business faster and better, you are more competitive.

◆ Statistically speaking, Lean Six Sigma enables you to "move the mean" of performance while also reducing variation around your key business, process, and product metrics.

◆ In the final analysis, Lean Six Sigma is about value creation—always improving the way you transform business inputs into outputs.

◆ The roots of both Lean and Six Sigma can be traced back to Scientific Management. The two methods evolved by virtue of the drive toward productivity (Lean) and quality (Six Sigma).

◆ You can use the Six Sigma DMAIC methodology to solve complex problems, or you can use a Kaizen Event framework for making important improvements. You can also blend the two approaches in certain situations.

# Part 2

# Defining and Measuring Performance

This is the beginning of your journey into DMAIC—the Lean Six Sigma project execution road map. This part covers the first two phases—Define and Measure—giving you the process to follow, the tools to use, and the outcomes to achieve. In Define, you're primarily concerned with selecting viable projects, completing plans for their execution, and creating a high-level map of how they function. In Measure, you're further documenting your current process or processes, identifying their primary metrics *(Y)* to be improved, and establishing their performance baselines. Think of Define and Measure as your way of getting to know your process; once you do this, you're in a position to make it change.

# Chapter 6

# Develop Project Opportunities

## In This Chapter

- ◆ Know what's critical
- ◆ The balanced scorecard
- ◆ Voice of the customer
- ◆ Keep the good projects
- ◆ Set your project priorities

Your first task in executing a Lean Six Sigma project is to select a "good" project in the first place. You certainly don't want to select the most obvious or intuitive project, or the first one that comes to mind. Instead, you'll want to bring reason and discipline to the way you select your Lean Six Sigma projects.

In this chapter, we'll guide you through the process of identifying appropriate Lean Six Sigma projects. We'll look at the factors you should consider in doing so. We'll give you tools and techniques for gathering project ideas, and for prioritizing the ones that promise to impact your business the most with the least amount of cost and effort.

# Figure Out What's Critical

The first principle you need to get when selecting a Lean Six Sigma project is *criticality*, meaning you have to select and define a project that is critical to the satisfaction of both your customers and your business. Otherwise, it's not worth your time, effort, or resources.

So what, then, do we mean by criticality? In Chapter 4, we briefly touched on the concept of CTs. These are the characteristics of your process or product that are "critical to" their success. The chart that follows shows some different types of CTs from both the business and the customer side of the coin.

*From a business perspective, it's critical to focus on low defects, short cycle times, and low cost. Customers, on the other hand, are concerned with quality, delivery, and price.*

| | Business | Customer |
|---|---|---|
| Process → | Low Defects | CTq Quality |
| Process → | Short Cycle Time | CTd Delivery |
| Process → | Low Cost | CTp Price |

Compared with CTs for specific products and services, these CTs are very high level. The customer demands high quality, a short order/delivery cycle, and high value for the price. To meet these expectations, the business must provide products and services with low defects, short cycle times, and low costs.

After identifying specific CTs, you (or the leaders of a business) must identify the business processes that control the performance of these business outcomes. In addition, the business leaders must identify the outputs of these critical business processes that are major contributors to the customer-focused CTs.

## The Customer View

Let's consider a bicycle courier service as an example. Many companies in large cities use such point-to-point couriers to deliver important documents to clients. From a customer point of view, what is critical to customer satisfaction?

- ◆ **Quality**—Every document must be delivered, complete and intact, to the correct address.

- ◆ **Delivery**—The courier must be available to pick up the package and deliver it to the client on very short notice.

- ◆ **Price**—While not inexpensive, it must be more cost-effective for the customer to use a courier service than to employ full-time couriers.

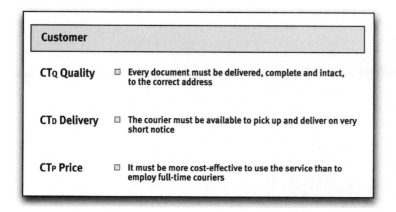

*Your project ideas should be directly related to what is important to your customers.*

To maintain a high-quality business, it's essential to meet these requirements for the customer. The courier service that best meets these criteria will own the bicycle courier business in the city.

## The Business Owner's View

Taking this a step further, from a courier service owner's perspective, what are some of the business outcomes that control customer satisfaction? For instance, what business processes are critical to quality? One major defect would be delivering the documents to the wrong address.

On the delivery dimension, you might look at your ability to service clients outside the range of bicycles, or you might have a process for making couriers available on standby if needed. On the price dimension, you'd need to look at how you can best utilize your courier staff, or how you can provide your service with the least amount of support and overhead.

*Your project ideas should also be directly related to what is important to your business.*

| Business |
| --- |

**CTQ Quality**
- ☐ Pick up at the right address
- ☐ Delivery to the correct address
- ☐ Delivery to the correct person
- ☐ Record of delivery details (when, to whom)

**CTD Delivery**
- ☐ Translating customer calls into dispatched couriers
- ☐ Having couriers available for immediate dispatch
- ☐ Transportation method suitable to time and distance

**CTP Price**
- ☐ High utilization of couriers
- ☐ Minimum support personnel
- ☐ Low cost transportation (bicycles vs. taxis)

Lean Six Sigma projects for the courier business would be aligned with these CTs. For any organization, the first step of project selection is understanding what's important to customers and to the business. Only after this are you ready to maximize performance in a way that satisfies both.

# Brainstorming Project Possibilities

If you're in the courier business, you might get some good project ideas from studying the preceding figures. Let's guess: you're not in the courier business, but you can still see how identifying all your CTs can put you on the right path in selecting good Lean Six Sigma projects. If you are in the courier business, all the better!

Often, defining your CTs is not enough to help you select the best Lean Six Sigma projects. This is because most business- and customer-level CTs are too broad for a single Lean Six Sigma project. Just to pick up the package at the correct address might require the good functioning of several processes, such as order taking, order entry, and dispatch. All three of these related processes (and others) have to work in flawless coordination to achieve the CT of "pick up (on time) at correct address."

Therefore, one great way to brainstorm project ideas is to use a CT Flow Down, shown here. This tool is related to "Five *Y*" analyses, whereby you start with a specific problem and "ask why five times"—all the while probing deeper and deeper into the chain of causation for any CT flow, process, problem, or issue. Following this progression, the upper branches of the CT Tree become your project families, while the lower branches become your individual projects.

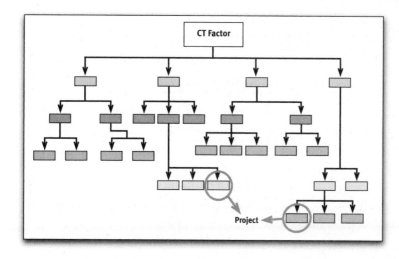

Project

*A tree diagram is a great tool for breaking down your CTs from the highest level of the business to the lowest level of the process where it makes the most sense to focus a project.*

In our courier example, we might have a CT identified: "quickly turn a customer call into a dispatched courier." We can break this CT down into two more CTs: 1) Having couriers available for dispatch and 2) Relaying accurate information from the customer to the courier. We might further break down each of these two CTs into lower-level CTs where it makes sense to focus a project.

Now you're generating a lot of project ideas! But remember, more is not always better. You only generate as many ideas as you can at first to make sure you don't miss any great project opportunities. After this, you'll go through a weeding-out process for keeping the viable project ideas and discarding the ones that don't make sense—or that won't pay off relative to the effort you'll expend.

> **Performance Pitfall**
>
> Don't shortcut your way through selecting Lean Six Sigma projects. If you do, you may be disappointed at the results you get. Instead, follow a proven process to pick the right projects from the beginning—and reap the rewards.

## More Idea Sources

Sometimes companies don't have their CTs identified or documented very well. And even if they do, there are many other sources for coming up with project ideas. Hang with us for the next few pages as we summarize some of these ways. There's really no end to where you can look for good ideas. (Also see Chapter 24 for more ways than we show here.)

## The Balanced Scorecard

Developed in the early 1990s by Harvard professor Robert Kaplan and Boston-area consultant David Norton, the Balanced Scorecard is a system of performance metrics. The reason it's called balanced is because, typically, companies manage themselves by looking in the rearview mirror—at their financial performance as it is reported to Wall Street.

The Balanced Scorecard approach includes the ultimate financial metrics but also includes other important business metrics that lead to healthy financials. Some of these metrics include those in the areas of customer satisfaction, internal business processes, and employee growth and development. The Balanced Scorecard approach connects all these many metrics in a cascading way, from the very top strategic priorities of an organization to its most fundamental operating processes.

The charts that follow show you how this system of performance metrics can lead you to new project ideas at the "actionable process level." Using a Balanced Scorecard approach to project identification ensures that you pay close attention to opportunities that are in direct support of your company's top strategic priorities.

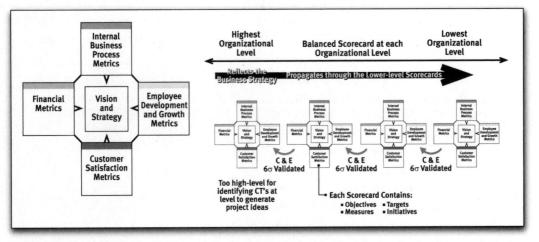

*Using a Balanced Scorecard to help you generate project ideas will ensure that you're focusing on what's most important to your business, employees, and customers.*

## Voice of the Customer

The success of any organization is directly related to how well it satisfies customers. With unsatisfied customers, no business can survive. With delighted customers, any business can thrive. Therefore, you can use the *Voice of the Customer* (*VOC*) to identify project ideas.

The key is to collect the VOC using a valid and repeatable measurement system. By doing so, you start to really understand what your customers think of what you do. As well as you think you know yourself, you will learn what others think, and especially what your customers think. Perhaps more importantly, you will learn about how they feel. Don't ever forget: customers buy mostly on the basis of emotion. Therefore, some sources of information, or ways to measure your customers' voice, are:

**Lean Six Sigma Lingo**

**Voice of the Customer (VOC)** refers to the collective needs, wants, and desires of your customer base. The VOC has to be captured, analyzed, and mapped to the processes of your organization—so you can deliver what the customer wants when they want it, in the way they want it.

- ◆ Complaint systems
- ◆ Technical support systems
- ◆ Sales reporting systems
- ◆ Observations
- ◆ Focused questioning
- ◆ Formal customer surveys

With this information you can develop performance metrics around customer satisfaction. By monitoring these metrics, you can learn how well you are doing in meeting your customers' expectations, and you can determine priority areas for improving their satisfaction.

Some of these priorities might include …

- ◆ Preventing the loss of an existing customer.
- ◆ Increasing business with an existing customer.
- ◆ Winning new customers.
- ◆ Developing new products and services.

Consider the example of a multiscreen movie theater. One of the business measures, of course, is the number of patrons. A theater decides to launch a program to make it the "theater of choice" for the area. A survey is designed to measure the Voice of the Customer.

Some of the survey results for what customers expect are predictable: matinee pricing, online ticket sales, convenient show times. But the theater owner is surprised that two of the larger complaints are dirty bathrooms and sticky theater floors.

*Often it pays to listen to the voice of your customers, and to institute a way to capture that voice accurately on a regular basis.*

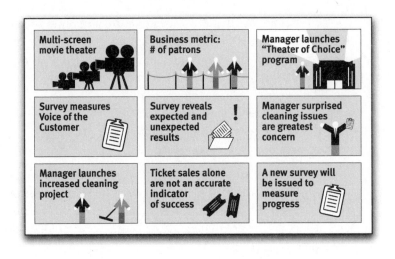

Needless to say, such issues at a movie theater would probably not require the horsepower of a Lean Six Sigma project. But you can see from this simple example how the Voice of the Customer might be helpful in exposing hidden opportunities for improvement.

## Value Stream Mapping

Another approach to project identification is using a Value Stream Map (VSM), which depicts how a process operates, with the added dimensions of documenting the people involved, inventory counts, queue times, process cycle times, and lead times. We will delve more deeply into the many functions and parts of a VSM in the Measure phase (discussed in Chapter 10).

For now, all you need is a high-level VSM to help you identify non-value-added activities that unnecessarily consume resources, increase cycle time, and compromise product quality. Such "broken" parts of the process can be good candidates for Lean Six Sigma projects.

Value Stream assessment at the business level focuses on the Value Stream activities, including:

◆ The people who perform the task and their knowledge and skills.

◆ The tools and technology used to perform the Value Stream tasks.

◆ The physical facilities and environment in which the Value Stream resides.

◆ The organization and culture of the enterprise that owns the Value Stream.

◆ The values and beliefs that dictate the corporate culture and behaviors that affect the way work is accomplished.

◆ The communications channel and the way information is disseminated throughout the enterprise.

◆ The policies, procedures, and processes that govern the activities of the Value Stream.

◆ The social systems that support the Value Stream.

The way in which all of these aspects are bound together and leveraged to achieve maximum customer satisfaction is the true focus of a Value Stream analysis. When you document and pick apart your Value Stream, you'll find problematic areas that are in need of improvement. These can become your golden opportunities for Lean Six Sigma projects.

## The Bigger Picture

Take a look at this chart, which shows you the many pathways and sources from which project ideas spring. There's a lot of hints and guidance in here that will help you generate great project ideas.

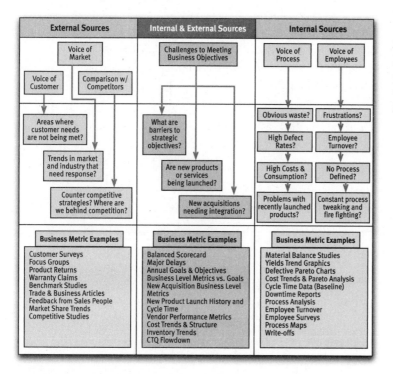

*There are plenty of places you can look to come up with great project ideas. Don't limit yourself to just one source or another. See the big picture and go from there.*

# Separate Wheat from Chaff

Once you have all your ideas for projects on the table, you have to weed out the ones you don't want and keep the ones you do. But don't jump too fast, and beware of your intuition. While sometimes your gut tells the truth, other times it misleads you. Therefore, you can use a Benefit/Effort Matrix to help you accomplish the important task of separating the wheat from the chaff.

Sometimes called an Impact/Effort Matrix, the Benefit/Effort Matrix enables you to determine which project ideas have the most value and which don't. Like anything in life, you want to invest in projects and activities that promise to bring you a payoff. When it comes to Lean Six Sigma projects, the Benefit/Effort Matrix makes your decisions easy.

**Lean Six Sigma Wisdom**

The Benefit/Effort Matrix can be drawn or created using many software packages, including Microsoft Excel or Microsoft PowerPoint.

Preferably working with a team, you build the Benefit/Effort Matrix by ascribing a Benefit scale to the *Y* axis, and an Effort scale to the *X* axis, as shown here. For this example, we then ascribe a scale of 1.0 to 5.0 for each axis. For *Y*, this scale most typically represents the financial benefit you can expect to enjoy from the proposed project.

*The Benefit/Effort Matrix helps you count the costs—and predict the outcome—before you commit to pursuing a Lean Six Sigma project.*

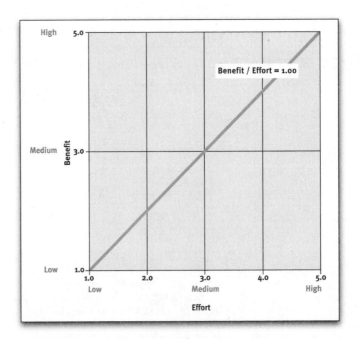

Often this scale has three range points of low (perhaps $100,000), medium ($500,000), and high ($1 million). But the actual dollar numbers associated depends greatly on your type of organization. A dry cleaner, for instance, might have a different financial definition of low, medium, and high than a jet engine maker.

On the $X$ axis you have a similar three-point system that forms a range for Effort, from low to medium to high. Often, Effort is synonymous with time or personnel or cost. Since different project ideas represent different types of benefits and effort, it's often best to stick with a generic numerical scale, or the simple low-medium-high scale for both axes.

Populating the matrix is primarily subjective (based on solid team member experience) and, therefore, is only a first-order estimation. Nevertheless, it's a critical estimation that will save you a lot of time and trouble later. Don't become bogged down in trying to determine the exact or actual numbers for Benefit/Effort with your team. This will unnecessarily slow down the process at this point.

Take a look at the following Benefit/Effort matrix, which is populated with many project ideas. What can you observe? Immediately you can see projects that are sprinkled all over the matrix. So which ones should you consider implementing and which ones not?

The short, uncomplicated answer—and the basic rule of thumb—is to use the projects in the middle as a relative standard for all the projects under consideration. Clearly, the objective is to disregard all project ideas that fall into the lower-right quadrant: those that require high effort but only yield low results. All other projects become legitimate candidates for Lean Six Sigma projects. And just in case you've been dozing, projects in the top left of the matrix are the best candidates—high benefit with low effort.

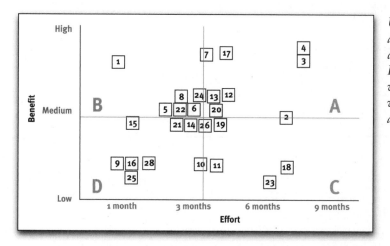

*Using a team process, you can allocate your project ideas into different areas of the matrix. Doing this gives you a great view into which projects are worth pursuing and which are not.*

Still, you have more to do in properly defining the most appropriate Lean Six Sigma projects. And a little more to do in deciding which ones you'll tackle first, second, third, and so on. The good news is that with this list of potential projects you are well on your way to making your process and organization better.

> **Performance Pitfall** _____
>
> Do not confuse the Benefit/Effort Matrix with a Prioritization Matrix. First you have to determine if a project is worth your time and attention at all (Benefit/Effort); then you need to figure out which projects to pursue right away (Prioritization).

# What's Most Important?

As much as you have to be disciplined about how you generate Lean Six Sigma project ideas, you have to do the same in deciding which project ideas are the best ones to implement. We call this "project prioritization," and the general rule of thumb is that you should start working on the projects that give you the best buck for your bang.

But what exactly that buck and bang is can be ambiguous if you don't define it. Like anything in life, you need a set of criteria to guide you. And this is all the more true when you have many people in many different areas of a company all selecting Lean Six Sigma projects at the same time.

Basically, there are three broad criteria by which you can make certain projects a priority and other projects not:

1. **Strategically critical:** The boss or leadership team deems a project important for the success of the business.

2. **Tactically necessary:** Customers require that you do something and this puts you in urgent firefighting mode.

3. **Methodically determined:** A business team decides which projects are a priority based on a structured selection process using a Prioritization Matrix.

Remember that CTs drive much of what you do in a business, including the generation of project ideas. Recall that you have CTs for the business, as well as CTs for customers. Generally speaking, the former are strategic in nature, while the latter are tactical in nature. As shown in the diagram here, the key is to be aware that each of these project types will pay off on different timelines to different degrees.

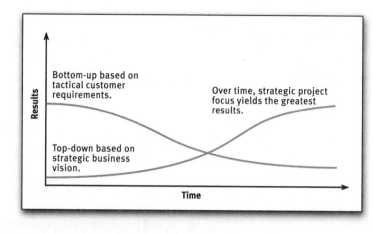

*A good combination of longer and more strategic projects, in addition to some short-term and tactical projects, is preferred because you are capitalizing on critical opportunities today while still working on the keys to success for tomorrow.*

# The Prioritization Matrix

You'll want to know this tool well if you want to be intelligent about the way you pick your projects. We all want to be intelligent, right? Well, if you use the Prioritization Matrix properly, you'll look like the smartest one around. Reason? The matrix enables you to narrow a long list of potential projects down to the ones you want to implement right away.

In the following figure, you can see what a Prioritization Matrix looks like and how you would use it to determine the best projects from a list of possibilities. Here's how it works:

1. Document business and customer CTs.

2. Rank the CTs against each other.

3. List project opportunities.

4. Estimate bottom-line dollar impact.

5. Identify appropriate resources.

6. Define the scoring criteria.

7. Score opportunities against CTs.

8. Calculate priority numbers and sort by these numbers.

9. Assign resource type to lead the project.

10. Repeat quarterly with business management.

 **Lean Six Sigma Wisdom**

While you may have many Lean Six Sigma project ideas, you can only implement a few at a time. Therefore, you have to pick the best ones first and go from there.

*Using the Prioritization Matrix in a team environment enables you to be as methodical as possible in determining where to focus your improvement efforts.*

| Prioritization Matrix | Rating of Importance to Business | Process | Estimated Cost Savings | 2 - 4 Months | $575,000 PTOI Minimum | 70% Defect Reduction Possible | Minimum Capital Required | Cost of Effort worth Benefit | Hard vs. Soft Savings | Internal Focus | Baseline Data Available | Capacity | Lower Unit Costs | Critical to Customer - Quality | Critical to Customer - Deliver | Total Project Points | Lean Six Sigma Belt |
|---|---|---|---|---|---|---|---|---|---|---|---|---|---|---|---|---|---|
| **Lean Six Sigma Potential Projects List** — Sort and rank by total project points. As a business team, rate each project to the CT | | | | 8 | 10 | 5 | 7 | 10 | 10 | 3 | 7 | 10 | 8 | 10 | 7 | | |
| 1. Project 1 | | Sheet | $5,100,000 | 9 | 3 | 2 | 9 | 9 | 3 | 5 | 5 | 9 | 9 | 0 | 9 | 735 | Brown |
| 2. Project 2 | | Sheet | $310,000 | 8 | 3 | 9 | 9 | 9 | 9 | 9 | 3 | 9 | 9 | 9 | 9 | 631 | Parker |
| 3. Project 3 | | Sheet | $3,100,000 | 9 | 9 | 3 | 9 | 9 | 9 | 9 | 9 | 5 | 1 | 0 | 9 | 671 | Brown |
| 4. Project 4 | | Sheet | $400,000 | 9 | 9 | 3 | 4 | 3 | 9 | 9 | 9 | 9 | 9 | 0 | 9 | 640 | Land |
| 5. Project 5 | | Sheet | $808,000 | 9 | 3 | 3 | 9 | 9 | 9 | 9 | 9 | 9 | 3 | 0 | 9 | 627 | Gaesser |
| 6. Project 6 | | CDMC | $180,000 | 3 | 9 | 9 | 9 | 9 | 9 | 9 | 9 | 3 | 3 | 9 | 3 | 683 | Carlson |
| 7. Project 7 | | Sheet | $662,000 | 9 | 9 | 3 | 9 | 9 | 9 | 9 | 3 | 3 | 3 | 1 | 5 | 681 | Mead |
| 8. Project 8 | | Sheet | $600,000 | 9 | 3 | 3 | 9 | 9 | 9 | 9 | 3 | 3 | 9 | 0 | 9 | 573 | Mead |
| 9. Project 9 | | Sheet | $175,000 | 0 | 9 | 3 | 9 | 9 | 3 | 9 | 3 | 3 | 1 | 9 | 3 | 485 | Parker |
| 10. Project 10 | | CDMC | $1,623,000 | 3 | 3 | 3 | 3 | 3 | 3 | 9 | 3 | 3 | 9 | 3 | 3 | 351 | Meissner |

0 = No correlation to CT     1 = Project only remotely effects CT     3 = Project has a moderate effect on CT

9 = Project has a direct and strong effect on CT

Don't develop a project Prioritization Matrix once and never look at it again. It should be reviewed and revised at least quarterly to maintain a list of the right projects.

## The Least You Need to Know

- An organization can only afford to focus its improvement efforts on processes that are critical to customer satisfaction or the viability of the business.

- There are many ways to generate Lean Six Sigma project ideas, and many different sources for project ideas.

- Two of the most important and useful ways to generate project ideas are through a CT Flow Down and the Voice of the Customer (VOC).

- Before you actually choose a Lean Six Sigma project, you have to separate your viable ideas from those that are not worth your time and effort.

- You can use a Prioritization Matrix to methodically determine which projects are best to focus on right away.

# Chapter 7

# Clarify the Problem

## In This Chapter

- Problem statements
- What is the current process?
- Spaghetti Diagrams
- Kano Model

This is the point in the Lean Six Sigma process when you formally enter the Define phase, which we cover in this and the next two chapters. In this chapter, we'll focus on taking your prioritized project ideas and turning them into problem statements. From there, we'll show you how to document your processes at 50,000 feet.

With these two pieces of the puzzle in place, you'll be well on your way to understanding what needs to be done to make your desired improvements. And if you remember anything about the Define phase of Lean Six Sigma, remember this: you need to answer the question "What is broken?" If you don't know exactly what's broken, you can't fix it.

# Introducing Define

The Define stage of Lean Six Sigma is when you set up your team for success in achieving your planned improvements. Since you've already gone through a structured process for selecting your project topic, or one has been assigned to you by a Lean Six Sigma Champion, you're ready to jump forward. But before you do, check out this flow chart—it spells out the key steps for defining your project right the first time.

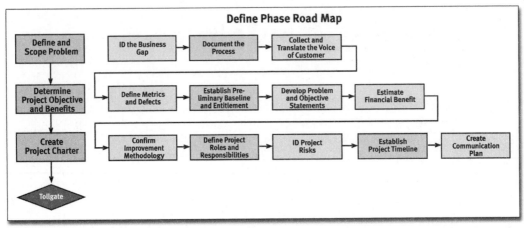

*This is the general process for defining a Lean Six Sigma project. Depending on your unique situation and experience, you may or may not strictly follow these steps in a set sequential fashion.*

# Write Problem Statement

Your first task is to compose a statement that clearly defines your problem and communicates it to others. In doing this, you should meet the following criteria.

**What** is the problem? What is the defect? What products or processes are defective? Examples:

◆ "Customers are not satisfied with my ordering service."

◆ "Equipment availability is poor."

◆ "Document correctness is insufficient."

**Where** does the problem occur? What part of the product or process is "broken"? In what geographical area or facility does the problem reside? Examples:

◆ "Customers in the Midwest region are not satisfied with my ordering service."

◆ "Equipment availability for Urgent Care is poor."

◆ "Document correctness is insufficient in Billing."

**When** was the defect first observed? What is the history? Is there a pattern? Examples:

◆ "Customers in the Midwest region are not satisfied with my ordering service, starting in January."

◆ "Equipment availability for Urgent Care is poor since the consolidation of services."

◆ "Document correctness is insufficient in Billing after the introduction of flexiforms."

**How extensive** is the problem? How many products are defective? How often does the process function improperly? What is the trend? Examples:

◆ "Customers in the Midwest region are not satisfied with my ordering service. Starting in January, complaints have increased 15 percent."

◆ "Equipment availability for Urgent Care is poor. Since the consolidation of services, delays caused by lack of availability have increased by 40 percent."

◆ "Document correctness is insufficient in Billing. After the introduction of flexiforms, errors have increased 28 percent."

**How do you know** the problem is a problem? What performance standard is missed by virtue of the problem? Examples:

◆ "Customers in the Midwest region are not satisfied with my ordering service. Starting in January, complaints have increased 15 percent at a time when complaint rates from other regions have remained static."

◆ "Equipment availability for Urgent Care is poor. Since the consolidation of services, delays caused by lack of availability have increased by 40 percent when the patient traffic has increased by only 5 percent."

**Lean Six Sigma Wisdom**

A problem statement does not include the causes of the deficiency. It does not include likely actions or corrections. A good problem statement is clear, concise, and specific.

♦ "Document correctness is insufficient in Billing after the introduction of flexiforms. Errors have increased by 28 percent when the goal of the project was to reduce errors by 90 percent."

Another criterion that guides your composition of a problem statement is maybe obvious, but how often do we humans miss the obvious? That criterion is **why** the problem is important to solve. Or what will happen if you don't solve it? The standard answer to "why" is to determine the importance of the problem to customers and to the business.

# Define the High-Level Process

Now you're getting into the details of process documentation, without which you are simply lost. So please don't take it lightly and remember this principle: if you don't document how you do business, then you probably don't do it very well or consistently.

You've heard the phrase "It is what it is." Well, too often organizations operate by the phrase "We do what we do." That's just not good enough if you want to be world-class at what you do. If you want to be among the best, you will document every one of your processes, and you will use that documentation to improve what you do over time.

## It All Comes Down to Processes

When we talk about improving performance, we're always talking about improving either products or processes. That's everything! An organization or company either makes a product or enacts a process.

Often, the latter (process) is referred to as a service or a transaction. A masseuse, for instance, follows a process when giving a massage, which some might call a service. An online brokerage company also follows a process when executing stock transactions.

Perhaps more interesting, an organization follows a process when it makes a product. In fact, that's the only way a company can make products that consistently meet customer requirements. You have to design and follow a set process over and over again, and you have to improve that process over time.

# The SIPOC Map

Your best tool for beginning to document your process is the SIPOC Map, short for Suppliers-Inputs-Process-Outputs-Customers. An example is shown here; the value of the SIPOC Map is to define the boundaries of your process, and to help you make sure your project intention is not too broad or too narrow.

This is an important precept in defining Lean Six Sigma projects: you don't want to boil the ocean and bite off more than you can chew with just one project. That's why, often, organizations deploy many different projects just to improve one large process that spans multiple departments or functions.

When you move into the Measure phase of Lean Six Sigma, you'll be exposed to more tools that can help you refine your project scope. Some of these include Pareto Charts, Fishbone Diagrams, Affinity Diagrams, and CT Trees. For now it's best to stick with the SIPOC Map, as it gives you the broad definition you need to move forward in the process.

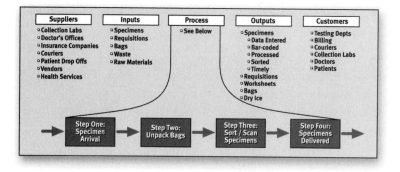

*The SIPOC Map is used to identify the boundaries of your process, as well as the key suppliers, inputs, outputs, and customers.*

The process for completing a SIPOC Map:

1. Identify the process beginning and ending steps. Fill in the process steps (keeping to a high level of three to seven steps). Are multiple products/services outputted by the same process? If so, use a Product Family Matrix to help determine what product goes with what steps of the map.

2. Identify the output of the process and its customers. An output is the finished product or service from each process step. A customer is the user of the output, and can reside within or outside the organization.

*The Product Family Matrix is used when several products or services are made using the same process.*

| Products | | Main Process Steps | | | | | | | |
|---|---|---|---|---|---|---|---|---|---|
| | | Cutting Room | Dying | Washing | Pre-Sewing | Final Cut | Sewing | Inspection and Packaging | Shipping |
| | Pants (Wool) | X | | X | | | X | X | X |
| | Pants (Casual) | X | X | X | | | X | X | X |
| | Shirts (Dress) | X | X | X | X | X | X | X | X |
| | Knits | | X | X | | X | X | X | X |
| | Infant | | X | X | X | X | X | X | X |
| | Pullovers | | X | X | | X | X | X | X |

3. Identify the inputs to the process and their suppliers. An input is what flows into the process. This can include personnel, material, equipment, information, etc. A supplier is a person or organization that provides inputs into the process.

## Document the Process

After you have created your SIPOC Map, you are ready to put more details to your process steps … but not too many at this point. Right now, your main objective is to gain agreement on how the process currently operates so you know where to go to get the data you will need later as you measure the performance of your process.

You'd be surprised. Often the simple exercise of creating a high-level process causes disagreement and controversy amongst those who work in that process. This disagreement should be your clue that it's no wonder you may be having problems. More often than not, team members who work in the process can't even agree at first about how the process currently operates!

 **Technically Speaking**

There are many different kinds of Process Flow Maps, not just one. Some are called Process Flows, others Value Stream Maps. Still others are called Swim Lanes. More on these in the Measure phase, and specifically in Chapter 10.

Think of it this way. You have some problem to solve, such as: "Equipment availability for Urgent Care is poor. Since the consolidation of services, delays caused by lack of availability have increased by 40 percent when the patient traffic has increased by only 5 percent."

Okay, so why is this happening? If you knew the answer, you wouldn't have a problem, and you certainly wouldn't need Lean Six Sigma to solve it. So you create a simple process flow as part of your SIPOC activity, and this flow then gives you clues and places to look for the answer to the question "why?"

Later, in the Measure phase, you will make your Process Map more sophisticated, and you will detail it out to the next level. In other words, for every one process step of a macro process, there are usually many smaller steps within. However, even high-level Process Maps, like the one shown in the SIPOC diagram, can expose areas of obvious waste.

These are the process loops, unnecessary transportation, and rework moments that kill productivity and numb employees. Teams building process maps quickly come upon these wasteful steps and are eager to eliminate them. These "ah-ha" moments are wonderful opportunities to eliminate easy problems and challenges.

The good news is that many process problems can be solved at this stage. In fact, many quick-hit challenges can be solved in days or hours rather than weeks or months. Other challenges that become obvious during the process mapping stage will require a more focused and time-consuming approach.

## Value-Added, Non-Value-Added

When examining your current high-level process, or "the way you do business," take time to reflect and look for what is valuable to the customer. This is a critical Lean Six Sigma concept: only those steps in the process that are absolutely necessary in providing the customer what he or she wants, and is willing to pay for, are considered to be value-added steps. Cutting a diamond, for instance, adds value to the raw stone.

In addition to the notion of value for the customer is the notion of value to the business. Therefore, such typical actions as performed in accounting, payroll, human resources, and other departments are critical to the functioning of the business. Many of these activities, still, are business-required non-value-added. This means that even if they are required by the business, their time and cost can be minimized.

Of course, non-value-added activities are any work the organization performs that does not add value. Using the cutting diamond example, any secondary cutting due to rework is non-value-added activity. The rework is certainly necessary if the job wasn't done right the first time. But customers expect you to do it right the first time, and the business should expect this, too. Therefore, all rework is non-value-added.

In the simple example that follows, a patient arrives at a clinic and goes through eight major process steps: sign in, waiting room, small waiting room, nurse, small waiting room, doctor consult, blood test, pay bill. Then the patient leaves.

In this case, value to the patient would be sign in, doctor consult, and blood test. Value to the business would be nurse (lower labor cost to perform certain functions), sign in, and pay bill. Non-value-added to the patient and the business would be waiting room, small waiting room, and small waiting room again. (Did you see the episode of *Seinfeld* when Jerry sarcastically asked why he had to go from the big waiting room into the smaller waiting room?) So much waiting in so many different areas!

*A Value Stream is the total set of activities, both value-added and non-value-added, that occur as a process unfolds.*

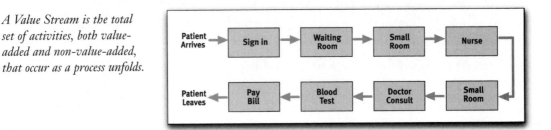

So what's the point for you as you define your project? Watch first for the non-value-added categories and work on reducing their waste factor. (Remember, waiting is one of the eight types of waste.) Work on the non-value-added areas first, then move on to optimizing the value-added steps.

## Spaghetti You Don't Eat

Another tool you can use to get a high-level view of your process is a Spaghetti Diagram, shown next. This tool comes in most handily when you are dealing with a process that entails a lot of people traffic in an office, or in a production cell. Especially when dealing with time-related problems, sometimes the creation of a Spaghetti Diagram can, in itself, enable you to solve your problem.

You'll note in the following example that the Spaghetti Diagram visualizes the waste of transportation and motion. You start by sketching all of the equipment and places the observed item (person or thing) travels through and around. Then you simply look for redundant trips and areas where the lines cross.

In some cases, by doing this you can straighten out the process with just a little thought and effort. For example, simply relocating a supply bin or a computer terminal for data entry can greatly reduce the distance a worker has to travel. In other cases, you will need more definition and data before you can reconfigure the Flow for optimum removal of waste.

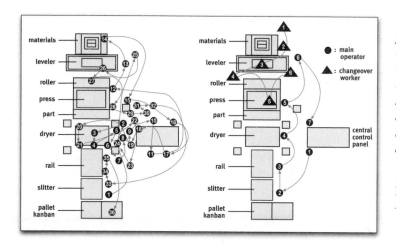

*You can see how much simpler and efficient the process becomes after it is redesigned using a Spaghetti Diagram. Still, remember that at this stage, you would employ the diagram to simply get a high-level view of how your process currently operates.*

*(Source: Sekine, K., and K. Arai, Kaizen for Quick Changeover, Productivity Press, 1992, p. 37.)*

# Collect the Voice of the Customer

All of business depends on having customers who are willing to pay for what you do. At work, you might think your boss is the boss, but your boss has a boss, and her boss has a boss, and so on right up to the owners of the business. Even so, the shareholders wouldn't hold anything of value if the company didn't have regular customers who are willing to pay for what the company does.

In this sense, we all report to our customers, and they can help us enormously in figuring out what is important and where to focus our improvement energies. We touched on this in Chapter 6 when discussing all the sources for Lean Six Sigma projects. Now we take you a step further in looking at what is important to customers and how that "voice" can empower you to define a Lean Six Sigma project.

Essentially, you want to use various means for collecting your customers' opinions about what you do for them. The most common means are questionnaires, surveys, focus groups, and customer complaints. A less common method, but one that can be very effective, is direct customer observation. Go and live with your customers and document their emotional responses to your product or service.

Clearly, these methods will surface all kinds of complaints, opportunities, and insights about what is important to your customers. And you should listen carefully to what they say, because they are the ones who are buying your products and services. You should also have a systematic way of organizing all your customer feedback into a framework that is actionable in the business.

In fact, there is a whole discipline around this called Quality Function Deployment (QFD). QFD is the science of systematically collecting and organizing your customers' voice (customer requirements)—then mapping what is important to them to the way you do business (functional requirements).

In association with this discipline, you may hear the term "House of Quality," which is a huge matrix that lists the customer requirements across the top, and the functional requirements down the side. By doing this, you gain visibility into what the business has to do to meet its customers' requirements. Of course you can learn much more about QFD by picking up a book or text devoted entirely to that subject.

## The Kano Model

For our purposes, we turn to the Kano Model, which is an interesting way of helping you figure out what is most important to your customers. The reason this model is so powerful is because it doesn't consider all customer requirements equal. Therefore, it helps you prioritize which requirements can catapult you to new heights of customer satisfaction (delighters), and which requirements can cause you to plunge to new lows in your customers' eyes (dissatisfiers).

In other words, how do you know that the metric you've chosen, or your expected performance outcome (Y), is the best one to focus on first? In the next chapter, we'll be looking at defining project metrics, but we don't want to determine these metrics blindly. As with everything Lean Six Sigma, rigor and discipline are the order of the day.

**Lean Six Sigma Wisdom**

The Kano Model is the work of Professor Noriaki Kano of Tokyo Rika University. Dr. Kano has been involved in the work of developing and spreading quality techniques since the 1970s.

As shown in the figure that follows, the Kano Model asserts that, for some customer requirements, satisfaction is proportional to the extent that the product or service is fully functional. These requirements, says Kano, are "one-dimensional." A 20 percent improvement in functionality results in a 20 percent improvement in customer satisfaction. A 10 percent increase in response time results in a 10 percent increase in satisfaction. And so on.

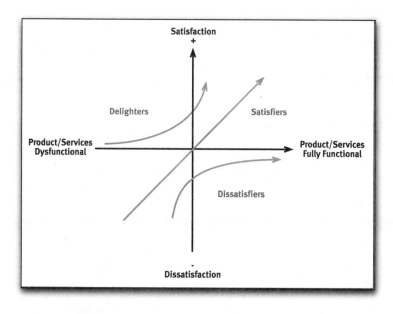

*The Kano Model shows how satisfaction rises proportionally with increases in functionality for certain characteristics, while satisfaction or dissatisfaction is affected disproportionately for other characteristics.*

## Focus on What Must Be

The other aspect to the Kano Model—and perhaps the more important one—is that certain requirements, called "Must Be," can only dissatisfy customers when not met, but cannot increase satisfaction when they are met. An example of this type of requirement is having coffee served hot. If the coffee is not hot, the customer will be dissatisfied. If it is hot, or very hot, the customer's satisfaction will not go up.

Delighters, on the other hand, are requirements that when met will increase customer satisfaction in a nonproportional way. And if a delighter is not present, the customer will not be dissatisfied. An example of this type of requirement might be what you get at a Red Robin restaurant: unlimited french fries. Not having unlimited fries will not make you dissatisfied; having as many as you can eat may delight you.

In the Kano Model, "indifferent" requirements are those that don't influence satisfaction or dissatisfaction when they are present or not. The color of the walls in a YMCA gymnasium, for instance, are probably not going to satisfy or dissatisfy the patrons. If you had to plot these types of requirements,

**Lean Six Sigma Wisdom**

You can use the Kano Model to prioritize customer needs, as well as to refine your ideas and problem statements to the point where they become more actionable—or definable as Lean Six Sigma projects.

they would fall directly on the X axis of the Kano Model. As you improve them, customer satisfaction remains the same—not affected.

So what to do with all this? For starters, know that there is a process and system you can employ to uncover the Must Be concerns of your customers, as well as their delighters and indifferences. This is important because you don't want to focus a project on items that you might think are important but your customers find unimportant (indifferent requirements).

What you do want to focus on first are the Must Be characteristics. That's why they're called Must Be! Then and only then, you'll want to shift your attention to the delighters, although often these become the subject matter of R&D projects or innovation projects. And these types of projects require another skill set we don't cover in this book.

## The Least You Need to Know

- ◆ Problem statements are necessary in setting you on the right course for improving your performance shortfall.

- ◆ The SIPOC Map, basic Process Map, and Spaghetti Diagram are used to document how you currently do business.

- ◆ In organizations, you have value-added and non-value-added activities, and you have to know which is which.

- ◆ The Kano Model is a strong tool for collecting the Voice of the Customer and determining what is most important to them.

# Chapter 8

# Set the Goal

## In This Chapter

- ◆ Know your scope
- ◆ Know your *Y* outputs
- ◆ Baselining performance
- ◆ Be very, very SMART
- ◆ Project your savings

We pick up in this chapter with the more quantitative aspects of the Define phase of DMAIC. Specifically, we'll look at some issues around scoping Lean Six Sigma projects, defining output metrics (*Y*-related), and verifying that those metrics are aligned with the key objectives of the organization.

Further, we'll show you how to establish your performance expectations and script out an objective statement for your Lean Six Sigma project. Finally, we'll give you some guidelines around how to calculate the expected financial benefits for your projects.

# A Note About Scope

Having documented your performance problem or issue, you're still a long way off from solving it. In fact, you're still pretty far from even properly defining it. Before you can do this, you have to be sure your project is properly scoped—and that you know which Lean Six Sigma approach and tools to apply to which types of projects.

In general, projects are either "a mile wide and an inch deep" or an "inch wide and a mile deep." Of course, most higher-level business goals are supported by a mix of both types of projects. In other words, it's not uncommon to encounter a big, long process that is a mile wide and an inch deep, but that also has several inch-wide, mile-deep problems that need to be solved.

For example, an auto manufacturer needed to reduce its cycle time for chassis assembly to meet market demand. The scope of this process was very broad, and improving it was primarily handled with Lean techniques and Kaizen Events that identified and eliminated non-value-added steps. But Six Sigma tools were also needed to solve deep, complex, $Y$-$x$ relationships within the welding and milling processes.

In other cases, the performance objective at hand is more clearly broad and not deep, so more Lean-like tools and Kaizen Events come into play. One grocery store chain, for instance, set out to reduce the cycle time for building new stores. As you can imagine, the lost revenue from just one day of nonoperation can be very sizeable. So in this case the project scope was very wide.

**Lean Six Sigma Wisdom**

Some project scoping tools include Pareto Charts, Affinity Diagrams, and Cause-and-Effect Diagrams. These tools are also useful in the Analyze phase, and for this reason we cover them in Chapters 13 and 16.

Finally, you have many problems that require mostly Six Sigma analytics because they are not so much related to cycle time, lead time, or work in process. Instead, they are related to complex defect or quality issues.

One aerospace engine manufacturer, for example, was having trouble with the reliability of its aircraft-engine combustors. But there were several types of combustors from several different suppliers, and you can't try to boil the ocean by trying to figure out such inch-wide, mile-deep problems at one time.

Therefore, the manufacturer focused its project on just one type of combustor at one supplier. It then further narrowed down the problem to a certain laser drilling machine operating in a certain process. When it was all done, the original complex problem was narrowly scoped by supplier, location, machine, and process type.

# Define Project Metrics

At this point, we take the next step in clarifying and defining the key metrics that you want to impact. Remember, no project is worth its effort if it doesn't do something significant for your business or organization. Therefore, defining and validating your project metrics will make it certain that your efforts are worth their time.

Lean Six Sigma is about impacting your organization's performance indicators. Lean Six Sigma, therefore, is about tracing the chain of causation down from your strategic priorities to your operational excellence indicators to your process performance to the specific features and functions of whatever it is your organization provides to customers.

## One Project, One Y

Generally speaking, whether the scope of your project is wide or narrow, it addresses only one output feature ($Y$) at a time. If you try to address more than one output feature with one project, you are likely to run into the problem of "scope creep."

Here in the Define phase, the key is to figure out which outcomes or features ($Y$s) your project directly addresses, remembering the rule of thumb that no more than one $Y$ per project is a good policy. Given this, what are some project metrics that might be appropriate for a Lean Six Sigma project? Maybe you can refer to the sample problem statements we provided in the section "Write Problem Statement" in Chapter 7, to get you going:

- Reduce customer complaints ($Y$) in the Midwest region.

- Increase equipment availability ($Y$) for Urgent Care.

- Reduce document errors ($Y$) in Billing.

Other $Y$-related project metrics might be along these lines:

- Increase customer retention for product line A.

- Reduce scrap rates of countertop installations.

- Lower processing time for indexed mortgage loans.

- Improve win rate for sales proposals in China.

- Reduce supplier cost for calcium dioxide product.

- Decrease engine noise in the riding lawnmower.

- Reduce falling injuries among the tree-trimming crew.

- Decrease abandoned customer calls for new service.
- Improve delivery time for groceries ordered on line.

Of course the whole thrust of Lean Six Sigma—and the remaining phases of Measure, Analyze, Improve, and Control—are geared toward moving from these *Y*s to the critical *x*s that influence them. When the *x*s influencing your *Y*s are intuitively obvious, and your intuition is correct, you won't need to use Lean Six Sigma. However, when the factors that cause your *Y* to perform or not perform are not so obvious, you'll need to dig deeper and deeper until you uncover the *x*s that make the *Y*s do what they do.

## Primary, Secondary, Consequential

Your other big concern around developing project metrics is making sure you are aware that for every *Y* you improve, it is possible you will also improve other *Y*s. These are called secondary metrics, because they are desirable performance side effects.

For instance, you may have a project that is focused on reducing cycle time for a certain process. As a result of doing this, you may also reduce backorders. Or you could execute a project that reduces defects per unit and, in doing so, also frees up available floor space for use (eliminate the need for a rework staging area).

Consequential metrics are different. Think of these like negative side effects. You "solve" your cost problem by selecting a cheaper vendor, but the product it supplies causes field reliability issues that cost even more money to fix. Oops.

**Lean Six Sigma Wisdom**

You can run a mini FMEA, or Failure Mode and Effects Analysis, to identify consequential metrics. More on FMEAs in Chapter 13.

Paying attention to consequential metrics is a pessimist's dream, and we should all be pessimists when it comes to performance improvement. Heed the words of Murphy's Law: "Whatever can go wrong will go wrong. And George Will's version: "The unintended consequences of an act will always be greater than the intended consequences." Or, if you prefer, "No good deed goes unpunished" (Clare Booth Luce).

## Verify Alignment to Business Metrics

Recall from Chapter 6 that you often use a CT Tree to generate project ideas, and that a CT Tree is essentially a hierarchical breakdown of an organization's strategic priorities into lower-level priorities and objectives. In this way, an organization ensures that its lofty goals get translated into actionable operational and process improvements.

At this stage, if you've designated an output metric for your project, it's probably aligned with your organization's business metrics. But this would not be the case if you haven't made the effort to ensure this, or haven't developed your project focus in accordance with your organization's needs.

In any case, to be sure your project is strategically aligned, and has value to your organization, validate where it fits in the overall performance scheme. For instance, look at the simple Tree Diagrams, which take two business metrics and show how they are broken down into supporting subcategories.

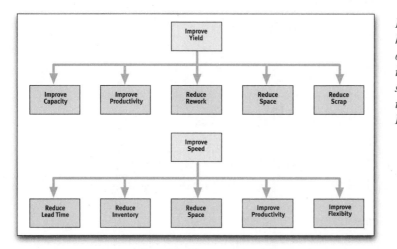

*Key business metrics are broken down into more narrow operational metrics, which in turn can be broken down into supporting process metrics that guide the definition of Lean Six Sigma projects.*

If you worked in a company that placed a strategic focus on yield or speed, your supporting metric hierarchy might look something like what's shown in the previous figure. Therefore, you'd have to work in close communication with your manager or Lean Six Sigma Champion to confirm that your project would directly support these improvement goals.

In some cases, even though your project addresses just one output feature, it can impact more than one strategic goal. Note the project shown in the next Tree Diagram—Reduce Changeover Time on Cartoner. Follow the metric breakdown back up the tree and see that this one project supports three strategic priorities.

*Using a Tree Diagram is a great way to confirm that your project is a good one. In this case, the identified project at the end of the tree supports three different strategic goals.*

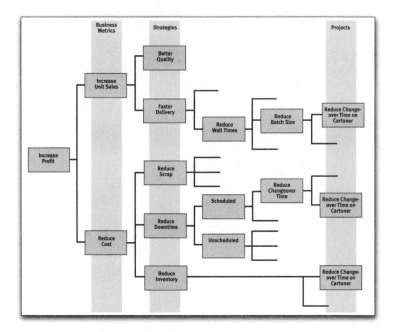

# Establish Baseline and Entitlement

We'll assume you have your *Y* defined now. So what's next? You'll have to collect some data on how your *Y* is performing over time. After all, that's the game. Remember, the Define phase is all about figuring out what is wrong with your process—at least in terms of its output performance. Therefore, you need to establish your *baseline performance*, and your Entitlement.

![Lean Six Sigma Lingo icon] **Lean Six Sigma Lingo**

**Baseline performance** is a snapshot of how well your process performs before you implement your Lean Six Sigma project and make your improvements. You always compare your post-project performance with your baseline to verify that you've made the difference you intended to make.

Doing this will accomplish four important goals. One, it will show you how bad or good your performance is and how much you need to improve (baseline). Two, it will tell you how much you can improve if you eradicate all the sources of variation (Entitlement). Three, it will tell you whether you'll need to reach beyond Entitlement to achieve your project objective. Four, it will give you a basis for determining the impact your project makes after it's completed.

Take a look at the next Time Series Plot related to lead time. You see that the baseline is the average of all the data points, in this case 34 days. You also see that the minimum time, or the best the process has performed, is 22 days. This is your Entitlement.

*This plot shows a series of data collected over time that tracks lead time for customer orders. Note that the baseline performance is 34 days (the average) and Entitlement performance is 22 days.*

## Calculate Your Standard Deviation

Also, you may want to calculate the standard deviation of your process performance, because that, too, is pertinent to your understanding of how your process is performing relative to its output metric. For quick reference, what follows is a simple formula for calculating the standard deviation of a population based on a random sample. (See the section "Sample Size Calculations" in Chapter 15, for some details about statistical sampling).

$$\sigma = \sqrt{\frac{\Sigma\,(x - \bar{x})^2}{n - 1}}$$

*This formula shows how to estimate the variance of a population based on a sample. Divide the sum of squared deviations by (n-1) rather than by n to create an unbiased estimator for the population variance.*

Where:

$\sigma$ = standard deviation

$x$ = the value of an individual data point in a sample

$x$-bar is the arithmetic mean of the sample

$n$ is the sample size

**Example:** As playground director, Maria wanted to calculate the variation in ages of children using the swings. She sampled eight children at random times of the day and found their ages were 4, 10, 5, 9, 7, 6, 8, and 7. The average age was 7. To calculate the estimated standard deviation of all children using the swings, she used the formula for a sample, first subtracting each age from the average and totaling the squared differences from the average:

$$(4-7)^2 + (10-7)^2 + (5-7)^2 + (9-7)^2 + (7-7)^2 + (6-7)^2 + (8-7)^2 + (7-7)^2 = 28$$

Dividing by n-1 (7) gives the sample variance = 4.0. The standard deviation is the square root of the variance = 2.0.

Maria now has an estimate of the variation in ages of the larger population of children who play on the swings.

 **Technically Speaking** _____

In addition to having a formula for estimating the population standard deviation from a random sample, there is also a formula for determining the population standard deviation if all the population is measured.

## Don't Forget to Benchmark

All done now? Hardly! You still have to determine your baseline and Entitlement for any secondary or consequential metrics. And if you really want to be good you'll look for benchmarking data around your primary and secondary performance metrics. Benchmarking is the practice of looking outside your own organization to those who are world-class at whatever it is you're trying to do.

In this case, you might find that a company in your industry has its lead times down to 12 days, whereas the best you've ever done is 22 days. This might give you the gold standard for how high you want to aim. It's one thing to know how well you've done in the past, and even another to aspire to greatness in the future. But on what basis can you reasonably set a performance goal for your process? Finding out how well others have performed your same process, or a very similar process, can help you do this.

# Develop an Objective Statement

With your performance metrics defined, you can now develop an objective statement for your project. Here is the template for doing so:

Improve [primary metric] from [baseline average] to [target] by [date].

It's as simple as that! You've done so much to understand your process, your customers, and the needs of your organization. And now that you've measured the performance of your process and collected some benchmarking data, you are ready to simply write your project objective statement, which will guide and drive you the rest of your way through the Lean Six Sigma process.

To do this properly, all you have to do is be SMART: Specific, Measurable, Aggressive (yet Achievable), Relevant, and Time-bound. For example:

♦ Increase the first-pass yield for the new client billing process from 81 to 90 percent by January 31.

♦ Decrease falling injuries among the tree-trimming crew from six per quarter to zero by October 31.

♦ Decrease changeover time for the milk production line from 96 minutes to 33 minutes by June 30.

So do we need to tell you that a bad project objective statement wouldn't be SMART? "Reduce billing errors" or "decrease injuries" aren't specific enough, or measurable, or aggressive, or time-bound—although they may be relevant. And one more thing: don't forget about your secondary metrics, and always keep an eye on your consequential metrics, too.

**Lean Six Sigma Wisdom**

If your organization has project tracking software, it's time to enter this information and begin using the tool to document and communicate the status of your project.

# Estimate Financial Benefits

Of course, the reason you do a Lean Six Sigma project at all is to ultimately impact one of the two most important metrics of your organization: cost and revenue. Even if you are a nonprofit or government organization, and your main concern is serving customers or citizens, you still want to do this in the most efficient and cost-effective way possible. At the end of the day, these efficiencies translate directly into higher resource utilization and cost savings.

Therefore, the question becomes, will your project impact revenue or cost? And by how much? So if your project involves reducing inventory, how will this affect the costs associated with housing inventory? If your project deals with increasing capacity, and that capacity is then utilized, how much more revenue will you enjoy as a result?

Same for projects focused on yield increases, defect reductions, safety, scrap, waste, and so on.

### Performance Pitfall

The requirement of estimating annual savings and benefits from your Lean Six Sigma projects is just that: an estimate. Don't spend oodles of time struggling to come up with exact, certain predictions. You only need a good first-order prediction now because your exact financial benefit will become much clearer as you move into the Analyze and Improve phases.

Your task is to estimate the savings or benefits that you expect to derive from your project and, ideally, go over these with your manager, boss, or Project Champion. You'll want to project your savings 12 months out so you can speak in terms of annualized savings and benefits to your organization.

The way to do this is to assume your project will enable your process to perform at its targeted level as per your objective statement. You'll have to get your finance department involved to help you estimate your projected savings, and to validate that you are on track to deliver your estimated benefits after you've implemented your process changes in the Improve phase of Lean Six Sigma.

## Savings, Cost Avoidance, and Revenue

There are many categories of savings and benefits you should know before estimating what your project will achieve. You can use these categories and scenarios as guides. And if you work in a company that is deploying Lean Six Sigma on a large scale, you'll surely need to work with your finance department to verify and approve your projections.

**Hard savings** are the quantifiable savings that result directly from a Lean Six Sigma project. Examples of hard savings could include savings in materials, man-hours, or overhead. Because of the method Lean Six Sigma Belts use to calculate Cost of Poor Quality (COPQ), not all of these savings will be reflected on existing accounting or financial reports.

**Soft savings** are intangible benefits derived from a Lean Six Sigma project, such as increased employee satisfaction. Soft savings are also tangible benefits that cannot be directly attributed to the project. For example, a customer can be happy and place two more orders, but you don't know that this was necessarily a result of your project, even though it could have been.

**Potential savings** are by-products of the process improvement that require subsequent action to be realized. Potential savings can include capacity (manpower/equipment/space) created as a result of a Lean Six Sigma project. Savings remain potential if the resources are not applied to another productive use. For example, if a piece of equipment is made surplus but it is not disposed, the savings are potential until the equipment is placed into productive service.

**Cost avoidance** is typically not a separate category on a Lean Six Sigma financial worksheet. Project benefits classified as cost avoidance will require evidence that the anticipated cost appeared in a current budget for spending or hiring. Once the cost is removed from the budget or hiring plan, the savings can be recharacterized as hard savings. If the amount was not budgeted, it becomes a management decision whether or not to include the amount.

**Revenue growth** is when your project directly impacts sales. This is often very difficult to establish scientifically. For instance, you may implement a Lean Six Sigma project to better target your advertising. But unless you can show that the new campaigns directly and solely caused increased sales, you are only making inferences.

## The Least You Need to Know

- Knowing if your improvement objective is "mile wide and inch deep" or "inch wide and mile deep" will help you scope your projects.

- Use your knowledge of business priorities to select the one output metric ($Y$) that your project will improve.

- Do some preliminary data collection regarding how your process and output metric is currently performing.

- Use your baseline performance, Entitlement, and benchmarking data to set the right performance target for your project.

- Make sure you write a formal objective statement for your project that is Specific, Measurable, Aggressive, Relevant, and Time-bound.

- Your project must return benefits to the organization in the form of hard savings, soft savings, potential savings, cost avoidance, or revenue growth.

# Finalize the Plan

## In This Chapter

- ◆ Pick team members wisely
- ◆ Who's for you and against you?
- ◆ What can go wrong will
- ◆ Plan your course
- ◆ Check your methodology

Several steps remain to complete the Define phase—the first of which is selecting your team members. No one makes a difference alone. You need others to be involved, and Lean Six Sigma improvements are always a team effort. Just the same, people can also hinder your progress and obstruct your pathway to the results you desire. Therefore, we'll tell you in this chapter how to identify who can help and who can hinder your project.

Also, we'll cover a nice tool for anticipating project risks, and how you can head off anticipated trouble. We'll further look at project planning principles and give you a template for chartering your project. Think of it as a mission document that provides everyone everything they need to know—at a high level. Finally, we'll use a decision flow chart you can use to validate that Lean Six Sigma is the right way to go with your project.

# Identify Project Team

Now that you've developed a project idea and have leadership support to make it happen, you need to create a team to work with you on the project. Since you'll be changing the way work gets done, you need the help of people who understand the process.

Basically, in selecting team members, you want to think through the type of knowledge and skills you will need. If your project is in an office environment, you may want to include people from such departments as IT, human resources, and other support functions—in addition to those who work or manage the process directly.

If you're in a production area, you may need to include the process owner, maintenance departments, someone from safety, and possibly a union steward (if a union shop). The purpose is to develop a crossfunctional team.

The suggested number of team members is anywhere from three to eight. If you have fewer than three, you risk not getting the benefits of multiple inputs and insights. When you have more than eight team members, these benefits become diminished, as the complexity of added numbers can start to slow you down.

The following graph highlights the emotions teams feel while working a project. At first, the rally cry can get everyone worked up and on board expecting great results.

**Performance Pitfall**

Team members are scarce resources in a business. Therefore, avoid using more team members than you need—and don't constantly use the same team members because you'll end up with a "group think" mentality. That is, everyone will think in the same way and possibly stifle needed creativity and new ideas.

Then the realities of the hard work and complexities of the problem will become foremost, and team members will begin to lose their optimism. Depending on how this is managed, spirits will fall. The question is how far, and what can you do as a team leader to mitigate this drop?

A good guide is to communicate with your team members clearly, consistently, and often. For those who've done their work correctly until now, there is good news. You have wonderful process documentation, and a clear mission in your project objective statement. It's best to just bring people back to the reason you are doing the improvement work, why it has to be done, and why it is important to do it well and on time.

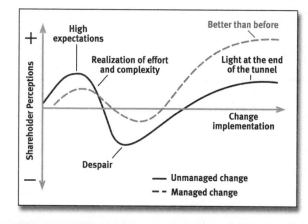

*Teams typically have high expectations at first, then plummet when they realize how difficult their task is, then rally to get the job done. This progression can be managed to speed the process of change and make it more effective.*

# Identify Stakeholders

Just like the show *Survivor*, to be successful with a Lean Six Sigma project, you have to know who is for you and who is against you. Figuring this out—knowing who's who—is called a Stakeholder Analysis, and the first part of conducting one is to simply identify your stakeholders.

Who are they? They are *anyone* who is impacted in *any way* by the changes you are trying to make. A practical definition of a stakeholder is any individual or group with an interest in the outcome of your project. And don't forget, a stakeholder is anyone who may be impacted by your project, like a Process Owner, as well as anyone with the ability to impact your project, like an executive who doesn't like you.

## Stakeholder Analysis

The chart that follows is an example of a Stakeholder Analysis, which you are advised to keep confidential. This is not a public document, but a tool you can use to help you work though political realities. Over time, you should adjust your analysis to reflect changing perceptions and attitudes.

| | Key Stakeholder | Role in Organization | Power/ Influence Category | Impact of Project on Stakeholder (H, M, L) | Current/ Desired Support | | | | | Reasons for Resistance or Support |
|---|---|---|---|---|---|---|---|---|---|---|
| | | | | | Strongly Opposed | Opposed | Neutral | Supportive | Strongly Supportive | |
| 1. | John Smith | Quality Manager | A | M | | | | O———→ | | T-Project will reduce most common defects. |
| 2. | Mary James | VP Operations | C | M | | O———→ | | | | T-Resultant yield increase. |
| 3. | Susan Davis | Production Supervisor | A | H | | | | ● | | T-Resultant yield increase. |
| 4. | David Kelly | Repair Tech | B | M | | ●———→ | | | | P-Changes imposed by others. |
| 5. | Mark Thomas | Quality Engineer | B | H | ●———————→ | | | | | Disagrees with priority of project relative to others. |
| 6. | Terry Nolan | Quality Engineer | B | H | | | | | ● | T-Project will reduce most common defects. |
| 7. | Wendy Ryan | Operator | B | H | | | | O | | Job will be easier. |
| 8. | Fred Granger | Inspector | D | H | ●———→ | | | | | P-Fears job loss. C-Feels left out of decisions. |
| 9. | Holly Lewis | Accounting Manager | C | L | | O———→ | | | | |

*Use this tool to identify your project's stakeholders and figure out who is for you and who is against you.*

# Power Influence Map

After you've completed your Stakeholder Analysis, you can use a Power Influence Map to plot the influence your stakeholders have—in other words, their ability to either help you or deter you from achieving your goal. Note in the sample Power Influence Map that follows, you can place your stakeholders into one of four categories.

**Quadrant A:** These stakeholders have both high organizational power and strong project influence. Ensuring their support should be a top priority.

**Quadrant B:** These stakeholders are not as high in the organization, but they have strong, often direct, influence over your project. Their support is also essential.

**Quadrant C:** These stakeholders have high organizational power, though they are farther removed from your project. While they need not be strong supporters, if they are opposed to the project, they can hinder or kill its progress.

**Quadrant D:** These stakeholders have lower levels of both organizational power and influence of the specific project. While their support is not required for project success, they could sabotage your efforts if they are strongly opposed to the project.

*Use this Power Influence Map tool to visualize the categories into which your stakeholders fall. This will help you manage your project.*

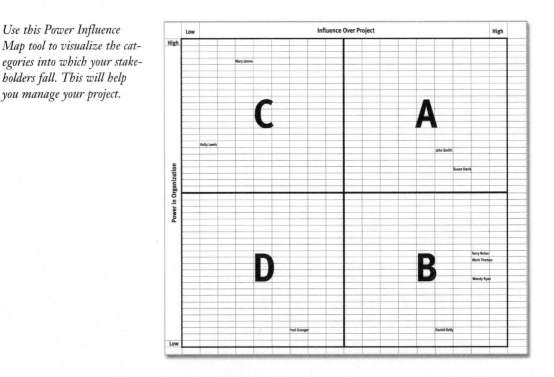

## Stakeholder Action Plan

As you determine how you can influence your key stakeholders, use a tool like the one that follows, the Stakeholder Action Plan. Remember that Lean Six Sigma projects should be completed in a timely manner, so don't get caught in analysis paralysis here. Only fill in the level of Stakeholder Action Plan detail you need to drive results.

To complete the action plan, identify each stakeholder's current position on the Power Influence Map. Then evaluate all stakeholders as to the kind of people who are using the DISC analysis. Based partly on this, then develop tasks or actions for moving each stakeholder into a greater position of support for your project.

| Rank | Stakeholder | Perceived DSC | Method of Communication | Leverageable Allies | WIIFS | Communication Tips and Reminders | Anticipated Questions and Your Responses |
|------|-------------|---------------|-------------------------|---------------------|-------|----------------------------------|------------------------------------------|
| 1. | | | | | | | |
| 2. | | | | | | | |
| 3. | | | | | | | |
| 4. | | | | | | | |
| 5. | | | | | | | |
| 6. | | | | | | | |
| 7. | | | | | | | |
| 8. | | | | | | | |
| 9. | | | | | | | |
| 10. | | | | | | | |

*Use this Stakeholder Action Plan tool to plan your actions for moving stakeholders into stronger positions of support for your project.*

| P/I Map Quadrant | Minimum Support Level | Desired Support Level |
|------------------|-----------------------|-----------------------|
| A | Supportive | Strongly Supportive |
| B | Neutral | Supportive or Strongly Supportive |
| C | Neutral | Supportive |
| D | Not Critical* | Neutral |

Extroverted, Verbal
Dominant, Risk-takers

Task-oriented,      D | I      People-oriented,
Suspicious, Wary,    |        Open, Trusting,
Less Approachable  C | S      Approachable

Introverted, Reserved,
Easy-going, Cautious

*What's In It For Stakeholders (WIIFS).*

# Identify Project Risks

Now that you've identified your stakeholders, and know how to deal with them, good project planning comes into play. And the first step of good project planning is to anticipate, once again, Murphy's Law: Whatever can go wrong will go wrong. This means you have to anticipate the risks that could end up derailing your project. Typical risks to consider are …

**Lean Six Sigma Wisdom**

One source of friction you may encounter is getting assigned a problem to solve that was already given to someone else or another department in the past. Therefore, view yourself as an additional resource to help, not a hotshot.

◆ What's the history of previous attempts to solve the problem?

◆ What constraints do you have on the project? Consider: capital spending limit, completion timing, and resource availability.

There are multiple tools that you can use to mitigate risk. One common tool is a Failure Mode and Effects Analysis (FMEA), but this we cover in Chapter 13. Perhaps a better tool—a simpler tool—to use at this stage is a Force Field Analysis, with an example shown next.

*You should know your supporting as well as opposing forces when trying to make any organizational or process change. Look at your force-field factors as levers you can press to influence your outcome.*

*(Source: Mind Tools: www. mindtools.com/pages/article/ newTED_06.htm#)*

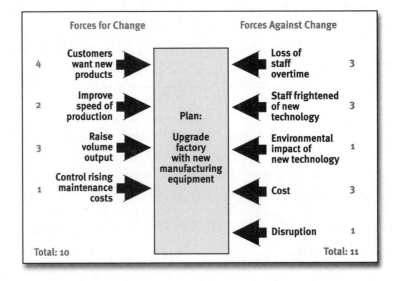

Here's how Force Field Analysis works. Create a table with two columns—one for all the reasons for change and the other listing all the barriers against change. Assign a value of 1 to 5 to these conditions, with 1 for "weak" and 5 for "strong"—referring to the degree of influence they have on the outcome, or plan. Add your totals to see how likely it is that your change will occur as you want.

Obviously, the more disparity there is between the negative and positive forces—in favor of the positive—the more likely it is that your project will be successful. If it appears that your project will not be successful, or is at risk, then you may need to revisit your Stakeholder Analysis and Action Plan and make some adjustments. Or find some additional alliances that can help you.

# Establish Project Timeline

The primary reason to develop a timeline is to ensure that you reach your project milestones in a reasonable amount of time. For a Lean Six Sigma project, it all depends on the difficulty of your problem, the amount of existing data you do or don't have, and other factors, such as whether your company allows you to work your project full-time or not.

What follows are some rules and guidelines for establishing your project timeline:

◆ Is the problem or opportunity well scoped or defined? (Then the project may not require a long time period in the Define phase.)

◆ Is the problem or opportunity tracked in a database? (If data needs to be collected or validated, the project may require more time in the Measure phase.)

◆ Is the problem or opportunity related to variation? (If variation occurs randomly, then again the Measure stage may take longer than expected.)

◆ Is the root cause easy to understand? (If a lot of investigation is required for analysis of root cause. or experiments need to be performed to understand the failure mode, the Analyze phase may be extended.)

◆ Is the improvement going to require capital expense or an Information Technology solution? (The time to implement now follows more of a traditional project management flow versus a process improvement flow.)

◆ Is there a high degree of culture change required? (This will affect the timeline based on how well the change is actively managed.)

Remember, you've already developed your project objective using SMART goal writing as a tool. The reason you now need a set timeline is because you have to create an expectation—for yourself, your team members, and your management. And to keep your team on track, communicate successes and obstacles both early and often.

# Create Project Charter

The purpose of a Project Charter template (shown in the following figure) is to create a contract for work between the Lean Six Sigma Champion and the Lean Six Sigma practitioner, or Belt. Regardless of your specific format, your Project Charter should reflect consensus on your problem statement, the scope of your project, and project objective—the details of which are in Chapters 7 and 8.

At this stage you can use this Project Charter template to guide you through the documentation aspects of work you've already performed. Among all the many elements of a Project Charter, it's desirable to state your business case. You may remember the catchphrase from the movie *Jerry McGuire:* "Show me the money." Everyone needs to know why the project is important and what it will do for your business.

| | Element |
|---|---|
| **Describe the Business Problem** | **What** is the specific problem (project idea) affecting the success of your business? |
| | **Who** is the internal or external customer most affected by this problem? |
| | Identify the **Critical to Customer (CTX)** category (Quality, Delivery or Cost) associated with this problem. |
| | Name the **business metric** associated with this problem (existing management performance indicator)? |
| | **Where** is the problem occurring (geographic or process location)? |
| | **When** was the problem first observed (specify month/year)? |
| | **How Much?** What is the extent or magnitude of the problem as measured by your business metric? |
| | **How do you know** this is a problem? What target is not being met? |
| | Write the **Problem Statement** in sentence format using the template ‹What›‹Where›‹When›‹How Much› ‹How do you know›. |
| **Scope Business Problem** | What is the output **product or service** delivered to the customer related to the business problem? |
| | **Name** the business process delivering the product or service. Think in terms of a process that can be mapped. |
| | Develop a high level (macro) **Process Map** of the above business process. This typically includes 5 to 7 major steps of a process. |
| | Name the product or service **features** (i.e., measurable characteristics) that may need to be fixed to improve the business problem. If more than 2 features are identified, the scope of the project may be too broad. |
| **Process Metrics & Objective Statement** | What is wrong with the features named above (i.e., what is the **defect** on this measurable characteristic that does not meet some requirement? |
| | Name the Primary Metric which measures the identified defect. The Primary Metric will be used to measure the success of the Lean Six Sigma project. |
| | Estimate the **Baseline** performance level of this Primary Metric. |
| | Can you estimate the **Entitlement** (best short term observed historical performance) of this Primary Metric? Yes or no? If so, what is the entitlement performance level? |
| | Name any **Consequential Metrics** which measure potential negative consequences of successfully improving the Primary Metric. |
| | Identify which **sources of data** (reports, collection sheets, inspection points, et) are available to measure the metrics above. |
| | Write a S.M.A.R.T. **Objective Statement** as follows: "Improve {primary metric} from {baseline level} to {target level 70% toward entitlement} by {timeframe MM?YYYY}. |
| **Financial Metric** | Who is the Finance Representative assigned to value the financial impact of this Lean Six Sigma project? |
| | Identify any potential **cost centers** that will be impacted by reducing this defect. |
| | Comment on application or extension of this project across other areas or locations of the organization. |
| | Complete the **Original Forecast** (80% confidence) with the Financial Representative. |
| **Team Assignment** | Does the project scope / complexity require a **Lean Six Sigma Belt?** Specify name. |
| | Identify the **Process Owner** (person with primary responsibility for ongoing operation of impacted process). |
| | Identify the **project team members** (typically 3-6 people who have a broad level of expertise or process knowledge). |
| **Project Launch** | Identify the **project approval team** (people required to approve the project before it can be started). If required in organization's project guidelines. |
| | Obtain the necessary **approval signatures** to launch the project. |
| | Are there other process initiatives (in work) that would be affected by this project? If yes, what are they? |

*Look at all the elements of this Project Charter template and ask yourself if you've got them covered before moving on in the process.*

Finally, to further create the needed sense of urgency, you will want to create a traditional project management Gantt Chart. We don't show one because they are so common in the business world. Just in case you don't know what one is, a Gantt Chart lists all the tasks to be performed down the left-hand side of a matrix. Also in rows, the Gantt displays who is responsible for the completion of the task. Then using horizontal bars, the chart shows how long the task should take and when it is due. Often, Gantt Charts also have a column for making status notes per task as the project moves forward.

# Choosing Your Methodology

In a very real sense, we can say that Lean Six Sigma is all about checks, double checks, and triple checks regarding your project, your process, your data, your performance, and so on. Well, here at the very end of the Define phase, we introduce a very important reality check: do you really need the power of Lean Six Sigma to solve your problem and improve your process as planned?

Here's the thing about performance improvement, and even about business in general: you should never expend more capital, money, or resources to do anything more than what is required. Therefore, if you can solve your problem without the Lean Six Sigma process, now is the time to determine that once and for all.

As well, your particular improvement objective may require a heavy-duty set of skills and tools related more to innovation or R&D than to improvement. If that's the case, you won't want to waste your time trying to apply DMAIC to a non-DMAIC type problem. Other tool sets would be more appropriate.

**Lean Six Sigma Wisdom**

If you're a Lean Six Sigma practitioner, you don't have to worry or pay too much attention to this business of how to allocate different projects. In a company that's deploying Lean Six Sigma, your Champion will simply assign you an appropriate project.

Generally speaking, as the following chart shows, you want to take yourself through a decision pathway to confirm that Lean Six Sigma is the way to go. First, ask yourself if you have a basic process management system in place. If yes, fine. If no, create one. If you've followed the process thus far, you have the early makings of a process management system.

Then the rest of your confirmation activity hinges around whether the root cause of your performance problem is known or not. If it is, and the solution to your problem is obvious, you Just Do It—meaning you simply implement the changes you know you need.

If your root causes and solution are not known, then you will need either some solution brought on by innovation methods, or some solution brought on by Lean Six Sigma. Once you get to this point in the flow chart, your decision is simple. If your root cause is not known, you need to implement a DMAIC Lean Six Sigma project. If it is known (but not the solution), then you need to implement a Lean Six Sigma Kaizen Event. If the root cause is known, and you need a brand-new process or product, then you turn to Design for Six Sigma or some other innovation method.

*Use this flow chart to confirm that you need Lean Six Sigma to solve your problem, and to determine if you need a full-blown DMAIC approach or a faster Kaizen Event.*

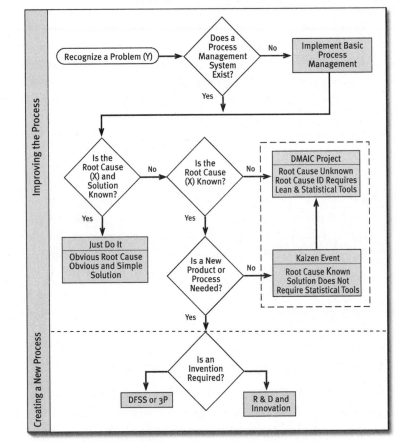

# Communicate, Communicate, Communicate

Remember that there's no one perfect way to communicate.

The primary goal of developing a communication plan is to keep all the stakeholders informed of your project's status, and to ensure you get any help you may need to finish the tasks on time.

You don't need to overwhelm your audience with too many statistics and terms. Often the best communication tool is a picture, like a simple before-and-after shot of what you've accomplished. Too many people are heavy on terminology and light on substance—don't you know that!

In general, know what you have to communicate, and do it through vehicles or a mix of vehicles that will be most effective—meetings, e-mail, formal presentations. Whatever your selected venues, communicate consistently, substantively, clearly, and often. And be sure to include all stakeholders in your communication plan.

 **Quotable Quote**

Of all of our inventions for mass communication, pictures still speak the most universally understood language.

—Walt Disney

# Conduct Tollgate Review

At the end of each phase of DMAIC, you need to conduct a tollgate review that ensures you've accomplished all your critical tasks and are ready to move on in the process. Such reviews should be attended by your Lean Six Sigma Champion, your Process Owner, team members, and other key stakeholders.

At your tollgate meeting, review your Project Charter, performance metrics, and other relevant information and data. Obtain concurrence to continue with your project. If concurrence is not obtained, clarify and resolve the issues before proceeding past the Define stage. If your company tracks projects with software, enter your project data into the application.

Otherwise, here are some tollgate questions and hints about how you can answer them:

- What is your $Y$? (Answer: The specific outcome your project aims to improve.)

- How did you determine this? (Answer: Show linkage of your process metric with business metrics.)

- How is your $Y$ relevant to your company and your customers? How do you know? (Answer: Typically assigned by Champion with a linkage to the strategic goals.)

◆ Is your *Y* measurable? (Answer: Data should be collected or a strategy developed to measure prior to the Measure phase.)

◆ What are the potential benefits (financial and other) of improving this *Y*? (Answer: Meet with finance department and determine savings or use internal metrics to calculate savings.)

◆ What is your project timeline? (Answer: On the charter.)

◆ What is the scope of your project? (Answer: On the charter and demonstrated by a Process Map or SIPOC.)

◆ What is your goal for your *Y*? (Answer: This is on the charter.)

◆ Is this goal attainable? (Answer: Review baseline, Entitlement.)

◆ Do you have sufficient support from your Champion and Process Owner? (Answer: This requires a nondefensive position from the Champion and Process Owner.)

◆ Are all data fields in your project tracking tool current with your most recent project progress? (Answer: Hopefully yes. If not, enter data.)

## The Least You Need to Know

◆ Recruit project team members who have the knowledge and skills you need to complete your project.

◆ Make sure you know who all your stakeholders are. These are people who can either make or break the success of your project.

◆ Use a Force Field Analysis or FMEA to identify and deal with project risks. Know that there will be risks, and you cannot escape them. You can only address them.

◆ A good Project Charter states the problem and the project objective. It also identifies your key process metric and the financial benefits you expect to achieve.

◆ Don't proceed unless you know for sure that you need either a DMAIC project or Kaizen Event to make your improvement.

◆ Complete a tollgate review to help move the project through its life cycle. Don't proceed to Measure until this review is done.

# Measure the Process

## In This Chapter

- ◆ Creating a process flow
- ◆ Swim Lanes and Value Streams
- ◆ The 8.5-by-11 syndrome
- ◆ Make your fast improvements now

We are now transitioning from the Define phase of Lean Six Sigma to the Measure phase. Remember that the goal of Define is to identify just what's wrong with your process. The goal of Measure extends this to include figuring out just how bad your process is. We know this sounds harsh, but if all your processes were running perfectly, you wouldn't need Lean Six Sigma.

Warning: you may begin to notice overlap in content with this chapter and preceding chapters. Don't be fooled. If we talk about Process and Value Stream Maps in this chapter (which we will), that doesn't mean you don't need to pay attention. Even though we touched on Process and Value Stream Maps in Chapter 7, we need to revisit them here—in more detail.

In this chapter, we'll look at the high-level road map for the Measure phase of Lean Six Sigma, DMAIC. This will set the course for this and the next two chapters. We'll also give you all the basic details of Process Mapping and Value Stream Mapping. And we'll show you how you can use these maps to make rapid, immediate improvements.

# Introducing Measure

The rest of this chapter, and ones to follow, will take you on a more detailed tour of what it takes to effectively complete the Measure phase of Lean Six Sigma. Let the flow chart that follows be your guide.

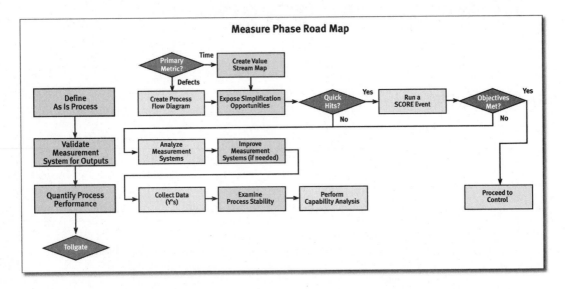

This is the general process for the Measure phase of DMAIC. Depending on your experience and unique situation, you may or may not strictly follow these steps in a set sequential fashion.

# Knowing What to Improve

The essence of the Measure phase of DMAIC is figuring out exactly what to improve. As we discovered in previous chapters, it's easy to say you need to "improve customer satisfaction" or "increase capacity at factory A." Even when you've spelled out your project objective statement, and have your baseline performance measures, you'll still need to collect more data.

The key deliverables for the Measure phase are a clearly defined performance metric and an understanding of how your process currently performs. In other words, you need to know exactly what is wrong and how wrong it is.

In Chapter 3, we talked about the Six Sigma principle of "$Y$ is a function of $x$," and we made the point that every effect has one or more critical causes. At this stage of the Lean Six Sigma game, you are primarily concerned with characterizing the output of your process, or its performance, or the $Y$ of concern. As we delve more deeply into the DMAIC process in later chapters, we will transition our focus from the $Y$s to the $x$s.

 **Performance Pitfall**

Remember that Lean Six Sigma projects are only necessary when the problem at hand is too difficult to solve without data and analysis. If you don't need data to solve your problem and install the best solution, don't measure what you don't need.

## Not as Easy as You Think

Depending on your process of concern, performance metrics are not as easy to develop and track as you might think. Some metrics are very precise and are captured automatically (e.g., length of time customers wait on hold). Other metrics are far less precise and much more subjective (e.g., degree of frustration among lab technicians).

Any type of metric is legitimate if it has a significant impact on the performance of a process, or on the satisfaction of an *internal* or *external customer*. The key is to identify and define your metrics, then determine how accurately you can measure them over time.

Measuring performance prior to, and after, an improvement effort gets to the heart of what Lean Six Sigma is all about. If you don't have at least relatively objective measurements, you can't ever say you've really improved. On the other hand, if you have accurate measurements, you can always clearly display your improvements. This will go quite a long way in winning over any skeptical observers.

Still, while concrete data present a compelling story, they also have a dark side.

 **Lean Six Sigma Lingo**

An **internal customer** is someone who needs the output of the previous step in the process to do his or her job. For example, a news anchor is the customer of the person entering the script into the teleprompter. An **external customer** is the person who purchases the final product or service.

Sometimes the creation of elaborate proof through extensive measurement of the process can take on a life of its own. This risk is especially likely when one or more team members is particularly keen on reporting and analysis. Another trap is when an especially doubtful stakeholder uses "lack of data" as a reason to object to the effort overall.

To best apply Lean Six Sigma, and solve the problem at hand, the team must strike an acceptable balance between intuitive assessment and precise data analysis. Therefore, an appropriate degree of data collection is essential; but excessive focus on perfecting your data will only stall progress and decrease your chance of making the desired improvement.

## Four Things to Do

The real work of Measure begins with a high-level understanding of your process. In the Define phase, we gave you a tool called a SIPOC Map (refer to Chapter 7), which helped you identify the boundaries of your process, its suppliers, key inputs and outputs, and major process steps. Now is when you take that high-level map and start to put some detail on it.

This is your first "must-do" measurement activity: *create a map of your process* so everyone understands how it works. If a picture is worth a thousand words, then a process map is worth a thousand hours of verbal communication. Even the simplest map is a major step toward understanding what does or doesn't happen in your process.

Your second need-to-do is to *collect empirical data* regarding how your process is functioning and performing. As you will see in the pages that follow, data collection is time-consuming. Therefore, you have to collect the right data correctly the first time. When you collect the wrong data, you end up doing it over again, and this is a drain on team morale that you don't want.

Third, you need to *make sure your measurement system is valid.* If your measurement system is making the process appear to run well or poorly when it really isn't, this will only botch up your improvement efforts. If your measurement system is inaccurate enough to warrant the effort, you may need to improve or replace it.

Finally, during the Measure phase, you will *quantify your process performance.* In Lean Six Sigma terms, this means you will "characterize" your process performance. In doing so, you will determine if your process is stable and capable. If it is stable, that means it doesn't vary unexpectedly over time. If your process is capable, then it meets its performance specifications.

# Primary Metric Defects or Time?

The first action step in Measure is to determine whether the primary performance metric is related to defects or time. While defects are instances of something in the process going wrong, time is when the process takes too long. When not up to expectations, both forms of nonconformance cause customer dissatisfaction.

But wait a minute—when a process takes too long, isn't that a defect, too? After all, any instance in which a process doesn't meet its specifications or requirements is a defect, right?

The answer is yes—but we make the distinction because that tells us which type of process map to build.

If your primary metric of concern is non-time-related defects, then you will use a Process Flow.

If your metric is time, then you will use a Value Stream Map.

## Flow the Process Flow

Assume that your primary metric is defects (something is going wrong and you don't know why). This would lead you to create a Process Flow diagram of the current "as-is" process. Remember that at this stage, you are creating a Process Map that reflects what the actual process is—not what one person thinks it is or what you want it to be.

Process Flow diagrams, or detailed Flow Charts, are very useful tools for seeing a breakdown of how the process works. They can and should be fairly detailed maps that answer the "who," "how," and "in what order" questions about the various steps of the process. The figures that follow demonstrate a simple Process Flow for baking crackers and common Process Map symbols.

W. Edwards Deming, the quality guru and process excellence expert, repeatedly told managers and employees alike that their mission was to have "profound knowledge" of the process before tinkering around with it. Profound knowledge, while sounding almost like a spiritual term, means knowing what actually goes on in the process and not depending on anecdotes and hearsay.

The second law of thermodynamics tells us that all systems tend toward entropy, or disorder. So, hot things cool down, neat things get sloppy, and organized work flow gets disjointed. This is just one great reason why anyone who does anything in an organization needs to flow out their process. Especially, organizations need to create Flow maps of their key processes that span many functions, departments, and people.

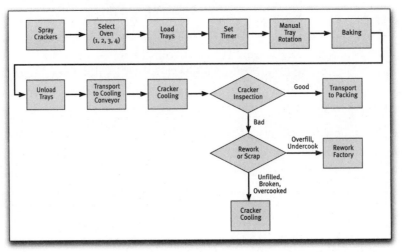

*This flow depicts the process of baking crackers. Note the difference between the squares, or action steps, and the diamonds, which represent decision points.*

*These are some of the more common symbols you might use in building your Process Map. There are others you can use depending on your process and the software you might use.*

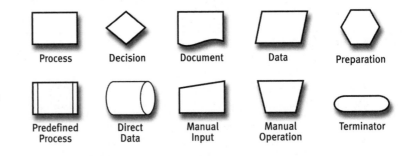

## Swimming in Lanes

The most useful form of Process Flow Map is called a Deployment Flow Chart or Swim Lane Flow Chart; these are one and the same. Both charts break down the process into the smallest meaningful steps and show ownership of the various steps by way of Swim Lanes across the page.

What follows is a simple Swim Lane Map for setting up a software demo. You can see how this map delineates the different functions and departments/people involved in moving from customer interest to the setup for the demo. As with process maps, Swim Lane Maps can be a lot more complex than this one.

On the left-hand side of the chart are the names of the functions that take part in the process (such as Sales, Marketing, Operations, Customer Service, Finance, Shipping, etc.). And across the horizontal flow is time. But you can also use the Swim Lane approach by listing your functions across the top horizontally, and then leaving the vertical flow to depict time, as shown in the Swim Lane example here.

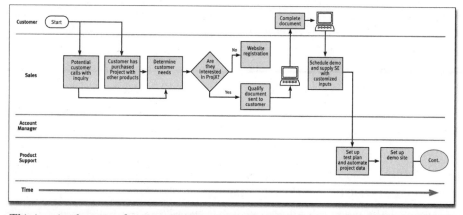

*This is a simple process for transitioning a customer inquiry into a product (software) demo. Note the Swim Lanes for each function and constituent involved.*

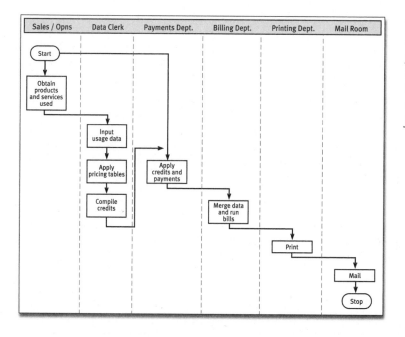

*This tool is a simple Swim Lane Map depicting a billing process. Note that the lanes in this case run vertically instead of horizontally. Also note the number of handoffs from one lane to another.*

By following the process Flow from step to step and across lanes, we see how many times the process is "handed off" to someone else. Handoffs are the first place to look for problems and are not nearly as visible in basic Flow Charts.

The reason we want to closely scrutinize handoffs is displayed at the Olympic track and field championships. One of the highlights of the summer games is the 4×100 meter relay race. In this race, four world-class runners per country compete by running 100 meters, then handing off a lightweight metal baton to the next runner.

Do you think the country with the fastest runners always wins? If you do, you'd be wrong. In nearly every Olympic Games in the last century, this pivotal race has been won or lost on the ability of the runners to smoothly hand off that baton. In many tragic cases, the fastest team has lost the race because they dropped or bobbled the baton.

The difference in the speeds of the runners can be and often is grossly overshadowed by their ability to work as a team. The baton is the measure of their performance. It's ironic when you consider it is called a sprinting race, not a "baton pass." We can quickly apply this baton analogy to fit businesses and most organizations.

In all likelihood you have some very good people working in your organization; they may even be world-class at what they do individually. But as the economy becomes flatter and flatter, and your competition gets broader and broader, you are being forced to compete with other world-class organizations who are able to hand off their processes smoothly.

## The 8.5-by-11 Syndrome

While a Flow Chart is a great place to start, it's not enough. To highlight why, let's talk a bit about the 8.5-by-11 syndrome. This is the tendency for people to try and squeeze their Process Flow Charts into an 8.5" × 11" piece of paper. Certainly all processes should be described with a single sheet of paper, right? Wrong!

Let's talk about why just one page is a bad idea. The goal of documenting your process is to make change, not to create something pretty that people with no patience for detail can enjoy. Building pretty 8.5" × 11" slides will not help you to solve your process problem, delight your customer, or make your organization any more money.

You need to build the level of Process Chart necessary to see the problems. The best way to do this is on *big* paper with lots of notes and explanations. Think wall size if possible. The more detail you have, the better chances you have of someone seeing what is wrong.

## Significant Other Test

The final test of your Process Map, before you dig in to further clarify your improvement opportunities, is what some call the "significant other test." But before you enact this test, be warned that it contains a high risk for personal embarrassment. Here it is:

1. Create a process map with your team of subject matter experts.

2. Invite your significant other to walk you through the map with no guidance or information from you.

3. Capture where he or she did not understand your process or your map.

4. Go back to your team and add the missing or new details.

## Value Stream Maps

If your primary $Y$ metric is time rather than defects, you'll want to use a Value Stream Map (VSM) instead of a Process Map. A VSM is similar to a Swim Lane Map in that it aims to document the entire process. The difference is that a VSM has more features than a straight Process Map.

Basically, the VSM depicts the Flow of a process but also the Flow of people, materials, information, equipment, products, parts, and "engineering" (or policies and procedures). In this sense, a VSM is more complex than most Process Maps, although Value Stream elements can be added to Process Maps if need be.

Referring to the sample VSM charts that follow, here are the steps for building a VSM:

1. Place each of the process steps in order from first to last in the center of the document.

2. Place the substeps under the major steps in a vertical stack.

3. Label each process step with who does the step.

4. Indicate any rework loops by drawing lines back to any place in the process where work must return based on inspection or any other decision criteria.

5. Identify any supplier or recipient of information or material from the process, and draw a separate icon to represent each one.

6. Draw a line in the direction of the material or process flow from or to the outside entity with an arrow. Use icons to help clarify in what format the information is moving (for example, use an envelope to indicate it is being mailed, and an envelope with an $E$ in the middle to indicate it's e-mail).

> ### ⟨σ⟩ Technically Speaking
>
> You can create all kinds of wonderful Flow Charts using different software packages. The main ones used by Lean Six Sigma practitioners are Visio, PowerPoint, iGrafx, SigmaFlow, and ProcessModel. Still, some of the most usable Flow Charts are those created on butcher paper hanging on walls.

7. Insert an arrow in between each major step indicating process flow (left to right generally).

8. Insert any queues in between the steps and use the queue symbol.

9. Collect basic data around how long it takes to complete the major steps or column of steps. Fill in any times or piece count information in the relevant steps (e.g., 10 orders/hour). Write the process cycle times on the bottom of the baseline chart. (Cycle time is how long a step spends on one unit, not including how long the unit is in a queue, or waiting for work to be performed.)

10. Measure any inventory waiting at any step. Insert the inventory icon with the average piece count above it.

11. Measure the wait times for any of the steps and insert on the top of the baseline chart.

12. Calculate the total queue times and the total time for the process, and display this in a timeline at the bottom of the chart. This distinctive timeline is found on all Value Stream Maps, and at a glance it shows how much of the total elapsed time (lead time) is value-added.

*Note:* If you chose to build a Value Stream Map with Swim Lanes, then the center section of your Value Stream Map will look very similar to a standard Swim Lane Chart. The difference will be the sources and recipients of information at the top of the chart and the baseline process and queue time at the bottom of the chart.

*These are the initial steps involved in building a Value Stream Map.*

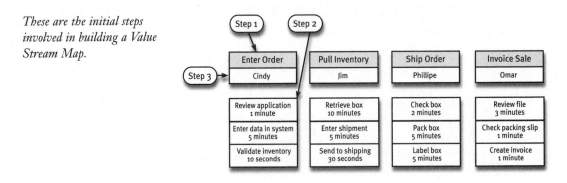

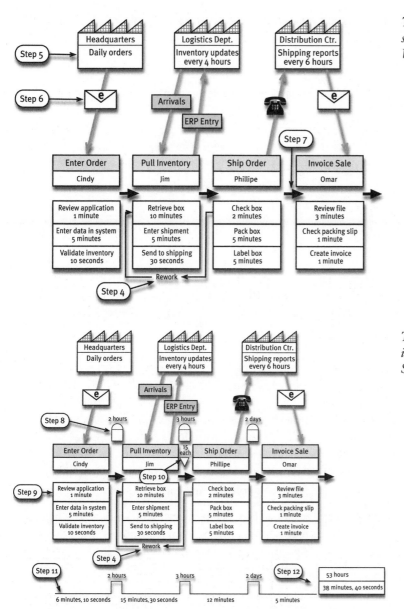

*These are the intermediate steps involved in building a Value Stream Map.*

*These are the final steps involved in building a Value Stream Map.*

Here are some of the most common symbols you can use when building your Value Stream Maps.

*These are some of the more common symbols you might use in building your Value Stream Map. There are others you can use depending on your process and the software you use.*

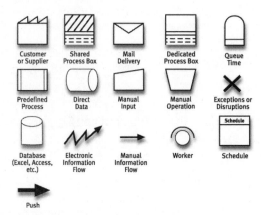

# Expose Simplification Opportunities

With your Process Map or Value Stream Map completed, you are ready to expose simplification opportunities. These are defects, wastes, bottlenecks, issues, inefficiencies, and other problems that can be solved with little additional effort and analysis. In other words, use the knowledge you gain from documenting your process to improve it immediately!

Do you remember the eight types of waste discussed in Chapter 2? Waiting, Overproduction, Rework, Motion, Processing, Inventory, Intellect, and Transportation. Do you see any of these in your process? If you do, then do what you can about them right away. Remember, you only need to progress further and further into the Lean Six Sigma methodology if you need to. If you can solve your project objective now, do it!

*Use the tool of brainstorming* to facilitate ideas from your team members about what you can do immediately based on your process and Value Stream Mapping work. Gather all the ideas you can. Give everyone an opportunity to express their ideas. No idea is a bad idea, and all team members should respect all other team members.

Also, and perhaps more importantly, *apply value-added and non-value-added labels* to all the various steps and activities of your process. The idea is to focus first on non-value-added activities because they hold your greatest opportunity for improvement. Here are some further criteria you can use to determine which steps of your process are value-added and which are not:

◆ **Value-Added:** 1) Done right the first time; 2) Customer is willing to pay to have it done; 3) Step actually transforms the item/transaction in some way.

◆ **Non-Value-Added:** Does not meet the three value-added criteria.

◆ **Value-Enabling:** Steps that do not meet the value-added criteria but must be done in order to meet some legitimate requirement (e.g., Sarbanes Oxley). Sometimes these steps and processes are referred to as Business Value Added.

Again, take your team through the Process Map or Value Stream Map and determine which steps actually add value to the process and which are clearly not adding value. Rework and approval loops are usually easy pickings here. The challenge is to help people understand that just because certain activities are non-value-added doesn't mean they aren't necessary. And especially make sure people know that if they work in a non-value-adding step doesn't mean they are non-value-adding people.

## Executing Quick-Hit Opportunities

In some cases, quick improvements can be made with little planning, additional thought, and team resources. This is the significant effect of simply defining and mapping your process. In other cases, you don't need the power of the full-blown DMAIC methodology, but you do need some extent of teamwork, data, and rigor to break through to the next level of performance.

In Chapter 9, we discussed the framework and process involved in allocating projects into different buckets: "Just Do It," basic process management, innovation, and Lean Six Sigma. We also mentioned that Lean Six Sigma projects don't have to be full-blown DMAIC projects; instead, you can perform a Kaizen Event with Six Sigma components (as well as the other way around).

This is the time you would do so if you have enough evidence to suggest that you don't need the further investigative power for uncovering the root causes of your performance problem. In other words, if you know what is causing your problem now, you can probably fix it by conducting a Kaizen Event.

The key is to know that these events occur usually within one week's time in a war-room-like environment. Everyone who impacts the process, and can implement improvements, basically gathers in the same room and focuses intensely on making the necessary changes.

 **Quotable Quote**

> Kaizen Events are used in Lean transformations to break down the project mentality of the organization and create a bias toward action.
>
> —Wes Waldo, *A Team Leader's Guide to Lean Kaizen Events* (Breakthrough Performance Press, 2006)

Conducting a structured Kaizen Event is really like doing a mini-DMAIC project in itself. The stages of a Kaizen event can be summarized using the acronym SCORE, as follows:

- *Select* the appropriate project on which to work.

- *Clarify* the process and goals.

- *Organize* the appropriate people, time, and resources.

- *Run* the event.

- *Evaluate* the results.

## Where Do I Go From Here?

Many projects need go no further than what we have accomplished up to this stage. The key question to ask yourself and your team is: "Does the process now meet our objectives?" If the answer to this question is yes, then the project team needs to shift immediately into the Control phase (see Chapter 20), and establish a reliable means to maintain the gains achieved.

## The Least You Need to Know

- When you begin your Measure activities, you are focusing mostly on your key performance metric, or expected outcome. This is also known as your major $Y$ of concern.

- To properly measure performance, you need a detailed map of how your process works. This in and of itself can be enlightening and lead you to make immediate improvements.

- If your key project metric is related to defects, you need to create a Process Map. If your key metric is related to time, then you need a Value Stream Map.

- A Swim Lanes Diagram can be used to depict the different people and departments, and therefore handoffs, involved in a process.

- Often you can conduct a Kaizen Event to make fast improvements that don't need the rigor of further data collection and statistical analyses.

# Validate Measurement Systems

## In This Chapter

- ◆ What is a measurement system?
- ◆ Attribute and variable data
- ◆ Gage R&R
- ◆ Accuracy versus precision
- ◆ Using customer requirements

You have exploited your quick-hit opportunities by employing the simpler tools and leverage of visual process analysis. But you still don't quite know what your problem is despite your detailed visual and rudimentary data analysis of your process.

Therefore, this chapter gives you the basics of measurement systems: what they are, why you need them, how they are validated, the nature of different kinds of data, key concepts, and specific tools for operationalizing your customers' requirements.

# Identify Existing Measurement System

Here in the Measure phase, you are still primarily concerned with your outcome measures, or *Y*s. And as much as you documented the way your current process operates, you now have to document your current measurement system. In other words, what data do you have and how is it collected, reported, and managed? How do you know that the data you have is valid? How do you know that your data-generating tools and gages are accurate?

> **Lean Six Sigma Lingo**
>
> **Key Performance Indicators (KPIs)** are leverage variables in the chain of causation we call "business success." Often we refer to the entire set of KPIs as one's "system of indicators."

Hmmm. That's a good one. Why make assumptions? Why make foolish assumptions that the data you have is good data? Why not question everything? What are your *Key Performance Indicators* (*KPIs*)? Is it enough to just collect data on the performance of your ultimate *Y* metric, or might there be a progression of *Y*-related metrics that you will need to know, validate, and track?

After all, if you want to impact yield in a specific way, then what are the components of yield? Rework? There's another factor to measure. Scrap? That affects yield, too. At the same time, these factors are caused by even more factors. And so on down the chain where every key input is the output of some lower-level set of inputs. Think about that.

The key is to make sure that your data is clearly and unambiguously defined so all know what it is and what it means. There is a story of a satellite launched into orbit and lost in space because the wrong definition of data was applied to the design and building of the rocket.

The data (specifications on the engineering diagram) said the rocket should be built to send a 225-pound satellite into space at a certain altitude. The problem was that the satellite weighed 225 kilos, not 225 pounds! This error caused all the trajectory calculations to be wrong, and the expensive satellite was lost in space.

# Analyze the Measurement System

Once we've assured that the definition, process, and procedures for collecting measurements are clear, we then test the measurement system for performance. All measurement systems have errors. Some errors are significant and some are not. For example, most home weighing scales are not perfectly accurate, but they do meet the needs of the users. (Unless, of course, you purposely set the scale to always read 10 pounds lighter!)

The makers of home scales know that customers can live with an inaccuracy of plus or minus half a pound. On the other hand, a scale used at the local butcher shop to measure filet mignon or lobster tails must be much more accurate. These scales have better accuracy built into them because this is demanded by customers and regulators.

But back to our key point that all measurement systems have errors. Like people, no one is perfect. Your job is to figure out how perfect your measurement system needs to be to accomplish your business goals, and the goals of your Lean Six Sigma project.

Validating the amount of error in a scale is called Measurement Systems Analysis, or MSA. If you want to be world-class in the way you go about making improvements in your organization, you have to conduct an MSA before you proceed. Otherwise you're introducing performance-improvement risk, and you don't want that.

Therefore, conduct one of two types of MSAs based on the type of data you have, either attribute or variable in nature. Attribute data is discreet in nature and is gathered into categories, such as large/small, on/off, red/blue, pass/fail, and so on. Variable data is also known as continuous data, and it is gathered according to a scale, such as time, weight, length, etc.

---

**Attribute Gages ■ Attribute measurement systems**

- ☐ Go/no-go gages
- ☐ Feeler gages
- ☐ Visual inspection (pass/fail)

**Variable Gages ■ Variable measurement systems**

- ☐ Voltmeters
- ☐ Calipers
- ☐ Graduated cylinders
- ☐ Pressure gages
- ☐ Thermometers
- ☐ Weight scales
- ☐ Clocks

---

*Your test for whether data is attribute or variable in nature is this: can it be divided in two? If yes, then it is variable. If no, then it is attribute.*

## Attribute MSA

MSA for attribute data is the easiest to understand and conduct. The process is simple: multiple people collect data on the same process, then compare their answers to each other and to the actual verifiable value, or "truth." The two important dimensions we are trying to verify are *repeatability* (the same person can get the same measurement result more than once) and *reproducibility* (different people can get the same measurement result at different times).

The spreadsheet example here gives you a nice view of how you might go about capturing and calculating gage repeatability and reproducibility for an attribute measurement system.

The correct answer is recorded in the column named Attribute (column D in the spreadsheet). Then operators 1, 2, and 3 each do two separate measurements of the process at different times and record their answers (repeatability). The last two columns are used to capture whether all the operators agree (reproducibility), and whether all the operators agree with the standard (accuracy).

*An attribute Gage R&R enables you to test for the repeatability, reproducibility, and accuracy of your measurement system.*

| | Known Population | | Operator #1 | | Operator #2 | | Operator #3 | | Y / N | Y / N |
|---|---|---|---|---|---|---|---|---|---|---|
| | Sample # | Attribute | Try #1 | Try #2 | Try #1 | Try #2 | Try #1 | Try #2 | Agree | Agree |
| | 1 | pass | pass | pass | pass | pass | fail | fail | N | N |
| | 2 | pass | pass | pass | pass | pass | fail | fail | N | N |
| | 3 | fail | fail | fail | fail | pass | fail | fail | N | N |
| | 4 | fail | fail | fail | fail | fail | fail | fail | Y | Y |
| | 5 | fail | fail | fail | pass | fail | fail | fail | N | N |
| | 6 | pass | pass | pass | pass | pass | pass | pass | Y | Y |
| | 7 | pass | fail | fail | fail | fail | fail | fail | Y | N |
| | 8 | pass | pass | pass | pass | pass | pass | pass | Y | Y |
| | 9 | fail | pass | pass | pass | pass | pass | pass | Y | N |

As we move to the bottom of the worksheet, shown in the example that follows, we calculate the various dimensions of system performance, as follows:

◆ The *Appraiser Score* shows us how many times an individual operator agreed with himself when taking a measure of the same thing.

◆ The *Score vs. Attribute* is the calculated percentage of times the operator agreed with himself and the known truth, or correct answer.

◆ The *Screen Effective Score* calculates the percentage of times all the operators agreed with themselves as well as each other.

◆ The *Screen Effective Score vs. Attribute* is a total system metric that is the percentage of times all operators agreed with themselves, each other, and the truth. This cumulative analysis is how often you can expect all operators using the same measurement system to get it all right.

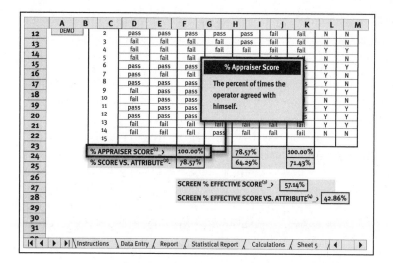

| | A | B | C | D | E | F | G | H | I | J | K | L | M |
|---|---|---|---|---|---|---|---|---|---|---|---|---|---|
| 12 | DEMO | | 2 | pass | pass | pass | pass | pass | fail | fail | N | N |
| 13 | | | 3 | fail | fail | fail | fail | pass | fail | fail | N | N |
| 14 | | | 4 | fail | fail | fail | fail | fail | fail | fail | Y | Y |
| 15 | | | 5 | fail | fail | fail | | | | | N | N |
| 16 | | | 6 | pass | pass | pass | | | | | Y | Y |
| 17 | | | 7 | pass | fail | fail | | | | | Y | N |
| 18 | | | 8 | pass | pass | pass | | | | | Y | N |
| 19 | | | 9 | fail | pass | pass | | | | | Y | Y |
| 20 | | | 10 | fail | pass | pass | | | | | N | N |
| 21 | | | 11 | pass | pass | pass | | | | | Y | Y |
| 22 | | | 12 | pass | pass | pass | | | | | Y | Y |
| 23 | | | 13 | fail | fail | fail | fail | fail | fail | fail | Y | Y |
| 24 | | | 14 | fail | fail | fail | pass | fail | fail | fail | N | N |
| 25 | | | 15 | | | | | | | | | |

*% Appraiser Score*

*The percent of times the operator agreed with himself.*

| % APPRAISER SCORE[1] > | 100.00% | | 78.57% | | 100.00% | |
| % SCORE VS. ATTRIBUTE[2] | 78.57% | | 64.29% | | 71.43% | |

| SCREEN % EFFECTIVE SCORE[3] > | 57.14% |
| SCREEN % EFFECTIVE SCORE VS. ATTRIBUTE[4] > | 42.86% |

Instructions \ Data Entry / Report / Statistical Report / Calculations / Sheet 5

*The percentage scores on the bottom of the worksheet tell you how effective your attribute measurement system is. Obviously, the closer to 100 percent, the better.*

At this stage, the process improvement team must make a decision about the usefulness of the current system. Generally, a system with a 90 percent overall effectiveness score is considered acceptable. However, if the process and data are critical or related to life-and-death issues, then this may not be good enough. Your specific circumstances will dictate just how good your attribute measurement system needs to be.

# Variable MSA

The next type of MSA is for variable data, which have five key dimensions of performance, listed here. As we said previously, performing MSAs for variable data is more difficult and complex than it is for attribute data. Therefore, make sure your variable MSA meets these five criteria:

1. **Accuracy**—Measurement system outcomes are, on average, close to the truth.

2. **Precision**—Measurement system outcome variation.

3. **Stability**—Measurement system performance over time.

4. **Linearity**—Measurement system error at the various points along its scale (accuracy at various points along a scale).

5. **Reproducibility and Repeatability**—Performance of the measurement system for more than one person (reproducibility), and measurement system consistency when used again by the same person (repeatability). (Both are components of precision.)

**Accuracy.** Accuracy is perhaps the easiest to understand and measure. The concept is simple: how do the values you get from the measurement system compare with the truth? In evaluating accuracy, you want to take several measurements, then find out how far the average of all measurements varies from the truth. The less they vary, the more accurate your measurement system is.

**Precision.** Precision is the quantification of measurement-system variation independent of its accuracy. Using a bulls-eye analogy, precision is how closely grouped your measurements are using the same system. In evaluating precision, you want to take several measurements, then determine how widely those measurements vary *from each other.* The less they vary, the more precise your measurement system is.

**Technically Speaking**

Manual accuracy and precision calculations can be very time-consuming and onerous. The good news is that you can quickly perform these calculations with a desktop statistics package like Minitab.

*In this scenario, the measurements taken from the system are accurate because, on average, they are close to the truth (the bulls-eye). But the measurements are not very precise.*

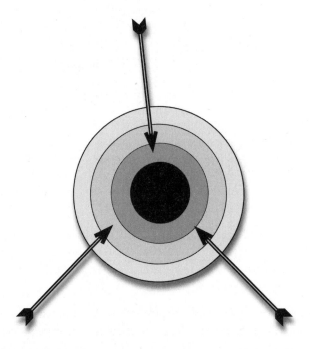

**Stability.** Stability is the quantification of measurement error over time, and one real-world example of this is measuring swim meet times all over the country. Specifically, in all places where the pool is not equipped with a touchpad electronic measuring system, the times are recorded the old-fashioned way.

*In this scenario, the measurements taken from the system are precise because they are clustered in the very same area (they have little variation). But the measurements are not very accurate.*

*In this scenario, the measurements taken from the system are accurate and precise, because they are clustered together and their average is very close to the truth (bulls-eye).*

Three parents standing at the end of the pool dutifully start their stopwatches at the same time the starting gun is fired. They watch the swimmer come to the end of the pool and then, leaning over the edge, stop their watches when the swimmer touches the side.

The stability problem is not easy to solve. As the morning wears on and parents get tired of standing in the sun, how are their measurements impacted? Are their reflexes slower? Are they faster? Who knows? This illuminates the concept of measurement system stability and explains why we use touchpads in the Olympics. In any case, you need to make sure your measurement system is stable over time.

**Linearity.** Another type of accuracy issue is called linearity, which is the difference in the bias of a gage through the expected range of the gage. Huh? Let's look at an example that we'll all understand.

Let's assume we have a scale that measures human weight. It is said to work for children that are over 25 pounds and adults as heavy as 250 pounds. We could test if, in fact, this weight scale works as well for measuring children as it might for measuring adults.

We could select one child whose true weight is 48 pounds and put him on the scale. If we put him on the scale and measure him 5 or 10 times, we may obtain an average value of about 50 pounds. That would suggest that at the lower end of our measurement system, our scale has a bias of 2 pounds.

In the same manner, we can take an adult whose true weight is 145 pounds. If we measure that adult 5 or 10 times, we may observe that his average weight on our scale reads at 150 pounds. That would mean the offset or bias of our measurement system at the higher end of the device is actually 5 pounds.

Because the bias at the higher end of the scale is larger, we imply that our measurement system has a linearity issue. The offset is not linear—it is not the same throughout the range of readings.

**Reproducibility and Repeatability.** Reproducibility and repeatability are essentially the same for variable data as they are for attribute data. The point is to determine what amount of variation is introduced by having two or more people take the same measurement (reproducibility), and to determine the amount of variation from the same person taking the measurement more than once (repeatability).

Remember the parents at the swim meet? Typically, when any two of the three parents get the exact same time on their stop watches, a celebration ensues. Most of the time, all three values are different, and the solution is to take the middle time as the correct time.

Remember that with attribute data the observers or operators could either get the measurement right or wrong with no in-between. With variable data, the observers are unlikely to get exactly the same answer very often. For instance, one observer may say the measurement is 13.6 centimeters, while the next observer may say the measurement is 13.65 centimeters.

The good news is that variable data always has the potential to tell us much more about the process than does attribute data.

# Improve the Measurement System

The outcome of analyzing your measurement system is to determine how well it works and how much you can rely on it. A reasonable rule of thumb is that if more than 20 percent of the total variation in your process is due to the measurement system, you need a new or improved measurement system.

Before embarking on a massive data collection effort or MSA study and improvement project, the team should carefully scrutinize the process for additional changes made viable by the Process Mapping and procedure studies done earlier. Substantial rework of the MSA system, or creation of a data collection system with statistically reliable data, should only be undertaken when the need for good, clean data is concrete.

This is one advantage of the merger of Lean and Six Sigma into one methodology. Classically, when employing the DMAIC method, practitioners would sometimes expend Herculean effort to get clean, useable data, first by expending great time, effort, and resources to generate that data, and second by improving the measurement systems to make them more reliable and usable.

All this is good when it is absolutely necessary to solve your problem or make your designated improvement. But this more statistically driven Six Sigma mentality can sometimes give way to the more immediate and practical value of the classic Lean approach. Even so, you still need good data, typically. But you may not need as much as you otherwise would to implement such Lean solutions as Pull, Flow, or Mistake Proofing systems.

But if these won't work and you need clean, reliable data, then you will need to improve your measurement system. And you do this just like you do any other Lean Six Sigma project: you move through the DMAIC process for your measurement system.

Therefore, you *define* what you are trying to measure. You *measure* how your current measurement system is performing. You *analyze* why the system is failing. You *improve* the system to meet the *20 percent rule*. And you *control* the system so it remains accurate, precise, and reliable over time.

Doing this entails analyzing the entire data collection and measurement process, looking for ways to make it give you solid data. A good place to start is with a Fishbone Diagram, or Cause-and-Effect Diagram. This powerful tool, an example shown here, helps teams visually see what may be causing the problems in any process.

 **Lean Six Sigma Lingo**

The **20 percent rule** says that when more than 20 percent of the variation in your process is due to measurement error, you may need to improve the measurement system.

*This simple example shows how the Fishbone Diagram can be used to brainstorm possible causes of measurement system failure.*

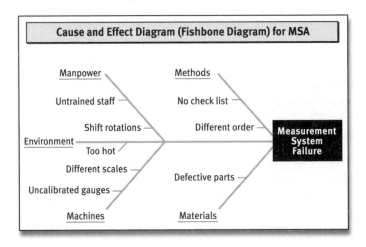

# Validate Customer Requirements

Hopefully, everything a Lean Six Sigma practitioner does and thinks is based on customer requirements. You examine these requirements when you generate ideas for your project funnel. You look at what your customers want when you separate the good project ideas from the not-so-good ones. You consider your customers when writing your problem statement and your project objective statement.

Further, you identify your customers and their requirements when creating a SIPOC Map, as we covered in Chapter 7. Then when you draw your Process Flow, you have your customers in mind. In fact, many steps in your process entail handing off work outputs from one department or person to another. Each time, you experience a transition that requires you understand the needs of the next step in the process—your customer.

Don't forget: customers are internal as well as external. That means the person paying you for your product or service is only the last customer (external) in a long chain of customers (internal). All customer requirements have to be met all along the chain—starting with the requirements of the external customer and working backwards through the system from those ultimate requirements all the way back through the interim requirements of everyone in the process.

As far as we're concerned here, we go back to our original question, the one we asked in the last chapter: is your improvement project based on decreasing defects, or time?

## Defect-Based Requirements

If your process and project are focused on defects, then you confirm that your measurement system is capable of detecting your defects of concern. But you also confirm that the customer requirements on which your project is based are valid. Think of it as a double check at this point, or as further refinement of your project focus.

Therefore, what are the CTs (Critical-To's) that your project addresses? Are you measuring exactly the right characteristics? Do you have the right performance target identified? You have to make certain you know the answers to these questions before moving on and collecting even more data on your process performance.

Therefore, the rule of thumb is to *operationalize* your customer requirements. It's okay to know that you want to increase customer satisfaction by 30 percent for your coffee product by June 30. That is your project objective. But now that you have defined your process and validated your measurement system, what exactly are the dimensions of that satisfaction? In other words, on what exactly are you going to focus all your data collection and analysis activities?

"Hot." "On time." "Served with a smile." Those are certainly a few dimensions, or characteristics, you may have surfaced from your Voice of the Customer analysis (refer to Chapter 7, the section, "The Kano Model"). So if "hot" is a big priority for the customer, you have to operationalize this; you have to move it from a lofty notion to an executable specification.

Therefore, you test the meaning of "hot" with a wide and representative range of customers to come up with a specific definition, say, between 168 and 172 degrees. Now you know exactly where to focus your remaining Measure, Analyze, and Improve activities.

## Time-Based Requirements

If your primary project metric is time, then you confirm that your measurement system is capable of quantifying this. And you also confirm that the customer requirements on which your time metric is based are valid. To do this you will need to understand a very important Lean Six Sigma formula called *Takt Time*.

Think of Takt Time as the underlying rhythm of a process that beats to the drum of customer demand. While the customer has his or her terms for how that time is defined and guided, the business has its terms. At a high level, the formula looks like this:

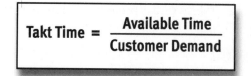

$$\text{Takt Time} = \frac{\text{Available Time}}{\text{Customer Demand}}$$

*Takt Time is available time divided by customer demand.*

So your customers tell you they want five applications completed every morning. Or they want one manufactured unit per day. Or they want to be fully checked into their hotel rooms in 10 minutes. Once you know what the customer needs, then you can determine how that need translates into your process Takt Time.

**Lean Six Sigma Lingo**

**Takt Time** means to "keep in step," or "keep time," as in keeping up with customer demand. Of German origin, the word *takt* literally means "beat" or "rhythm."

Let's take an example. Customers demand that you make 100 personal computers every day. There are 8 hours in a work day, or 480 minutes. To meet the customers' needs, the process will have to deliver 100 computers in 480 minutes, or $480/100 = 4.8$ (one computer in 4.8 minutes). The Takt Time for the whole process, then, is 4.8 minutes.

What does this mean? Anyone? Anyone? It's very simple. You have to make one computer every 4.8 minutes to keep pace with customer demand. This means that if every person in the process were to have a balanced amount of work, they would each spend no more than 4.8 minutes before handing off their output to the next person in the process.

This simplistic example calculation assumes that the process pipeline is filled when the day begins and, of course, that all handoffs are seamless and immediate. More on Takt Time in Chapter 14. Here, all you need to know is how to calculate it for the purpose of translating your customer requirements into your process requirements.

## The Least You Need to Know

◆ To do a Lean Six Sigma project, you must have a valid and reliable measurement system in place. This means it gives you good data consistently over time.

◆ Any data you collect is either attribute or variable in nature. The former refers to discreet categories, while the latter refers to a continuous scale.

◆ You have to treat your measurement system like anything in your organization: a process or system to be improved using the DMAIC methodology.

◆ Like the focus of your processes and your projects, the main focus of your measurement system is either on monitoring defects or time.

◆ Takt Time is an important Lean Six Sigma formula. It tells you how fast you have to be to meet customer demand.

# Chapter 12

# Characterize the Process

## In This Chapter

◆ Planning for data collection

◆ Random sampling techniques

◆ Watching process stability

◆ What's your capability?

◆ The ideal process

Now you are ready to collect more data on how your process functions. Everything you've done to this point is ensuring that the efforts you now make to gather data are properly focused and engineered for the payoff you want. There's a lot of risk associated with performance improvement and Lean Six Sigma: you can always get off course and waste time, energy, and resources you don't have to waste.

Therefore, in this chapter we guide you through the pathways of data collection and sampling. We look at tools you can use to measure process stability (Run Charts, Control Charts, and Histograms). And we show you how to calculate your process capability, or sigma level. Finally, we give you a set of tollgate questions you can ask, and answer, before moving on to the Analyze phase of DMAIC.

# Collect Data

The focus of this activity is on your primary, secondary, *and* consequential metrics. If your customer is most concerned, say, about the temperature of coffee, then your primary metric is the specific range you've identified (say 168–172 degrees). This is your output metric, and tracking it will tell you how often you are meeting your customers' needs.

It's also important to collect data on any secondary metrics that might be positively affected by your work on improving the primary metric. In our coffee example, it's possible that efforts to make sure the coffee is hot (primary) will also make it taste better (secondary). While customers may not have expressed this as a priority need, they do care whether the coffee tastes right or not.

And you can't forget to collect data on your consequential metrics, or those that could be negatively affected by your efforts to improve your primary metric. Let's stick with our coffee example and say that our barista wants to reduce the amount of time it takes to make a cup of latte. Therefore, his primary metric is time.

Our eager barista wants to delight his customer by being the fastest guy in town. So he figures that the time it takes to make the drink can be accelerated if the milk is pre-heated or perhaps kept hot all day, and then just quickly brought to a steam for each customer. Similarly, the coffee could all be ground the day before and save the time of freshly grinding it in batches throughout the day.

The problem is that this now makes our former secondary metric, taste, a consequential metric. If the barista doesn't heat the milk fresh each time, or grind the beans each time, the taste may suffer. So while our barista is measuring the time it takes to serve the customer, he's overlooking the consequence on taste. Therefore, robust data collection accounts for the primary, secondary, and consequential metrics of any given improvement project.

## Make a Plan

The first step is to create a plan that will guide you in collecting consistent, reliable, and repeatable data. Such a plan has four key elements, as follows.

**What are you going to collect?** As defined by a clear and easily understood definition of what you are measuring.

**How are you going to collect it?** Clear and written procedures for how to collect your data, what tools you will use, what good versus bad data means, how to read the gauge or measurement tool, what forms or templates you will use to capture the data.

**When will it be collected?** Detailed descriptions of what times the data will be collected. Will it be every item or will it be by some random sampling technique?

**Who will collect it?** Description of who the person is who will actually do the data collection.

## Sampling

Most often, you won't be able to collect data on every single action, process step, product, or transaction. Some credit-report organizations, for instance, process in excess of 30,000 reports per hour. Do the math. That's 240,000 reports in an eight-hour period. Surely, if your project has to do with such a high-velocity and volume process, you'll be taking random data samples.

When sampling from a data set, there are two major decisions to make. The first is how to sample or what process to follow. To this end, here are some guidelines:

**What you want to do:**

◆ Collect the data randomly—the data should be representative of the process.

◆ Use a systematic approach—as in take a sample every five units, or take one sample every 5 minutes.

**What you don't want to do:**

◆ Collect the data based on how easy it is to collect—easy data doesn't represent the whole process.

◆ Be arbitrary or inconsistent—such as taking too many samples in the morning and none in the afternoon, or taking all samples on Monday and none on Friday.

The second major decision is around sample size, which should be just large enough to draw the conclusions you'll need (about the population). The rule of thumb is that the larger your sample, the more certain you can be that it is representative of the population from which it's drawn.

 **Technically Speaking**

Statistical sampling is a science that has been studied and refined over years, and is a whole field in and of itself. Depending on the objective of study for which the sample is gathered, the type of data involved, and the certainty with which you wish to draw conclusions (confidence level), you can calculate your minimum sample required.

The following formulas are good rules of thumb for calculating sample sizes.

For continuous data, the formula is:

*Use this formula to determine your minimum sample size for estimating the mean of a continuous data population.*

$$n = (\frac{1.96s}{E})^2$$

Where:

**n** is the sample size. If *n* is less than 30 from the calculation, upgrade to a sample size of 30.

**1.96** is a constant used for a 95 percent confidence interval (e.g., you will capture the true mean of the population within the confidence interval 19 out of 20 times).

*s* is an estimate of the standard deviation of the population. A representative sample of 30 data points should be adequate to estimate *s*. You can also use calculations of the standard deviation from control charts or other studies.

E is the Margin of Error—the interval of certainty you want to achieve (e.g., +/– 2 pounds)

For discrete data, the formula is:

*Use this formula to determine your minimum sample size when dealing with discrete data for defectives (binomial data).*

$$n = (\frac{1.96}{E})^2 P(1-P)$$

Where:

**n** is minimum sample size.

**P** is an estimate of the proportion defective (e.g., 25 defectives in 100 units = 0.25). The sample size to estimate the proportion should be large enough to contain at least 5 defective units.

**1.96** is a constant used for a 95 percent confidence interval.

E is the margin of error—the interval of certainty you want to achieve (e.g., +/– 0.02 = +/– 2 percent).

For example, newspaper political polls frequently report a margin of error of +/– 3 percent, reflecting a sample size of 1,067 people polled based on this formula.

# Examine Process Stability

You have collected meaningful, representative data about your process, and you can see how it is performing relative to your selected metrics. Your next move is to watch how your process performs over a certain period of time. This means you want to see how stable your process is. Which *doesn't* mean it doesn't fluctuate or vary.

Having a stable process only means you can predict its outcome within a known range of possible outcomes. You can generally only look for root causes or issues in a process that is behaving in a stable manner. Therefore, you must determine or establish stability before you dive deeply into the Analyze phase.

Three tools in particular will help you examine process stability: Run Charts, Control Charts, and Histograms.

## Run, Run Chart, Run

A Run Chart visually plots data in time sequence order as the process "runs." Run Charts display variation quickly and help us make fast determinations about stability. We do this by applying time-proven rules to Run Chart data. See the sample Run Chart that follows, which plots the cycle time of loan application approval at a bank.

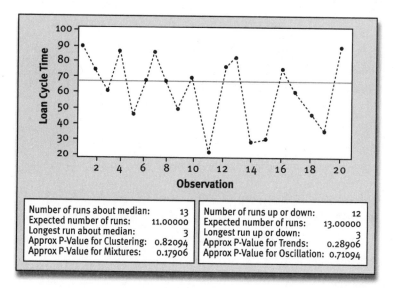

*This depicted process for loan cycle time is showing a stable process. None of the conditions for clustering, mixtures, trends, or oscillation are present.*

| Number of runs about median: | 13 |
|---|---|
| Expected number of runs: | 11.00000 |
| Longest run about median: | 3 |
| Approx P-Value for Clustering: | 0.82094 |
| Approx P-Value for Mixtures: | 0.17906 |

| Number of runs up or down: | 12 |
|---|---|
| Expected number of runs: | 13.00000 |
| Longest run up or down: | 3 |
| Approx P-Value for Trends: | 0.28906 |
| Approx P-Value for Oscillation: | 0.71094 |

Stability is determined by the existence of one of four major potential problems:

1. **Clustering**—the unnatural grouping of values around a certain point.

2. **Mixtures**—the unnatural absence of significant occurrences of values above or below the median.

3. **Trends**—the unnatural existence of trends going up or down.

4. **Oscillation**—the unnatural occurrence of values that swing up and down.

This analysis comes from the statistical tool, Minitab. It highlights both the visual performance of the data and some simple analyses of the values. The median of the values is plotted in the center of the plot. The analysis compares the values entered with statistical expectations for random data. The p-Values are statistical inferences about the data.

For now, all you need to know is that a p-Value below 0.05 means you have a problem in that area. In our example, all the p-Values are above 0.05, so we are safe to say that our process is stable.

# Control Chart

The other tool we use to determine stability is a Control Chart. If we produce a Control Chart for the very same loan approval data, we will uncover even more information about our process. The Control Chart that follows is a combination of individuals (I) and moving range (MR). It plots the individual data points in the top portion of the graph, and the value of the range of successive points in the bottom of the graph.

Most importantly, a Control Chart calculates upper control limits (UCL) and lower control limits (LCL) from the data. As a practitioner rather than an academic, there is no good reason you should know how to calculate these values. Suffice it to say that the UCL and LCL are the smallest and lowest values your process will produce if it remains in control. Values outside these limits would indicate that the process was out of control, or unstable.

As you can see, there are no out-of-control points in the individual portion of the chart. That means for 30 observations, or times driven to work, there wasn't one instance in which the driver was too early or too late. In terms of variation, however, as shown in the MR portion of the chart, there was one out-of-control condition.

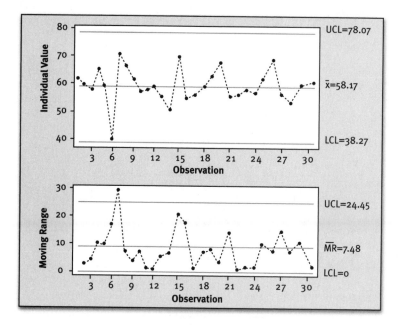

*This I-MR Control Chart shows drive time to work in terms of minutes, and shows an upper control limit of 78.07 minutes and a lower limit of 38.27 minutes.*

Once you've created a process baseline by collecting data and plotting it on a Run or Control Chart, you can use it for comparisons going forward. If possible, you want to create these charts for all the metrics you choose to observe. They will provide very useful and ongoing information about your process. They are also the cornerstone of any data-based improvement efforts you pursue.

## Histograms

We must look at another tool, the Histogram, for organizing and displaying data. The Histogram shows data on two dimensions: the $X$ axis shows the actual value of the data points, while the $Y$ axis shows the number of times the data occurred (frequency).

In the example that follows, we have plotted drive time to work by grouping different times into 5-minute categories. You can see that once it took about 40 minutes to get to work, no times about 45 minutes, three times about 50 minutes, 11 times about 55 minutes, and so on. Note, too, the "fuzzy eyeball" comparison to the normal distribution, which helps you detect the presence of any special causes.

Using the histogram, we want to identify any "odd" data. Odd in this case would be outliers, or data that don't look right. For example, we may find that there are one or two values that are dramatically higher or lower than all the rest. These should be looked at closely to determine if they are real values (meaning collected correctly) or special-cause variation. If we determine that Special Cause variation is the culprit, then we want to find out what we can do to control that cause.

*Use a Histogram to plot the number of times certain data occur. This example shows a visual depiction of the mean time (58.17) and standard deviation (6.818).*

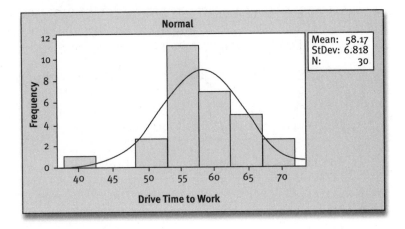

# Perform Capability Analysis

Now that we know our process is stable, or we have made the changes necessary to make it stable, we want to know if our process is capable. This is when you determine just how often your process is meeting the customer's needs so you can improve it going forward. There are many ways to analyze and display the data, all of which will tell you a great deal about your process. What you want to be able to say with some confidence is something like this:

*The difference in the stated sigma levels and the potential process capabilities is due to the expected 1.5 sigma shift from short-term to long-term performance.*

| Project Type | Capability Statement (Plain English) | Capability Statement (Lean Six Sigma) |
|---|---|---|
| Defect Based | The process meets the customer's CTs 99.379 percent of the time. | The process is performing at 4.0 Sigma with a potential process capability of 2.5. |
| Time Based | The process meets the customer timeline 99.865 percent of the time. | The process is performing at 4.5 Sigma with a potential process capability of 3.0. |

A sigma score is obtained by converting the percentage of time the process performs correctly into a sigma value. In practice, this means that you compute what percentage of the time your process gives you an acceptable output (meets customer's specifications), and then look it up on a sigma chart. (See Appendix C for a sigma conversion chart.)

So if your process performs as designed 93.32 percent of the time, this converts into a sigma score of 3.0 (for the short term). Without going too far into why, know that you can expect some mild "shifts and drifts" over time that amount to a difference of about 1.5 sigma between short-term and long-term performance (see the section "Beware of Shift and Drift" in Chapter 4 for more information).

In practice, this means your short-term data make you look better than you really are over the longer haul. You can take your process output data and run it through a statistical package like Minitab, which will quickly produce a sigma score. The following table shows the parameters we enter into Minitab:

| Parameter | Entry |
|---|---|
| Raw data | 50 drives to work |
| Lower specification | 30 minutes |
| Upper specification | 71 minutes |

Then Minitab outputs a screen, as shown in the figure that follows, providing a wealth of information—actually more than you probably need in most cases. The most important metrics to focus on at this stage are the overall capability numbers (see callout on chart). Here we find that our process is currently performing at a 1.85 sigma level (Z.Bench).

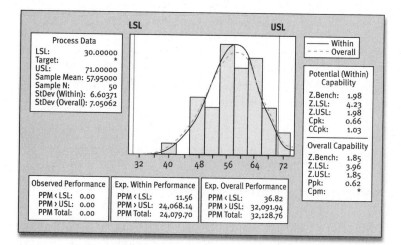

*Using statistical software makes the job of calculating your sigma score easy. Here we see that performance for driving to work is at 1.85 sigma.*

# Why Sigma Score?

So why all the trouble to translate a simple percentage, like 99 percent good, into a sigma score? It could seem excessive to the casual observer. Two reasons.

One, at the higher range of performance (world-class levels), the difference between 99.9770 and 99.9997 good can be significant, even though it seems incredibly insignificant. A score of 99.977 good is five sigma good, while 99.9997 good is six sigma good—a whole one-sigma difference.

The other reason to convert from a straight performance percentage to a sigma score (or Z-score) is because doing so enables you to compare your performance to everyone else's performance. Every process has a Z, no matter if it is in manufacturing or accounting or assembly or anywhere else in the organization. With your sigma score, you can benchmark yourself with other processes in other places.

## Process Capability and Time

If your process metric is time and multiple workers are involved, you want to look at how your process compares to the ideal. In this case, what we mean by the ideal is a process that is nearly perfectly aligned to deliver goods or services at the Takt Time the customer wants (remembering that Takt Time is the pace at which your customers demand what you provide them).

In the chart that follows, you see a Takt Time line that indicates the amount of time available for each operation if the process delivers perfectly in line with customer needs. The bars for Operator 1 through Operator 6 represent how long each of their steps currently take. In this scenario, the process is operating just under Takt Time, which is nearly ideal.

Every process needs some form of downtime when operators can attend to unexpected events or nonprocess activities (like the restroom or phone calls). This process has a good utilization percentage going. A good benchmark is 85 to 90 percent utilization to allow for real-world interruptions.

*This is a good scenario. The cycle times for operators 1–6 in the process are all functioning just below the Takt Time line.*

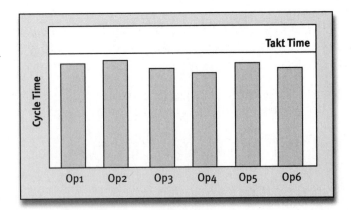

On the other hand, the process depicted in the next chart is in need of improvement. Here we see that many operators have too much time on their hands, and a few are near or over the breaking point. Clearly, we need to think about process improvement and workload balancing if we intend to meet the customer's requirements.

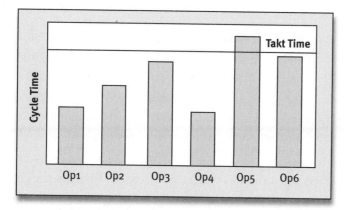

*This is a process in need of improvement. Only two operators in the process are functioning desirably. All other operators are either taking too long or have too much time on their hands.*

Remember that we are in the Measure phase. What we want now is a clear picture of what the process looks like and how it is performing today.

As you complete Measure and move into the Analyze phase of DMAIC, you will have ample opportunity to slice and probe your data, digging deeply for the root causes of your performance problems. First things first, though. We need to semiformally close out the Measure phase. We do this via a tollgate with our key stakeholders.

# Conduct Tollgate Review

Before moving on to the Analyze phase in the next chapter, you need to conduct a tollgate review that ensures you've accomplished all your critical tasks. This review should be attended by your Lean Six Sigma Champion, your Process Owner, team members, and other key stakeholders. Some questions to ask, and answer, at your review include:

◆ Is your primary metric related to defects or time? (Answer: If defects, then you should have drawn a Process Map; if time, then a Value Stream Map.)

◆ Did you include the flow of people, materials, information, equipment, products, parts, and procedures in your Value Stream Map? (Answer: Yes, to the extent required for the project.)

◆ What quick-fix opportunities did you discover and what did you do about them? (Answer: Execute quick-hit or "just do it" efforts to implement easy solutions.)

◆ Do you have a measurement system, and how do you know it is working properly? (Answer: We conducted a Measurement Systems Analysis and have the data to prove it.)

◆ What is the Takt Time for your process? (Answer: We calculated it and displayed it against our time-related performance.)

◆ What are your customers' requirements for the performance of your *Y*? How do you know? (Answer: We assessed the voice of our customers and operationalized their requirements.)

◆ What is the current performance of your *Y* in short term? How did you determine this? (Answer: Collected data via rational sample and examined it using various tools like Run Charts, Control Charts, and Histograms.)

◆ What is your process capability? (Answer: Used Minitab or comparable statistical software to determine this, and understand the difference between the short- and long-term.)

◆ Who will measure this process going forward? (Answer: The Process Owner.)

◆ Are all data fields in your project tracking tool current with your most recent project progress? (Answer: Hopefully yes. If not, enter data.)

◆ Are you satisfied with the level of cooperation and support you are getting to solve your project in a timely manner? (Answer: If yes, great; if no, revisit Stakeholder Analysis and Action Plan.)

◆ Is your project still on track to meet the scheduled completion date? (Answer: If yes, great; if no, remove roadblocks, accelerate pace, lead, revisit Stakeholder Analysis.)

◆ Has your financial forecast changed by more than 20 percent? If yes, what is the new validated forecast? (Answer: With the finance rep, we updated the project forecast.)

## The Least You Need to Know

◆ A primary metric is the key *Y* of concern; a secondary metric is another *Y* that is positively affected by the primary *Y*; a consequential metric is another *Y* that is impacted negatively by the primary metric.

◆ The data you collect has to be clean, meaning if you take a random sample it has to be valid and based on proven guidelines and formulas.

◆ Your process must be stable before moving into the Analyze phase. A stable process doesn't mean it doesn't fluctuate; it means you can predict its outcome within a known range of possible outcomes.

# Part 3

# Analyzing, Improving, and Controlling Processes

Your work in Define and Measure has given you a clear mission for what you need to improve ($Y$ metric), and you may even have some hunches about how to do this. In this part, we give you the guidance you need to formulate and test those hunches. Even better, we give you a methodical process for identifying, narrowing, testing, and validating exactly how you need to change your process to ensure it performs much better. In the Lean Six Sigma world, this means you're moving through the Analyze and Improve phases of DMAIC. Then, after you've improved your process beyond the shadow of a doubt, you lock in your improvements during the Control phase.

# Chapter 13

# Identify Potential Causes

## In This Chapter

- ◆ Brainstorming root causes
- ◆ Wayne and Fred's fishing expedition
- ◆ Affinities, Fishbones, and FMEAs
- ◆ Selecting the vital few
- ◆ Time or defects?

Congratulations! You know a lot about $Y$ (your primary metric). You know why the customer wants improvement in $Y$ from the Define phase, and the Measure phase documented the as-is process for producing $Y$. You determined the best way to measure $Y$, and you now know the capability of $Y$ to meet your requirements (internal or external). In Analyze, your focus turns to the $x$s (inputs, process controls, decisions) that influence the behavior of $Y$.

In this chapter, our investigation of potential causes begins—much like a TV crime show—by gathering evidence and clues. From there, we use special tools and technology to identify potential $x$s, recognizing that each Lean Six Sigma project is unique and the investigative tools will vary from project to project.

Specifically, we'll look at such tools as brainstorming, Affinity Diagrams, Fishbone Diagrams, Failure Mode and Effects Analysis, multivoting, and the C&E Matrix. Of course, there are other Analyze tools in the Lean Six Sigma arsenal, but these are the ones that are the most basic and typically used.

# Introducing Analyze

As depicted by the road map that follows, the Analyze phase of Lean Six Sigma is when you surface all the potential inputs (xs) that could be causing your $Y$ to fluctuate, or perform below its level of Entitlement. As well, the Analyze phase is when you investigate the significance of your xs, finding out which ones are more important than others.

Finally, in the Analyze phase, you come to the point where you discover the xs that are the most critical and powerful in determining the behavior of your $Y$. This is your first big grip on the leverage you need to solve your performance problem. In the Improve phase, you will refine your understanding of your x-Y relationships and generate solutions to change your process.

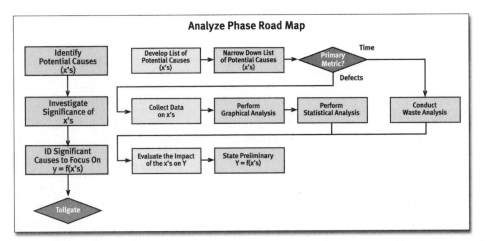

*This is the general process for analyzing the relationships between your Ys and xs. Depending on your experience and unique situation, you may or may not strictly follow these steps in a set sequential fashion.*

# Focus on the xs

The focus of Analyze is to discover the $Y = f(x)$ equation—or the output is a function of the inputs. The $Y$ is the primary metric, or any other measurable characteristic of interest. The $x$ is an assignable cause that influences the behavior of $Y$ in a desirable or undesirable way. As we investigate and verify the influence of $x$ on $Y$, we will be able to explain a percentage of the variation in $Y$ that can be tracked to variation in the $x$s.

Regardless of your effort, some unexplained (random) variation will remain. Think of this as error that goes unexplained by the $Y = f(x)$ equation. Your goal is to understand how to put $Y$ on target and reduce the unexplained variation, whether the objective is cycle time, defects, or variability in $Y$.

Probably everybody on your team thinks they know the potential causes of variation in $Y$. Some have knowledge from the process design, some from working in the process, and some from observing the process. Each person brings valuable information to the project, but everyone doesn't always agree, and superstitions abound. The first goal in listing potential causes is to generate the main categories or "themes" of causes. Later, the most likely causes will be probed in more detail.

A variety of tools exist to identify potential causes and, as a successful practitioner, you'll need to apply those that are most applicable to your project and team. Use of multiple tools allows your team—and other stakeholders—to view the problem from differing viewpoints. The key Lean Six Sigma Analyze tools also help you continue to build project momentum and increase the buy-in of all team members.

## Wayne and Fred

Take a step back from your project and think of this scenario: catching big fish and winning a bass fishing tournament. Many tournaments can be won by catching five fish that average 4 pounds. First-, second-, and third-place prizes are doled out by weighing the largest (heaviest) five fish one catches in the tournament.

Wayne and Fred decided to take on a personal Lean Six Sigma project to improve their bass fishing techniques to catch large fish in a short time. We'll follow their project and how they use some of the Lean Six Sigma tools. Their team consists of buddies that have fished for years, including one that works at a bait-and-tackle shop.

Wayne and Fred have two metrics. The primary metric is the weight of each fish. The goal is to average 4 pounds or more, so they established a lower spec limit of 3.75 pounds. The secondary metric is elapsed time. They want to catch as many fish as possible, in the shortest intervals possible, to increase their chance of having five whose total weight wins the top prize.

Consequential metrics for Wayne and Fred are: 1) to not increase the cost of fishing, 2) to not incur capital expenses over $1,000, 3) to not have fish die after they're caught and before they're presented to the tournament officials for weighing.

We'll showcase snippets from Wayne and Fred's project sporadically throughout this and the next several chapters. But we'll also provide plenty of other examples that demonstrate the use of Analyze and Improve tools in different organizational environments.

## Extracting Causes from Process Mapping

The detailed as-is Process Maps you created in the Measure phase will pay large dividends in identifying potential causes of delays, defects, excessive inventory, rework, and hidden factories. Capability Analysis and time series (or Control Charts) of the Y data can help identify outliers and trends not apparent to the casual observer.

Outliers are data points that appear far removed from the main body of data. An example might be a computer information system showing repair truck in-route time of 1,000 hours when the typical in-route time is 1 to 4 hours! Outliers abound in information systems, sometimes as true outliers but other times as just plain bogus data. Beware!

## Brainstorming Techniques

Brainstorming sessions for Lean Six Sigma projects are a means to elicit a wide range of potential $x$s related to the primary metric. By casting a large net, the likelihood of having to revisit potential $x$s in the project is minimized, and this is a good thing. You don't want to perform rework on DMAIC and have to recycle through Analyze more than once.

An idea trigger session is a simple procedure for your team. After assembling the team and handing out sticky notepads to each person, give them two minutes to write down all the causes they can think of that would affect the variation in Y. Write down one cause per sticky note. After the two minutes are up, have each person in rotation read one cause and post the sticky note on the wall. This ensures that each person has a voice in the process. After the first round, continue until all sticky notes have been read and posted.

## Affinity Diagrams

The next step is to construct an Affinity Diagram to organize the causes into groups. Under a vow of silence (avoid discussions that might lead to minutiae), all team members look for similarities of the causes and place them next to each other. Groups of causes will start to appear. When the activity dies down, look at each grouping and add a header for each group indicating the theme, process step, or other label that describes the group.

| Research | Technical Aids | Location | When to Fish | Bait | Line Prep | Depth |
|---|---|---|---|---|---|---|
| Stocking Schedule | Fish Finder | Lake Estes | At Dusk | Match the Hatch | Hook Size | Trolling |
| Gomer's Feeding Chart | Down Rigger | Lake Palmer | Phase of the Moon | Minnows | Sinker Position | Fish at Fish Level |
| Ask Locals | Speedboat to Get Back Fast | Lake Granby | Weather | Worms | Stay Hooked Up | Fish on Bottom |
| Fishing Guide | Reel Type | Shadow Mountain | Early Morning | Sucker Bait | Trailer Hook Lock | Find Best Depth |
| Bait Shops | Trolling Motor | Kiddie Pond | Just Before Tournament Ends | Power Bait | Clean Knots | On Surface |
| | Bass Boat | Fish From Pier | | Lures | Marmot Indicator | Multiple Depths Same Line |
| | | | | Scents | Spider Jigs | |
| | | | | DuPont Spinners | | |

*The Wayne and Fred Team identified Research, Technical Aids, Location, When to Fish, Bait, Line Prep, and Depth as category headers for the potential xs affecting fish weight.*

# Fishbone Diagrams

Fishbone Diagrams are akin to Affinity Diagrams, but focus on a very specific characteristic *(Y)* in an organized format. They relate causes *(xs)* to an effect *(Y)* in a structured manner. The beauty of Fishbone Diagrams is that they generate stakeholder buy-in and are easy to learn. Beyond this, they're wonderful visual representations of stratified data that set you up for further probing of your *xs*.

Generating an initial Fishbone Diagram for potential *xs*:

1. State the quality characteristic *(Y)* and place it in a box on the right-hand side of the diagram.

2. Review available information relating to the performance of *Y* from the Measure phase (e.g., capability, Control Charts, etc.).

3. On the left-hand side, draw arrows to the *Y* box and list potential causes *(xs)* under key categories. Common categories for manufacturing projects are materials, machines, methods, measurement, people, and environment.

**Lean Six Sigma Wisdom**

The Fishbone, or more formally the Cause-and-Effect Diagram, was first developed by Dr. Kaoru Ishikawa in 1943. We asked our friend Ike, a rocket scientist, what his company uses to uncover potential causes of an undesired effect. His reply: "We fishbone a lot."

Common categories for transactional projects (e.g., finance, retail, service, health care) include policies, procedures, places, and personnel. The categories are not rigid—you might even use customized headers derived from an affinity exercise.

4. Take each category and brainstorm potential $x$s that might influence the $Y$. Keep the pace moving, and record all $x$s, even if they "belong" in a different category.

5. Review the diagram for additional $x$s. Review with other stakeholders for additional $x$s also.

6. Keep the fishbone visible—a fishbone in a computer only stifles additional input.

7. Prioritize the $x$s to narrow the scope of the first investigations.

In the first session for generating potential $x$s, try to avoid probing too deeply into each $x$. The risk is that detailed discussion of a particular cause might bog down the process and leave other potential $x$s unstated. Later investigations will prioritize which $x$s require further probing.

It's also not essential to make sure each $x$ is in the proper category. If an $x$ seems to fit in more than one category, don't waste time debating; put it in every category in which it fits, or in a category in which it doesn't really fit. Your biggest concern should be in not leaving out any potential $x$s.

Finally, use good team-facilitation skills to ensure that one team member doesn't dominate the process. To gather balanced input, you might use the idea-trigger-session process explained in the "Brainstorming Techniques" section earlier in this chapter.

We close this discussion of Fishbone Diagrams with an example that shows how the tool was used to uncover potential causes of "mail misfeeds" (sending mail to wrong locations) in a large organization. The first fishbone shows a higher-level treatment of identifying the potential $x$s, while the second fishbone shows how detailed you can get with tracing further and further down the chain of causation.

*This Fishbone Diagram explores the higher-level possible causes of a mail misfeed problem.*

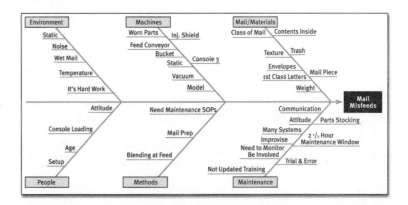

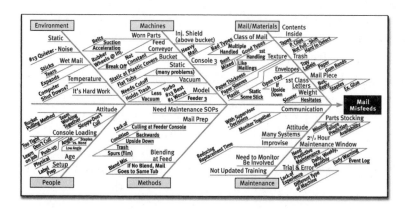

*This Fishbone Diagram shows many more possible causes further down the chain of causation. The input from operators, supervisors, maintenance personnel, and design engineering was gathered in less than one hour.*

## Ask Why Five Times

A very old performance-improvement convention is to ask why five times. Doing so enables you to probe deeper into cause-and-effect relationships, particularly when the team is generating *x*s at a superficial level (symptoms, not causes). Put the *Y* on the left side of the diagram and keep asking "why" until you reach an actionable root cause. Often the tree will go five layers deep, thus the common problem-solving phrase: ask why five times.

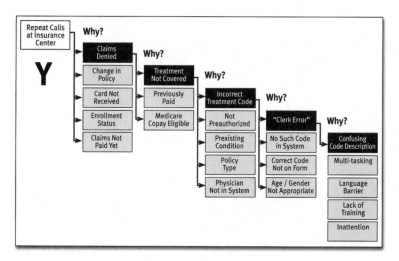

*Drilling down by asking why is like peeling an onion to uncover potential root causes. This call center example illustrates that the root cause is frequently buried in the system (poor description of treatment codes).*

# Failure Mode and Effects Analysis

FMEA reviews a process—step by step—and asks, "What can go wrong?" That's the failure mode. It then asks what happens if it fails (how severe is the effect?). Next, potential root causes of the failure are listed and the frequency of occurrence is determined. The ability to detect (or prevent) the failure is also reviewed for the current process.

These three criteria, Severity (S), Occurrence (O), and Detection (D), are rated on scales of 1 to 10, with a 1 representing only a minor incidence and 10 representing a catastrophic event for S, very frequent occurrence for O, or inability to detect the failure for D. The product of the three S\*O\*D ratings becomes the Risk Priority Number (RPN). Higher RPNs prioritize the need to eliminate the cause, reduce the frequency, or improve detection and prevention of the failure mode.

### Lean Six Sigma Wisdom

FMEA was developed by the U.S. military in 1949, and used by NASA for Apollo space missions and by Ford to reduce the risks of failure. Other industries adopted FMEA methods and applied them to products and processes. Performance-improvement practitioners use FMEA to detect critical xs and prevent potential failure modes.

The second part of a FMEA form is to determine action steps to reduce the RPN for those items selected. Once actions are taken, the S\*O\*D ratings and the RPN are revised. We will revisit the FMEA in the Improve phase, but for now see the charts that follow for 1) a depiction of the rating scale and 2) a stylized, real-life example of a FMEA for emergency-room operations.

*Most organizations develop rating scales specific to their processes, products, and services. This rating scale example is typical of process FMEA applications.*

| Rating Scale | Severity Examples | Severity Examples | Occurrence Description | Occurrence Examples | Detection/ Prevention | Detection Examples |
|---|---|---|---|---|---|---|
| 9 - 10 | Catastrophic event | - Death<br>- Epidemic<br>- Severe injury | Very frequent | - Hourly-daily<br>- 1 in 5 - 10 patients | No detection | - Customer sues<br>- Malpractice |
| 6 - 8 | Major event | - Long term recovery<br>- Widespread outage | Regular occurrence | - Weekly-monthly<br>- 1 in 50 - 100 patients | Detect after event occurs | - Patient returns<br>- Found on audit |
| 3 - 5 | Moderate event | - Long waiting room delay<br>- Repeat visit | Infrequent occurrence | - Quarterly-yearly<br>- 1 in 500-patients | Detect and correct as event occurs | - Corrected before patient leaves |
| 1 - 2 | Minor event<br>Mild or no dissatisfaction | - Slight waiting room delay<br>- Small $ loss | Extremely rare event | - Once every 10+ years<br>- 1 in 10,000 patients | Predict and prevent before event can occur | - Mistake-proofed<br>- Advance notice in time to fix |

Take heed of these guidelines while building your FMEAs:

◆ Conduct a FMEA for process steps that are key to improving your primary metric. Your project purpose is to investigate failure modes related to your primary metric, not to document all failures for each step of the entire process.

| Process Step | Potential Failure Mode | Potential Effects of Failure | S Severity | Probable Causes | O Occurrence | Process Controls/ Detection | D Detection | RPN Risk Priority Number |
|---|---|---|---|---|---|---|---|---|
| Admit Patient | Delay in admitting (> 10 minutes) | Possibly serious injury, not treated quickly | 9 | - Volume | 9 | - Log sheet - Crosstrain | 3 | 243 |
| | | | | - Staff not on duty | 4 | - Call button | 4 | 144 |
| Triage Patient | Delay in triage | Treatment delay | 7 | - Volume - Staff | 5 | - Visual check only | 8 | 280 |
| | Incorrect diagnosis | Wrong treatment infection | 7 | - Staff knowledge - Language | 2 | - On patient return or callback | 10 | 140 |
| Run Lab Tests | Lab not open | Repeat visit | 6 | - Late night lab hours | 4 | - On call | 7 | 168 |
| | Need to rerun lab test | Longer wait in ED | 4 | - Machine operation - Lab tech | 7 | - When tests come back | 5 | 140 |
| Treat Patient | Drugs not in pharmacy | Patient pain call local | 6 | - Out of stock - Rare drug | 2 | - Standard prescription - At exit | 6 | 72 |
| Instruct patient on care | Patient doesn't understand | - Longer recovery - Repeat visit | 7 | - Language - Age - Patient leaves | 8 | - Instruction sheets-multi-lingual - Follow-up | 5 | 280 |

*Look for "clusters" in RPN ratings. In this example, three high RPN values stand out, with values of 243–280. Each should be reviewed for potential actions to reduce the RPN values. Also, particular attention should be given to any failure mode that is very high on the Severity scale.*

- Keep the team on track. Extensive review of potential causes in the first meeting or debates on exact ratings might slow the process down—and you might be focusing too much attention on low RPN failure modes.

- Remember that FMEA can be dominated by opinions. Gather data to support your ratings.

- Keep the S*O*D rating scales in balance. Heavy weighting in one of the categories can bias the final RPN value.

# Narrow the Potential Causes

By now, you should have 25 to 50 potential $x$s identified that might affect $Y$, and it's time to prioritize the list for investigation. Basically, you want to identify the vital few $x$s that create most of the variation in $Y$. The team needs to narrow the list of potential $x$s down to a workable size, say 15 or fewer $x$s. The list should be focused on potential causes, not just the easiest $x$s to investigate or the $x$s that have the most data available.

As chief detective on your project, you need to decide where to perform the investigation. In other words, you slice open your fishbone and decide where to probe more deeply. With this knowledge, you can make a case for taking action (in the Improve phase) on the $x$s that most greatly influence your $Y$.

## Multivoting

One method to get the pulse of the team is to use consensus techniques, such as multivoting. Each team member is allocated five tick marks to place on the fishbone for prioritizing the investigation. The members may use multiple ticks on a particular cause or assign one tick to each of their top five. Discussion around the causes with the highest number of tick marks will help to prioritize the first investigations.

## Cause-and-Effect Matrix

A Cause-and-Effect Matrix (C&E) provides a more rigorous display of the $x$-$Y$ relationships. Recall that a fishbone diagram focuses on one $Y$ at a time. On the other hand, the C&E Matrix allows the team to display relationships with multiple $Y$s.

**Performance Pitfall**

Use of consensus techniques requires a balanced team that represents all views of the process, and is not influenced by rank in the organization. For example, a lopsided team comprising five members from marketing and only one from customer service will probably have a biased viewpoint.

The usual convention is to display the effects in columns across the top of the matrix, with the team rating the importance of each $Y$ on a scale of 1 to 10 (10 is the most important). Then, process steps are listed in order in blocks down the left side of the matrix, with the potential $x$s listed in rows for each step (see the example that follows).

The team examines each potential cause with each effect, and determines the relationship of the $x$ to influence the variation in $Y$. The influence is first labeled as strong, moderate, weak, or none—and a symbol is assigned for each relationship. The use of symbols creates a good visual picture of the relationships and avoids prolonged discussions about what number to assign in each cell.

After the symbols are placed in the matrix, numbers can be assigned for the calculations (strong = 9, moderate = 4, weak = 1). The numeric scores can be further refined or fine-tuned prior to calculating the total priority.

For each row (cause), the influence rating in each cell is multiplied by the importance for each effect and summed in the far-right column. Potential $x$s that have the highest total rating are the highest priority for investigation. Look here to see how Fred and Wayne used the C&E Matrix.

| Process Step | Process Input | Output Metrics | | | | | | | Total |
|---|---|---|---|---|---|---|---|---|---|
| Relationships: ⊙ = Strong, ○ = Moderate, △ = Weak, - = None | Importance | Fish Weight 10 | Fish Type 9 | Elapsed Time for Each Catch 7 | Total Time Fishing / Day 3 | Variable Cost (per fish) 4 | Capital Investment 6 | Relaxation 8 | |
| Research Lake | Map | ⊙ 9 | ⊙ 9 | ⊙ 9 | ○ 4 | △ 1 | △ 1 | - | 256 |
| | Observation | ⊙ 9 | ⊙ 9 | 4 | ○ 4 | △ 1 | △ 1 | - | 221 |
| | Fishing Guide | ⊙ 9 | ⊙ 9 | ⊙ 9 | ⊙ 9 | ⊙ 9 | - | ⊙ 6 | ○ 4 | 329 |
| | Stocking Schedule | ⊙ 9 | ○ 4 | - | | ○ 4 | - | - | - | 138 |
| | Time of Day | ○ 4 | ○ 4 | ⊙ 9 | ⊙ 9 | △ 1 | - | ○ 4 | 202 |
| Acquire Bait | Type | ⊙ 10 | ⊙ 9 | ⊙ 9 | ○ 4 | ○ 4 | △ 1 | △ 1 | 286 |
| | Freshness | ⊙ 8 | ○ 4 | ⊙ 9 | ○ 4 | △ 1 | △ 1 | ○ 4 | 233 |
| Pack and Go | Weather | ⊙ 9 | ⊙ 9 | ⊙ 9 | ⊙ 9 | △ 1 | △ 1 | ⊙ 9 | 343 |
| Go to Fishing Spot | Boat | ○ 4 | ○ 4 | ⊙ 9 | ⊙ 9 | ○ 4 | ⊙ 10 | ⊙ 9 | 314 |
| | Parking / Launch | - | - | - | ⊙ 9 | ⊙ 9 | - | ○ 4 | 59 |
| | Fishfinder | ⊙ 10 | ⊙ 9 | ⊙ 9 | ○ 4 | △ 1 | ⊙ 8 | ○ 4 | 340 |
| | Anchor | ○ 4 | ○ 4 | ⊙ 9 | - | | △ 1 | △ 1 | 153 |
| Prepare Line | Jigs | ⊙ 8 | ⊙ 9 | ⊙ 9 | △ 1 | ⊙ 9 | △ 1 | △ 1 | 277 |
| | Sinkers | ⊙ 8 | ⊙ 9 | ⊙ 9 | △ 1 | ○ 4 | - | - | 243 |
| | Hook Size | ⊙ 7 | ⊙ 9 | ○ 4 | △ 1 | ○ 4 | - | - | 153 |
| | Bait Preparation | ⊙ 9 | ⊙ 9 | ⊙ 9 | ○ 4 | △ 1 | △ 1 | △ 1 | 264 |
| Cast | Rod & Reel | ○ 4 | ○ 4 | ⊙ 9 | ○ 4 | △ 1 | ⊙ 9 | ○ 4 | 241 |
| | Downrigger | ⊙ 9 | ⊙ 9 | ⊙ 9 | ○ 4 | △ 1 | ⊙ 9 | ○ 4 | 336 |
| Set Depth | Depth | ⊙ 10 | ⊙ 10 | ⊙ 9 | △ 1 | - | △ 1 | △ 1 | 270 |
| | Troll | ⊙ 10 | ⊙ 10 | ⊙ 9 | ○ 4 | - | ○ 4 | △ 1 | 297 |
| Wait for Bite | Beverages | △ 1 | △ 1 | ○ 4 | ○ 4 | ⊙ 9 | △ 1 | ⊙ 9 | 173 |
| | Patience (time) | ⊙ 8 | ⊙ 7 | ○ 4 | ○ 4 | ○ 4 | △ 1 | - | 219 |
| Hook & Reel In | Technique | ⊙ 9 | ⊙ 9 | ⊙ 9 | ○ 4 | ○ 4 | △ 1 | - | 322 |
| | Net | △ 1 | △ 1 | ○ 4 | △ 1 | △ 1 | △ 1 | ○ 4 | 92 |
| Go to Weigh Station | Boat (speed) | ○ 4 | △ 1 | - | | ⊙ 9 | ○ 4 | ⊙ 10 | 184 |
| | Weather | ○ 4 | ○ 4 | ⊙ 9 | ⊙ 9 | △ 1 | △ 1 | △ 1 | 184 |

*For demonstration purposes, both symbols and numerical ratings are shown on this diagram. The numerical ratings are multiplied by the importance of each output and totaled on the right-hand side for each input. Inputs with the highest total ratings include Fishing Guide, Weather, Boat, Fishfinder, Outrigger, and Technique.*

# Pick Your Analyze Tool Set

Once again we return to the question of whether your project deals with time or defects—and once again this determines whether you use more Lean-oriented tools or more Six Sigma–oriented tools in the Analyze phase. If your primary metric is time, then the Lean tools of waste analysis (see Chapter 14) will prevail. If your primary metric is defects, then you'll wield the Six Sigma tools of root cause analysis (see Chapters 15 and 16).

Think of the Analyze phase as detective work. As you search for clues, you might use a logical flow of the crime (Lean) or forensics (Six Sigma) to solve the case. You'll likely pursue leads that don't pan out. The challenge is to sift though the leads (potential causes) in an efficient and reliable manner to find the significant evidence (vital few *x*s). Of course, both tool sets are process-focused and provide a synergy when applied in any given project.

## The Least You Need to Know

- The first part of the Analyze phase is to identify potential $x$s—the inputs, process controls, and decisions that might affect the $Y$.

- Input is needed from several viewpoints to generate a comprehensive list of potential $x$s. Such input is generated using Affinity, Fishbone, and Tree Diagrams.

- The DMAIC practitioner must determine the best brainstorming and selection techniques to prioritize the investigation of potential $x$s. Some of these include multivoting and the Cause-and-Effect (C&E) Matrix.

- If the primary metric is focused on defects, select the Six Sigma toolbox. If the primary metric is focused on time, Lean analysis tools are appropriate. Both tool sets focus on reducing variability. Remember: variation is evil in the Lean Six Sigma world!

# Chapter 14

# Conduct Efficiency Analysis

## In This Chapter

- ◆ Looking for waste
- ◆ Value-added/non-value-added analysis
- ◆ Inventory, queues, and batch sizes
- ◆ Balancing workloads
- ◆ Reducing setups and changeovers
- ◆ Dealing with bottlenecks

In practice, you never use purely Six Sigma approaches, and you never use purely Lean approaches. Yet when it comes to rooting out waste and analyzing inefficiencies, the Lean toolkit takes precedence. That's why this chapter will focus almost exclusively on Lean approaches, techniques, and tools.

Lean tools are used to answer questions like: How many people do I really need to perform the work demanded by customers? What should management expect of the people in the process? How can I improve the flow of my processes? How much inventory is required to sustain flow in the process? Do I have enough equipment processing capacity to meet customer demand?

To answer these questions, we'll get into some details of Value Stream Mapping, Takt Time analysis, inventory levels and Queuing Theory, Little's Law, Kanban calculations, Workload Balancing, Standard Work combinations, equipment effectiveness, Fast Changeover, and Total Productive Maintenance. If all this sounds foreign, good. That means you'll benefit from further reading.

# Name That Waste

In chapters past, we touched on the twin Lean concepts of Flow and Pull. *Flow* is making sure your workloads are even and humming along at full utilization in a steady way. *Pull* is the dynamic by which you store, use, and produce what you need only when you need it, in real time ideally, or as close to this as possible.

> ## Lean Six Sigma Lingo
>
> *Mura* is when your operations flow unevenly and therefore aren't utilized at their full capacity. Often mura is a root cause of **muda,** or waste. For instance, if you have too much inventory at any one time, it might be because your operations are not flowing well.
>
> *Muri* is when your people or machines are overburdened and therefore cost you more time and money in the long run. Often muri is a root cause of muda, or waste. For instance, if your people are overworked, they might make mistakes that later have to be rectified with rework.

With this in mind, let's take another look at the notion of waste, or *muda*, from its Japanese origin. The key at this stage of the game is to use various approaches to find and eliminate waste (and inefficiency). But before we get into the many ways this can be done, we should point out that *muda* is not the only form of waste you need to tackle. There are two other important forms as well: *mura* and *muri*.

*Mura* is *unevenness in operations* (poor Flow), and *muri* is the *overburden of people or machines*. If you focus only on *muda*, or waste reduction, then you might inadvertently create uneven flow or overburden people or machines. You don't want this, because the goal of Lean Six Sigma is always to be as efficient as possible with the least amount of waste, rework, and variation.

For example, sometimes a company will artificially reduce materials just to meet inventory targets at the end of a quarter. They stop ordering the materials they need just to make a number. Doing this then greatly overburdens the organization, which works twice as hard at the beginning of the next quarter until they rebalance the supply. This also causes Flow issues as production starts and stops while the rebalancing occurs.

In other cases, organizations perform end-of-the-month miracles to meet schedules while ignoring maintenance schedules, incurring overtime, and compromising quality standards. While this feels good at the time (or not so good), there are consequences. While the customer is temporarily satisfied, your long-term ability to achieve good quality, perfect delivery, and lower costs is jeopardized.

Therefore, don't just be a loose-cannon waste warrior. When you conduct your waste analysis, you have to understand the true causes of that waste. How can you ensure good Flow? How can you avoid overburdening your people and equipment? These are good questions to ask as you go about looking for and ridding waste.

Be systematic and recognize that, often, *mura* creates *muri* that causes *muda*. Only when *mura* and *muri* are under control will your efforts to take *muda* out of the process be effective. And sometimes unaddressed *mura* creates *muri* that *undermines* previous attempts to eliminate *muda*. If all this sounds confusing, good. You know you've still got a ways to go before you master the Lean Six Sigma Lingo.

# Value Analysis

The opposite of waste is value, which we defined in previous chapters as activities that are necessary to transform inputs into outputs for which customers are willing to pay. When we say that an activity is *value-added*, we mean it's absolutely necessary. For instance, squeezing juice out of an orange is value-added; the customer is willing to pay a price for that, and the business makes money doing it.

Other activities or steps in a process are *non-value-added*. This includes waiting time for people and materials, like when parts wait in a queue before their assembly. It includes the costs associated with storing excess inventory, and the time involved in changing over from one mode of production to another. Of course, rework performed to fix mistakes or errors is non-value-added, too.

We touched on the use of a Value Stream Map (VSM) in Chapters 6 and 7, and we gave the details of building a VSM in Chapter 10. Here we just want to mention that you use the VSM to identify opportunities related especially to such non-value-added activities as inventory levels, waiting queues, cycle times, setup times, processing times, wait times, customer demand rates, process yields, capacities, and numbers of people.

# Examining Inventory Levels

Many Lean Six Sigma practitioners will talk about doing Kaizen Events to reduce or eliminate inventory. This is a good thing, but it's dangerous because inventory issues are usually the result of other issues. Removing the inventory without first eliminating the sources of unevenness might pose delivery issues, and can create nervousness and resistance as the inventory security blanket is removed.

If you really want to reduce inventory down to its bare required minimum (which you do), then you'll have to dig a little deeper. One way to do this is to "walk the process" to account for *work-in-process inventories*, as well as measure traditional warehouse inventories tracked by accounting. Work-in-process inventories are potential signs of bottlenecks, rework, products not in demand, poor ordering or scheduling, or hoarding items due to just-in-case, pseudo emergencies.

**Lean Six Sigma Lingo**

**Work-in-process inventory** is any materials or needed inputs that reside, virtually or physically, at different points in the process.

To minimize operational costs, you need to minimize the quantity of things (inventory levels) inside your process without putting your output in jeopardy.

If you make the causes of problems go away, then inventory can be reduced. This includes such issues as long changeover times, poor work balance, unreliable quality, and frequent equipment failures. Ultimately, this all boils down to improving Flow, one of the five key Lean principles.

## Queueing Theory

Queuing Theory is the mathematical science of organizing the flow of people, material, information, data, supplies, and other items through a process. Properly designed queues (or waiting lines/areas) create harmony because they create a constant flow and balance of whatever the process needs to perform its function.

Service operations build inventories of customers waiting for service (think long lines at a fast-food restaurant), or inventories of resources that are unused. Unlike production inventories, service inventories can suddenly disappear—that's not always a good thing. Customers might give up on the service (abandon) and go to your competitor, or they might be blocked from the service (not enough bandwidth to handle the service). Manufacturing operations can build inventories of product, which often leads to increased damage or spoilage.

Queueing models use statistical distributions used to answer a variety of important questions. How many customers or items will be waiting in the queue? How long will a customer or item have to wait in line to be processed? What is the average utilization of servers in the process? What is the probability of waiting longer than some specified time? How does absenteeism affect service levels?

Since different situations have unique mathematical queuing models, we could get overwhelmed quickly. Rather than pursue this complexity, in our next section we'll look at Little's Law, which has universal application.

**Real-Life Story**

An Internet service provider identified dramatic swings in customer service times. By asking why, they found that service reps were not trained to field questions about new features; long customer queues resulted from this lack of training.

## Little's Law

It's called Little's Law, but it's big—because Little's Law desribes the relationship between lead time, work in process, and completion rate. Here's an illustration: if the rate of arriving patients is high (work in process), and it takes a long time to process each patient (completion rate), then the inventory of patients in the waiting room will be high—and they will have to wait longer (lead time).

Generically, you can think of Little's Law like this: the average number of customers (or things) in a system is equal to their average completion rate, multiplied by their average time in the system.

The same relationship applies to all service, transactional, and manufacturing processes. For instance, if the rate at which customers phone in to a call center increases while the staffing level remains the same, and the average handling time for each call stays the same, then the average time on hold (wait time) will increase.

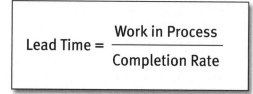

$$\text{Lead Time} = \frac{\text{Work in Process}}{\text{Completion Rate}}$$

*Little's Law is a formula that shows the relationship between lead time, work in process, and completion rate.*

The simplest practical application of Little's Law is calculating wait times in your VSM. If you count the number of items in each queue and have the cycle times for the process each queue is feeding, then you can multiply them to get the wait time for each process. Then, by adding the cycle times and wait times, you can see the overall process lead time.

Viewing the following small section of a VSM, we find the wait time consumed by the three pieces of inventory is equal to 3 pieces × 2.5 minutes per part in the next operation, which equals 7.5 minutes.

*This part of a Value Stream Map provides the visual correlation to Little's Law. It shows total wait time of 7.5 minutes and total cycle time of 2.5 minutes.*

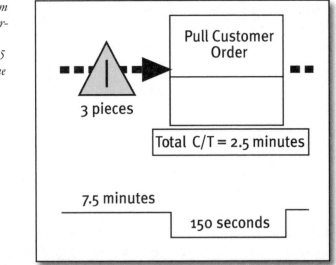

Therefore, we can determine our total lead time by adding the wait times to our total process cycle times (2.5 minutes), as shown by the following formula.

*Lead time is the sum of all wait times plus the sum of all cycle times for a given process.*

$$\text{Lead Time} = \sum \text{Wait Times} + \sum \text{Cycle Times}$$

## Takt Time Analysis

*Takt* is the German word for the beat an orchestra conductor uses to regulate the speed at which musicians play. Without *takt*, we only have noise and confusion. So what sound does your process make? Is it beating along at the same rate your customers demand? Or does it feel disjointed, overwhelmed, or underutilized at different times?

We introduced the notion of Takt Time in Chapter 12, and showed you how it relates to process cycle time. The idea is to match your process cycle time as closely to your Takt Time as possible. But to do this you first have to calculate your Takt Time, which is done like this:

$$\text{Takt Time} = \frac{\text{Available Work Time}_{\text{per Time Period}}}{\text{Customer Demand}_{\text{per Time Period}}}$$

*Takt Time is calculated by taking your available amount of work time (within a certain time period) and dividing it by your customer demand (for the same time period).*

So say your available time is 12 hours per day, 5 days per week to make a product, or deliver a service, or conduct a series of steps in a process. Available time is the actual amount of time you have to perform value-added work, excluding lunches, breaks, and scheduled team meetings that result in planned machine and process stoppages.

So our availability is 12 hours × 5 days × 60 mins/hour = 3,600 minutes per week. And let's also say that we have 410 units of demand from the customer each workweek. Our Takt Time is 3,600 minutes per week divided by 410 units per week, which is equal to 8.78 minutes per unit. Our Takt Time of 8.78 minutes is the average pace of customer demand.

You may have heard the mantra of cycle time before—doing what you do and operating your process faster and faster. Generally this is a good thing, but you have to realize that the fastest doesn't always win the game. Just ask the three guys who were out in the woods camping when the bear began to chase them down. In that scenario, you don't have to outrun the bear. You only have to be faster than the slowest guy!

Business survival is much the same. Your process doesn't have to be "fast," but only in step with the rhythm of the customer. Knowing your Takt Time can greatly help you determine such key process variables as staffing and equipment levels, and work-in-process levels. The goal is to balance the workload and make your process as consistent with customer demand as possible over time.

## Do You Kanban?

*Kanban* is a Japanese word that literally means "sign" or "signal card." In the context of performance improvement, Kanban systems are inventory replenishment systems that function on the basis of customer demand. When stock batches of raw materials reach a certain level of depletion, the system signals the need to order or replenish stock using some kind of visual sign, like a colored card.

You know when you reach that place in your checkbook where you see a check reorder form? That's a Kanban—a visual signal telling you it's time to replenish your inventory.

Kanban systems are a subset of Just in Time operations—the practice of using only what you need when you need it, and minimizing all inventory and waiting queues. If you know how much stock to keep on hand at every part of the process, and you keep inventory moving through the process at the rate it runs, you never store more than you need, and you never run out of stock, either.

Comparing current batch sizes, or materials on hand, to Kanban calculations enables you to uncover the root causes of inventory problems. This typically leads to changes in your ordering and scheduling processes, and helps you determine your ideal batch sizes for inventories throughout the process. The formula you'd use is this:

*This is the formula for analyzing ideal inventories and determining the number of Kanbans you need in a process, or at various stages in a process where materials and inputs are needed to perform work.*

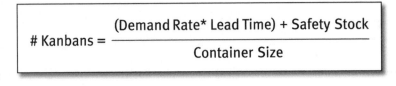

$$\# \text{ Kanbans} = \frac{(\text{Demand Rate* Lead Time}) + \text{Safety Stock}}{\text{Container Size}}$$

In our analysis, a container is the device created to house the units in process, often organizing and protecting them during internal handling. Containers can be baskets or custom racks for parts, a mail pouch, or a stock card on the shelf of the office supply store. The number of Kanbans is the number of these containers, or handling units, that we have in process. Because of this relationship, we often think of the Kanban as the container itself, but actually the Kanban is a visual trigger.

In the formula, demand rate is influenced by fluctuations in Takt Time. Lead time is influenced by supplier delivery timing. Safety Stock is influenced by tolerance for outage, likelihood of an outage, fluctuations in Takt Time, supplier delivery history, and defects. When these are unknown, you should start with 15 percent as safety stock.

# Analysis of Resource Usage

Just like inventory issues, resource (staffing) issues are usually the result of other, deeper problems. The good news is that you have a number of Lean-type techniques at your disposal to analyze your resources and determine their optimum use. These include Ideal Manning Calculation, Workload Balance, and Standard Work Combinations. You'll find that all these techniques lead you to the root of what it takes to best utilize your resources.

## Ideal Manning

Every process requiring humans has to be staffed with people who are capable of doing their respective jobs. But you never want to understaff or overstaff, so it pays to use a formula to determine your ideal manning levels. See the formula that follows.

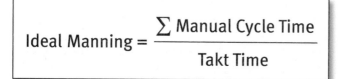

$$\text{Ideal Manning} = \frac{\sum \text{Manual Cycle Time}}{\text{Takt Time}}$$

*You determine your Ideal Manning Levels by dividing the sum of your manual cycle times (time required to perform a job) by your Takt Time (rate of customer demand).*

Summing cycle times provides the total work content time, while Takt Time (customer demand rate) gives you the number of people required to produce to that demand rate. This is your Ideal Manning Level. The implication is that you can't achieve or sustain your Ideal Manning Level without also addressing all causes of *mura*, or unevenness in Flow. A process must be approaching near zero downtime, zero rework, and zero defects to sustain ideal manning.

## Workload Balance

Workload Balance is the distribution of total work cycle time, and the pacing of that work content to the customer demand rate. This process helps eliminate bottlenecks, unevenness in Flow (*mura*), and overburdening of people and machines (*muri*). Workload Balance is done through Cycle Time Bar Charts to identify imbalances in equipment, workers, and process times.

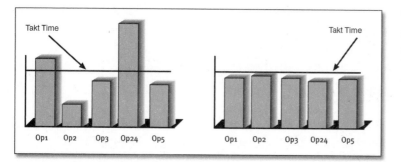

*The chart on the left is without Workload Balance; the chart on the right is with Workload Balance.*

You can see from the previous charts that your goal is to engineer staffing levels to utilize people at their fullest capacity as close to Takt Time as you can.

Here's how it works: you plot the manual cycle times for each operator (staff) on a bar chart against the upper limit of the Takt Time. In principle, you have cycle times at or below the Takt Time to assure you have the capacity to service the demand rate of the customer.

Let's consider an automotive example. As vehicles move through an assembly line, workers have a fixed amount of time to complete their work at each step. Imagine the problems and amount of waste created if the windshield installation step takes 20 percent longer than Takt Time. By the time you get to the sixth vehicle, you are one car behind schedule, and you are faced with a tough choice: stop the line, skip a car, or put the car in the parking lot with no windshield and work overtime to catch up every day.

## Analyzing Standard Work Combinations

Standard Work Analysis breaks down process steps in small increments and compares performance to the Takt Time. By doing this you eliminate the overburdening of people (*muri*), and you identify worker variations that can be smoothed and made consistent. Such an analysis, an example shown following, helps you determine the best arrangement of work tasks for optimum performance.

## Spaghetti Diagrams

Analysis of Spaghetti Diagrams (covered in Chapter 7) provides a great visual image of the flow of materials, people, forms, and even customers. The purpose of the Spaghetti Diagram in the analyze phase is to visualize the waste of transportation and create strategies for reducing distance. Physical layouts of equipment and resources can be analyzed and improved using Spaghetti Diagrams.

*Standard Work Analysis is useful for arranging work tasks and for keeping each worker's responsibilities below the customer demand rate.*

| # | Description | Manual Task Time | | | sub total for ref. | Auto Run Time | Time (draw red vertical line at takt time) |
|---|---|---|---|---|---|---|---|
| | | value-add | non-v-add | walk time | | | |
| | **Take Customer Call** | | | | | | |
| | Greet Customer | 8 | 15 | 15 | | | |
| | Determine Need | 25 | | | | | |
| | Capture Information | | 5 | | | | |
| | Look Up Request | 45 | | | | | |
| | Determine Price | 4 | | | | | |
| | Determine Availability | | 5 | | | | |
| | Process Invoice | 15 | | | | | |
| | **Pull Parts for Invoice** | | | | | | |
| | Remove Ticket from Printer | | 4 | | | | |
| | Walk to Part Location | | | 67 | | | |
| | Locate Parts | | 45 | | | | |
| | Pull Part | 5 | | | | | |
| | Walk to Dispatch Area | | | 28 | | | |
| | Put Parts and Invoice on Shelf | | 4 | | | | |
| | **Stage Order for Delivery** | | | | | | |
| | Evaluate Customers & Locations | 5 | 53 | | | | |
| | Group Delivery Routes | | 23 | | | | |
| | Assign Drivers | | 30 | | | | |

# Overall Equipment Effectiveness

If people have to be utilized well, so do machines, because both are necessary in most businesses and processes. That's why the Lean Six Sigma Master is concerned with analyzing Overall Equipment Effectiveness (OEE)—the percentage of value-added time for the equipment.

Low OEE values are symptoms of poor scheduling, material shortages, excessive changeover times, inaccurate standards, surprise maintenance, and rework. Stratifying the categories of nonvalue time on equipment can direct the investigation to the critical $x$s.

OEE takes into account losses in availability (like planned downtime, setup time, unplanned downtime, or breakdowns), performance rate (like reduced speed, minor unrecorded stoppages), and quality rate (like rejects, rework, yield, and start-up losses). OEE is a clearly defined measure of actual process/asset performance relative to its maximum capability.

You can use the following equations to calculate your OEE:

$$\text{OEE} = \text{Availability} \times \text{Performance} \times \text{Quality Rate}$$

Where:

**Availability** is Actual Run Time/Total Time in Period

♦ *Actual Run Time* is the time that the machine produces product.

♦ *Total Time in Period* is simply the actual amount of time in the period.

**Performance** is Actual Production Rate/Expected Production Rate

♦ *Actual Production Rate* is the actual pace that product is generated.

♦ *Expected Production Rate* is the pace that internal standards dictate.

**Quality Rate** = Percent Acceptance/100 Percent

♦ Percent Acceptance is typically referred to as the First Pass Yield.

For example: A wire manufacturer runs its operation 24 hours a day, five days a week. The current-year production standards state that each machine should be able to make 225 meters of wire per hour of operation with perfect quality. For the last

28-day month, they ran 20 days and averaged only 200 meters of wire per hour, with a 2 percent reject rate.

$$\text{OEE} = \frac{480 \text{ hours}}{672 \text{ hours}} \times \frac{200 \text{ meters/hour}}{225 \text{ meters/hour}} \times \frac{98\% \text{ FPY}}{100\%}$$

OEE = 71.4% × 88.9% × 98.0%

OEE = 62.2%

# Quick Changeover Opportunities

Changeover is an important non-value-added activity that most organizations have to perform to be competitive. Changeover is downtime: while it's happening, no product is made and no service is delivered to the customer.

You clean your juicers when switching from making grape to making raspberry. You clean the airplane, gas it up, and ready it for its next load of passengers. You clean up and prepare the operating room for its next patient.

All these necessary activities do not add value for the customer, but they have to be done. Therefore, the goal is to minimize the time it takes to perform changeovers, or eliminate the downtime involved altogether, if possible. This is known as Fast Changeover, and the Lean Six Sigma practitioner applies many techniques, such as videotaping, to reduce setup times.

For manufacturing processes, standardized equipment and changeover processes can reduce changeover times by 90 percent. Changeovers in transactional processes can have dramatic impacts also. Southwest Airlines, for example, is known for the way it unloads passengers, cleans planes, restocks supplies, and loads baggage and passengers for the next flight.

When videotaping or analyzing changeovers, you want to classify steps into two categories: internal and external. Internal changeover steps are activities that must be done while the process is idle. To change the battery, we must shut down the computer. External changeover steps are activities that can be done while the process is running. To add or remove USB devices, we can simply unplug them from the computer.

Your strategy is to externalize as many changeover steps as possible, and to keep the process producing good product for as long as possible. Also, your strategy is to, in advance, organize and stage all materials necessary to perform your changeover activities, external or internal in nature.

## Total Productive Maintenance (TPM)

The goal of Total Productive Maintenance (TPM) is to make all equipment downtime 100 percent predictable and minimized. In other words, you want to make processes better than new, not simply restore them.

For example, if we look at one part of the 5S activities (Sort, Store, Shine, Standardize, Sustain), the Shine activity, we might find a leak, and we would use the TPM activity to diagnose the underlying cause of that leak. We'd also use TPM to correct the problem at its source (Improve) to fix it and to avoid future leaks.

A subset of TPM is Autonomous Maintenance, the goal of which is to make the worker the first line of maintenance, performing routine tasks (like adding toner to a copy machine), identifying problems early (detecting low tire pressure before it goes flat), and making minor adjustments (aligning rollers before the paper jams).

Close observation of the process, and rigorous review of maintenance records, can reveal the critical *x*s for any maintenance issues you have. This is the Analyze aspect of TPM; we cover more of the Improve aspect of TPM in Chapter 17.

# Identifying Bottlenecks in the Process

We mentioned earlier in this chapter that bottlenecks often cause inventory problems. At the same time, bottlenecks are caused by still deeper issues related to manning levels, Flow, equipment effectiveness, changeover issues, rework, and anything else that causes you to wait. In essence, bottlenecks are what happens when processing time exceeds Takt Time.

The result is bumper-to-bumper traffic on the highway, long lines at an amusement park, long waits to purchase concert tickets right after they go on sale—even online—for a popular band. In manufacturing, bottlenecks come in the form of work (parts, assemblies, people) that is queued up to the point where it prevents subsequent steps in a process from getting needed inputs in a timely manner to maintain Flow.

In writing this book, we had many consultants draft and provide material. Sometimes these consultants were busy teaching Lean Six Sigma to clients for weeks at a time. While we tried to schedule their tasks and inputs in a flowing manner, sometimes the

**Performance Pitfall**

Don't fix your bottlenecks too much, especially if it takes more time and effort. All you have to do is fix them enough to meet your Takt Time. Anything beyond this will only create capacity you can't use because the customer demand is not there.

assignments backed up because the consultants were booked for billable business with clients. Therefore, their book-related tasks took a backseat, creating bottlenecks.

So how do you analyze bottlenecks and solve them? Go to the *Genba*—the "actual place" where the work is performed. There you use observation, interviews, the Five Whys, and other techniques to find out why the bottlenecks occur. Most likely this will lead you down a chain of bottleneck causation. Unlike stubborn defect issues where the root cause is not known, usually you can figure out how to fix bottlenecks through pure observation and simple investigation.

## The Least You Need to Know

- If your primary metric is time, the Lean toolbox offers your best bet for analyzing what you need to do.

- Focus on reducing waste to improve flow and remove non-value-added activities as much as possible.

- Analysis of queue flow delays and batch sizes can reduce inventories.

- Smoothing flow through any process requires a balance of equipment, materials, and resources in step with the Takt Time of the customer.

- Quick changeovers reduce the need for large batches and improve responsiveness to customer needs.

- Most of all, you can see a lot by observing, or by going to the Genba (walking/ observing the process where it is).

# Chapter 15

# Find Significant *x*s

## In This Chapter

◆ Collecting data for analysis

◆ The basics of experimental design

◆ Know your sample size

◆ Risk comes in alpha or beta

◆ Calculating sample sizes

◆ Testing your hypotheses

Now the real detective work begins. You have a lot of leads from brainstorming, fishboning, process mapping, and failure mode analyzing. Your evidence is still circumstantial, and you need the hard facts to prove your case to the judge—the almighty Process Owner. You also need to present your case to the jury (stakeholders), so they can understand and take action.

In this chapter, we'll show you how to slice and probe your data until you can explain much of the variation in *Y*, leaving little to the imagination. You'll determine what data needs to be collected to examine the potential *x*s you've already generated and prioritized. The Lean Six Sigma analysis toolbox is full of methods to get to the root of the *x*-*Y* relationships.

# Collect Data on the xs

Using good data collection methods will simplify and improve the accuracy of your analysis. It takes a world-class statistician to extract information from an unorganized data set, but precise data collection and a few simple graphical tools can pop those critical xs out of a haystack of organized data with minimal effort.

Any data collection system requires accurate and precise information for both the input (x) and output (Y)—and operational definitions and methods of recording data must be standardized up front. A Measurement System Analysis (MSA) should be conducted on key inputs and on all outputs to verify the integrity of the data. We covered MSA in Chapter 11.

*One data collection method does not satisfy all characteristics desired for analysis. This relationship matrix shows the strengths of various collection methods.*

| Strength of Relationships:<br>⊙ = Strong<br>○ = Moderate<br>△ = Weak<br>− = None | Data readily available | Detailed x-level data | High integrity | Quick analysis | Wide range of x's | Long-term data | Stakeholder involvement | Appropriate sample size | Few pitfalls |
|---|---|---|---|---|---|---|---|---|---|
| **Collection method** | | | | | | | | | |
| Computer databases | ⊙ | ○ | ○ | ⊙ | △ | ⊙ | △ | ⊙ | ○ |
| Logs (logbooks & logsheets) | ⊙ | ○ | ○ | △ | △ | ⊙ | ○ | △ | ○ |
| Data collection forms | ○ | ⊙ | ○ | ○ | ○ | ○ | ⊙ | ○ | ○ |
| Checksheets | ○ | ○ | ○ | ○ | △ | ○ | ⊙ | ○ | ⊙ |
| Control charts | ○ | △ | ○ | ⊙ | △ | ⊙ | ⊙ | ○ | ○ |
| Observation of processes | ○ | ○ | ⊙ | ○ | ○ | △ | ⊙ | ○ | ⊙ |
| Internal or external audits | ⊙ | △ | ⊙ | ○ | △ | △ | △ | ○ | ○ |
| Special studies | ○ | ⊙ | ⊙ | ⊙ | ⊙ | △ | ⊙ | ⊙ | ⊙ |

*Table title: **Key Metrics for Data Collection***

Let's explore some of the potential data collection methods that might apply to your project.

## Computer Databases

Computer databases can track process parameters automatically by capturing times, test results, scrap costs, order delays, service times, response times to nursing call lights, project completion dates, and even repeat calls from the same telephone number. Summary reports are issued, helping managers identify opportunities for improvement.

Computer databases are relatively easy to download for analysis in spreadsheets or statistical software packages. With the help of the IT department, more frequent reports or special inquiries can provide specific data for your project.

Rookie Black Belts believe that there's a magic database waiting for them that includes all the potential *xs* they listed on their fishbone diagram. Reality sets in quickly, and they learn that other methods are needed to get the proper information.

## Logs (Logbooks and Log Sheets)

Logbooks are commonly kept by maintenance, production, customer service, nursing, and many other functions. The intent is usually to communicate specific problems and actions taken. Extracting data from logbooks usually takes extra effort from a team member who is familiar with the logbook.

Log sheets are kept for process steps by those most closely associated with specific tasks (e.g., operators, clerks, lab technicians, dispatchers). The format is usually in rows and columns, with time or changeovers defining the rows and specific *x* and *Y* measurements, or comments, for the columns. Log sheets provide more specific and easier-to-extract data on *xs* than logbooks do.

Logs (logbooks and log sheets) are usually readily accessible and tell the history of process steps from an insider's viewpoint. Comments in logbooks and log sheets can provide valuable insights to defects, rework, and hidden factories.

| Logsheet - Injection Press | | | | | | Machine Settings | | | | | Dimensions | | Test |
|---|---|---|---|---|---|---|---|---|---|---|---|---|---|
| Date | Time | Operator | Material | % Regrind | Inj. Press | Hold Press | Material Temp. | Speed | Back Press | Mold Temp. | Diameter | Thickness | Torque |
| 3/13/06 | 7:00 | Ted | UCP | 5% | 1250 | 1400 | 450 | 8 | 25-50 | 140 | 3.145" | 0.060" | 45.1 |
| | 7:45 | | | 5% | 1250 | 1400 | 450 | 8 | 25-50 | 140 | | | |
| | 9:22 | | | 5% | 1250 | 1400 | 450 | 8 | 25-50 | 140 | | | |
| | 9:58 | | | 12% | 1400 | 1400 | 450 | 8 | 75-100 | 140 | 3.145" | 0.060" | 40.8 |
| | 10:36 | | | 12% | 1400 | 1400 | 450 | 8 | 75-100 | 140 | | | |
| | 11:25 | | | 12% | 1400 | 1400 | 450 | 8 | 75-100 | 140 | | | |
| | 1:00 | | ORA | 0% | 1350 | 1400 | 450 | 8 | 25-50 | 140 | 3.142" | 0.062" | 42.2 |
| | 2:45 | | | 0% | 1350 | 1400 | 450 | 8 | 25-50 | 140 | | | |
| | 3:00 | Arnie | | 0% | 1250 | 1700 | 470 | 9 | 25-50 | 140 | 3.140" | 0.058" | 44.4 |
| | 5:30 | | | 0% | 1250 | 1700 | 470 | 9 | 25-50 | 140 | | | |
| | 9:00 | | | 7% | 1250 | 1700 | 470 | 9 | 25-50 | 140 | 3.140" | 0.059" | 41.1 |
| | 10:05 | | | 7% | 1250 | 1700 | 470 | 9 | 25-50 | 140 | | | |
| | 11:20 | Boxer | | 7% | 1400 | 1500 | 450 | 8 | 25-50 | 150 | 3.148" | 0.061" | 40.6 |
| | 12:30 | | | 7% | 1400 | 1500 | 350 | 8 | 25-50 | 150 | | | |

*Manufacturing operations frequently use log sheets for operators to record machine conditions. This log sheet for producing plastic parts shows data for many of the xs listed on the team's Fishbone Diagram.*

## Data Collection Forms

Data collection sheets are very similar to log sheets, but are designed to collect detailed information on the potential *xs*, focused on the problem at hand. The intent is to get specific *x-Y* data for analysis. Data collection sheets might be used to study task times, control settings for producing a product, or factors under study in a clinical environment.

Data collection sheets are intended to be used for a short period of time to study the process in detail. Typically, the data collection sheet is designed by the Lean Six Sigma team after generating potential $x$s. The more detailed the collection form, the more likely assistance from team members will be required to collect the data.

## Check Sheets

Check sheets are designed to collect data with minimal effort but high visibility. They can vary from simple tally sheets to custom-designed forms to solve a specific problem. Categorical (attribute) data can be quickly recorded by line personnel close to the process.

*This tally sheet for a call center used customer service representatives to record the type of call and if the call was a repeat from a customer for the same problem. The Lean Six Sigma project goal was to reduce repeat (unresolved) calls.*

| CSR | Time Start | Time End | Billing All | Billing Repeat? | Subscription All | Subscription Repeat? | Outage All | Outage Repeat? | Tech Service All | Tech Service Repeat? | Misc/No Code All | Misc/No Code Repeat? | Totals All | Totals Repeat? | Comments |
|---|---|---|---|---|---|---|---|---|---|---|---|---|---|---|---|
| Monique | 7:00 AM | 8:00 AM | | | | | | | | | | | 24 | 10 | Tech service-connectivity |
| Monique | 8:00 AM | 9:00 AM | | | | | | | | | | | 29 | 13 | Tech service-connectivity |
| Monique/Fred | 9:00 AM | 10:00 AM | | | | | | | | | | | 27 | 14 | |
| Monique | 10:00 AM | 11:00 AM | | | | | | | | | | | 14 | 6 | |
| Monique/Fred | 11:00 AM | 12:00 PM | | | | | | | | | | | 9 | 3 | |
| Fred | 12:00 PM | 1:00 PM | | | | | | | | | | | 25 | 8 | |
| Monique | 1:00 PM | 2:00 PM | | | | | | | | | | | 13 | 4 | Outage-system down |
| Monique | 2:00 PM | 3:00 PM | | | | | | | | | | | 19 | 5 | Outage-most from CSI, inc. |
| Fred/Jo Bob | 3:00 PM | 4:00 PM | | | | | | | | | | | 14 | 8 | |
| Jo Bob | 4:00 PM | 5:00 PM | | | | | | | | | | | 4 | 1 | |
| Jo Bob | 5:00 PM | 6:00 PM | | | | | | | | | | | 17 | 3 | |
| Jo Bob | 6:00 PM | 7:00 PM | | | | | | | | | | | 21 | 3 | |
| Fred | 7:00 PM | 8:00 PM | | | | | | | | | | | 36 | 11 | |
| Jo Bob | 8:00 PM | 9:00 PM | | | | | | | | | | | 35 | 10 | New features-new layout |
| Jo Bob | 9:00 PM | 10:00 PM | | | | | | | | | | | 29 | 2 | |
| Jo Bob | 10:00 PM | 11:00 PM | | | | | | | | | | | 30 | 8 | |
| **Total - All** | | | 20 | | 15 | | 45 | | 62 | | 19 | | 346 | | |
| **Total - Repeats** | | | | 10 | | 1 | | 19 | | 26 | | 2 | | 109 | |
| **% Repeats** | | | | 50.0% | | 6.7% | | 42.2% | | 41.9% | | 10.5% | | 31.5% | |

## Control Charts

Control Charts provide time-ordered data on shifts, drifts, and unusual events for specific process measures. The data from Control Charts are usually focused on output ($Y$) characteristics (e.g., defectives, dimensions, service time) and do not inherently contain detailed information on the $x$s.

The benefit of Control Charts lies in the feedback from those closest to the process. The impact of specific $x$s can be identified by associating shifts, trends, and outliers with specific observable changes in the $x$s (inputs, environment, or process controls). See Chapter 21 for all the details on Control Charts.

## Observation of Processes

Independent observation of processes can provide an unbiased view of the process and record events not recognized by those closest to the process. Standard forms might be used to observe task times or methods used in a process. One example is the Standard Work Combination form common to Lean, recording tasks within each process step in detail (see Chapter 14). Videotaping of processes (or going to the Genba) is another observation technique that allows more than one person to view the same activities. By reviewing how each operator differs in methods, critical differences can be identified.

# Special Studies

You can undertake specific studies to manipulate xs and determine the resulting behavior in Y, which gives you knowledge of your transfer function, or $Y = f(x)$. Another advantage of special studies is that they can be conducted quickly and at the convenience of the team.

The key with special studies is that you are looking for the critical few x variables that exercise the most influence over your Y of concern, your output metric. Lean Six Sigma is all about leverage, and about finding the leverage, especially when it comes to solving complex defect and performance issues.

With special studies, you can home in on the xs you believe have the most signifcant effect on Y, and prove or disprove those assumptions. You can also home in on the xs you think have the least significance, or influence on Y, and test those assumptions as well. Both ways, you begin to formulate a scientifically valid picture of how your xs impact your Y.

The most common and powerful tool for conducting special x-Y studies is Design of Experiments, or DOE for short. When applicable, you use DOE methods to examine multiple xs in a concise set of experiments. Getting ready for DOE, we revisit our fishermen friends, Wayne and Fred, to view their following data collection sheet.

| Trials | x's | | | | | Y's | |
|---|---|---|---|---|---|---|---|
| RunOrder | Time of Day | Location | Bait | Depth | Fisherman | Time | Weight |
| 1 | 6:30 AM | Elephant Island | Minnows | 15 | Wayne | | |
| 2 | 6:30 AM | Elephant Island | Minnows | 40 | Fred | | |
| 3 | 7:30 AM | South End | Minnows | 40 | Wayne | | |
| 4 | 7:30 AM | South End | Worms | 40 | Fred | | |
| 5 | 8:30 AM | South End | Minnows | 15 | Fred | | |
| 6 | 8:30 AM | South End | Worms | 15 | Wayne | | |
| 7 | 9:30 AM | Elephant Island | Worms | 15 | Fred | | |
| 8 | 9:30 AM | Elephant Island | Worms | 40 | Wayne | | |
| 9 | 1:00 PM | South End | Worms | 15 | Fred | | |
| 10 | 1:00 PM | South End | Worms | 40 | Wayne | | |
| 11 | 2:00 PM | Elephant Island | Minnows | 15 | Fred | | |
| 12 | 2:00 PM | Elephant Island | Minnows | 40 | Wayne | | |
| 13 | 3:00 PM | Elephant Island | Worms | 15 | Wayne | | |
| 14 | 3:00 PM | Elephant Island | Worms | 40 | Fred | | |
| 15 | 4:00 PM | South End | Minnows | 15 | Wayne | | |
| 16 | 4:00 PM | South End | Minnows | 40 | Fred | | |

*Design of Experiments (DOE) methods manipulate factors (xs) in specific patterns to ensure independence of xs and integrity of data. In this DOE, Wayne and Fred examined the Time of Day, Location, Bait, Depth, and Fisherman in 16 balanced trials.*

We're going to give you more details in the next chapter, showing you more about how to run a simple DOE. Note that the DOE subject matter is broad and deep, and you can find entire texts devoted to them if you want more.

# Sample Size Calculations

To conduct special studies, you have to calculate your sample sizes, and to do this you need to employ statistical sampling methods. In this vein, you ask one important question: How much evidence do I need to convict a particular $x$ of exercising significant influence over $Y$? Answer: You need enough evidence to make the arrest and bring the case to court. And to do this, using statistics, you must manage your risk of making incorrect decisions. So before you calculate your data sample sizes for special studies, you have to determine the level of risk—or uncertainty—with which you're willing to live. Then you adjust your sample size accordingly.

So first, here is what you need to know about risk:

**Alpha ($\alpha$) Risk** is the risk of making a *Type I error*—detecting a false difference or declaring that the $x$ influences $Y$ when it's only random variation. If you were on a jury, this is the risk of convicting an innocent defendant.

**Confidence** is the likelihood of not making a Type I error, defined as $(1-\alpha)$.

**Beta ($\beta$) Risk** is the risk of making a *Type II error*—not having enough evidence to detect that $x$ really does influence $Y$. Back to the jury—this is the risk of letting a guilty person go free for lack of sufficient evidence.

**Power** is the probability that we would detect a specific minimum difference in the populations with a given sample size, defined as $(1-\beta)$.

When the $Y$ is a continuous distribution, we might look for changes in shape (normal versus not normal), location (average or median), or spread (standard deviation). When the $Y$ is attribute data, we might compare samples from populations to detect differences in proportions. Specific comparison methods will be covered soon, in this chapter.

To calculate an appropriate sample size to determine statistically significant differences in $Y$, you first need to determine …

- The type of comparison you are making—averages, variability, proportions, etc.

- The smallest change in $Y$ that you need to detect, delta ($\Delta$).

- An estimate of the variability of $Y$ (i.e., standard deviation, $s$).

- The acceptable alpha risk of making a Type I error. For initial screening of $x$s, we might set the alpha risk between 0.05 and .15 (i.e., between 5 and 15 percent chance we might label an $x$ significant when it's not).

◆ The acceptable beta risk of making a Type II error. For initial screening, we don't want to hastily ignore significant *x*s, so we might set the beta risk at 0.10 (i.e., a 10 percent chance we might not have sufficient data to identify a significant *x*, thereby mistakingly placing it in the "no effect" pile).

As with many other Lean Six Sigma tools and techniques, sampling techniques and calculations can be complex and varied. For example, you use different sampling techniques for different types of data: averages, standard deviations, and percentages. We'll give you some details for the more common scenarios of calculating sample sizes for averages and percentages.

## Comparing Averages

Averages can be compared to each other or to some target or historical value. It's convenient to standardize the difference in averages by estimating a Z-score, which is done by dividing delta (Δ) by the estimated standard deviation (*s*). The Z-score allows us to use standard statistical tests and tables and simplifies the process.

| Δ Desired Minimum Difference in Averages | s Estimated Short Term Standard Deviation | z score = Δ/s Difference in Standard Deviation Units | n Sample Size, Number of Observations from Each Group |
|---|---|---|---|
| 0.25 | 1.00 | 0.25 | 275 |
| 0.50 | 1.00 | 0.50 | 70 |
| 0.75 | 1.00 | 0.75 | 31 |
| 1.00 | 1.00 | 1.00 | 18 |
| 1.50 | 1.00 | 1.50 | 9 |
| 2.00 | 1.00 | 2.00 | 6 |

Recommended sample sizes to compare averages of 2 populations ($\alpha = 0.05$, $\beta = 0.10$).

*This table provides sample sizes for comparing averages of samples from two populations based on the estimated Z-score. Reducing variability has a large impact on reducing sample size for detecting smaller differences in average. For a reduction of 50 percent in variability, the sample size recommended is reduced by about 75 percent.*

For example: Wayne and Fred want to compare the fishing near Elephant Island of Grand Lake to the south end near the inlet. They are hoping to find at least a 0.25 pound difference between the shores. From previous fishing in the one spot with the same bait, they estimated the short-term standard deviation to be 0.25 pounds. How many fish do they need to catch from each spot in the lake?

Z-score = 0.25 lbs. /0.25 lbs. = 1.00

Using the previous table, they should catch 18 fish from each spot to compare the populations of fish at each end of the lake. This would give them a 90 percent (1-β) probability of detecting at least a 0.25 pound difference, and they would have 95 percent (1-α) confidence that they won't be misled by the data if no difference exists.

If the difference was 0.375 pounds between the populations, then the Z-score = 0.375/0.25 = 1.50, and it would only take nine fish at each spot to detect that there is a statistically significant difference in average weights.

## Comparing Percentages (Proportions)

When your data is not measured on a continuous scale, you might measure the results as pass or fail. The table that follows shows recommended minimum sample sizes to detect a 50 percent reduction in defectives.

*When the process is running at a lower proportion of defectives, the sample size required increases dramatically.*

| $p_1$, Baseline Proportion | $p_2$, 50% Reduction | n, Recommended Sample Size |
|:---:|:---:|:---:|
| 0.005 | 0.0025 | 5185 |
| 0.01 | 0.005 | 2582 |
| 0.02 | 0.01 | 1281 |
| 0.04 | 0.02 | 630 |
| 0.08 | 0.04 | 304 |
| 0.16 | 0.08 | 142 |
| 0.32 | 0.16 | 60 |

Recommended sample sizes to detect a 50% reduction in proportion defective ($\alpha = 0.05$, $\beta = 0.10$).

For example: A package-sorting operation currently missorts 1 percent of the packages to the wrong destination. If the process is reduced to a 0.5 percent missort level, how many samples would be recommended to affirm the statistical significance of the improvement? Using the previous table, the proportion defectives would be reduced from 0.01 to 0.005, and a sample size of 2,582 would be recommended to compare the new process to the previous process historical proportion missorted.

# Graphical Analysis

Okay, you've got the data you need, and the evidence is clear to you. Or is it? You have data on so many $x$s that you need to sort out the significant ones for trial. If a picture is worth a thousand words, then a graph is worth a thousand data points. A good graphical picture of the data will make the significant $x$ pop out of the crowd. That's what you're after!

But, still, not so fast. Before you present your summation to the jury, you will need to use statistical analysis to confirm hypotheses you make from the graphs.

So back to the graphs. You're looking for solid evidence that *Y* moves when *x* is changed, and to do this you have a whole slew of graphical tools at your disposal. To sort through these tools, and select the right one(s), you need to determine what type of *x*s you're examining (continuous or discrete), and what type of data you've recorded for *Y* (continuous or attribute).

Reminder: Continuous *x*s are measured on a continuous scale (e.g., time, temperature, age, distance). Discrete *x*s are those that are grouped into distinct categories (e.g., transaction type, day of the week, gender). The selection matrix that follows will assist you in selecting the right tool for the job.

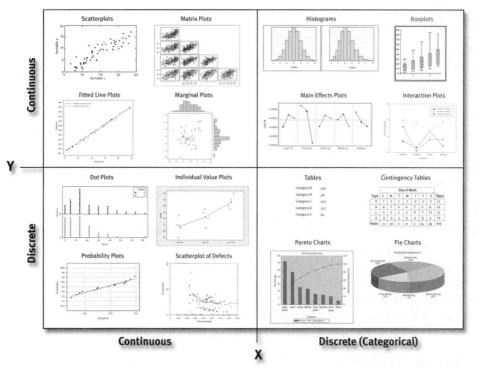

*Minitab software offers a variety of graphs that can be quickly created to identify potential significant xs. This chart summarizes some of the most common graphs you can use, depending on the nature of your x and Y data.*

Graphs may represent all the data points, showing the density and spread of the data. These include Histograms, Scatter Plots, Dot Plots, and Box Plots. Other graphs focus on such summary statistics as averages or variation. Summary graphs include Main Effect and Interaction Plots, confidence intervals, and Pareto Charts.

Scatter Plots display pairs of continuous $x$ and $Y$ data. When examining a lot of $x$ and $Y$ relationships, Matrix Plots can be used to view many Scatter Plots at once. With the use of regression or lowess techniques, a best fit line can be drawn to help identify the $Y = f(x)$ relationship.

Boxplots display quartiles of data with the lower and upper 25 percent represented by the whiskers and the middle 50 percent of the data points within the box, including a line for the median (middlemost) value. They are so frequently used to display the differences of categorical $x$s that one Lean Six Sigma Black Belt wanted to name his first child "Boxplot."

Main Effects Plots are free from the usual clutter of individual data points. Interaction Plots display averages of the combinations of two $x$s and help identify any additional combined effects of the $x$s.

### Performance Pitfall

Graphs that average individual raw data can create a false impression of x-Y relationships. Small sample sizes, outliers, and highly correlated input variables (e.g., shoe size and height) can distort the relationship to the point of misidentifying ($\alpha$ risk) or not identifying ($\beta$ risk) the critical xs. To reduce the risk of this pitfall, construct graphs diplaying individual data points, and use statistical analysis to confirm your conclusions. Consult your friendly statistician frequently.

### Real-Life Story

Neural network software, such as RapAnalyst, has been used by Lean Six Sigma practitioners to process enormous amounts of data, and to visually display their relationships. Such analytical horsepower comes in handy when you need to find meaningful x-Y relationships amongst very large populations of variables.

Probability Plots for discrete $Y$ values show the "best fit" relationship of the probabilities that an event (e.g., bankruptcy) will occur, given predictor variables ($x$s) that are continuous (e.g., debt to equity ratios) or discrete (e.g., marital status).

Various tables displaying and summarizing the relationship of discrete $x$s and discrete $Y$s can be created in spreadsheets (e.g., pivot tables) or statistical software (e.g., contingency tables).

Pareto Charts display the counts of discrete categories of events in a descending order. The visual display of high counts on the left helps identify the largest categories for investigation. The 80/20 rule frequently applies to Pareto Charts.

# Conduct Statistical Analysis

Statistical analysis is the grand jury of the Analyze phase—do you have enough evidence to pursue the case for or against your many *x*s? Do you know enough to convict the alleged *x* suspect of its crime in causing your defect?

Some statistical orientation is needed here. We are concerned with getting the correct decisions a high percentage of the time using the factual evidence collected (how often do you make good decisions based on opinions?).

To test whether the *x*s are truly significant, we state two hypotheses—*different* or *not different*—similar to a jury that will conclude a defendant is guilty or not guilty. Does the jury ever say "innocent"? No; you're either guilty (responsible) or not guilty (not responsible).

In essense, statistical tests tell you if there is any significant difference in one population (*Y*) over another based on changes in some *x* or set of *x*s. For example, if task cycle time is your *Y* metric of concern, and you think training can significantly shorten this time, you can test for this by examining the population cycle times for the trained (group A) and the untrained (group B).

If you turn up no statistical (significant) difference, then you are very sure that training (*x*) does not exercise leverage over your cycle time (*Y*). If there is a statistical difference, then your *x* of training is responsible, so you know what to do to make the change you need: conduct more training.

# p-Values and Hypothesis Testing

For statistical tests, a common method for determining if one population is different from another is to calculate a p-Value. A common decision point is to call the populations different if the p-Value is less than 0.05. This would equate to a 95 percent confidence that the populations are different.

Hypothesis testing uses samples from populations to compare the populations to standards or other populations and make statements of statistical significance about the populations.

Before the data is examined, both a Null Hypothesis and an Alternate Hypothesis are stated, together with the risk levels we assign to our decision.

The Null Hypothesis ($H_0$) is a statement of no difference or independence—that the *x* does not affect *Y*. If we are testing samples from two populations of data, the Null

Hypothesis might be that the averages of the populations are equal (not different). Innocent until proven guilty—right?

The Alternate Hypothesis ($H_A$) is a statement of difference or dependence: that changes in $x$ do affect $Y$. For our example, the Alternate Hypothesis can be stated that the average task time of the population of trained employees is less than the average task time of untrained employees.

Through appropriate statistical tests, you calculate a p-Value, which represents the probability that the Null Hypothesis is true. If the p-Value is less than your alpha risk, you reject the Null Hypothesis and accept the Alternate Hypothesis that the populations are different.

Remember that alpha risk ($\alpha$ risk) is the risk we are willing to take that we conclude there is a difference between the populations (a Type I error), when in truth there is not a difference. The beta risk identifies the chance of making a Type II error—not identifying a statistical difference in the populations when in truth they are different.

Type II errors can occur because there isn't enough evidence (sample size) to conclude that the $x$ significantly influenced the $Y$. The evidence could also be insufficient to overcome the *background noise* (e.g., standard deviation) of the sample data. This would be like trying to convict a defendant who was involved in a gang rumble. So many $x$s are involved—which ones really did the damage?

# Statistical Analysis Methods

Recall that a statistic is a calculated value derived from a set of sample data used to describe a characteristic of a population. A statistic might be the average (arithmetic mean), standard deviation, proportion defective, or count of defects per unit. Statistics can also describe the shape of data distributions (e.g., normal, gamma, weibull, binomial, Poisson).

Statistical tests have been developed by statisticians over the centuries based on sampling behavior probabilities. Tables of probabilities have now been converted to algorithms in software programs for ready reference in summarizing results of hypothesis tests. Common tests used in statistical analysis for DMAIC are shown in the chart that follows.

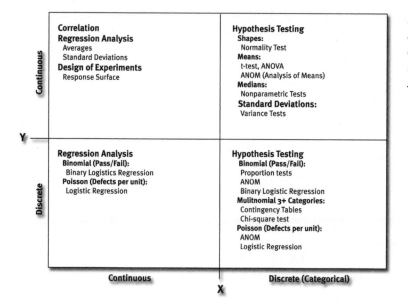

*Hypothesis tests have been developed for a wide variety of analysis combinations. This table shows the most common statistical tests used.*

As with sample size calculations, statistical tests exist for a wide variety of data and conditions. There are statistical tests for distribution shape, for averages, for variability, for proportions, and for testing hypotheses that entail multiple *xs*. For simplicity's sake, we'll only cover some details of statistical tests for averages and for proportions—as we did previously for calculating sample sizes.

## Tests for Averages

The most common test to compare averages is the *t*-test. Normality of the population distributions is assumed in calculating *t*-test statistics.

For example: Wayne and Fred caught and weighed 16 fish from one area of the lake. The average weight was 4.20 pounds, and the standard deviation was 0.50 pound. They wanted to determine if they had enough evidence that the population average was greater than 4.0 pounds.

The statistical software calculated a *t*-statistic as follows:

$$t_{Statistic} = \frac{\triangle}{\left(\frac{s}{Sqrt(n)}\right)} = \frac{(4.20 - 4.0)}{\frac{0.5}{4}} = 1.60$$

The software cross-referenced a *t*-table and returned a p-Value of 0.065 (a 6.5 per-cent chance that the sample data could have come from a population averaging 4.00 pounds). Since Wayne and Fred had established an alpha risk of 0.05 for 95 percent confidence, they decided that they needed to fish some more to get a larger sample size and test the hypothesis again.

When comparing averages of three or more groups of data, the appropriate method is Analysis of Variance (ANOVA), if each distribution is normally distributed. If distri-butions are not normally distributed, tests for the medians of populations are usually used.

## Tests for Proportions

Hypothesis tests for pass/fail data require larger sample sizes than tests for averages, medians, or standard deviations. In a recent election, 1,200 potential voters were polled to determine which candidate they favored; 47 percent favored one candidate, 44 percent favored another, and 9 percent were undecided.

A hypothesis test was conducted to determine if the population contained a higher proportion of voters for the first candidate. With a p-Value of 0.07, the test deter-mined that the associated margin of error placed the candidates in a "virtual statistical tie" prior to the election.

## The Least You Need to Know

- ◆ Good data collection includes detailed data on the *x*s with good measurement systems. Be wary of historical data—there may be errors and pitfalls.

- ◆ To make sound inferences about your data populations, you must follow the rules and formulas for calculating sample sizes.

- ◆ Alpha risk is the risk of falsely declaring that an *x* influences *Y* when it doesn't. Beta risk is not ascribing responsibility to an *x* that does significantly impact *Y*.

- ◆ Graphical methods abound for comparing discrete or continuous *x*s to discrete or continuous *Y*s. Tell the story with graphs and charts—back up your conclu-sions with statistics.

- ◆ Statistical analysis gives you the examination of evidence to sort out critical *x*s, but you will probably need special studies to derive a good $Y = f(x)$ relationship.

# 16

# Solve the Problem

## In This Chapter

- ◆ Getting your priorities in order
- ◆ Torturing the $x$s to get a confession
- ◆ Experiment like you never have before
- ◆ Simulate processes to gain profound knowledge
- ◆ On the road to $Y = f(x)$

Reviewing log sheets, analyzing computer databases, detailing failure modes, and conducting special studies should be giving you a clue about the $x$s that have the most impact on $Y$. So far you've collected data and analyzed, but you really haven't changed much. The latter part of the Analyze phase and the Improve phase focus on manipulating the $x$s and detailing the results.

In this chapter, we crank it up a notch. We'll bring in the most likely $x$ suspects and torture them until they finally confess. Which ones are significant? Which have the leverage? This is our focus in this chapter. To accomplish this, we'll cover such key Lean Six Sigma tools and techniques as correlation, Design of Experiments, Analysis of Variance, and simulation.

# Prioritize the *xs*

Early in Analyze, you identified potential *xs* using a Cause-and-Effect Matrix, mostly with opinions from your team. You also examined failure modes using FMEA techniques and established Risk Priority Numbers (RPN) based on the Severity, Occurrence, and Detection of process failures. Your review of the process through Lean glasses identified waste, Flow, and efficiency issues. Now it's time to bring that analysis together and track down the really important *xs*.

*Initial Cause-and-Effect Analysis in the Measure phase should identify a vast number of potential xs. The Analyze and Improve phases narrow the list down to the vital few that make the most significant impact.*

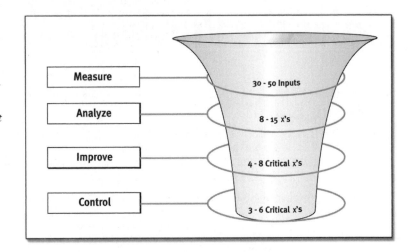

## Focus on the Primary Metric

The success of your project relies on the team's ability to improve the primary metric *(Y)*. Your initial opinions on the fishbone diagram directed your data collection. The data became information through process, graphical, and statistical analyses. You now need to turn that information about the process into knowledge. The next step will be to turn the knowledge into action—the Improve phase of DMAIC.

The Critical *X* Worksheet is a log of your analysis to date, sorting out the significant *xs* from those that don't have leverage to impact your process. As you can see from the following sample, the Critical *X* Worksheet summarizes the impact of each *x* on *Y*, and shows the evidence supporting that claim.

**Real-Life Story**

A team focused on improving the flatness of the disk in a hard disk drive—a key component of performance. The initial fishbone identified 30 potential xs that might affect flatness. Through a series of designed experiments, the team investigated each x and found that number 17 had the biggest impact on flatness, and a breakthrough was achieved!

| Process Step | Potential X | Impact on Y (repeat calls) | Evidence | Priority/ Action Plans |
|---|---|---|---|---|
| Answer Call | Time to Answer | Call Drop | Opinion- No Data | Special Study- Call Drops |
| Receive Information | Account Number | Research- Might Call Back | QA Sampling 7% of Calls | Increase |
| Code Problem | Clarity of Codes | Wrong Solution- Repeat Call | MSA: 67% Agreement with Standard | Revise Code Structure? |
| Assign Ticket | Not Logged | 13% of Tickets Incorrect | Review of January Tickets | Revise IT Format? |
| Provide Instructions | No Follow-up | Repeat Call for "Next Step" | CSR Checksheet | New Script for CSRs? |

*This Critical X Worksheet sample shows five critical xs that were surfaced as a result of analysis.*

## Revisit the Cause-and-Effect Matrix

The Cause-and-Effect Matrix shows the impact of each *x* on all the *Y*s. Early in Analyze, you developed a C&E Matrix with the team, with the best knowledge at hand. Now that your knowledge is more refined, you need to update the C&E Matrix. The C&E Matrix is an evergreen document—it should be updated whenever the knowledge of the *x-Y* relationships is improved.

# Evaluate the Impact on Y

Databases, log sheets, and observations can surface the high-level suspect *x*s from the crowd, but you need more than that. You need to verify the impact of those *x*s on your primary metric. Statistical analysis of historical data can yield *correlation* of *x* variables with *Y*, but often the *x* variables are also correlated with each other, leaving doubts about which *x* might cause *Y* to vary.

The correlation coefficient *(r)* is used to quantify the linear relationship of the variables. The correlation coefficient varies between –1 and +1, with 0 representing no correlation. If the variables are plotted on

 **Lean Six Sigma Lingo**

**Correlation** is the strength of the relationship between two variables. Correlation can be used to identify *x-Y* relationships, or *x-x* or *Y-Y* relationships. A high correlation does not necessarily imply that one variable causes the effect of the other variable.

a Scatter Plot and all the points fall perfectly on a straight line, the correlation coefficient will be –1 if the slope is negative, or +1 if the slope is positive.

Wayne and Fred collected detailed data for a day of fishing. They correlated two *Y*s (Fish Weight and Time to Catch) to five *x*s (Time of Day, Depth, Bait, Location, and Sky). Fish Weight had a high correlation with each of the *x*s, but the *x*s were also highly correlated with each other. Which *x* really caused the *Y* to change? Even sophisticated regression analysis can't sort this one out.

*This Matrix Plot shows the various correlations between Wayne and Fred's five xs and two Ys. It also shows the correlations of all five xs with each other.*

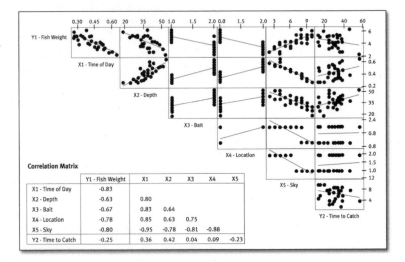

**Correlation Matrix**

|  | Y1 - Fish Weight | X1 | X2 | X3 | X4 | X5 |
|---|---|---|---|---|---|---|
| X1 - Time of Day | -0.83 | | | | | |
| X2 - Depth | -0.63 | 0.80 | | | | |
| X3 - Bait | -0.67 | 0.83 | 0.64 | | | |
| X4 - Location | -0.78 | 0.85 | 0.63 | 0.75 | | |
| X5 - Sky | -0.80 | -0.95 | -0.78 | -0.81 | -0.88 | |
| Y2 - Time to Catch | -0.25 | 0.36 | 0.42 | 0.04 | 0.09 | -0.23 |

Since correlation coefficients examine one *x* at a time versus *Y*, you need to watch out for four possible pitfalls that can occur in the analysis:

◆ Variation in other *x*s can mask the correlation of the *x* under examination.

◆ Correlation of input *x*s can lead to mistaking the effect of one *x* for the true effect of the critical *x*.

◆ Two *x*s might combine to produce a significant interaction effect in *Y* that is not apparent for either *x* when examined individually.

◆ Nonlinear effects do not show up as strong linear correlations.

Correlation studies are most useful when only one or two *x*s create most of the variability in *Y*. When multiple *x*s are under investigation, you need more sophisticated methods like Design of Experiments (DOE), Analysis of Variance (or ANOVA), or simulation methods. We'll look at each of these now.

**Real-Life Story** _____

An analyst was trying to correlate the impact of several operations on the end result—late mail. Substantial information on 16 metrics had been collected and each was tested individually for correlation. None were significant. When the analyst used multiple regression analysis that included all the xs, significant effects were found. The multiple regression partitioned the effect of each x so that it would not mask the effect of other xs.

# Design of Experiments

At some point, you'll need to experiment with xs in the process—and you need to do so in the most reliable and cost-effective way possible, with experiments that yield easy-to-understand conclusions. DOE methods do just that—*if* you can properly manipulate your xs for special study.

Design of Experiments uses specific design combinations (arrays) of changes (levels) of input factors (independent variables) to observe changes in output responses (dependent variables). A key characteristic of DOE is to eliminate any correlation of input factors and to extract the contribution of each factor.

DOE can be used to stratify the effects of each input factor independently of the other factors. This is accomplished by the use of orthogonal arrays that are analyzed for the effects of each factor, and any interactive effects. The simplest design would be a two-factor design, with each factor varied over two levels.

To demonstrate a simple DOE, here is an actual example. One of the authors of this book was driving from Pittsburgh to Denver in his van and thought a DOE on gas mileage would be entertaining. He selected two inputs he could control—Gas Octane at two levels (86 versus 91) and Speed at two levels (55 mph versus 65 mph). All combinations of the factor levels would require four trials, as shown by the following figure.

**Lean Six Sigma Wisdom**

Design of Experiments techniques were first used in the 1920s to improve crop yields in England by Sir Ronald Fisher. Since that time, the methods have been used by American universities and by many industries around the world to develop and improve products and processes.

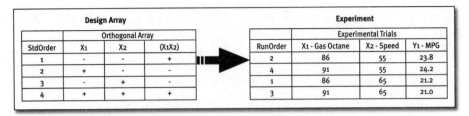

| Design Array | | | |
| --- | --- | --- | --- |
| | Orthogonal Array | | |
| StdOrder | X₁ | X₂ | (X₁X₂) |
| 1 | - | - | + |
| 2 | + | - | - |
| 3 | - | + | - |
| 4 | + | + | + |

| Experiment | | | |
| --- | --- | --- | --- |
| | Experimental Trials | | |
| RunOrder | X₁ - Gas Octane | X₂ - Speed | Y₁ - MPG |
| 2 | 86 | 55 | 23.8 |
| 4 | 91 | 55 | 24.2 |
| 1 | 86 | 65 | 21.2 |
| 3 | 91 | 65 | 21.0 |

*The design array for a two-level design is typically written as "–" for the low level of a factor and "+" for the high level. The four combinations shown are translated into the actual experimental conditions. Other columns can be calculated to represent interaction effects (X1X2) but are not needed to set up the experiment.*

For this experiment, gas mileage varied from 21.0 mpg to 24.2 mpg—more than expected. To analyze the results, we calculate the difference in averages for each factor level.

The average with 91 octane is 22.6 mpg, and the average for 86 octane is 22.5 mpg. The difference of 0.1 mpg seems rather small. For speed, the average at 65 mph is 21.1 mpg and the average at 55 mph is 24.0 mpg—a difference of –2.9 mpg!

The effect of the interaction can also be calculated using the "+" and "–" levels of the interaction (see the following diagram). The "+" level averaged 22.4 mpg and the "–" level averaged 22.7 mpg—a difference of –0.3 mpg—negligible compared to the speed impact alone.

*The Main Effects Plot shows the averages for each factor level. The Interaction Plot shows the combination effects of two factors.*

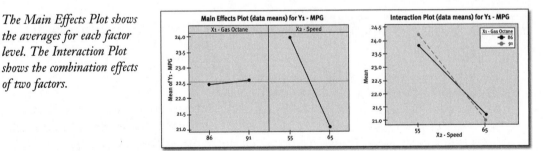

By viewing the Main Effects Plot, we can conclude that speed affects gas mileage significantly, and that the octane level does not affect gas mileage significantly. We can also conclude that *the combination of speed and octane level* produced no significant interaction effect. (Parallel lines on an *Interaction Plot* indicate no interaction effect.)

Maybe we can provide you a few helpful hints about how to make your DOE as smooth, efficient, and errorless as possible. Here's some simple advice:

- **Don't put all your data eggs in one basket.** Projects have relied on downloading computer databases only to find that many of the $x$s were not in the database.

- **Make sure measurement systems are accurate and precise.** Poor measurement and recording of $x$s causes biases and lack of precision in the data, leading to analysis errors.

- **Drill down to find the critical $x$s.** Teams that don't stratify the layers of $x$s gloss over significant differences and abandon the hunt for the critical $x$s.

- **Go beyond the typical variation in $x$s if necessary to see the $x$-$Y$ relationships more clearly.** If the $x$s vary little in your data, you may need to manipulate them to uncover the relationships.

- **Take sufficient samples before running statistical tests.** Not collecting enough data is coming to court with no evidence—the guilty $x$ is likely to go free!

- **Involve stakeholders in the data collection plan.** People in the process can identify flaws in the plan and identify other significant $x$s.

# Analysis of Variance

Analysis of Variance (ANOVA) is the statistical method used to test the hypothesis that changes in levels for each $x$ factor cause changes in the response variable $Y$. ANOVA partitions the *explained* variation in the response variable for each factor or interaction, and also creates an error category for *unexplained* variation.

For each factor, the explained variation is weighed against the unexplained variation to determine if the results are statistically significant for the amount of data collected. A p-Value is calculated for each factor to determine the risk of making a Type I error (calling a factor significant when it is not). Generally speaking, a factor is considered significant if its p-Value is less than 0.05.

Many factors can be investigated at many levels in designed experiments. Experiments that test all combinations of factors and levels are called full-factorial designs. Fractional factorial designs are also available to significantly reduce the number of trials, while retaining the integrity of a statistically designed experiment.

# Simulation

While DOE methods, including ANOVA, provide solid evidence for identifying the critical *x*s, the resources required might be prohibitive. (Running such statistical tests can be expensive and time-consuming.) Another alternative for process analysis is the use of simulation techniques, such as *Monte Carlo Simulation*, when the parameters and relationships of the *x*s are known, but the overall system is complex.

**Lean Six Sigma Lingo**

Monte Carlo Simulation uses mathematical models, probability, decision rules, and induced variabililty in inputs to simulate real-life scenarios and identify variability in outputs.

The advantage of simulation compared to deterministic spreadsheet models is that a range of inputs are investigated, and the range of outputs are quantified, versus a single output from a deterministic model. Therefore, the sensitivity of the outputs to variation in inputs can be identified and prioritized. For example, let's examine a loan approval process to determine where the overall cycle time can be improved.

*This six-step process takes 100 hours on average, according to the average of individual process steps. Simulation of the process using Monte Carlo methods includes the rework in the process, variability, and distribution of process times.*

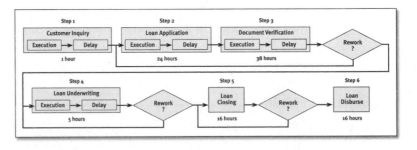

*This output from Crystal Ball® software shows the variability of loan cycle times based on variability and defect levels for the six process steps. We added the sensitivity analysis to show that the total cycle time is predominantly dependent on delays in document verification.*

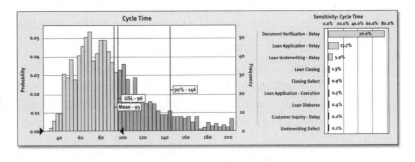

Monte Carlo Simulation is not limited to process analysis. It can also be used for tolerance design of parts, probabilistic models (e.g., on-time air travel), and a variety of other investigations. To develop a good simulation model, the team must first detail the as-is process prior to playing what-if scenarios or redesigning the process.

Switching gears, Discrete Process Simulation models show the visual flow of materials through the process to help identify bottlenecks and utilization of resources. The model is based on a process flow model, with the ability to incorporate decision rules, queues, assignment of resources, and work schedules. An example of Discrete Process Simulation follows.

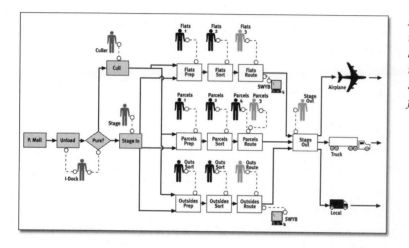

*A Priority Mail team used the process flow diagram and ProcessModel software to conduct Discrete Process Simulation analysis of a new facility.*

Prior to building facilities to process Priority Mail, an improvement team used Discrete Process Simulation models to determine the flow of mail, and to identify bottlenecks in the proposed process. Inputs were based on the operations in current facilities and experimental trials for process changes.

Resources were assigned by the software for each process step, and task time distributions and volume fluctuations were included in the model. Bottlenecks and the impact of defective units were identified through the simulation.

The model showed that mail arriving on the last truck of the night needed to be processed through a different flow to meet the outbound schedules. It also showed that a large bottleneck would occur at final dispatch late in the shift. The process was redesigned, which led to the avoidance of the bottleneck at the opening of a new facility.

# State the $Y = f(x)$ Equation

The $Y = f(x)$ equation represents the dependence of the output response on the input factors. The output might be a probability of occurrence or a continuous response.

The input factors might be continuous or discrete (categorical). Some of the input factors identified will be controllable, others might be noise (e.g., temperature, or arrival rates of customers).

For many projects, a specific mathematical $Y = f(x)$ equation can be stated. Other projects may find the impact of critical $x$s is well understood, but trying to put them all into a single mathematical equation just doesn't work. In these cases, knowledge of the impact of each $x$ can still be used to improve and optimize the process.

Designed experiments produce results that can easily be transformed into $Y = f(x)$ equations. If the $x$s are continuous, the equation can be written as a true mathematical equation. If the $x$s are discrete, the equation looks a little different—the effect of each depends on which categorical level is chosen.

Good analysis of data, experimental trials, and simulations can weed through the previously unexplained variation and explain why the variation occurs. Regression analysis and ANOVA separate the total variation into two components—factor effects (explained) and error (unexplained variation).

A company that manufactured water meters discovered that the see-through lids were cracking when the screws were tightened down. The team developed a torque test to investigate the settings and material on the plastic injection molding machine that produced the lids. Having identified 11 potential $x$s on the molding machine alone, the team conducted a screening DOE consisting of 12 trials. The results from the experiment identified three critical $x$s, leading the team to produce lids that didn't crack on assembly.

*This was a 12-run Placket-Burman screening design. Eleven factors (X1—X11) were run at two levels each. Instead of running all 2,048 combinations, the highly fractionated factorial design only required 12 experimental combinations.*

| | Design Factors | | | | | | | | | | | Responses |
|---|---|---|---|---|---|---|---|---|---|---|---|---|
| Material | Booster Timer, sec | Inj. P-Booster | Holding Press | Ram Speed | Mat'l Temp | Mold Temp-F | Mold Temp-B | Extr. RPM | Back Press | Cooling | | Average Torque |
| X1 | X2 | X3 | X4 | X5 | X6 | X7 | X8 | X9 | X10 | X11 | | Y |
| Current | 1 | 1250 | 1700 | 8 | 450 | 140 | 90 | 20 | 30 | Air | | 43.33 |
| Current | 1 | 1250 | 1700 | 8 | 470 | 150 | 120 | 70 | 80 | Quench | | 40.20 |
| Current | 1 | 1400 | 1400 | 9 | 450 | 140 | 90 | 70 | 80 | Quench | | 42.30 |
| Current | 3 | 1250 | 1400 | 9 | 450 | 150 | 120 | 20 | 30 | Quench | | 28.30 |
| Current | 3 | 1400 | 1700 | 9 | 470 | 140 | 120 | 20 | 80 | Air | | 28.30 |
| Current | 3 | 1400 | 1400 | 8 | 470 | 150 | 90 | 70 | 30 | Air | | 40.30 |
| High % | 1 | 1400 | 1400 | 8 | 450 | 150 | 120 | 20 | 80 | Air | | 37.60 |
| High % | 1 | 1400 | 1700 | 9 | 470 | 150 | 90 | 20 | 30 | Quench | | 36.80 |
| High % | 1 | 1250 | 1400 | 9 | 470 | 140 | 120 | 70 | 30 | Air | | 35.70 |
| High % | 3 | 1400 | 1700 | 8 | 450 | 140 | 120 | 70 | 30 | Quench | | 35.22 |
| High % | 3 | 1250 | 1400 | 8 | 470 | 140 | 90 | 20 | 80 | Quench | | 38.70 |
| High % | 3 | 1250 | 1700 | 9 | 450 | 150 | 90 | 70 | 80 | Air | | 25.80 |

DOE uses ANOVA to separate the statistically significant $x$s from other unproven $x$s. For our injection molding example, 12 data points were recorded, allowing for 11 terms in an equation plus a constant. Variation is stratified for each of the 11 factors by using a Sum of Squares accounting method.

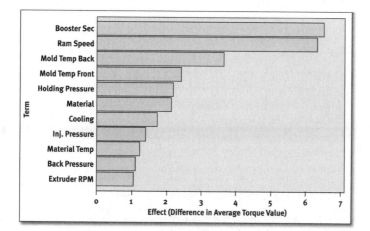

*The differences in average torque were calculated by comparing the means of the + level to the – level of each factor. Three factors show more than a 3-torque unit's effect on the average torque values: Booster Seconds, Ram Speed, and Mold Temp-Back.*

The following ANOVA table is then constructed by separating out the major contributors to variability (explained variation) and pooling the variation from minor contributors into error (unexplained variation). The explained variation is compared to the unexplained variation using an *F-test* and results in a p-Value for each factor. The p-Value represents the alpha risk of calling the factor significant when it is not. Confidence in your decision is defined as (1-$p$).

### Technically Speaking

The **F-test** is used to determine if variances are different comparing variability between means of multiple populations (variance between groups) to the variability within the populations (variance within groups).

It's really great to have a $Y = f(x)$ equation finally, but do we really have the whole picture? Using a table of level effects, which follows, predictions can be made about the torque values for any of the 2,048 possible combinations, even though only 12 experimental combinations were run.

| Source | DF | Sum of Aquares | Mean Square | F Ratio | p-Value |
|---|---|---|---|---|---|
| Booster Sec | 1 | 128.773 | 128.773 | 14.06 | 0.006 |
| Ram Speed | 1 | 121.285 | 121.285 | 13.24 | 0.007 |
| Mold Temp Back | 1 | 40.004 | 40.004 | 4.37 | 0.070 |
| Error | 8 | 73.27 | 9.159 | | |
| Total | 11 | 363.332 | | | |
| S = 3.03 | | R-Sq = 79.8% | | | |

*For the injection molding example, the ANOVA table was reduced from 11 factors to 3 major contributors, and 8 terms were placed in error. The result was an R-squared value, showing that 79.8 percent of the variation in the experiment was explained by the three major terms. The 20.2 percent unexplained variation is assumed to be random error and contributes an estimated standard deviation of 3.03.*

| Injection Molding (Placket Burman Screening Design) | | | | |
|---|---|---|---|---|
| Factor | Factor Name | Levels | Level Means (Avg. Torque) | Level Effects |
| X1 | Material | - Regular<br>+ High% | 37.12<br>34.97 | 1.08<br>-1.08 |
| X2 | Booster Timer | - 1 sec<br>+ 3 sec | 39.32<br>32.77 | 3.28<br>-3.28 |
| X3 | Inj P-Booster | - 1250<br>+ 1400 | 35.34<br>36.75 | -0.71<br>0.71 |
| X4 | Holding Press | - 1700<br>+ 1400 | 34.94<br>37.15 | -1.10<br>1.10 |
| X5 | Ram Speed | - 8 - Slow<br>+ 9 - Fast | 39.23<br>32.87 | 3.18<br>-3.18 |
| X6 | Mat'l Temp | - 450 deg<br>+ 470 deg | 35.43<br>36.67 | -0.62<br>0.62 |
| X7 | Mold Temp-F | - 140<br>+ 150 | 37.26<br>34.83 | 1.21<br>-1.21 |
| X8 | Mold Temp-B | - 90<br>+ 120 | 37.87<br>34.22 | 1.83<br>-1.83 |
| X9 | Extr. RPM | - 20<br>+ 70 | 35.51<br>36.59 | -0.54<br>0.54 |
| X10 | Back Press | - 30<br>+ 80 | 36.61<br>35.48 | 0.56<br>-0.56 |
| X11 | Cooling | - Air<br>+ Quench | 35.17<br>36.92 | -0.87<br>0.87 |
| | | Grand Average | 36.05 | |

*A table of level effects shows the mathematical effect of changing levels for each factor tested. A conservative approach to making predictions would be only including factors found to be statistically significant.*

To predict the best combination of settings from our example, we would select the levels of the three significant factors that increase torque values:

| | |
|---|---|
| Grand Average | = 36.05 |
| Booster Timer @ 1 sec | = +3.28 |
| Ram Speed @ 8-Slow | = +3.18 |
| Mold Temp–Back @ 90 | = +1.83 |
| Predicted Average | = 44.34 |
| Predicted Standard Dev. | = 3.03 (from ANOVA) |

Based on the analysis, you can also make predictions for other combinations, and you can run verification trials to confirm the predictions. At the end of the rainbow, you still might not be able to state the exact $Y = f(x)$ equation—but that's your goal, and you shouldn't stop your analysis until you can do this.

# Conduct Tollgate Review

Before moving on to the Improve phase in the next chapter, you need to conduct a tollgate review that ensures you've accomplished all your critical tasks. This review should be attended by your Lean Six Sigma Champion, your Process Owner, team members, and other key stakeholders. Some questions to ask, and answer, at your review include:

◆ Has your problem or objective statement changed? (Answer: If not, great. If so, reflect changes on your Project Charter.)

◆ How did you identify potential $x$s? (Answer: Show correct use of Process Map, Brainstorming, Affinity Diagrams, Fishbone Diagrams, etc.)

◆ What $x$s were verified with data? What evidence do you have? (Answer: Used Scatter Plots, Hypothesis Testing, ANOVA, Regression, etc.)

◆ What are the top potential process steps, based on RPNs, that you have identified from your FMEA? (Answer: see completed FMEA.)

◆ What has the performance been, by week, for the metrics tracking your primary metric? (Answer: We maintained a Control Chart or Time Series Plot.)

◆ If you have completed the Analyze phase, what are your conclusions? (Answer: We know what our critical $x$s are with a specified degree of confidence.)

◆ Was a preliminary $Y = f(x)$ equation developed (to be refined in the Improve Phase)? (Answer: Yes, and here is the proof.)

◆ Have you developed a plan for and conducted Design of Experiments? (Answer: We did, and here is our data and conclusions.)

◆ Are all data fields in your project tracking tool current with your most recent project progress? (Answer: Hopefully yes. If not, enter data.)

◆ Are you satisfied with the level of cooperation and support you are getting to solve your project in a timely manner? (Answer: If yes, great; if no, revisit Stakeholder Analysis and Action Plan.)

◆ Is your project still on track to meet the scheduled completion date? (Answer: If yes, great; if no, remove roadblocks, accelerate pace, lead, revisit Stakeholder Analysis.)

◆ Has your financial forecast changed by more than 20 percent? If yes, what is the new validated forecast? (Answer: With the finance rep, we updated the project forecast.)

## The Least You Need to Know

◆ You cannot investigate all the $x$s—you need to prioritize your investigations to the most likely.

◆ Continue to update the Cause-and-Effect Matrix and FMEA to document your knowledge of the process.

◆ Pitfalls in correlation analysis can be prevented by using Design of Experiments methods and ANOVA analysis.

◆ Simulation techniques can provide insights to the critical $x$s when physical trials are prohibitive.

◆ Advanced statistical tools such as regression analysis, DOE, and simulation can develop $Y = f(x)$ equations. Verification of the predictions is mandatory.

# Create the Future State

## In This Chapter

- ◆ Envision your future state
- ◆ *Seiri, seiton, seiso, seiketsu, shitsuke*
- ◆ Developing standard work procedures
- ◆ U-shaped work cells
- ◆ Improving equipment and maintenance
- ◆ Do you have the Kaizen Event in you?

You've left the Analyze phase and are now entering the world of Improve—the time when you ultimately end up with the exact equation $Y = f(x)$ for your performance problem. In other words, you now know a lot about why your performance problem exists, and it's time to carry that knowledge to its final destination: the place where you know exactly what needs to be done to solve your problem.

In this chapter, we cover some of the main Lean techniques you use to improve your process. As we have stated in prior chapters, you primarily use the Lean tool set when dealing with issues related to time (as opposed to defects). Still, even when pursuing time improvements, and their related efficiencies, you may need to integrate Six Sigma thinking and tools.

With that in mind, stay tuned as we cover the creation of a Future State Value Stream map, details about the Five Ss, and such other techniques as the Multiple Skills Map, Mistake Proofing, cellular operations layout, and Total Productive Maintenance for increased Overall Equipment Effectiveness. Finally, we'll give you a rundown on how to conduct a Kaizen Event.

# Introducing Improve

As depicted by the road map that follows, the Improve phase of Lean Six Sigma is when you review and consolidate your analysis work. You use the outputs of your analysis to generate solutions to your performance problem, and you then develop an Implementation Plan to enact the associated changes.

Part of your implementation might include a full-blown Kaizen Event, which we'll tell you how to run at the end of this chapter. Otherwise, during Improve, you'll build your future-state Value Stream Map; generate, narrow down, and test your possible solutions; select the best solution to your problem; and conduct other activities that are necessary in making the transition from Improve to Control.

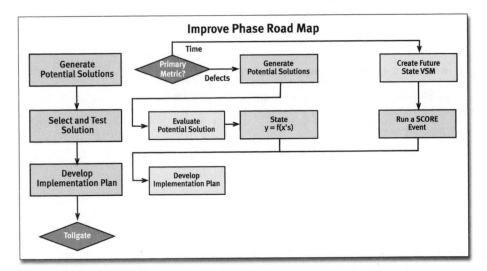

*This is the general process for the Improve phase of DMAIC. Depending on your experience and unique situation, you may or may not strictly follow these steps in a set sequential fashion.*

# Your Future State

Whether your problem is time or defect related, you know enough now to begin revising your Process Map or Value Stream Map (VSM). While you haven't fully confirmed the critical variables in your new process, you have a pretty good idea about what needs to change. Therefore, update your Process Map or VSM accordingly. (See Chapter 10 for details of building and revising Process Maps and VSMs.)

## What Needs to Change?

For your future state, you want to design the perfect vision of what the customer values and the business needs to provide. By working through DMA, the first three phases of DMAIC, you've completed the discovery and development process; you've discovered a new way of working and providing value to your customer. Now you can map this new vision on paper, and set it beside your old process. This in and of itself should be inspiring.

Wow, you couldn't have imagined the old process and the new process could look so much different. You couldn't have dreamed of making the changes you now know you need. The future state looks so obvious, but the obvious often eludes until after it becomes known. Back when you started your project, the answers weren't so clear!

In Chapter 20, we show you a before-and-after Value Stream Map example, so you can see the difference between the current and future states of a process. In this example, the process had already transitioned through the Improve phase altogether, and all future-state improvements had been made.

In the Improve phase, your future-state map enables you to project differences in lead time, inventory, head count, and your value-to-non-value ratio. By using the data and knowledge you've gained thus far, you can estimate your new lead times and inventory levels. You can estimate any space savings. You can predict your new quality levels, and calculate cost-savings forecasts.

## Which Path to Take?

Your future-state map is still only a highly educated vision; it is not a reality yet. You still have to clarify how you'll improve the process to achieve this future vision. If time is your objective, you would bias your performance intervention toward Lean-oriented concepts and tools. If defect reduction is your goal, then your bias would be toward Six Sigma-oriented concepts and tools. Ultimately, however, you won't think in terms of Lean or Six Sigma; you'll just tackle all time and defect issues simultaneously with one tool set: Lean Six Sigma.

For now, we'll give you a rundown of key improvement techniques for your time-related problem. Then we'll summarize the process involved in conducting a Kaizen Event, which can be used to make quick improvements during the Measure phase without the further work and analytics involved in Analyze and Improve. (That's right, sometimes you essentially skip over the Analyze and Improve phases and go right to Control.)

# The Five Ss

In former chapters, we touched upon the Five Ss, which are disciplines that can transform a messy, cluttered, and inefficient process into one that is clean and streamlined.

The five disciplines are *seiri, seiton, seiso, seiketsu, and shitsuke*—the Romanized versions of the five Japanese words for the concepts of Sorting, Storage, Shining, Standardization, and Sustaining.

*Words are just words unless you bring them alive. The Five Ss are those kind of words: words with the power to transform your process.*

| Japanese | English | Description |
|----------|---------|-------------|
| Seiri | Sort | Eliminate unneeded items |
| Seiton | Store | Orderliness for ease of use |
| Seiso | Shine | Cleanliness to observe deviations |
| Seiketsu | Standardize | Cleaned up to retain standards |
| Shitsuke | Sustain | Discipline adhering to new standards |

The Five S disciplines, which establish the foundation for a visual Lean workplace, are often mistaken as "extreme housekeeping." But the Five Ss are not about making the workplace look more orderly, even though they usually have this effect. If you want a work environment that is simple, efficient, and safe, the Five Ss are for you.

## Sort (Seiri)

Simply arranging things in neat rows and stacks is not Sorting. People (and organizations) are often pack rats, keeping things that have no use for extended periods of time. Sorting is about keeping what you need to perform the process activity and removing everything else from the work area.

The Sorting step is usually done with an activity called a *red tag event*. For every item in the workplace, you ask: "Do we use this every time we do the process?" If the answer is no, then the item is tagged and removed to a holding area for disposition. Excess supplies are also red-tagged for disposition as possible waste.

## Store (Seiton)

The Store step is about creating standard locations for everything used in the process (a place for everything, and everything in its place). This way, everyone who needs items can locate and use them when needed. The more frequently you use an item, the closer it should be to the work space. Conversely, the less often you use an item, the farther away from the work space it should be.

Shadow boards with "dead-man" outlines are sometimes used to indicate the proper location for items. These simple visuals help you know when things are missing, or the proper location for your items. In terms of efficiency and waste removal, this beats having to become a veteran at finding what you need to do your work.

## Shine (Seiso)

Once you've organized your work space to include only what you need on a regular basis, it's time to Shine. This is when you make your work area clean and tidy, and make everything like new. The basics here are activities like wiping down counters, cleaning computer monitors, throwing away old notes from the desk, sweeping and mopping floors, and cleaning debris from drilling or cleaning oil drips.

You should integrate Shining into each day's work routine by establishing clear owner-ship of daily cleaning tasks. Many cities, for instance, have Shining programs that look for and quickly repair broken windows in unoccupied buildings. Your business should be no different; seek out areas of debris and disorderliness and Shine them up, regularly and without fail.

**Lean Six Sigma Wisdom**

Shining implies a certain amount of attentiveness to the way work is performed. As you go about your cleanup, look for causes of the mess. And by all means, fix them!

## Standardize (Seiketsu)

Once you've Sorted, Stored, and Shined, you have to Standardize—which is to insti-tute a way of making sure everyone keeps the work space in its new state over time. If Shining is the act of cleaning up, Standardization is the act of getting everyone to adopt the practice of cleaning up, or following the new procedures for Sorting and Storing. When you Standardize, you set everyone on the same course so there are no surprises and everyone knows what to expect when they come to work.

Part of standardization could entail Mistake Proofing—installing a foolproof system for ensuring people follow your new procedures. We give you a bunch of Mistake Proofing guidelines and examples in Chapter 20. Often checklists are used as Mistake Proofing devices for ensuring process activities are completed on time and without fail.

**Lean Six Sigma Wisdom** _____

The concept and practice of Standardization isn't just what you do after you've Sorted, Stored, and Shined. It's also what you do after you've solved a difficult performance problem (defect), revamped a process through deeper analytical means, and are looking to keep your new process in control (stable with acceptable variation).

**Performance Pitfall** _____

Sustaining Five S improvements over time requires a certain disdain for shortcuts that cheapen the resulting product or output. You put a lot of work into improving your process. Don't mess it up by getting lazy at the end.

## Sustain *(Shitsuke)*

The time and effort required to Sort, Store, Shine, and Standardize are wasted unless management takes actions to Sustain the improvements over long periods of time. Such actions can include the development of performance dashboards, training, and Standard Operating Procedures. These are management (not worker) activities that require commitment and discipline. In fact, sustaining improvement often entails continually identifying new opportunities for improvement.

# Standard Work

Standard Work operations are an effective combination of people, materials, procedures, and equipment to create a product or service in minimum time with minimum resources. Standard Work has three elements: 1) Takt Time, 2) work content and sequence, and 3) standard in-process inventory. The purpose of standard work operations is to answer the following questions:

1. What quality standards must be met by the product or service?

2. How much should it cost to make the product or service?

3. How many products or services do you need delivered and by when?

4. Is the work itself safe?

In Chapter 14, we introduced the concept of Workload Balance to establish measures for job duty breakout and work cycle timing. And we analyzed work content and sequence using the Process Flow or Value Stream Map, and the Standard Work analysis. We also showed you a little bit about how to design standard in-process inventory using Little's Law to set up Kanbans and queues.

Here in the Improve phase, when you're ready to implement Standard Work, take heed of these guidelines:

◆ Standard Work must be established in an operation throughout the Value Stream and for all products. Process workers cannot maintain standard operations without management making a conscious decision to support them.

◆ Standard Work must be understood at all levels for management to appropriately support, and workers to appropriately perform.

◆ Standard Work must be integrated into such sustaining practices as hiring and recruiting, and training practices must establish skill competency.

◆ Visual process controls are required for making it much easier to do the job right than wrong.

◆ Management is accountable for assuring Standard Work is maintained. Besides, Standard Work enables management to interface with workers in a positive manner because you have a basis for performance evaluation.

◆ Improvements must be integrated into the Standard Work content on an ongoing basis.

## Managing Standard Work

The Process Control Plan is the basic tool used to manage Standard Work and conforms to the Shewhart cycle of Plan-Do-Study-Act, as shown by the following figure. A flow chart (or checklist) provides work content and sequence information for the process. The measurement indicators are key process or input variables that provide information about the health of the process. The control actions provide action instruction and accountability, should the measures fail to meet performance criteria.

How you get to the control actions is the important part. Use of the FMEA, your process risk mitigation tool, identifies and quantifies process risks, and prescribes predetermined actions should the process go wrong. We give you more details of building a Control Plan in Chapter 21.

*Managing Standard Work is a matter of sufficiently meeting the intent of the Plan-Do-Study-Act cycle.*

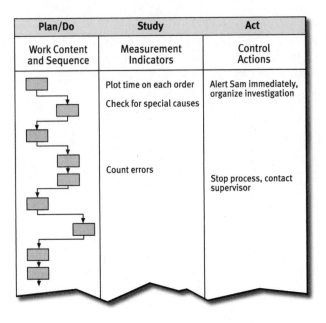

| Plan/Do | Study | Act |
|---|---|---|
| Work Content and Sequence | Measurement Indicators | Control Actions |
| | Plot time on each order | Alert Sam immediately, organize investigation |
| | Check for special causes | |
| | Count errors | Stop process, contact supervisor |

# Multiple Skills Matrix

Another tool for managing and sustaining Standard Work and process performance is the Multiple Skills Matrix, an example shown following. This matrix is used by managers to create employee development plans, and to plan training and cross-training activities. Once the training is completed, a proficient operator would know what to do, and a good process would prevent making errors.

*You can use a Multiple Skills Matrix to plan for training, and to firmly establish Standard Work as "the way we do business."*

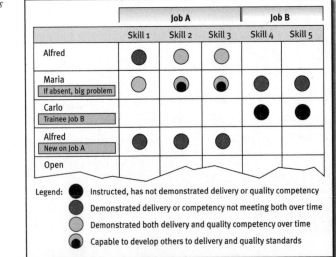

|  | Job A | | | Job B | |
|---|---|---|---|---|---|
|  | Skill 1 | Skill 2 | Skill 3 | Skill 4 | Skill 5 |
| Alfred | ● | ● | ● | | |
| Maria — If absent, big problem | ○ | ● | ● | ● | ● |
| Carlo — Trainee Job B | | | | ● | ● |
| Alfred — New on Job A | ● | ● | ● | | |
| Open | | | | | |

Legend:
● Instructed, has not demonstrated delivery or quality competency
● Demonstrated delivery or competency not meeting both over time
○ Demonstrated both delivery and quality competency over time
◉ Capable to develop others to delivery and quality standards

Looking at the previous Multiple Skills Matrix, the jobs (Job A and Job B) might be a loan approval process, or an entire subassembly. The skills in a loan approval process might be identity confirmation, credit verification, and collateral risk assessment. The skills in a subassembly might be assemble belt and winder, run compliance verification test, and enter compliance data in tracking system.

# Cellular Layout

During the Analyze phase, when your performance issue is related to time, you engage in a number of calculations to help you optimize Flow and Pull in work processes. We looked at many of these calculations in Chapter 14 (Takt Time, Kanbans, Little's Law). We also looked at analysis methods for balancing workloads and utilizing resources—again for the purpose of improving Flow and Pull.

Sometimes such analysis and calculations lead you to redesigning the physical layout of your process in a way that minimizes space, time, equipment, and inventory. And much more often than not, this can happen through the use of U-shaped work cells, sometimes called cellular operations, or cellular manufacturing.

Straight lines create waste by making people walk farther between steps and after the last step in a process. Implementing a cellular layout can greatly minimize the waste of unnecessary transportation and motion—the movement of people, things, and information through a process. Work cells also increase the efficiency of communication and coordination of work, and improve the ability of a team to solve performance issues.

## Rebalance Equipment

Often the move to cellular layout necessitates the right-size equipment to support the more efficient layout and use of space, time, and inventory. All, of course, in the name of better Flow. The key is to synchronize your new operational cycle time, including machining time, with your Takt Time.

Example: A large coating machine handled minimum batches of 500 metal parts, which often "puddled" and became stuck together. Inspectors had to sort the parts, and either scrap them or scrape the coating globs and recoat. The coating machine manufacturer designed a smaller machine that handled the parts individually in the work cell. This eliminated defects and the need for inspection and rework. It also eliminated the need for material-handling fork trucks and cranes. Plus, it eliminated the space required for storing the larger batches of inventory.

Example: To eliminate configuration errors caused by a 2-D modeling system, a 3-D system was designed to run on special high-end graphics workstations. However, the automated configuration step took more than 20 minutes to run—a 100 percent increase in time. A software graphics accelerator was installed that achieved the desired Flow. The resulting solution cost a fraction of the alternatives and was faster to implement.

## Quick Changeover

We covered the principle of Quick Changeover (or Rapid Changeover) in Chapter 2, and we addressed the way you study and analyze changeovers in Chapter 14. By the time you get into the Improve phase, you should be ready to implement your new changeover process. Often this is done in conjunction with reconfiguring the layout of your process into a more cellular shape or design. As with any change, you'll need to test and pilot your new changeover process before implementing it and training operators on the new procedures.

## Implementing TPM

We covered Total Productive Maintenance (TPM) in Chapter 14 (part of the Analyze phase), but we mention it here to remind you that the system you designed has to be implemented. Remember, TPM is the prevention of equipment deterioration or breakdown so you can process your transactions or goods according to a predictable and reliable schedule, or expected capacity utilization rate.

For example, a productive car is one that's ready to go where you want it to go and when; but this doesn't mean your car has to be available 100 percent of the time. You have to take your car off-line sometimes to change the oil and conduct maintenance that will prolong its deterioration and ensure its long-term reliability.

Overall Equipment Effectiveness, which we showed you how to calculate in Chapter 14, is a measure that tells you how well TPM is working. And to make it work well, practice these eight core activities of TPM:

1. Focused improvement for eliminating waste.

2. Autonomous maintenance to prevent equipment deterioration.

3. Planned maintenance for achieving zero breakdowns.

4. Education and training for increased productivity.

5. Early equipment/product management to reduce waste during the implementation of a new machine or production of a new product.

6. Quality maintenance (Mistake Proofing) to achieve zero loss by taking necessary measures to prevent downtime.

7. Institution of a safe, hygienic work space for achieving zero work-related accidents and for protecting the environment.

8. Office process simplification for support processes that could otherwise constrain equipment performance.

# Kaizen Events

You should think of a Kaizen Event as an intensified session whereby a team uses a war-room-like environment as a base to identify and make a needed improvement. As we covered in Chapter 5, you conduct Kaizen Events to make rapid improvements, especially when the root cause of your performance problem is known, or when your primary objective is to take waste and time out of your process.

Essentially, a Kaizen Event augments the DMAIC approach by acting faster on opportunities with known solutions that don't require extended, in-depth statistical analyses. (But don't be misled: full-blown Kaizen Events typically require a significant degree of data and analysis, but just not necessarily as in-depth as you'd need for a full-blown DMAIC project.)

Conversely, your DMAIC projects might incorporate the Kaizen Event approach at various stages. When collecting data in the Measure phase, for instance, you may want to set up a data collection war room to intensify that activity. Or, in the Improve phase, you may want to utilize a Kaizen Event approach to pilot and roll out your solution.

That said, a good Kaizen Event adheres to these guidelines:

**Lean Six Sigma Wisdom**

If you want a good resource for running Kaizen Events, go to Amazon.com and order *A Team Leader's Guide to Lean Kaizen Events.* Waldo, Wes, and Tom Jones. (Breakthrough Performance Press, 2006)

**Kaizen Events are thorough.** The devil is always in the details. Kaizen Events are fast-paced, and there is no time for major adjustments once they are underway. Therefore, do your homework and preparation up front. Consider all of the variables, people, and interactions prior to the event kickoff.

**Kaizen Events require training.** This includes training and knowledge of many Lean Six Sigma tools and techniques; you can't expect people to make improvements if they don't know how to think about and apply Lean Six Sigma techniques.

**Kaizen Events require change management.** While some people are born leaders, you can learn and teach people how to manage change. Aside from the technical and mechanical knowledge required, your ability to lead and motivate people—and keep them on track—will be the determining factor in your success.

**Kaizen Events require participative management.** In normal business life, managers "decide and direct" and workers "do." During a Kaizen Event, managers are much more concerned with getting everyone's participation than telling people what to do. And workers are much more involved in creating solutions than they are in the rote aspects of their jobs.

Once you've made all your preparations, and you know what needs to be improved, you can often complete a Kaizen Event in just one week's time. On Monday, you assess your current situation, which includes reviewing the team charter that has been prepared by the team leader. On Tuesday, you make the changes you need to make. On Wednesday, you run the new process and confirm that it is producing the planned improvements. Thursday is for documenting your standard operating procedures, while Friday is when you present your new process and results to management.

Naturally, to get this much done in one week, the team leader needs to have good intelligence and direction beforehand. As we said, usually, when the Kaizen Event is a viable option, you already know what needs to be changed and why; you just need a dedicated period of time in which to make the changes.

## The Least You Need to Know

- Redraw your Value Stream Map to reflect the future state of your process. This will guide you through the Improve phase.

- The Five Ss (Sort, Store, Shine, Standardize, Sustain) are simple but powerful disciplines you can use to rid waste, gain efficiency, and even solve the cause of certain performance issues.

- Instituting Standard Work procedures is a critical aspect of sustaining improved performance.

- Cellular layouts are fantastic ways of reducing time, space, and inventory—and this applies for production as well as office environments.

- Kaizen Events are your way of getting major improvements done in a very short period of time, especially when you don't need to engage in extended periods of data collection and analysis.

**18**

# Generate and Evaluate Solutions

## In This Chapter

- ◆ Homing in on your solutions
- ◆ Experimenting with the $x$s
- ◆ Refining $Y = f(x)$
- ◆ Narrowing solution options

If your project has required deeper Six Sigma statistical analysis, you've been waiting for this time ever since you started your project. Everybody on your team, the Process Owner and all the stakeholders, have ideas about how to fix the process and solve the problem. Each of your team members has probably kept a list, or parking lot, of solutions in his or her head or on paper. Some of these ideas were disproved through data collection and analysis, while others were reinforced.

Now is the time to generate several possible solutions to your problem, along with their corresponding action plans. That's why this chapter will show you how to refine your $Y = f(x)$ pathway, driving all the way to the point where you know the ultimate answer to your performance problem!

If you know the answer, you can develop different solution alternatives, ultimately choosing the best for full-scale implementation.

# Generate Solutions

As you review and consolidate your analysis work, solutions will fall into three categories: 1) the solution will be obvious, so just do it! 2) the team knows where to focus but needs to refine the solution(s) and corresponding Implementation Plan; 3) you need a miracle or an innovation to solve the problem.

Regardless of your pathway, you want to find solutions that are long-lasting and permanently address the root cause of your problem. You either want to eliminate that root cause or change the process to function as desired regardless of that cause (robust design). In any case, you'll want to update your Critical $X$ Worksheet (from Chapter 16) to reflect what you've learned and confirmed since the Analyze phase.

## Still Need Solutions?

Your goal is to generate a complete list of possible ways to solve the problems at hand, using the investigations and factual data you've collected. Your list of potential solutions is probably not complete, and your team needs to expand its solution ideas before rushing into the first one it has. Brainstorming and inventive problem-solving techniques can provide unique solution ideas.

## Brainstorming

By solving your primary problem, it's likely that you'll surface other, lower-order problems that need to be solved. In addition to solving your primary problem, your proposed solutions will also have to address these related but subordinate problems. Hint: If the subproblems are extremely difficult or complex, they might require a separate or parallel DMAIC effort. If not, you can usually address them using simple brainstorming.

Start by identifying these lower-order problems and ask "How to …" in front of each one. This will focus the brain on coming up with necessary solution actions, which later can become the line items of your Implementation Plan.

For example:

◆ How to reduce variation in the measurement process?

◆ How to Mistake Proof data entry?

◆ How to maintain proper equipment in the service truck?

◆ How to collect insurance copays after emergency room care?

Brainstorming techniques open up the creativity side of your brain, bringing out unique perspectives for solving problems. Most brainstorming techniques are divergent in nature, meaning they expand your list of possibilities according to some spawning mechanism. Some of these methods include ...

◆ **Idea Trigger Sessions**—Rapidly generate potential solutions.

◆ **Mindmapping**—Diagramming concepts and relationships stemming from an original problem statement.

◆ **Six Thinking Hats**—Viewing the problem from distinctly different perspectives (Analytical, Emotional, Critical, Positive, Creative, Managed).

◆ **Random Word**—Incorporating a random word into the thinking pattern to generate new thought patterns.

## Structured Innovation

To achieve a breakthrough in your solutions, sometimes an innovation or invention is needed. While the multitude of brainstorming techniques tend to be focused on expanding your thought horizon, a handful of techniques are available that rely on inventive benchmarking for similar problems. Such benchmarking is convergent rather than divergent in nature—you work your way to a specific solution through the use of established inventive principles and the use of thinking by analogy.

The Theory of Inventive Problem Solving (a.k.a. TRIZ) was developed by Genrich Altshuller after studying the principles behind thousands of patents worldwide. TRIZ focuses on specific problems, leading the practitioner to a proven matrix of generic solutions, which then are translated into specific solutions via analogical thought.

To generate potential solutions, TRIZ starts with the Ideal Final Result (IFR)—a perfect solution with no trade-offs or negative consequences. TRIZ measures the deviation (trade-offs) of proposed solutions from the IFR; these potential trade-offs then become contradictions for TRIZ to solve.

Once the contradictions have been formed into a problem statement, they are rephrased as conflicts between generic

**Lean Six Sigma Wisdom**

For a great summary of TRIZ, pick up *Insourcing Innovation*, a book written by David Silverstein, Neil DeCarlo, and Michael Slocum. You can find this book at Amazon.com.

**Real-Life Story** _____

A circuit board manufacturer used the TRIZ process to come up with a new surface mounting technology that eliminated field failures, saving $9 million in the first year. In doing so, the company relied on the TRIZ inventive principle of spheroidality.

parameters, of which there are 39 in the TRIZ system. The TRIZ practitioner then references the parameters in a contradiction matrix to reveal the inventive principles by which others have solved similar problems (contradictions) in other environments at other times.

Using these principles, the innovator can then analogously reason his or her way back to a specific solution to a specific problem. That, in a nutshell, is a convergent approach for coming up with viable inventive ideas for solving problems. TRIZ and other structured innovation approaches are a burgeoning field as extensive and deep as Lean Six Sigma.

## Applying Lean Concepts

You can also use Lean concepts and techniques to come up with potential problem solutions, especially when trying to improve Flow and Pull for the purpose of reducing waste and increasing efficiency. We covered the most widely used techniques in Chapter 17, so check out that chapter for more details.

## Process Thinking

In Chapter 17, we talked about creating a future-state Value Stream Map as a framework within which to guide solution generation. Here we revisit this theme with the following guidelines, in case you need more help using process thinking to generate potential problem solutions.

- ◆ Should some steps be eliminated as non-value-added?
- ◆ Should the steps of the process be rearranged?
- ◆ Should steps be combined or broken apart?
- ◆ Is there a lot of cross-department flow on the Swim Lane flow chart?
- ◆ Where are the bottlenecks? Is line balancing needed?
- ◆ Is too much/too little information required at any particular step?

# Evaluate Potential Solutions

So you've got a bagful of solutions now, or at least a couple of solid options. Of course, all your solution-generation activities have been constrained by your discovery during

Analyze and Improve. So all possible solution options should be solid, and you should have a high degree of confidence that they will solve your problem and improve performance.

Still, not all solutions can be put into action plans immediately. You have to evaluate the viability of implementing each of your proposed solutions in the spirit of managing limited resources, avoiding unnecessary risk, and accomplishing your gains in a realistic time frame.

# Find Affinities and Consolidate

Once a number of alternative solutions have been identified, similarities between solutions can be identified through Affinity Diagrams. If you're not familiar with this tool (Affinity Diagram), see Chapters 13 and 22 for some details. Basically, Affinity Diagrams enable you to organize your brainstormed solutions into proposed Action or Implementation Plans.

**Performance Pitfall**

For each potential solution, identify any critical concerns. These are potential showstoppers that could prevent the solution from its implementation. If the critical concern can't be resolved, generate and evaluate alternate solutions.

# Potential Solutions Matrix

Another way to narrow down your solution options is to subject them to two simple criteria: their quality (Impact) and their efficiency of implementation (Ease). Just plug your potential solutions into the following Ease/Impact Matrix to see where they fall in the resulting nine-box grid.

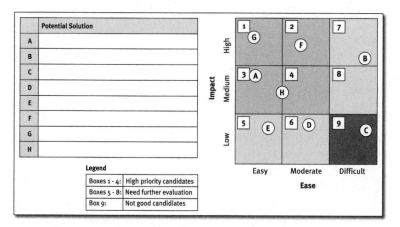

*The Ease/Impact grid compares the impact of each potential solution and the ease of getting the solution in place. Relative positions on the grid help determine the priority of each solution.*

The Impact of a solution is estimated by projecting its benefits according to project metrics, and its longevity. Of course, the acid test for Impact is to evaluate the solution 12 months after its full implementation. But right now that's getting the cart a little before the horse.

Ease is focused on the politics, technology required, difficulty of implementation, and time frame required for implementation. Just Do It solutions rate on the easy end of the spectrum. Solutions with political, technical, or cultural barriers rate as difficult. Solutions requiring high capital investment or long lead times also rate as difficult.

So here's the skinny. Solutions in boxes 1 through 4 are high-priority candidates. Solutions in box 5 might get some quick wins, but have little impact on your metrics. Solutions in box 6 should be further evaluated to see if they can be combined with other solutions to achieve a stronger impact. Solutions in boxes 7 and 8 might need intervention by a Champion to improve the ease of implementation. Finally, solutions in box 9 are not good candidates for adoption.

# Conduct Experimental Trials

Experimental trials in the Analyze phase were primarily focused on screening out insignificant $x$s and finding the critical $x$s. Now that you have more direction with the potential solutions, you'll probably need to refine your knowledge of the critical $x$s before proceeding with pilot trials and a specific solution Implementation Plan.

## Simulations

We introduced Monte Carlo and discrete simulations in the Analyze phase (Chapter 16). The first step was to model the As-Is process and identify bottlenecks and sensitivity to critical $x$s. Using simulations, you can manipulate the critical $x$s to see how they impact the overall process. If one process step has large variation, the simulation can examine the impact of reducing that variability or adding additional resources.

If the results of the simulation are positive, you can seek solutions to reduce the variability of the process step. Of course, the solutions will still require validation prior to pilot trials of the revised process. For more complex analysis, simulations can be combined with DOE methods to identify the solutions with the greatest impact.

## Mathematical Models

Well-designed experiments extract concrete evidence of the $x$-$Y$ relationships and provide clean data for defining $Y = f(x)$. Once again, DOE is the answer. Specifically, you can use Response Surface Methods to examine for responses that have curvature and/or interaction effects.

Let's look at an example of trying to adjust the friction index of a brake lining. The goal is to center the friction index on a target of 25 with minimal variation. Three critical *x*s were identified in the Analyze Phase: Temperature, Time, and Pressure.

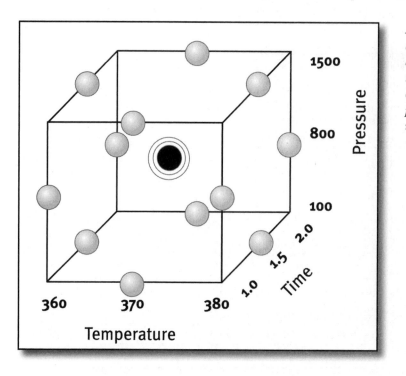

*A Box-Behnken Design is chosen for the response surface design setup. This design incorporates three levels of each factor and three center points—a total of 15 combinations.*

The use of the Box-Behnken Design provides clean data, free of correlation between input factors, while providing the necessary trial combinations to establish higher-order quadratic and interaction terms in the equation.

| RunOrder | Design Combinations | | | Test Results | | | Friction Index | |
| | Temperature | Time | Pressure | F1 | F2 | F3 | Mean | StDev |
|---|---|---|---|---|---|---|---|---|
| 1 | 370 | 1.5 | 800 | 25 | 23 | 21 | 23.0 | 2.00 |
| 2 | 380 | 1.5 | 1500 | 20 | 21 | 20 | 20.3 | 0.58 |
| 3 | 360 | 1.5 | 1500 | 45 | 24 | 39 | 36.0 | 10.82 |
| 4 | 370 | 1.5 | 800 | 21 | 20 | 22 | 21.0 | 1.00 |
| 5 | 370 | 1 | 100 | 12 | 25 | 13 | 16.7 | 7.23 |
| 6 | 380 | 1.5 | 100 | 20 | 21 | 17 | 19.3 | 2.08 |
| 7 | 360 | 1.5 | 100 | 29 | 37 | 34 | 33.3 | 4.04 |
| 8 | 370 | 1 | 1500 | 15 | 15 | 19 | 16.3 | 2.31 |
| 9 | 360 | 2 | 800 | 42 | 40 | 38 | 40.0 | 2.00 |
| 10 | 360 | 1 | 800 | 30 | 25 | 16 | 23.7 | 7.09 |
| 11 | 370 | 2 | 100 | 35 | 33 | 31 | 33.0 | 2.00 |
| 12 | 380 | 1 | 800 | 10 | 15 | 10 | 11.7 | 2.89 |
| 13 | 370 | 1.5 | 800 | 19 | 21 | 28 | 22.7 | 4.73 |
| 14 | 380 | 2 | 800 | 26 | 29 | 26 | 27.0 | 1.73 |
| 15 | 370 | 2 | 1500 | 32 | 29 | 29 | 30.0 | 1.73 |

*The 15 combinations in the Box-Behnken matrix include settings at three levels for each factor and multiple center points. The trials are run in random order to guard against correlating other "noise factor" effects with the experimental factor effects.*

# State the Y = f(x)

Once a prediction equation is developed, optimization methods or Monte Carlo simulations can direct the team to optimal conditions for the process. For our friction index example, three samples were tested for each trial (F1, F2, and F3). The mean and standard deviation for friction index were analyzed using Regression Analysis.

*The low p-Values from the regression analysis identify terms that should be included in the equation.*

**Estimated Regression Coefficients for Mean**

| Term | Coef | SE Coef | T | P |
|---|---|---|---|---|
| Constant | 22.2222 | 0.8752 | 25.390 | 0.000 |
| Temperature | -6.8333 | 0.5360 | -12.749 | 0.000 |
| Time | 7.7083 | 0.5360 | 14.382 | 0.000 |
| Pressure | 0.0417 | 0.5360 | 0.078 | 0.941 |
| Temperature*Temperature | 3.3056 | 0.7889 | 4.190 | 0.009 |
| Time*Time | 0.0556 | 1.7889 | 0.070 | 0.947 |
| Pressure*Pressure | 1.7222 | 0.7889 | 2.183 | 0.081 |
| Temperature*Time | -0.2500 | 0.7580 | -0.330 | 0.755 |
| Temperature*Pressure | -0.4167 | 0.7580 | -0.550 | 0.606 |
| Time*Pressure | -0.6667 | 0.7580 | -0.880 | 0.419 |
| S = 1.516 | R-Sq = 98.7% | | R-Sq(adj) = 96.5% | |

The regression model is reduced to the significant terms and a prediction equation is written in uncoded terms (i.e., actual units) for temperature and time.

$$\text{YMean} = 4605.41 - 24.208*\text{Temp} + 0.031786*\text{Temp2} + 15.4167*\text{Time}$$

Performing regression analysis on the standard deviation for each trial showed that temperature and time were significant terms. Interaction and quadratic terms were not statistically significant and not included in the equation.

$$S = 85.1263 - 0.208436*Temp - 3.01521*Time$$

## Contour Plots

The contour plot for the average friction index, following, shows curvature from the quadratic Temperature term. The contour line at 25 shows the multiple combinations of Temperature and Time that can be used to set the process mean on target. The contour plot for standard deviation shows a linear relationship, with lower variability in the upper right-hand corner of the plot.

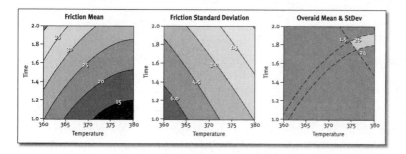

*Contour plots can graph equations for varying levels of two factors, with the response variable shown in the contour regions.*

By overlaying contour plots, the region of most interest is highlighted—on target with low standard deviation. This technique is handy with two dominant factors, but more complicated with multiple critical factors.

## Optimization

Optimization routines use linear algebra or more complex search methods to determine the best settings of factor levels to meet performance criteria. Comprehensive statistical software packages can seamlessly optimize the settings after analysis of designed experiments. Upwards of 20 $Y$ responses can be optimized with upwards of 20 input factors with relative ease.

Verification trials should always be run to confirm the output of the optimizer before proceeding to pilot trials.

*Optimization of responses using Minitab™ quickly determines the best settings for each factor to meet the specified responses. This optimization recommends Temperature at 380 degrees and Time at 1.8514 minutes to average 25 and minimize variability.*

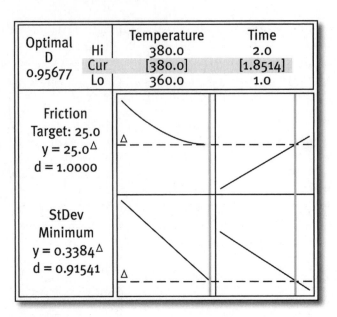

## Monte Carlo Simulation

Monte Carlo Simulation uses fundamental models incorporating variability in factors to generate results based on the $Y = f(x)$ equations. Input factor levels can be varied with realistic distributions, decision rules, and constraints to simulate the real process. Many simulation packages also include search methods to pinpoint optimal conditions based on the models.

*This output from Crystal Ball® software compares two feasible solutions to meet the average friction index. Input Temperatures and Times were varied through specified input distributions to simulate process operating conditions.*

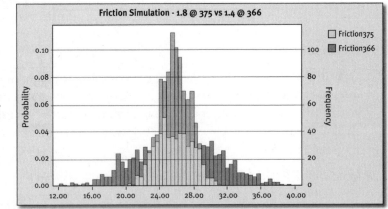

## DOE Methods for Multiple Solutions

DOE can also be used to evaluate multiple solutions to a problem on a small scale prior to piloting the solutions. If multiple individuals are working in the process, DOE combinations can be divided amongst them to match the design combinations.

As shown by the following table, each solution is placed in the design matrix as a factor, with the levels set at either adopting (New) or not adopting (Current) the solution. The advantage of the DOE, versus trying one factor at a time, is that each solution has been tried multiple times in combination with other solutions.

| Combo | Solution A | Solution B | Solution C | Solution D | Repeat % |
|-------|-----------|-----------|-----------|-----------|----------|
| 1 | Current | Current | Current | Current | 18.4 |
| 2 | New | Current | Current | New | 9.3 |
| 3 | Current | New | Current | New | 13.7 |
| 4 | New | New | Current | Current | 20.2 |
| 5 | Current | Current | New | New | 9.8 |
| 6 | New | Current | New | Current | 15.1 |
| 7 | Current | New | New | Current | 19.7 |
| 8 | New | New | New | New | 10.8 |

*Four proposed solutions were compared in eight combinations via a designed experiment. The levels for each solution were to stay with the current or implement the new solution.*

Example: A project team was working to reduce the number of repeat calls from 18 to 8 percent at its customer service centers. In the Improve phase, the team identified four independent solutions that would require varying levels of training and resources to implement.

A designed experiment was created to evaluate the potential solutions in eight total trials. Customer service representatives at one of the centers were divided into eight groups and the eight combinations of solutions were tried for three weeks.

The results showed that one solution reduced repeat calls by 7 percent, while another increased repeat calls by 3 percent. The other two solutions had smaller, but positive impacts on reducing repeat calls. Two of the solutions were implemented and the goal was reached.

## The Least You Need to Know

◆ There are many techniques to generate solutions—generate first, critically evaluate second.

◆ Structured innovation techniques can help you find specific solutions to difficult problems or contradictions.

◆ A nine-square Ease/Impact Matrix helps you visualize which solutions are best and ready to implement.

◆ Design of Experiments methods and simulations can provide breakthroughs by defining $Y = f(x)$ equations that optimize process settings.

◆ Objective criteria are required to select the best solutions and ensure the permanence of the solutions.

◆ *Always* verify your results and run verification trials.

# Implement the Solution

## In This Chapter

◆ Deciding on the best solution

◆ Anticipating what could go wrong

◆ Revisiting your stakeholders

◆ Designing your Implementation Plan

If your problem is stubborn, complex, and related to errors or defects, you've used more Six Sigma-like tools to get to the bottom of what's causing it. And you've identified a variety of potential solutions. However, not all possible solutions are equal. Some will work better for you than others. But how will you know? This is tricky ground.

You'll have to pilot your potential solutions to figure out which one is best. Which ones can be implemented with the least effort and expense, yet return the greatest benefits. As usual, you'll anticipate problems and issues, count the costs, and disable the risks. Then you'll develop an Implementation Plan that will ensure you enact all the changes you've come up with to improve your process.

# Select the Solution

All your work in Analyze has led you to the real root cause of your performance issue or problem—and it's enabled you to generate a set of potential solutions. Now you have to make a choice: run with one best solution and leave the others behind. But consider certain factors before you do this. What is your budget for implementation? Do you need new technology? How much time will the changes take? What are the political ramifications of the change?

## Ease, Permanence, Impact, and Cost

Selecting solutions isn't quite as easy as it sounds. Each solution will require an Implementation Plan to get it in place, and possibly some additional resources. To ensure that you rationally select your solution, develop good criteria for evaluating your options. Typical criteria include the following:

**Ease of implementation:** Will the solution be readily accepted by stakeholders? Is the path long and difficult, or is it a Just Do It? Are technical, cultural, or political barriers in the way?

**Permanence of the solution:** Is your solution merely an interim solution to mask the symptoms, or a real corrective action driving to the root cause? Is your solution robust (takes a licking and keeps on ticking)? Are there critical concerns or assumptions that might render the solution useless? Does the solution depend on a key person to keep it intact?

**Impact on the metrics and savings:** Will your solution achieve the goal of the project? What is the impact on savings? What other benefits will result from the solution? Can the solution be replicated to other processes?

**Cost of implementation:** Is the solution low cost to implement and maintain? Is capital approval needed for the solution? Will production or sales suffer as the solution is implemented?

Other specific criteria are as follows: Is safety a concern? Will regulatory or legal review be required? Is the solution fair and ethical?

You can embody these criteria in an EPIC Solution Matrix. That's E for Ease, P for Permanence, I for Impact, and C for Cost. The example that follows shows you what a completed EPIC Solution Matrix might look like.

| Potential Solution | Ease | Permanence | Impact | Cost | E*P*I*C | Critical Concerns/Other |
|---|---|---|---|---|---|---|
| Change Mail Route | 5 | 2 | 2 | 5 | 100 | Low Impact - Just Do It |
| Revise Letters | 3 | 3 | 4 | 4 | 144 | Legal Approval |
| Reassign Work | 2 | 4 | 3 | 2 | 48 | Departmental Changes |
| Customer Training | 2 | 5 | 5 | 2 | 100 | Need to Construct eCourse |
| CSR Training | 3 | 3 | 3 | 3 | 81 | 600+ to Train |

*Rating solutions on a five-point scale, then multiplying (E × P × I × C) gives you the intelligence you need to prioritize possible solutions.*

# Selecting Competing Solutions

Some solutions go head to head with each other and need a comparison to determine which is the best choice. Several methods are available for this type of comparison, but the Pugh Matrix is most commonly used.

As shown by the following example, the Pugh Matrix compares competing solutions against a set of evaluation criteria. Each solution is compared to a reference (usually the current situation)—as the same (S), better (+), or worse (–) for each criterion.

| Critieria | | Reference (Fred's Boat) | Wayne's Boat | Fish on Shore | New Bass Boat | New Power Boat | New Pontoon Boat | Canoe (Borrow Jim's) | Rent Boat - Power | Rent Boat - Pontoon |
|---|---|---|---|---|---|---|---|---|---|---|
| | Big Fish | S | - | + | S | S | S | + | + |
| | Find Fishing Spot Fast | S | - | + | + | - | - | - | + |
| | Catch Fish Fast | S | - | + | S | S | S | S | S |
| | Launch Time | S | + | S | S | - | + | + | + |
| | Travel Time | + | - | S | + | S | - | S | S |
| | Keep Alive | S | S | + | S | + | - | S | S |
| | Total Time on Lake | S | S | + | + | S | - | + | + |
| | Make Spouse Happy | S | S | - | - | + | S | + | + |
| | Cost | S | + | - | - | - | S | - | - |
| | **Total +'s** | 1 | 2 | 5 | 3 | 2 | 1 | 4 | 5 |
| | **Total -'s** | 0 | 4 | 2 | 2 | 3 | 4 | 2 | 1 |

Header row: **Solutions**

*Wayne and Fred used a Pugh Matrix to decide what type of boat was best for fishing tournaments.*

One advantage of the one-on-one comparisons with the Pugh Matrix is the potential generation of a hybrid solution, which, in Wayne and Fred's case, is not the best way to go. Other methods are also used, including criteria–solution ratings similar to Cause-and-Effect Matrices, and pairwise comparisons.

# Pilot the Solution

Now that you've chosen the appropriate solution, or combination thereof, it's time to turn it loose—try it out and see if it works. Think of those warning labels you see on consumer products urging you to test the product on a small area before applying it to the entire surface. You need to try your solution in a limited environment to validate that it works.

If it does work, great. Go implement your solution on a full scale. If you selected a solution that doesn't work, then you can quickly pilot another solution, returning to your Solution Selection Matrix and picking the next one in line.

Let's talk about what a pilot is and what it isn't. A pilot is a small-scale test of the new change applied to the real process, not a hypothetical or simulated process. You want to find out if real people taking real actions with real machinery will really yield the changes you desire in your output metric $(Y)$.

Taking this seriously, you create a pilot Implementation Plan and train your operators on the new process. This pilot plan doesn't need to be fancy or elaborate; we'll save that for the final Implementation Plan you'll assemble later. However, your plan should be detailed enough to ensure the new changes are executed properly. Remember that you're testing your new Implementation Plan in addition to your new process.

> **Performance Pitfall**
>
> Don't ruin a good solution with a bad Implementation Plan. Sometimes the solution can be good, but the plan to implement it is shoddy. Make sure you know the difference.

The pilot is not complete unless you can reliably measure the outcome of the new improvement. Specifically, you need to collect good data, and enough of it, to ensure you've impacted your $Y$ metric, or expected process outcome.

# Evaluate Pilot Performance

Evaluating the performance of your piloted solution is very similar to the way you evaluated the performance of your process at the outset of your project. Recall that the most important metric is your primary *Y*—the improved outcome you desire. But you also have your secondary and consequential metrics to evaluate.

Secondary metrics are performance outcomes that could be affected (positively) by improving your primary metric. Making the water colder also makes it taste better— that kind of thing. Consequential metrics, on the other hand, are negative outcomes that happen by virtue of your improving your primary metric. Making the water too cold causes brain freeze.

By using the same metrics you've been watching all along (primary, secondary, and consequential), you can directly compare your new process with your old process. Hopefully, you'll find a big improvement, or at least an improvement large enough to satisfy your predicted (or needed) improvement level.

One simple but powerful tool you can use to make this comparison is a Box Plot, which visually displays two performance samples next to each other. In the following example, a team tested its solution for increasing the flip angle of a V-belt to solve an assembly line problem affecting about 1 in 20 cars. The tested solution was effective and solved an important reliability issue for the customer.

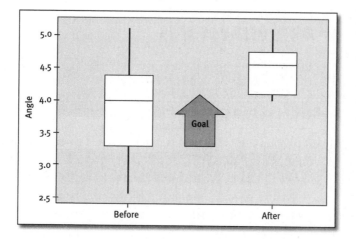

*After the solution was piloted, the team found that the mean flip angle was increased by 0.7 degrees, and variability was decreased by 42 percent, making the V-belt more stable.*

In some cases, you may be disappointed. You may find that the data associated with your new process is not much different than the data from your old process. All that work and nothing! Well, not so fast. First, you have to make sure the new solution is the right solution. Second, you have to make sure the pilot solution was implemented properly according to the plan, and that the plan itself is sound.

Third, sometimes the improvement you were seeking turns out to be too ambitious and a smaller improvement is all you can make without completely redesigning your process using DFSS (Design for Six Sigma) or other innovation techniques.

Fourth and finally, you can't really conclude that your improvement is significant without more verification using such statistical tools as a $t$-test. In Chapter 15, we covered the $t$-test formula and used it to determine if population means are significantly different.

Here you would use a $t$-test to test your hypothesis that your before-and-after results are statistically different or not, of course within some level of certainty, or confidence (p-Value). Even though you might have a difference that is practically significant, you might find that your sample size is too small to determine statistical significance. Or, conversely, you might have achieved statistical significance, but the difference is not meaningful in a practical sense.

Obviously you have to keep refining your solutions, piloting them, and testing their implementation until you are sure you have the right solution in place—and the right plan for implementing that solution.

# Identify Risks and Countermeasures

Now that you've chosen and piloted a solution to your problem, and proven that the new performance level is better than the old, you want to make sure your revised process can be maintained over time. You want to make sure you know your new process can be reliably adopted as the way the organization does business.

There are many reasons why this may not be the case, so you want to question what can go wrong, and revisit your FMEA (Failure Mode and Effects Analysis). If you've been reading this book in sequence, you know that you should develop and update your FMEA throughout the DMAIC process. Here in the Improve phase, you will use the FMEA tool to anticipate what could go wrong as you implement your new process.

First, you'll list all the potential ways your project could go wrong. "All the ways" does not mean you include the possibility of alien life arriving on the planet and disrupting your whole operation. But it does mean you include all the *reasonable* things that could go wrong.

Once these are listed, each potential failure mode is rated for its severity (how bad it would be), how likely it is to occur, and how easy or not it would be to detect. For instance, aliens would probably be easy to detect, but not necessarily! We gave you details of how to complete a FMEA in Chapter 13, so go there to see how it's done in more detail.

The key is to identify your top implementation risks, then develop countermeasures to reduce those risks. For instance, if the night shift nurse is known to never fill out checklists, and your new process involves filling one out, then you have to address this. Make sure the nurse's supervisor gets involved, or find some other way to ensure compliance.

Sometimes your FMEA can cause you to second-guess your solution altogether. This is okay. Better to redesign your solution now than to implement it full force only to experience a disaster. Look at your FMEA and decide if the expected benefits outweigh the risks involved. If so, great; if not, you might have to go back and reconfigure your Implementation Plan—or even make changes to your new process that are less risky to implement.

# Develop Implementation Plan

Now that you've tested your pilot solution, and it works, and you've updated your FMEA, it's time to roll out your solution to its full scale. In theory, this should be easy since your solution has been tried and tested; in reality, you'll encounter some challenges in getting many people (possibly in many locations) to adopt and adhere to the new way.

The next few chapters cover the all-important Control phase of DMAIC. These chapters will give you a lot of tools and knowledge for transitioning the new process from the project leader (Belt) to the Process Owner. For now, you'll have to worry about developing a full-scale Implementation Plan that documents all the many actions required, when they are to be done, and by whom.

The following is an example Implementation Plan for a project solution. Note that the plan designates the actions required, who is responsible, how the actions get completed, and what the schedule is. Many times, you can use standard project management tools and software to document your Implementation Plan and manage its rollout.

*This is a simple example of a solution Implementation Plan. If your project and solution are more complex, your plan will be more complex, too.*

| What (Action) | Who (Owner) | How (Process) | When (Schedule) | | | | |
|---|---|---|---|---|---|---|---|
| | | | Week 1<br>M T W T F | Week 2<br>M T W T F | Week 3<br>M T W T F | Week 4<br>M T W T F | Week 5<br>M T W T F |
| Update Process Map | Black Belt | - Update Map and Post New Version | ■ | | | | |
| Produce Final SOP's | Project Team | - Make Electronic SOP's<br>- Print for Training | ■ | | | | |
| Train Business on New Process | Project Team | - Use Simulated Process with Real Forms or Steps | | ■ | | | |
| Train Connecting Functions | Project Team | - Use Simulated Process with Real Forms or Steps--Focus on Inputs/Outputs | | | ■ | | |
| Schedule Operating Reviews | Project Leader | - Create Forms for Key Measures<br>- Pre-build Templates for Reports | ■ | | | | |
| Conduct Kick-off Meeting | Process Owner | - Lock in Dates with Stakeholders<br>- Identify "Must Attends" and "Optional" | | | ■ | | |
| Celebrate First Successful Unit/Service Delivered | Project Team | - Plan Party to Suit Budget | | | | | ■ |
| Shut Down Old Process | Process Owner | - Physically Stop Old Process | | | | | ■ |
| Update/Execute Communications Plan | Project Team | - Send eMail, Post Notes, Town Hall Meeting, etc. Give Out Toys! | ■ | ■ | ■ | ■ | ■ |

# Update Stakeholder Analysis

Remember, it's possible you'll still have certain stakeholders sitting on the fence, doubting that the new change will ever come to pass. In some cases, they've been waiting—dare we say even to watch your project fail. Therefore, you'll be wise to revisit your Stakeholder Analysis and update it, or create a new one for the rollout of your project, especially if you expect to run into any resistance.

# The Training Plan

You'll also want to train all the operators or people involved in the new process, and you'll want this to be part of your Implementation Plan. Who needs to be trained and how? When? What training methods will you use to ensure that the new knowledge and procedures are reinforced? Training is about getting people to change their behaviors, and this isn't always easy. Having a plan that ensures the new knowledge is learned and applied is the best way.

# Systems and Supports

Change and the ongoing maintenance of a new process is best managed with the help of systems and supports. For example, if the process for scheduling service calls changes, you can support that change by modifying the scheduling system (software). If the process for equipment changeover changes, you might want to implement some form of Mistake Proofing, like a tray with set indentations for your changeover tools. Of course, Kanban systems are great for signaling and reinforcing new behaviors associated with new process changes.

## Communicate

As usual, you have to communicate the new changes to all stakeholders and, preferably, the entire organization. This is your chance to blow your own horn, so don't be shy. The more you broadcast the new change, the more likely it is that people will adopt and practice it. Publish your project story in your company newsletter; talk about it in staff meetings; recognize and reward team members for making the change. Build the Lean Six Sigma culture!

# Conduct Tollgate Review

Before moving into the Control phase, you'll want to conduct a Tollgate Review—just as you do after every phase of DMAIC. If your organization is serious about Lean Six Sigma, and is deploying it on a large scale, this is the required discipline. After all, you're now at the stage when your process change is no longer on the white board or in the test tube. It's final, and officially the new way you're going to do business.

If a Lean Six Sigma Project can be compared to a wedding, then this is the time to speak or forever hold your peace. So who exactly are you waiting to hear from then? Bring your stakeholders back together, especially the Project Champion, Process Owner, Master Black Belt, and anyone else who's affected by the change. Or anyone else who will be needed to implement and sustain the change.

You'll want to take your stakeholders through the milestones of your project using a PowerPoint presentation, or the like. As you do, cover these points:

◆ Has your problem or objective statement changed? (Answer: It needs to change; you discovered it needs to during Improve.)

◆ Describe your experiment(s). (Answer: Provide an overview of DOE, Simulation, other statistical analyses used.)

◆ What were the statistical and practical conclusions from your experiment(s)? (Answer: State the impact on your Primary Metric, significance levels, and contribution of each factor studied, including factors found not to be significant.)

◆ Summarize which $x$s you have selected, based on your analysis, to provide a solution to the problem. (Answer: Include data and graphical/statistical analysis to support your selection of $x$s.)

◆ What possible solutions did you consider? (Answer: Refer to Solution Matrix.)

◆ Do your solutions drive to lasting improvement? (Answer: Indicate if solutions are corrective—directed at the root cause of the problem—or interim band-aids.)

◆ What did you learn from the Pilot test? What is the full-scale implementation plan? (Answer: Pilot was evaluated using Capability Analysis or equivalent, and Implementation Plan designates who, what, when.)

◆ What had the performance been, by week, for your primary metric? (Answer: Refer to Control Chart, Time Series Plot, or Pareto Chart.)

◆ If you have completed the Improve phase, what are your conclusions? (Answer: We know exactly what we have to do to fix the problem or process.)

◆ Are all data fields in your project tracking tool current with your most recent project progress? (Answer: Hopefully yes. If not, enter data.)

◆ Does it look like you will have any difficulties in implementing your solution? (Answer: Discuss barriers with Process Owner and Champion and revise Stakeholder Analysis.)

◆ Is your project still on track to meet the scheduled completion date? (Answer: If yes, great; if no, remove roadblocks, accelerate pace, lead, revisit Stakeholder Analysis.)

◆ Has your financial forecast changed by more than 20 percent? If yes, what is the new validated forecast? (Answer: With the finance rep, we updated the project forecast.)

If you've accomplished these points with substance, then you'll be ready to move on to the Control phase. Hopefully, the stakeholders at your presentation will point out any limitations or missing pieces in your Implementation Plan, if there are any. And they will help you fill these gaps and update your plan accordingly.

## The Least You Need to Know

◆ Every problem usually has more than one solution. Develop options, then select the best one based on time, risk, and cost to implement.

◆ The only way you'll know if your solution will work is to test it. Therefore, do this to confirm you can implement your solution on a full scale.

◆ What are the risks involved with implementing your solution? Know these and have a plan for minimizing or neutralizing them.

◆ Pay attention to your stakeholders—the people you need to successfully implement your solution, and the people who will be affected by your new process.

◆ Make sure you have training and communication plans in place to ensure the new process is known and faithfully adopted by all.

# Chapter 20

# Develop the Control Plan

## In This Chapter

- ◆ The road map for Control
- ◆ Mistakes are not an option
- ◆ Updating your Process Flow
- ◆ Writing good procedures
- ◆ Securing commitment to excellence

Feeling done? Not so fast. The method is not called DMAI. There's a C in DMAIC to remind you that your improvement project isn't done until you've installed mechanisms for holding your gains. The natural state of any process is decay, so you have to fight this tendency with deliberate actions to lock in the gains you've made. Doing this keeps your process humming at its new and improved level.

In this chapter, we'll cover the initial process and tools you need to sustain your gains. Since you've completed the hard work of DMAI, and since you'll surely be pulled in another direction to solve another problem, you have to insist that you first seal up the deal, and do what you have to do to keep your good results from eroding away.

# Introducing Control

Before you launch into all the specifics of Control, you can see the big picture, shown here. This is the macro road map for the Control phase—it shows you what you need to accomplish before you can say you're truly a control freak. That's one who refuses to believe the gains one has made will be maintained by others in one's absence.

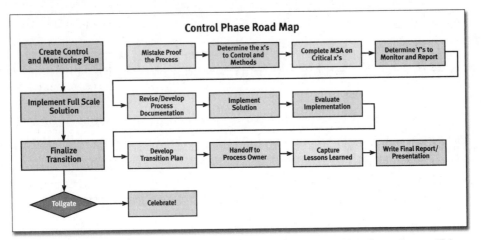

*This is your road map for moving through the key steps of Control. Follow this and you will be successful in locking in the gains you've worked so hard to make.*

Establishing sufficient process control will require discipline on your part, and support from your Project Champion. After all, results usually don't begin to decay immediately. Only after time passes do your performance advancements become challenged by the natural course of erosion. Just remember: it's not a matter of if, but when.

So unless you want to fight the same battle all over again, take note of the hard lessons others have learned. Take note of the Control road map and do what it tells you to do before moving on to the next big problem or performance-improvement challenge.

# Control *x*, Monitor *Y*

A huge part of any Lean Six Sigma project is discovering the critical few *x*s that drive your *Y* metric of interest. Therefore, your work in the Control phase begins by listing the *x*s you've found to be so important; these are the objects of the Control Plan we will show you how to build at the end of this chapter.

Yes, you will want to monitor your $Y$ and make sure it continues at its new level. But the true essence of control is in monitoring the $x$s that affect your $Y$. That's why people who've lost weight due to diet and exercise are well advised to keep watching their food intake and workout routines, rather than just stepping on the scale every day.

Here's a good place to revisit the Measurement System Analysis (MSA) tool we discussed earlier in Chapter 11. In the Measure phase, you used MSA to make sure you had an adequate measurement system for measuring $Y$. Now, you'll want to make sure your critical $x$s are measured with the same confidence of repeatability and reproducibility.

Take a lesson from one team that determined viscosity was the critical $x$ causing too much variation in coating weight $(Y)$. A MSA of the viscosity measurement found that 80 percent of the variation was due to measurement error, making it impossible to know what the true viscosity was. Technicians were actually making viscosity variation worse by adjusting the process based on faulty measurements!

The viscosity measurement was improved to only 20 percent of the total variation by adding temperature control to the test device. The project was a roaring success, meeting the project goal of reducing coating weight variance by 50 percent.

## An Ounce of Prevention

The simplest and most elegant control method is called Mistake Proofing—which means making it impossible, or nearly impossible, to make a mistake. Why incur the cost of inspection when you can remove the need for inspection via Mistake Proofed system designs? It's far less costly to prevent a problem from occurring than to add another inspection step.

Years back, in the old days of the typewriter, a major daily newspaper did a DMAIC project to reduce spelling errors. Of course, the initial thought was to add another proofreading step. Proofreading, editing, audits, and approvals are all just another name for inspection.

But this was an enlightened project team, and they pushed for a Mistake Proofing approach. The solution was to convert the process from using typewriters to using PCs, which at the time could be equipped with an early form of the spell checker we all take for granted today. Back then, however, the spell-check function was a breakthrough Mistake Proofing solution.

**Lean Six Sigma Wisdom**

Mistake Proofing (a.k.a. poke-yoke) was coined by the Japanese engineer Shigeo Shingo, who wanted to describe the technique of changing the process to prevent mistakes from occurring.

Another example comes to us from manufacturing, where a project reduced the downtime involved in changing over a packaging line to a different carton size. The solution included Mistake Proofing the machine parts that had to be changed out. Prior to Mistake Proofing, one could put the part in backwards and not discover the problem until the line was restarted. The Mistake Proofing solution was to add a locator pin on one side of the part so the part would only fit in one way—the right way.

Take time with your project team brainstorming how to Mistake Proof your solution. Review the list of process changes you are making. List the ways the new solution could be done incorrectly, and recognize that it's natural for people to make mistakes. Then consult Mistake Proofing resources to find the best way for ensuring your new process operates as intended.

For now you can examine the following table, which gives you some Mistake Proofing principles, and examples of their application.

| Mistake Proofing Principle | Examples |
| --- | --- |
| Orientation and Placement | The use of templates, such as a plastic frame people use to affix mailing labels at the correct place on each box for shipping. |
| Dispensers | Hand-soap dispensers that supply the correct amount of soap per squeeze. Metal scoops at McDonald's for filling french fry bags. |
| Lock-ins/Lock-outs | Lotte World theme park in Korea sewing shut the pants pockets of employees so they don't stand around with their hands in their pockets. |
| Control Physical Space | Chains that border off waiting lines, such as those at airport security. |
| Detect Presence or Absence | Use of floodlights while working at night. Taking one's blood pressure before seeing the doctor. |

| Mistake Proofing Principle | Examples |
|---|---|
| Use of Unusual Physical Attributes | Beepers on ATMs to warn customers they left their card in the machine. |
| Improve Visibility | A major medical center uses colored lines on the floor to direct patients to different areas of the sprawling hospital. |
| Go/No-Go Gauging | Amusement park height gauges that make sure someone is big enough for the ride. |
| Baiting | Offering customers a free gift or benefit when filling out a comment card. |
| Interlocks | Similar to lock-ins and lock-outs, this adds another step to release the lock, such as the use of a key. |
| Task Substitution | A bank requires tellers to check a box indicating customers' eye color to ensure the advent of making eye contact. A press operator has to activate the machine by pressing two buttons, one with each hand, thereby ensuring hands are not in danger of the operation. |
| Kits | Surgeons are provided with all the necessary instruments for particular operations in a kit. |
| Arrangement | Placing gardening tools on a pegboard so they can be easily located. |
| Counting and Ordering | Take-a-number systems at deli stores. Sewell Cadillac places color-coded numbered markers on cars as they arrive to ensure first come, first served. |
| Layout Mats | Child-care centers use layout mats to indicate where toys should be returned after their use. |
| Checklists | Instead of grouping physical items, checklists group information. Blank spaces on checklists indicate the need for action. |
| Make Information Stand Out | A trucking company uses egg-crate-like partitions in boxes to make it clear that the correct quantity was packed. |

# Update Your Process Flow

After you've made your process changes, you need a new and improved Process Flow or Value Stream Map to reflect those changes. Surely you can't control your new process if you can't see it or don't have it documented.

Therefore, revise your Process Flow (Value Stream Map or Process Flow Diagram) to reflect the new reality. By having both a before and after depiction of the process, you have an excellent way to educate stakeholders about what's been changed.

The updated diagram also serves as an excellent training tool for any new people coming into the process. And if that's not enough, your updated flow chart or Value Stream Map helps identify remaining opportunities for future project work.

*Note that lead time for this process is 23.6 days, and the value-add time of 188 seconds. This was how the process looked before it was improved.*

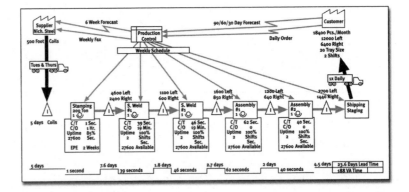

*Note the new lead time of 5 days, and value-add time of 166 seconds, for the new and improved process.*

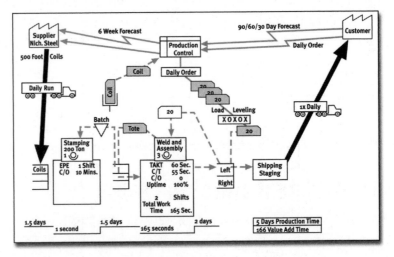

## Update Your FMEA

Remember Failure Mode and Effects Analysis, or FMEA? You do if you read Chapter 13 and completed a FMEA for your process in the Analyze phase. Here in Control, you need to update your FMEA because you've changed your process. By doing so, certain risks may have become less important while other risks may have become more important. And you may need to add new risks you didn't have before based on your new process changes.

As shown in the matrix that follows, the "Recommended Actions" section of the FMEA is a history of the work conducted. Of course, you want to make sure your updated FMEA shows the work actually completed (Responsibility and Completion Date column). Then you want to list the Actions Taken and calculate your new Risk Priority Numbers (RPNs) for all your risks. Remember, RPNs are calculated by multiplying the SOD ratings (S*O*D).

| Recommended Action(s) | Responsibilty and Completion Date | Action Results | | | | |
|---|---|---|---|---|---|---|
| | | Actions Taken | Severity | Occurrence | Detection | Risk Priority Number |
| What are the actions for reducing the severity and occurrence of the identified risk, and for improving its detection? | Who is responsible for the recommended action(s)? | List the completed actions that are included in the re-calculated RPN. Include the implementation date for any changes. | What is the new severity? | What is the new process capability? | Are the detection limits improved? | Recompute RPN after actions are complete. |
| Add auto-sensor for voltage/current | B. Carlson 6/8/07 | Sensor added, software up-graded 7/7/07 | 5 | 3 | 5 | 75 |
| Establish Forecast and Auto-ship with supplier | C.S. Soo 9/2/07 | Auto-ship system in-place 10/1/07 | 7 | 2 | 3 | 42 |

*Revisit your Failure Mode and Effects Analysis to see if you still have the same risks you did before you made your process improvement. Take action on any risks with higher RPNs.*

# Be Consistent and Standardize

Actions don't happen on a consistent basis unless you build a system for making them happen on a consistent basis. That's why most companies have standard operating procedures (SOPs), otherwise just called procedures, or policies and procedures. In any case, most Lean Six Sigma improvements require a change in SOPs that, when followed, allow the new process to operate reliably over time.

Of course, Mistake Proofing is the ultimate remedy, because then you don't have to rely on SOPs to guide the actions of people, machines, processes, and systems. But often the Mistake Proofing solution has yet to be discovered, and the best you can do is develop good SOPs, then train people to adhere to them over time.

To help you, here are some tips on creating good SOPs:

♦ Build on existing SOPs. Modify and update them instead of inventing new ones. You'll simplify the rollout and maintenance of the SOP if it's part of an existing, healthy system.

♦ Write the procedures in brief, simple language. The test should be: "Can someone new to the area understand and follow the procedure?"

♦ Keep the detail at the appropriate level. Too much detail will make the document long and discourage its use. Too little detail will miss the key changes that need to be made to control your critical *x*s.

♦ Make liberal use of diagrams, flow charts, and digital photos. Remember the adage that a picture's worth a thousand words when you create your new SOPs.

♦ Include a mechanism for regularly updating your SOPs.

SOPs are your current best approach for performing your process and, as such, they're the repository of your knowledge (intellectual property) about how your process should work. When an organization's procedures are covered in dust and more than five years old, what does that say about its learning rate?

Preparing good SOPs is necessary but not sufficient. To state the obvious, they must be put into use—and we all know that humans tend to resist standards, especially in cultures that value and reward individualism. You'll have to overcome such resistance, so check out the following tips:

♦ Involve the people performing the procedure(s) to help create the new procedure(s). Remember that people like changing but just don't like being changed.

♦ Include the reason for the procedure in the SOP. Clarify what problem is solved by the new procedure by answering the question "Why is this important?"

♦ When people say the SOP stifles their creativity, push back. You don't want people doing something different just to be different. Work with folks to apply their creativity to new problems while applying the current best approach via the SOP.

◆ Create a simple and clear way for updating SOPs when data show a better way. The SOP should be a living document and always represent the current best knowledge about how to do the work.

◆ Incorporate the new SOP as the routine first step when investigating problems. The question should always be "Did we follow the SOP?" If not, why? If the SOP was followed and there's still a problem, what needs to change? This brings relevance to the SOP, reinforces its use, and provides a steady stream of updates to keep it a living document.

◆ Train people on the new SOP. Even experienced employees need to learn the new actions, steps, or methods. Focus your training on the critical aspects of the change. In your training plan, include a measurement by which you can determine how well the new SOP is used.

 **Performance Pitfall**

Don't expect everyone to learn everything in a single training session. Remember that most learning occurs on the job. Combine up-front training with job aids, on-the-job coaching, performance measurement, and follow-up training sessions.

# Plan for Control

Since you know process performance decays over time, you'll have to develop a plan that determines exactly how you'll keep your critical inputs ($x$s) and outputs ($Y$s) in control. You guessed it—we call this a Control Plan. Not a fancy name, but quite fitting nonetheless. Your Control Plan is the glue that pulls together all the key aspects of keeping your process on track and performing as intended.

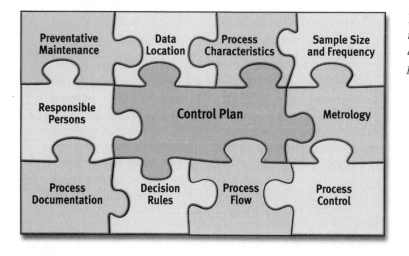

*Your Control Plan institutionalizes your new process and provides one-stop shopping for control information.*

The following table shows a small portion of a Control Plan (for baking crackers). In building your plan, you rely on the work you've done in Define, Measure, Analyze, and Improve. Your Process Map and your FMEA highlight the areas you'll need to control—while all your measurements and data studies (DOE, etc.) determine your operating windows and rational tolerances for your critical $x$s.

*This is a sample Control Plan for the baking of a cracker. It only shows one input and one output. Most Control Plans have about two outputs and six inputs.*

| ❶ Process Step | ❷ What's Controlled? | ❸ Input or Output? | ❹ Spec. Limits/ Requirements | ❺ Meas. Method | ❻ Control Method | ❼ Sample Size | ❽ Freq. | ❾ Who/What Measures? | ❿ Where Recorded | ⓫ Decision Rule/ Corrective Action | ⓬ SOP's |
|---|---|---|---|---|---|---|---|---|---|---|---|
| Bake | Bake Temp. | Input | 112 ± 3°C | Omega T/C Meter | PM Calib. | 100% | Weekly | Maint. Tech. | ASI | Adjust to Spec. | 9785-123 |
| | Thickness | Output | 195 ± 45nm | SP | SPC | 3 Sites/ Wafer | 1 Wafer/ Lot | Operator | Oracle | None | 9785-369 |

Let's walk through building a Control Plan, working from left to right across the table. In the example that follows, the project goal was to improve the percentage of crackers falling within their specification limits for thickness. The critical $x$ was determined to be baking temperature.

◆ Column 1 identifies the process step and should tie directly back to the Process Flow diagram.

◆ Column 2 identifies the metrics.

**Performance Pitfall**

Avoid monitoring too many items by focusing just on the critical xs and important Ys. Don't create more work for yourself than is necessary.

◆ Column 3 clarifies whether the metric is an input or an output for the process.

◆ Column 4 lists the target and tolerances for each metric.

◆ Column 5 clarifies what method is used to make the measurement.

◆ Column 6 identifies the method used to control the measure.

◆ Column 7 is the sample size. In our example, the sampling is 100 percent. In another case, a sample of 5 might be taken from a production process making 1,000 units an hour.

◆ Column 8 displays the sampling frequency. In this example, the input is measured weekly, and the output is measured at a rate of one wafer per lot.

◆ Column 9 is where you identify the important "who" that does the data collection.

◆ Column 10 identifies where the data will be recorded and stored. Often this is on a chart that is part of a visual controls display.

◆ Column 11 clarifies what action is required when an out-of-control situation is signaled in the data. More on this in the next chapter.

◆ Column 12 shows where the added details can be found for this control item. What documentation governs this control process?

Whew! Another plan made and more to do. That's the story of Lean Six Sigma: a never-ending journey toward perfection. Assuming you successfully lock in your gains on any one project, you'll soon be off to another. But not so fast; you still have to implement your Control Plan. Before you do, however, there's one more thing to do ….

You'll need to obtain the formal agreement and approval of your Lean Six Sigma Champion, Process Owner, and anyone else who's critical to the functioning of your new process. This is where the rubber meets the road when it comes to whether or not your process will stay in tip-top shape, or whether it will fall into bad health. So practice good management and leadership, and get it in writing.

| Approved by: | [Lean Six Sigma Black Belt] |
| Approved by: | [Lean Six Sigma Champion] |
| Approved by: | [Process Owner] |
| Approved by: | [Others as necessary] |

*Have key people sign off on your Control Plan. Better to get it in writing than to leave the continued maintenance of your hard work in jeopardy.*

## The Least You Need to Know

◆ Processes naturally decay. The purpose of the Control phase is to prevent this from occurring.

◆ Focus on ways to control the significant $x$s your project has identified. You'll still want to monitor $Y$ to ensure the gains are held, but $x$s are actionable and earlier indicators.

◆ Find as many Mistake Proofing solutions as you can, because Mistake Proofing is the surest and cheapest way to eliminate defects.

◆ Don't forget to update those Process Flow Diagrams and FMEAs. You want to leave the Process Owner with a picture of the new reality, and anticipate what could go wrong.

◆ It takes some work to do your standard operating procedures (SOPs) correctly, but they are essential when you find that the way a procedure is done is a critical $x$.

◆ Control Plans pull together all the elements of improvement sustainability into a cohesive whole. They are an important deliverable from the project team to the Process Owner.

# 21

# Use Control Charts

## In This Chapter

- ◆ Knowing when to let it go
- ◆ Calculating your limits
- ◆ Selecting the right chart
- ◆ Special Cause and Common Cause
- ◆ Outliers, shifts, trends, and cycles

Profound words were spoken when Yogi Berra said "You can see a lot by looking." When you want to understand how a process is behaving, Control Charts are the best way to look. Think of it this way. Data is how a process talks to us. Control Charts are the interpreter that translates that voice of the process into information we can use.

This chapter picks up with bringing the Control Plan (end of last chapter) to life using Control Charts. We'll show you why Control Charts are vital. We'll also show you a little bit about how to construct Control Charts, and how to interpret them. Based on this interpretation, you'll know how to sustain the wonderful improvements you've made.

# What Are Control Charts?

Control Charts tell you what you should expect from a process. They also tell you if something is wrong with the process so you can get it back on track. If you do have process variation, is it natural and expected, or is there something wrong that warrants special investigation?

Control Charts help a Process Owner break the bad habit of acting only on the most recent data point, which, of course, will almost always be different from the previous data point. Any grade-schooler can tell if the new number is better or worse than the old number. For example, sales yesterday were 35, and today they are 32. What does this tell you? It tells you that 32 is less than 35, but not why. The important question is not whether 32 is smaller than 35; the important question is "Has the process that produces the results changed?" The Control Chart enables you to really see if your process is in or out of control.

*This is an example of a stable process. Even though the sales numbers fluctuate over time, they do not do so beyond their expected variation.*

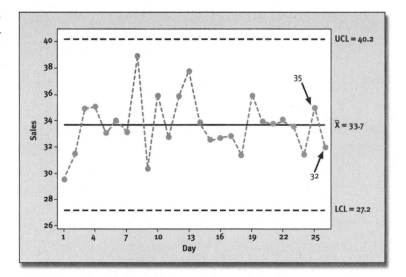

In the Control Chart, we've plotted the last 26 days of sales. Sales average 33.7 and seem to be stable around that average, because there are no data points beyond the control limits and no trends in the data. We expect the individual data points to fall between the upper control limit (UCL) of 40.2 and the lower control limit (LCL) of 27.2. Moving beyond our grade-school education, we can now see that there is no indication of a change in the process. No special action is required to investigate why 32 is less than 35. In fact, to do so would be a waste of time.

Control Charts tools tell us when to investigate what's changed and when to let it be. Think about that—a tool that helps you be more productive and not waste time. That's just what every Process Owner needs.

### Technically Speaking

There are many software applications you can use to create and monitor Control Charts. Some are devoted only to Control Charts, while others also include many other analytical/statistical functions. Some software even attaches directly to your process and gathers data automatically with no manual input, generates Control Charts, and even makes automatic adjustments in the process with no human involvement.

# Constructing Control Charts

Control Charts come in many varieties, but all Control Charts have some common features. The data is plotted in time order from left to right. A centerline is drawn to represent the calculated mean of the data. Each new data point is added as it is collected, and the chart is interpreted each time a data point is added.

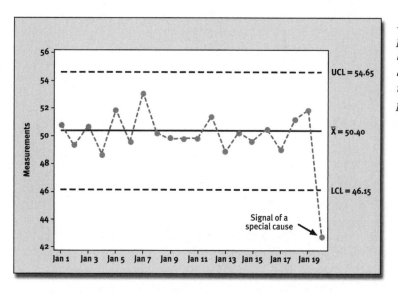

*In this example, the last data point plotted is below the lower control limit (LCL) and is thus worthy of investigating what changed in the process.*

All Control Charts show control limits that reflect the extremes (limits) for the expected variation, called Common Cause variation. As a rule, the limits are set at three standard deviations from the mean so that almost all the Common Cause variation is captured within the limits. It's highly unlikely that a stable process would have a data point beyond these control limits. When that occurs, we call it a Special Cause.

It's important to know that control limits are calculated on the basis of the variation in the data from the process. The control limits represent the voice of the process, telling us what extent of variation we can expect to see. Specification limits are different. They represent the voice of the customer and, as such, tell you what extent of variation that is desired.

# Individuals Control Chart

The Individuals Control Chart is the most often used and versatile control chart, particularly for monitoring $Y$. It's called an Individuals Control Chart because data is plotted individually, without grouping, and the Common Cause variation is estimated by calculating the moving ranges between those individual points.

Note that the moving range is always expressed as a positive value (called the "absolute value"), as shown in the following table. Then the mean of the moving ranges is inserted into the formula for control limits, also shown. If the data had more natural variation, the moving ranges would be bigger, and thus the control limits would be farther from the mean. Likewise, a process with less natural variation would have tighter control limits.

*The mean of the data becomes the centerline on the chart.*

| Date | Data | Moving Range |
|---|---|---|
| 1-Jan | 50.8 | N/A |
| 2-Jan | 49.4 | 1.4 |
| 4-Jan | 50.8 | 1.4 |
| 3-Jan | 48.8 | 2.0 |
| 5-Jan | 51.9 | 3.1 |
| 6-Jan | 49.6 | 2.3 |
| 7-Jan | 53.2 | 3.6 |
| 8-Jan | 50.3 | 3.0 |
| 9-Jan | 49.8 | 0.5 |
| 10-Jan | 49.9 | 0.1 |
| 11-Jan | 49.9 | 0.1 |
| 12-Jan | 51.5 | 1.6 |
| 13-Jan | 48.9 | 2.6 |
| 14-Jan | 50.3 | 1.3 |
| 15-Jan | 49.7 | 0.6 |
| 16-Jan | 50.6 | 0.9 |
| 17-Jan | 49.1 | 1.5 |
| 18-Jan | 51.3 | 2.2 |
| 19-Jan | 51.9 | 0.6 |
| **Mean** | **50.40** | **1.60** |

**For the Individuals Control Chart**

UCL = xbar + 2.66 (average moving range)
= 50.40 + 2.66 (1.60)
= 54.65

LCL = xbar - 2.66 (average moving range)
= 50.40 - 2.66 (1.60)
= 46.15

*The upper and lower control limits are calculated by multiplying 2.66 times the average moving range and adding it to the mean (x-bar) for the UCL, while subtracting it from the mean for the LCL.*

## Other Control Charts

The Individuals Control Chart is just one of a whole family of Control Charts. Fortunately, all Control Charts have this same format of centerline and UCL and LCL. And the objective of all Control Charts is to plot data so you can see if any Special Causes exist. Of course, the reason you interpret the control chart is to determine what actions you have to take, if any.

Other Control Charts include I & MR Charts, x-bar & R Charts, x-bar & S Charts, p-Charts, u-Charts, and so on. While all these charts show performance over time, their differences lie in the way the limits are calculated for different types of data.

Data come in many forms. Continuous data (also called variable data) may come one at a time or in subgroups. Discrete data may be a tally of defects or the proportion of units that are defective. Sample sizes may be constant or they may vary. No matter what the shape or fashion of your data, there's a Control Chart for you.

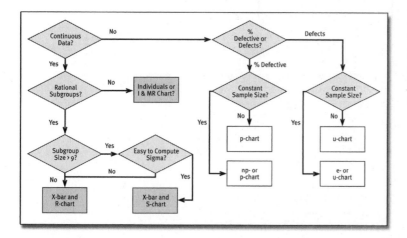

*You can use this flow chart to select the proper Control Chart for your data. There are many texts that can show you more particulars about each different Control Chart.*

# Interpreting a Control Chart

As a Process Owner, you want to properly interpret the Control Chart because that tells you what actions to take, or not to take. Variation always exists—so your job is to separate variation into its two categories of Common and Special Cause. Then you use your centerlines, control limits, and plots of data to make your interpretation. The following flow chart gives you a decision pathway for taking action on your process.

 **Performance Pitfall** _____

A common mistake is assigning someone to create lots of Control Charts. While the walls become covered with pretty charts, no one has responsibility to interpret and act on the charts. Acting on just one Control Chart is better than plastering the wall with many charts that go unattended.

*Use this flow chart to guide you in taking action, or not taking action, on your process. Note that Special Causes require special action, while Common Causes require Lean Six Sigma–type improvement.*

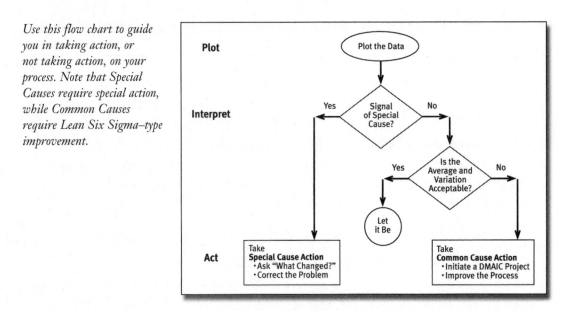

# Special Causes

Any occurrence or pattern in the data that isn't just random variation is called a Special Cause. Statisticians have created several signals for detecting Special Causes, the most common of which are outliers, shifts, trends, or cycles. Let's look at each one of these for a moment.

**Outliers.** An outlier is any data point that is above the UCL or below the LCL. Because the control limits are calculated from probability theory, an outlier is highly unlikely in a process with just Common Cause variation.

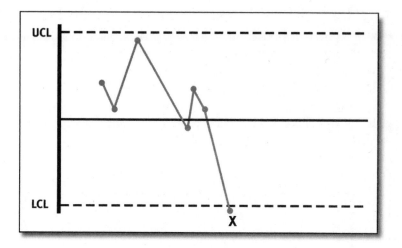

*This is a depiction of a data point outlier. Look for a large change in the process at the time of the outlier.*

## Technically Speaking

Special Cause signals are not necessarily bad news. For instance, the Control Chart on process yield may have a UCL of 92 percent. A data point at 93 percent would be a Special Cause and should be investigated to find out what has changed in the process. This can be very helpful in improving the process.

**Shifts.** The likelihood of a stable process generating nine points in a row on the same side of the centerline is like tossing a coin and getting heads nine times in a row. It's possible, but highly unlikely. Therefore, a run of nine consecutive points all on the same side of the centerline indicates a shift in the mean. This is a strong indicator that the process has changed and warrants investigation.

*This is a depiction of a shift in the process. Look for what is happening with your processes to explain shifts.*

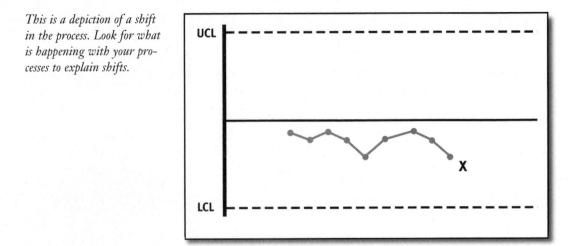

**Trends.** A trend is defined as six consecutive points, each higher than the previous point—or six consecutive points, each lower than the previous point. This indicates a Special Cause with a gradual effect. Look for a process change that began at approximately the start of the trend.

*This is a depiction of a trend in the process. Look for what is happening with your processes to explain trends.*

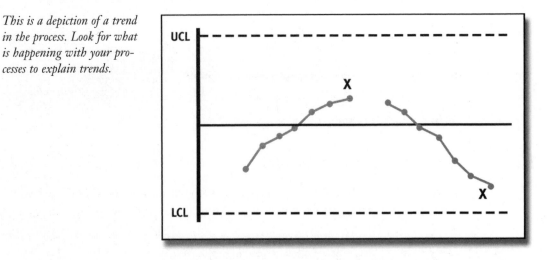

**Cycles.** Repeating patterns, called cycles, are signaled by 14 consecutive points that alternate up and down. This pattern signals cyclical change in the process that is repetitive and certainly warranting investigation. Possible causes include overadjustment, shift-to-shift variation, and machine-to-machine variation.

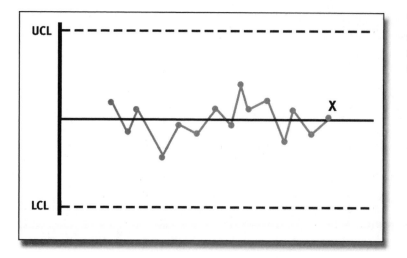

*This is a depiction of a cycle in the process. Look for what is happening with your processes to explain cycles.*

These signals (outliers, shifts, trends, cycles) apply to all Control Charts. When you're working with Control Charts for continuous data (also known as variable data), additional signals are available for your use. These added signals, such as the zone rules, make it easier to detect Special Causes for variable-data charts and related processes.

## Common Causes

When no Special Cause signals are present, we deem the process to be in control, not out of control. In other words, the process is stable and not changing—and only Common Cause variation is affecting its behavior. The first sample Control Chart in this chapter (sales) is a good example of Common Cause variation.

# Acting on the Interpretation

Okay, you've constructed your Control Chart, plotted your data, and even interpreted the chart for Special Causes. Surely you're done, right? Well, you guessed it—not quite.

Remember, Control Charts enable you to be more scientific about your process, and about taking action on your process—or not taking action.

If you detect a Special Cause, you want to ask yourself what changed. The Process Owner can determine this without the help of Lean Six Sigma. Even when your process changes positively in a special way, you want to investigate to find out why. However, your objective here would be to identify the source of the change and try to sustain it.

Often, you will plot successive data points and not get a Special Cause signal. This means your process is stable and no corrective action is required. This is why the Control Chart is an amazing productivity tool for the manager, who typically reacts emotionally to performance fluctuations. But the Control Chart prevents us from reacting to every data point.

A process can be in control (no Special Causes signaled) and yet the numbers are not acceptable. Maybe the average is lower than target. Or the variation is greater than the specifications allow. Trying to apply Special Cause actions will be futile.

A process that is "in control" can be improved, however. It does take more work, though. This is where you would charter a new project to address the gap using DMAIC if your goal is to reach Entitlement, or DFSS if your goal is to exceed Entitlement.

## The Least You Need to Know

◆ Control Charts are the tool of choice for monitoring $x$s and $Y$s in a Control Plan.

◆ The formulas for calculating control limits on Control Charts use the variation in the data to estimate the Common Cause variation.

◆ There are several different Control Charts so all types of data can be charted. Use the Control Chart selector tool shown previously to select the right control chart for your data.

◆ Plot the data. You can see a lot by looking. Interpret the Control Chart for any signals of Special Cause.

◆ Take the appropriate Special Cause or Common Cause action. Don't waste productivity applying Special Cause action to every data point.

# Chapter 22

# Lock In the Gains

## In This Chapter

- ◆ Reporting the financial benefit
- ◆ Storyboards and Final Reports
- ◆ Implementing standard operating procedures
- ◆ Capturing new improvement opportunities
- ◆ Transition planning

Many a relay race has been won or lost in the baton pass. As a project leader, you received the baton from the Project Champion back in the Define Phase. You've run the race well. You wouldn't be this far with your project if you hadn't. It's now the critical step in the race where you have the responsibility to get that baton into the hands of the next runner, the Process Owner.

While your work as a project leader is nearing completion, the process you've improved doesn't end. It continues on in its new and improved state—but only if you pass the baton with grace and efficiency. The information in this chapter will help you do this. We'll let you know what's important, showing you how to document your project results, create standard operating procedures, and transition yourself to the next project.

# Show Me the Money

The purist practitioner might say you do Lean Six Sigma to improve processes, and that practitioner would be right. Still, from a management perspective, the importance of Lean Six Sigma lies squarely in its ability to return financial benefits to the organization. This is why management decides to do Lean Six Sigma in the first place.

Therefore, you need to make sure you communicate the financial benefits of your project to management before moving on to another project. Imagine you are the Champion (or Black Belt) for the following four projects that were just completed in your business unit. You could forward a summary, like the one following, to your management team.

## Project Summary for Champion A

| Project | Before $Y$ | After $Y$ |
| --- | --- | --- |
| Reduce downtime at 200-count cartoner | 4 hr/day | 1 hr/day |
| Increase on-time deliveries of XYZ | 96% | 99.6% |
| Reduce dropped calls in call center | 33/day | 2/day |
| Increase Rolled Throughput Yield for 200 count | 72% | 82% |

Great stuff! Management is proud, very proud. But they wonder about the numbers. Not the performance numbers, as important as they seem. Management eats and sleeps on one thing only: the *financials*. Those are the numbers they care about, and that's the language of business leadership. Therefore, you might instead send a summary like the one following to your management team.

## Project Summary for Champion A

| Project | Before $Y$ | After $Y$ | Annual Savings |
| --- | --- | --- | --- |
| Reduce downtime at 200-count cartoner | 4 hr/day | 1 hr/day | $90,000 |
| Increase on-time deliveries of XYZ | 96% | 99.6% | $130,000 |
| Reduce dropped calls in call center | 33/day | 2/day | $450,000 |

| Project | Before $Y$ | After $Y$ | Annual Savings |
|---|---|---|---|
| Increase Rolled Throughput Yield for 200 count | 72% | 82% | $340,000 |
| Total Savings | | | $1,010,000 |

That's better. If I'm a manager, I now have the numbers in which I'm most interested. You added the right-hand column numbers for projects and answered the call of management: Show Me the Money.

Earlier in the Define Phase, the project leader, with assistance from a finance resource, estimated the financial impact of the project. The net benefits in savings and revenue increase were forecasted for the first 12 months after project completion. At that time, you only had firm data on the baseline, or "before" process.

Now you have both the before and the after results for the project. The financial impact, estimated during the Define Phase, should be recalculated based on the actual financial impact. This is done as a joint effort between the project leader (Belt) and the finance resource, with input from the Process Owner. The savings numbers are then entered into your project tracking software.

**Lean Six Sigma Wisdom**

An active, informed finance resource is an important asset for the project leader. Disputes about the determination of savings (between Black Belt, Process Owner, and finance resource) should be resolved by the Project Champion.

# Make It Known

Remember all those stakeholders you identified in the Define phase? It's time to pull out your documentation and provide an update to those stakeholders. Some may be aware of the financial results but not of the process changes you made that must be sustained. Some may know what they are now doing differently as individuals, but they aren't aware of all the implications of the change.

The best way to ensure that everyone is on the same page is to create a project Storyboard and a Final Report.

# Project Storyboard

What's a Storyboard anyway? It's a mostly visual depiction of a storyline, like when moviemakers sketch out scenes in advance before spending gobs of money on shoots. For a Lean Six Sigma project, the purpose of a Storyboard (usually a PowerPoint presentation) is to bring all stakeholders up to speed on what has changed, why, and the results.

**Lean Six Sigma Wisdom**

Start preparing and using your Storyboard in the Define phase. Update it as part of the tollgate for each phase.

Using the Storyboard approach, you can show the logic for why a change was made, show some of the important milestones, and provide only enough detail to secure buy-in to the change. Most DMAIC Storyboards require between 15 and 30 slides that can be posted in the work area and presented at meetings.

# The Final Report

*You're not done until the paperwork's done.* A fitting statement for the Lean Six Sigma practitioner. While the Storyboard is your abbreviated version of your project, the Final Report is the whole kit and caboodle. It includes all the graphs and pictures of your Storyboard, as well as a lot of additional information and narrative description.

Where the Storyboard requires a narrator, the Final Report should be written so it can be understood by anyone who might read and study the document, which is usually between 20 and 40 pages. Key sections and elements of a Final Report are as follows:

- Executive Summary (one page or less)
- Project Definition (details of the project charter)
- Deliverables and Conclusions for
    - Define (include problem and objective statements)
    - Measure (include baseline, Process Map, and MSA validation)
    - Analyze (include tools used and logic/process)
    - Improve (include detail on changes made)
    - Control (include detail on the Control Plan)
- Approval signatures (typically the Master Black Belt, Project Champion, and Process Owner)

The Final Report can be e-mailed to stake-holders and filed in a repository of reports for future reference. The objective is to spread knowledge, encourage replication, and avoid reinvention. Final Reports are an essential part of your organizational memory and are available for instant recall when necessary.

**Lean Six Sigma Wisdom**

Project tracking software makes writing Final Reports a breeze. It ensures the project is being documented as it is executed and the Final Report is prepared as a by-product.

# Herding Cats

A colleague once said that implementing standard operating procedures (SOPs) is as difficult as herding cats. Thank goodness she was exaggerating. But it isn't as simple as e-mailing the standards to everyone and naïvely expecting them to comply. You have to install systems and props to help people follow the new standards.

For example, a call center created a new SOP for how to schedule service appointments. A new script was created that emphasized a new feature. The project team had verified in testing that this change would improve customer satisfaction, the project's *Y* metric.

All 600 operators were given the new procedure at the launch meeting. Based on the test results, the team expected to see an improvement of 3 percentage points above the baseline of 80 percent. The following Control Chart shows the results.

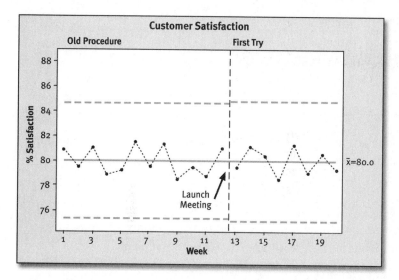

*Performance of following the new standard operating procedure prior to reinforcement. Note that there was no change in performance.*

Notice that the expected change did not happen. Fortunately for the project, the Control Plan included actions for monitoring customer satisfaction. While the results were disappointing, at least the team knew it was not yet time to declare victory.

Why was no improvement being seen? Every one of those call center operators had attended the launch session. Well, the project team did some spot checks and found that most operators had continued to use the old procedure, regardless. The reasons varied from "I forgot" to "It's not important to my manager."

That's enough to make a project leader or Process Owner mad. But soon getting over it, the project team gathered all the lead operators and supervisors together again, this time emphasizing the critical need to use the new SOP. Together, they created a more foolproof plan that reinforced its use. Here were the new results:

*Performance of following the new standard operating procedure after reinforcement. Note that performance got better.*

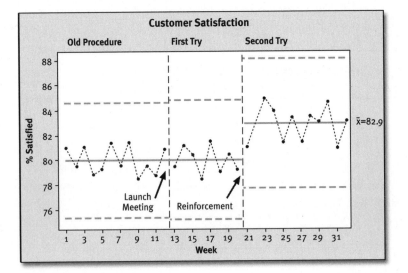

The expected benefit was seen immediately, and this teaches us an important lesson: even if you have the right solution, you still have to make sure it is implemented.

So how can you avoid making the same implementation mistakes? It's not enough to have a well-written, easily understood standard. That's certainly necessary, but not sufficient. Procedures have no effect unless they are followed. Try these guidelines:

◆ Explain the reason for the change.

◆ Don't try to teach people everything they need to know in a single training session. Combine up-front training with on-the-job reinforcement.

◆ Provide job aids that reinforce using the new procedure.

◆ Measure compliance with the new procedure; don't assume compliance.

◆ Schedule follow-up sessions after implementation. Collect feedback on the new standard. Listen for what makes the new standard difficult to use and make changes based on that feedback.

◆ Create a simple, robust method to update the procedure when an improvement is verified, with data. Ensure this updated method is known and accessible to all users of the procedure.

◆ Remember that most learning will occur on the job.

Your SOPs are the intellectual capital of your process. They represent your current best approach for doing the work. Given this, what would it say about your rate of learning if your SOP was last updated five years ago? Good SOPs are living documents, reflecting the continuous improvement of your processes.

# Opportunities and Obstacles

We've already talked about documenting the project. The Storyboard and the Final Report will capture the project work. But that's not all the project team has learned. They've also learned about 1) other opportunities for improvement in the process, and 2) obstacles to the efficient use of DMAIC.

## Opportunities

Lean Six Sigma projects are like knowledge: the more you know, the more you realize what you don't know. So the more projects you complete, the more you uncover opportunities for more projects.

Make sure you tell your Champion about what you find so he or she can feed this into the hopper of new project ideas. If you're a Champion, make sure you get enough data from the project team to roughly flesh out the potential for the proposed project.

 **Performance Pitfall**

Don't automatically assign the problem or new project to the person who surfaces it. That's like shooting the messenger and will stifle the input stream. Take time to consider who is the best project leader for the job before assigning it.

## Obstacles

Every time a team completes a project, they don't just learn how to improve their process; they also learn how to better utilize DMAIC. And this may be just as valuable to the organization—especially when you identify any obstacles that may have been encountered during the project. Then, of course, do something about those obstacles to make the DMAIC process smoother next time.

**Lean Six Sigma Wisdom**

Champions and business leaders are reminded that project teams are a gold mine of improvement ideas, and the Control phase is an excellent time to mine that gold.

The Lean Six Sigma deployment leader (manager in charge of the overall effort) will want to know what obstacles slowed the team's progress. Maybe it was hard to get time with the finance resource; maybe the project leader (Belt) was not dedicated full-time to the project; or maybe the original project scope was too broad. Good deployment leaders will use this feedback to continually improve overall project completion time and success rate.

By listening to all the project teams, the Champion is able to affinitize the feedback and identify the biggest pain points. You can use an Affinity Diagram to organize all the barriers surfaced. Affinitizing any information is a matter of grouping all the separate inputs into their natural, or logical, categories—then naming those categories with a title that characterizes them. We show an example here so you get the idea.

*Use an Affinity Diagram to organize all the project difficulties you encountered. Gather all your ideas, group them by affinity, then give each group a title.*

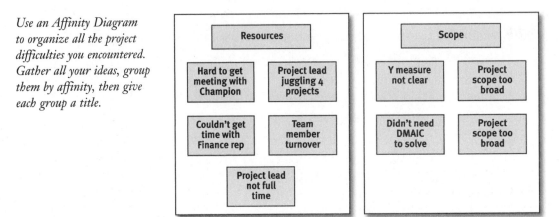

## Pass the Baton

Improvement is continuous, but an individual project has a beginning and must have an end. Still, have you ever been assigned to a project that never seemed to end? Meeting after meeting, month after month, with no end in sight, the project just idles along. If you're a project leader, don't let this happen to you. Complete your work and make sure the project gets transitioned right away to the Process Owner.

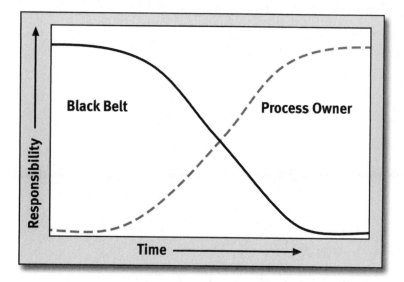

*Over time, responsibility for a project transitions from the Belt to the Process Owner. Know this and make the transition smoothly and effectively.*

The primary tool for this transition is the Control Plan.

Remember, the process will require some ongoing attention to sustain its gains and avoid decay. That's the ongoing work of the Process Owner, not the project leader, who needs to move on to the next project.

Sometimes there are a few remaining action items for the project. Perhaps it's a piece of machinery that needs to be installed when it arrives. Or maybe certain personnel on leave need to be trained when they return. Whatever it is, the list of actions needs to be fully documented and properly passed on to the Process Owner. You can use a document like the one that follows.

Project Title: _____

Transition Owner: _____

Plan Date: _____

| Actions Required for Completion | Action Owner | Initials | Scheduled Completion | Actual Completion |
|---|---|---|---|---|
| 1 | | | | |
| 2 | | | | |
| 3 | | | | |
| 4 | | | | |
| 5 | | | | |

*Make sure you document all the actions necessary to keep your project alive and sustain its improvements. The initials portion is where those responsible for actions sign and agree.*

It's critical that someone is held accountable for completing the remaining items in the Transition Plan. Like SOPs, you have to take extra steps sometimes to make sure the plan will be followed. Jointly completed by the project leader and Process Owner, the Transition Plan should include these elements:

◆ What tasks are required to complete the project?

◆ Who is responsible for each task?

◆ When will each task be completed?

◆ Who owns the plan? (Usually this is the Process Owner.)

A good follow-up approach is for the Process Owner to schedule periodic reviews of the Transition Plan until all items are completed. Each person with an action item should commit to the action, then be held accountable for their work.

# Conduct Tollgate Review

Before closing your project, you'll want to conduct your final Tollgate Review. Bring your stakeholders back together, especially the Project Champion, Process Owner, Master Black Belt, and anyone else who's affected by the change. Or anyone else who will be needed to sustain the change. Some questions to ask, and answer, at your review include:

◆ What process controls are being implemented to maintain the newly achieved level of performance? (Answer: See Control Plan.)

◆ Is the measurement system now in place adequate and in control to sustain the improvement? (Answer: Revisit Measurement Systems Analysis.)

◆ Has the Process Owner approved the implementation of your project results? (Answer: If no, explore and obtain approval.)

◆ Are there any follow-up actions to complete this project? What are they, who is responsible, and when will they be complete? (Answer: Project Transition Action Plan.)

◆ Who has the responsibility for maintaining the solutions your project has implemented, and are they aware that they have agreed? (Answer: Indicated in project Transition Action Plan, and yes, if you've made a good handoff.)

◆ What has the performance been of your primary metric? (Answer: See your updated Time Series Plot or Run Chart.)

◆ What is the final validated forecasted savings from this project? (Answer: Provide certified numbers from finance rep.)

◆ Have you updated all of your project documentation (FMEA, Process Flow, Control Plan, Procedures, etc.)?

◆ Are all data fields in your project tracking tool current with your most recent project progress? (Answer: Hopefully yes. If not, enter data.)

# Let's Celebrate

Good work should have its reward. A pizza lunch for everyone who was involved in the project is a proven winner. Dinner for the project team with the Champion is another proven approach. Small souvenirs, like T-shirts, are a good way to build pride in the accomplishment. Recognize the efforts of the project team, perhaps by putting a blurb in the company newsletter with a team photo.

The Champion of a project team at an insurance company was very pleased with the results the team achieved. He decided to have a catered barbecue lunch for everyone in the department to celebrate the success. Certainly, the project had touched almost everyone in the department, and it was appropriate to invite all these stakeholders to the lunch.

Celebration is an opportunity for the Champion to recognize the contributions of all participants in the project: publicly recognize the project team members. Make use of the Storyboard, and show the before-and-after results. Remind the guests why you're celebrating.

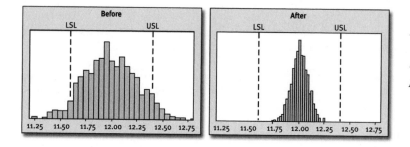

*It's all about making and sustaining the improvement. Document your before-and-after success and display it proudly.*

## The Least You Need to Know

- ◆ Calculating your project's benefit in financial terms is an important aspect of Lean Six Sigma success.

- ◆ Create a Storyboard and Final Report to document and communicate the project.

- ◆ Implementing standard operating procedures takes as much or more care as creating them.

- ◆ Get ideas for future projects from team members, and ask about any obstacles that impeded their DMAIC work.

- ◆ Plan and execute the transition of the project from the project leader to the Process Owner.

- ◆ Take time to recognize contributors and celebrate success upon project completion.

# Part 4

## Leading Lean Six Sigma Initiatives

While Lean Six Sigma is good in small doses, it's better when your entire organization is doing it. That's the difference between implementing a project and driving a corporatewide initiative, or program. In this part, we elevate Lean Six Sigma to the status of business transformation, showing you how it helps your company achieve its strategic objectives. We're not kidding around, and neither are the companies that improve quality and efficiency with a vengeance in everything they do. These organizations, and perhaps yours, make Lean Six Sigma *the way they do business*. Read this part to see how this happens.

# Chapter **23**

# Lean Six Sigma Deployment

## In This Chapter

- ◆ Enterprisewide transformation
- ◆ Enabling key processes
- ◆ An overall model for excellence
- ◆ Phases of deployment

Many corporations around the world attest to the benefits of enterprise-wide Lean Six Sigma deployment—the act of spreading, coordinating, and driving many improvements throughout an organization. When you think about Lean Six Sigma deployment, think twice. First, think of dramatically multiplying the number of projects you can execute at any one time. Second, think of the systems, structures, supports, training, management, and leadership needed to achieve such multiplication.

Like anything in our world, scale requires organization. It's one thing for a craftsman to make a single piece of furniture. It's quite another for a corporation to make 50 million units of furniture a year and distribute them all over the world. The former is a project, while the latter is an initiative.

This chapter shows you all the planks of a Total Performance Excellence (TPE) platform, of which Lean Six Sigma is just one. Context is everything, so we want you to know where Lean Six Sigma stands in the big picture of business. Also, this chapter will summarize a model for deploying Lean Six Sigma. Finally, we'll give you a set of critical success factors for ensuring your Lean Six Sigma initiative is successful.

# How Does a Business Excel?

Business improvement and transformation requires cultural and operational change—change in people, processes, and systems. Therefore, to implement an enterprisewide change strategy through Lean Six Sigma, you must first step back and understand how your business performance is linked to your business operating system.

In the following diagram, we assume that a business sets its strategy based on its capabilities, value proposition to customers, and competitive opportunities in the marketplace. This then becomes the way the business thinks, plans, and operates with its processes, systems, and people. Processes are the way a business creates value, while systems and people are enablers for the processes.

*Strategies, processes, systems, and people all work in lock-step to achieve results for the business and customers.*

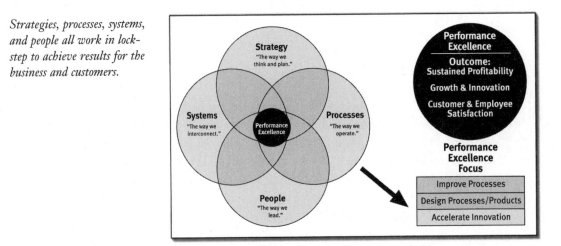

The focus of performance excellence is to improve processes, design new processes and products, and accelerate innovation. The better you do this, the more you will be able to sustain profitability, grow revenues, and achieve higher levels of customer, employee, and other stakeholder satisfaction. In short, performance excellence is about enhancing value for your customers and your business.

# Product/Service Life Cycle

As shown in the following figure, Lean Six Sigma is a subset of overall performance excellence deployment. The other key elements of performance excellence are innovation and design for Six Sigma. Presented as a continuum, or product/service life cycle, we view these elements as innovation processes, design processes, operational processes, and after-operation processes.

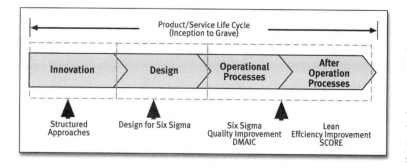

The work of providing products and services encompasses several life cycle phases. As the products/services move through these phases, different methods apply. When all methods are applied within a common framework, results are achieved in a fluid manner.

When these processes are planned and executed in an uncoordinated manner, organizations suffer waste, lack of profitability, customer dissatisfaction, and growth stagnation. Often, companies improve these processes in an ad-hoc rather than a holistic manner. As an alternative, a TPE framework allows you to plan and execute your key product/service life cycle processes in a way that yields world-class performance.

Let's therefore take a look at each life cycle phase, and find that end-to-end context we seek before deploying Lean Six Sigma. As with any organizational initiative, Lean Six Sigma can be expensive; it requires commitment, culture change, and resources. No sense in expending that kind of effort before understanding the big picture.

## Innovation and Growth

The essence of innovation is to discover, develop, and demonstrate new ideas—then bring them successfully into the marketplace. Unfortunately, innovation processes in most companies are very risky and difficult to manage, due to their unpredictable and unreliable nature. Plus, the key variables affecting innovation and growth are not well defined or understood by the average business manager.

*Structured methodologies exist to help you innovate better, more often, more extensively, and more reliably over time. Executing these methods in conjunction with Design for Six Sigma and Lean Six Sigma is a powerful combination.*

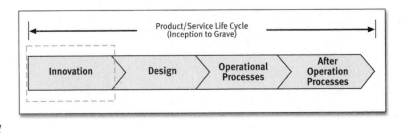

To be effective at innovation, you must have a way of measuring customer outcomes, not just the Voice of the Customer. For example, your customers might tell you they want a better watch. But focusing on customer outcomes, you might come up with a way for your customers to tell time without a watch at all. Just remember this question: What human need does the product or service fulfill?

In many organizations, innovation is considered more of an art than a science. While creativity and ideas are necessary ingredients of innovation, most organizations need a system and process for generating more valuable ideas more often. To this end, there are many structured innovation methodologies available, such as the Theory of Inventive Problem Solving or Innovation by Analogy, as discussed in "Structured Innovation," Chapter 18.

## Design and Development

The next phase of the product/service life cycle is your design and development process. After all, it's one thing to have a great idea (innovation), but quite another to transform that idea into a commercial product or service. And when you do, the better you design quality into your processes, the less you need to repair and fix them after they are launched into the market. In other words, a large percentage of products and services that need improvement using Lean Six Sigma are victims of poor design and development processes.

Often flaws in design and development processes start with a poor understanding of the Voice of the Customer (performance expectations). In addition, there is a lack of performance metrics around current design processes. Still other problems can be traced back to neglecting process capability during the design cycle. As a result, scrap and rework (waste) get designed into manufacturing and service processes. This then becomes part of a ship-and-fix mentality—the field is the test ground!

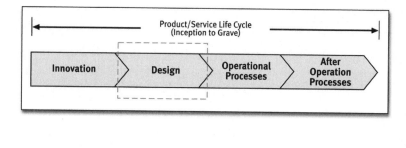

*Structured methodologies exist to help you optimize the design of your products, services, and processes. Applying these methods minimizes the extent to which you need Lean Six Sigma interventions after your processes are launched.*

Many organizations choose Design for Six Sigma (DFSS) to ensure that processes are equipped from the outset to produce high-quality products and services with zero or minimal waste. While Lean Six Sigma improves performance through Defect Reduction and efficiency improvement, DFSS strives to prevent defects and inefficiencies.

Therefore, Lean Six Sigma projects are launched to complete the design while also improving the capability of the process.

## Operations and Support

Once a product or service is launched, all the operational processes come into play, as well as the processes that support those operations. It's best to think of these processes in terms of what you do to create value for your customers.

For an automotive company, these processes would entail any that produce the cars or trucks, or service them after they are sold. For a grocery store, these processes would be those needed to acquire, sort, display, and sell the food. For a bank, operational and support processes include all transaction processing (loans, deposits, wire transfers, etc.), as well as marketing and sales (support) or investment counseling (support).

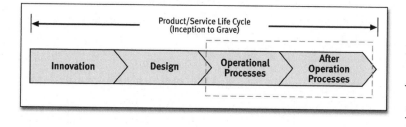

*Lean Six Sigma is an effective methodology for solving problems, reducing variation, ridding waste, improving flow, and generally increasing the effectiveness with which you transform operational inputs into outputs.*

Typically, operational and support processes don't function at their customer or business Entitlement levels. Reasons for this are that 1) we don't understand or measure customer expectations, 2) we fail to characterize the relationships of all the critical variables in the process, and 3) we lack an end-to-end view of the process.

Because of this, many companies spend most of their time fighting fires, which leaves little time for preventing fires. Since there is no time or resource available for systematic fire prevention, this only leads to more firefighting. Ultimately, the vicious cycle continues until an intervention approach such as Lean Six Sigma is deployed.

# Total Performance Excellence

Having defined the key elements of performance excellence, we transition to presenting a framework within which these elements are installed and managed in an organization. The figure that follows is a model for achieving excellence in every aspect of the performance life cycle: process innovation, process design, and process improvement.

*This is the big picture of total performance excellence. It provides the backdrop for Lean Six Sigma deployment, and it shows the phases and activities you have to lead and manage to be successful.*

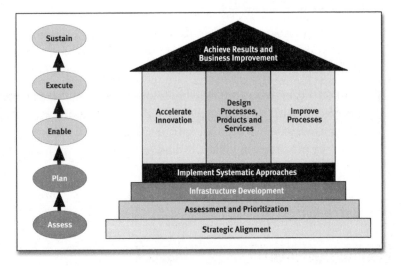

Note that these critical activities are all supported by several key performance-excellence enablers:

◆ **Strategic alignment**—Ideally, everything an organization does is aligned with its strategic intent.

◆ **Assessment and prioritization**—If you want your organization to perform better, then you have to know where to focus your efforts and resources.

- ◆ **Infrastructure development**—An infrastructure is an interconnected system of enablers that allow activities of great scale and import.

- ◆ **Systematic approaches**—When change needs to be widespread and fast in a competitive environment, you need the aid of proven, systematic approaches.

# Deployment Phases

Having a high-level deployment model enables you to chart your journey toward operational excellence as a series of interconnected steps. Therefore, the performance excellence framework (shown in the previous figure) can be followed even if you are only deploying and implementing the Lean Six Sigma component. As you can see, the major deployment phases are Assess, Plan, Enable, Execute, and Sustain.

## Assess Performance

The key objective of the Assess phase is to establish the case for change, and to evaluate how ready the organization is to make that change. Part of this entails gathering and organizing external data about the marketplace and the competition. Another part entails examining the resources and capabilities of the organization—and identifying the gaps that can be filled to improve competitive standing.

It's important during the Assess phase to identify the early adopters and resistors of the intended change. This analysis will reveal stakeholders that need to be converted into supporters if Lean Six Sigma change is to take hold.

The outcome of the Assess phase includes an initial list of opportunities, including financial benefits, that are catalogued for further prioritization and execution. At the end of the Assess phase, you have a compelling case for change and a list of opportunities for further refinement and prioritization.

## Plan Improvements

During the Plan phase, you establish and articulate your Lean Six Sigma deployment objectives. You also create your multigenerational plan, which identifies the sequence by which you deploy projects and events in different parts of the organization. For example, a leadership team may decide that the initial phase of Lean Six Sigma should focus on operations in the Southwest region.

**Lean Six Sigma Wisdom**

Many companies form a leadership steering committee to govern Lean Six Sigma deployment decisions and actions. The steering committee sets direction, establishes policies and guidelines, monitors performance metrics, enables ongoing progress, and holds leadership accountable for results.

For the success of any deployment, it's necessary to enlist the commitment and buy-in of an organization's leadership team. Project and practitioner objectives are reviewed and aligned with organizational strategies and priorities.

Another key task during this phase includes designing a governance model for Lean Six Sigma deployment. Such a model will define how projects are selected and prioritized; how Lean Six Sigma leaders and practitioners are selected, trained, and empowered to succeed; and how financial benefits will be determined.

## Enable Execution

The main activity of the Enable phase is establishing an infrastructure for widespread change. Key infrastructure elements are systems for training, finance, human resources, information technology, communications, and project management. Lean Six Sigma leaders, through a steering committee, develop policies and procedures that guide these systems. These policies and procedures are then published and made available to all interested parties.

It's most critical at this stage to provide all necessary Lean Six Sigma knowledge and skills to leaders and practitioners. This is when the organization engages in Lean Six Sigma Champion, Black Belt, and Green Belt training. In addition, Process Owners and team members are trained in the goals and means of Lean Six Sigma change.

To accomplish this, an organization develops training curricula, knowledge transfer plans, and knowledge delivery mechanisms. For example, you might customize or modify your training materials to include examples and case studies from your industry sector. If there are other performance improvement approaches that exist within your company, you might choose to integrate these with the Lean Six Sigma approach.

## Execute Projects and Events

This is when you execute the projects you've prioritized, and when you develop the many Lean Six Sigma practitioners responsible for those projects. By doing this, you begin to achieve demonstrated, quantified results for the organization through full-blown DMAIC projects as well as through more shotgunlike Kaizen Events.

Effective project and event execution is dependent on the influencing skills of Lean Six Sigma practitioners, team availability, data availability, executive and Process

Owner support, and the viability of improvement solutions. Master Black Belts and Project Champions should coach practitioners and remove any barriers or hurdles to easy project execution.

Further, validating financial benefits is a critical aspect of project execution—and in good companies this is done by a trained and designated financial representative before closing the project. Also during this phase, Champions lead the translation of solutions from one organizational area into other, related areas that can benefit.

## Sustain Improvements

No improvements made—large or small—are worth the investment if they are not sustained. While this is definitely common sense, you'd be surprised at how many organizations falter when it comes to sustaining the improvement they make. This is why we call out Sustain as a separate phase in your Lean Six Sigma journey.

Major activities during the Sustain phase include developing Master-level practitioners and trainers, conducting deployment health checks, and evolving and adapting the Lean Six Sigma approach. During this phase of deployment, redesigning and managing processes becomes second nature for the workforce, and Lean Six Sigma is embraced by the entire organization.

# Critical Success Factors

Before you launch into the specifics of Lean Six Sigma deployment, you should consider the following critical success factors. Take these factors seriously, because they're based on years of experience with both success and failure. And check out the table that follows; it goes into more detail about what makes for Lean Six Sigma success, and what makes for ruin.

- ◆ Align Lean Six Sigma objectives and plans with the strategic priorities of the business, generally with a sharp focus on financial results.

- ◆ Design a sound infrastructure system to support the governance, HR, IT, finance, communication, training, and project management aspects of Lean Six Sigma deployment.

- ◆ Designate dedicated, well-trained problem solvers who have the capability to become future leaders of the organization.

- ◆ Continue renewing a healthy pipeline of Lean Six Sigma projects, review these on a regular basis, and communicate success stories to the organization.

## Checklist of Best Practices and Pitfalls to Avoid

| Planning for Success | Recipe for Failure |
|---|---|
| Lean Six Sigma is promoted as critical to the success of the company, and as the framework for how to manage. | Lean Six Sigma is used to complement other initiatives and forced to not interfere with other efforts. |
| Hard sell with mandatory participation by all business units. | Soft sell with optional participation by business units. |
| Champions are chosen by senior executives and have significant business and P&L accountability. | Champions volunteer, are chosen because of availability, or because they're part of the quality organization. |
| Executives and Champions undergo extensive training to develop competencies. | Only Champions undergo competency training, while senior executives settle for awareness training. |
| Champions select Lean Six Sigma Belts from the best of the best. | Belts are chosen because they are expendable or available, or exclusive to the quality department. |
| The CEO or senior leader reviews and makes the final selection of Lean Six Sigma Belts. | The CEO or senior leader has no hands-on role in Belt selection. |
| Lean Six Sigma is broadly implemented. | Lean Six Sigma is selectively implemented (pilot) to satisfy certain stakeholders. |
| Lean Six Sigma Black Belt succession planning begins early. Skilled Black Belts are seen as future leaders. | Return of Black Belts to functional career paths. |
| All capable employees trained at Green Belt level and leading projects. | Green Belts seen as only limited support group for Black Belts. |
| Senior financial personnel establish guidelines and oversee financial analysis and tracking. | Finance organization not involved in process or treats process as extra work. |

| Planning for Success | Recipe for Failure |
| --- | --- |
| New Lean Six Sigma metrics used as significant business metric by CEO or president. | Lean Six Sigma metrics tracked for the sake of Lean Six Sigma only. |
| Assignment of Lean Six Sigma Belts viewed as gaining a more capable employee. | Sacrifice of Belt viewed as loss of available resource. |
| Assignment of personnel to support Lean Six Sigma teams viewed as opportunity for learning and process improvement. | Assignment of personnel to Lean Six Sigma teams viewed as a burden. |
| Training includes middle management. | Knowledge gap develops in middle management, between Black Belts and Champions. |
| Master Black Belt is a critical knowledge and mentoring resource to Champions and Black Belts. | Master Black Belt is a "staffer" who does errands and tracking exercises for the Champion. |
| New information systems designed around Lean Six Sigma metrics. | Lean Six Sigma viewed as separate program not worthy of IT changes. |
| Projects treated with a sense of urgency. | Projects pursued in a laissez-faire manner. |
| Lean Six Sigma leader has direct line of communication to the CEO or president. | Communication between Lean Six Sigma leader and CEO or president filtered through another leader. |
| Employee communication is proactively planned to usher the organization into Lean Six Sigma. | Communication is expected to happen by word of mouth. |
| Rewards and incentives are adopted to emphasize goals and congratulate achievements. | Lean Six Sigma is treated as just another difficult program that will eventually go away. |

## The Least You Need to Know

◆ All businesses, products, and services flow through a life cycle entailing innovation, design, operations, and support.

◆ For Lean Six Sigma to be effective on an organizational scale, you have to align your projects with your strategies, and build an infrastructure to support widespread change.

◆ Just like a Lean Six Sigma practitioner follows a structured project execution process (DMAIC or Kaizen Event), a Lean Six Sigma leader follows a deployment process (Assess-Plan-Enable-Execute-Sustain).

◆ If your Lean Six Sigma initiative is to be successful, you have to treat it as a top priority—which means putting your best people on it and driving it like your survival depends on it.

# Chapter 24

# Prepare the Path

## In This Chapter

- ◆ Conducting a Needs Assessment
- ◆ Performing a Stakeholder Assessment
- ◆ Evaluating competitors and customers
- ◆ Ten pathways for selecting projects

You can't get somewhere if you don't first evaluate your suitability for the journey. Nor can you make that journey if you don't have a clear sense of where you're going. That's why you need to assess where you are, where you'd like to go, and how well equipped you are to get there—before you take your first step. Especially if you're an organization that wants to achieve ambitious business goals.

In this chapter, we'll cover the basic concepts, activities, and tools involved in assessing your organization's readiness for change. We'll show you an assessment road map, and we'll cover the mountaintops of assessing your business needs, working culture, strategic intent, competitive position, and personnel. Finally, we'll summarize what's involved in surfacing opportunities for improvement that become Lean Six Sigma projects.

# Assess Road Map

Three activities are key for Lean Six Sigma leaders as they engage in the Assess phase of deployment. First, you assess your organization's readiness for change. Second, you evaluate your market, customer, and organizational situation. Third, you conduct an opportunity assessment that yields a list of Lean Six Sigma projects for practitioners to tackle.

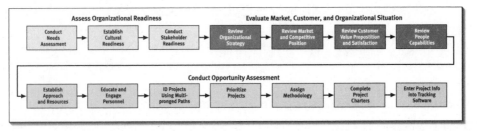

*Here are the steps you should follow in the Assess phase of Lean Six Sigma deployment. Depending on your experience and unique situation, you may or may not follow these steps in set order.*

# Assess Organizational Readiness

Your first assessment step is to define your organization's performance-improvement needs. From there, you can learn more about how ready your organization is for real change. Finally, you can figure out who your greatest change proponents are, and who will be slower to change. You'll have to work both ends of this spectrum to be successful with Lean Six Sigma.

**Lean Six Sigma Lingo**

A **burning platform** is a known need—or emergency—in an organization. For instance, if a key foreign competitor is killing you on price, then you can use this common burning platform to sell and sustain the Lean Six Sigma initiative.

## Conduct Needs Assessment

Regardless of the size and complexity of your organization, you need a rigorous and efficient assessment approach that will quickly define your current performance, and especially identify shortfalls. Basically, your Needs Assessment should look for *burning platforms*—reasons your organization needs to change significantly and quickly. Some of these could include increased competition, customer satisfaction issues, erosion of market share, need to cut costs, need to grow revenue, and desire to change the culture.

You'll need a burning platform for change to enroll your organization into the ways and means of Lean Six Sigma. And you need to enroll people convincingly because Lean Six Sigma involves a lot of discipline and extra effort for a lot of people. Basically, you're asking everyone in the organization to define, and refine, the way they think about and do their work.

## Establish Cultural Readiness

Most well-designed and well-managed performance-improvement initiatives have a significant impact on an organization's culture. And when this is the case, you can expect to encounter resistance. That's why you'll want to address this resistance by raising awareness of your Lean Six Sigma initiative as early in the process as possible.

The way you can assess your organization's readiness for change is to collect some data. Find out if the culture of your organization is geared for Lean Six Sigma. Use climate surveys, stakeholder interviews, and power and influence charts. Use, too, any lessons learned from past initiatives that succeeded or failed. Interview specific executives, managers, and employees.

Responses to the following questions can help you assess the cultural readiness of your organization for change:

◆ Are your organization's mission, vision, values, and strategic objectives clearly communicated? How are they measured and reported?

◆ How does your leadership cascade information throughout the organization? (Frequently? Visibly? Unambiguously?)

◆ Does your organizational structure and philosophy actively support change? (Rigid hierarchy? Networked? Project leaders empowered regardless of position?)

◆ Are people empowered, and is unconventional thinking encouraged? (Does management listen and act? Are ideas encouraged and collected?)

◆ Does your organization have a performance-oriented culture? (Goal setting for functions, processes, teams, and people? Regular performance reviews? Rewards and recognition?)

## Conduct Stakeholder Assessment

We covered a process and some tools for assessing Lean Six Sigma project stakeholders in Chapter 9. These include the Stakeholder Analysis tool, the Power Influence

Map, and the Stakeholder Action Plan. We refer you back to this chapter for details, because these tools also apply to assessing the stakeholders involved in a Lean Six Sigma initiative.

Using these tools, you should focus your stakeholder assessment on the executives and decision makers in your organization. As well, you should strongly consider using an objective party from the outside to help with this task. It's difficult to clear the way for Lean Six Sigma deployment without clearing certain hurdles at the executive level; and it's difficult to clear those hurdles without the involvement and initiative of an outside force.

Don't underestimate the importance of your stakeholder assessment and resulting Stakeholder Action Plan. Any initiative that requires significant change, such as Lean Six Sigma, must have strong, steady, and real support from leaders at all levels of the organization. Some pointers to this end include ...

- ◆ Meet with stakeholders—allow them the opportunity to express concerns and put them to rest.

- ◆ Understand what initiatives are underway currently (in all areas, such as technology, customer service, performance improvement, and so on).

- ◆ Understand the desire for change in the organization. (Can key stakeholders articulate a burning platform for change, sincerely? When asked why change is necessary, do you get any blank stares?)

- ◆ Understand current knowledge and use of Lean Six Sigma within the organization. (Past history and experience? Presence of Lean Facilitators and Six Sigma Black Belts or Green Belts? Managers and executives from Lean Six Sigma companies?)

- ◆ Estimate stakeholder support for Lean Six Sigma across the business. (Stakeholders show up for meetings? Express how Lean Six Sigma worked somewhere else? Show signs of disconnection through passivity?)

- ◆ Assess major roadblocks that may influence the deployment. (Any competing initiatives? Any personal in-fights between key people? Resource limitations?)

- ◆ Communicate current state of the deployment and intended next steps. (Communicate consistently, compellingly, clearly.)

- ◆ Understand the one-year expectations for the initiative (stated in specific, measurable terms at more than one level).

# Evaluate the Organizational Situation

Your next assessment step is to understand several important aspects of your current organizational situation. Specifically, this includes understanding your intended strategic direction. As well, you'll need to assess market trends and your competitive position in your industry. Further, you'll look at your customers' needs and wants, and how well you're meeting them. And finally you should conduct an assessment of your people: who are they, and how capable are they of leading and implementing Lean Six Sigma?

## Review Organizational Strategy

It's important to make sure your Lean Six Sigma deployment plans are aligned with your organization's strategic priorities. And you can achieve this by following a process that, while simple, requires a good deal of work, negotiation, communication, and tenacity. Generally speaking, here are the steps you should follow:

**Step 1.** Your leadership team is galvanized around a transformational vision.

**Step 2.** That vision is translated into a tree of business priorities that are cascaded through the organizational hierarchy.

**Step 3.** Metrics and accountability are attached to each objective.

**Step 4.** Specific methodologies, projects, and people are deployed to achieve the objectives.

**Step 5.** Periodic reviews are conducted to refine direction and objectives, and to ensure execution to plan.

Lean Six Sigma empowers steps 2 through 4, and arguably step 1 as well. It's easier to have a bold vision if you also have a way of achieving that vision. With Lean Six Sigma, you have a rational way to develop cascading business objectives and metrics. You also have the tangible skills and practitioners you need to translate strategy into action (Lean Six Sigma projects).

## Review Competitive Position

No one likes surprises—and this is especially valid when it comes to market changes and competition. That's why you want to assess your company's position in the competitive landscape. Then you can use this information to determine the focus and pace of your Lean Six Sigma rollout.

The key to assessing your market and competitive position is to manage the future by transforming information into intelligence, and transforming intelligence into strategic and tactical initiatives. The tools you can use to do this include Market Needs Analysis, Trend Analysis, SWOT (Strengths/Weaknesses/Opportunities/Threats) Analysis, Growth Analysis, and the Boston Consulting Group Segmentation Matrix.

## Customer Value Proposition

To cope with change, every business must regularly define and evaluate its customers' needs, wants, and desires. But this is only part of the equation. The other part involves looking at your products and services and assessing their value proposition to the customer. In other words, how well are your products and services positioned relative to the competition in providing customers what they want?

Some questions you can ask to help you figure out your customer value proposition are:

◆ What are the major products and services you provide to customers?

◆ What needs do these products and services fulfill for your customers?

◆ What are your customers' expectations of your products and services?

◆ What results do your customers want to achieve from your products and services?

◆ How satisfied are your customers with your products and services?

◆ How satisfied are your customers with your competitors' products and services?

Of course, these are very simple and broad questions, while the practice of customer assessment can be deep and extensive. This is especially true for larger organizations with so many different products and services and very large numbers of diverse customers. Therefore, the key to remember is: always listen to your customers and don't assume you know what they want or need. Ask them!

And don't assume they're happy with you, either. Create formal listening posts, like feedback cards, to measure how they feel. Find out where you're falling short, and target these areas as priorities for Lean Six Sigma.

## People Matter

As much as Lean Six Sigma is a critical method for improvement, you need the right people to really make it happen. Therefore, you need to assess your human resource capabilities prior to designing your specific deployment. This way you can determine where you are strong, and where you may have human resource gaps to fill.

The key to remember is that you need change agents to lead a Lean Six Sigma initiative, and also to implement the associated projects. So whatever assessment process or instrument you use, make sure it can identify the change agents as well as those who are not as open to change. You'll have to be aware of who's who in both categories and take actions to 1) empower the change agents and 2) contain those who could oppose change.

**Quotable Quote** _____

According to Gallup Poll data, just 29 percent of U.S. employees are energized and committed at work. In other words, about half of the U.S. workforce is effectively neutral, and the remaining employees are disengaged. These disengaged folks have a profound impact, says Gallup, which estimates they cost companies around $300 billion per year in lost productivity.

—Source: Fleming, J.H. et al., "Manage Your Human Sigma," *Harvard Business Review,* July-August 2005

Needless to say, strong and tangible commitment to a Lean Six Sigma initiative precedes its success and sustainability. Without a doubt, disengaged leaders and project team members can stall or cause an initiative to fail. On the other hand, positively engaged project team members will yield better and faster results.

# Conduct Opportunity Assessment

Your final assessment step is fully defining and clarifying what needs to be done to achieve the objectives you identified during your Needs Assessment. Essentially, this boils down to defining opportunities for Lean Six Sigma projects that are in direct support of your organization's strategies and business needs. To this end, there are a number of tasks you need to accomplish. The rest of this chapter outlines those steps.

## Establish Approach

The following chart shows the steps you go through to select Lean Six Sigma projects. As you do this, you need to communicate often with all your stakeholders. You need also to identify the resources (people) that will be necessary to execute your projects, and to keep the Lean Six Sigma initiative alive.

*The key to opportunity assessment is moving through a process that translates business problems into Lean Six Sigma projects.*

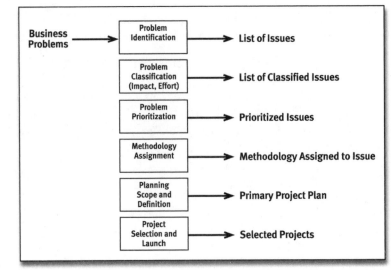

## Educate and Engage Personnel

Research shows that 75 percent of the problems companies face when making improvements are due to their inability to properly manage change. To make organizational improvements sustainable, companies need strong and capable change leaders who know how to enroll others and accelerate acceptance across the organization.

**Lean Six Sigma Wisdom**

The ongoing process of identifying potential projects is critical to the sustainability of your initiative.

Because of this, every successful Lean Six Sigma initiative begins by assembling key business leaders, and setting them on the right conceptual path. And it's best at this point to hire a powerful consultant who can work with your senior leaders to truly win them over to the Lean Six Sigma philosophy and approach. Without such buy-in and support, your efforts are doomed.

Here are some specific messages you'll want to get across to your Lean Six Sigma steering committee:

◆ Continuous improvement is a core business philosophy. Build understanding about what Lean Six Sigma is and its importance to your mission and strategic agenda. Demonstrate exactly how the former enables the latter.

◆ The focus is on cost benefit rather than savings. Lean Six Sigma is about improving both the bottom and top lines.

◆ This is not just a corporate headquarters initiative; we want everyone to do continuous improvement, not just talk about it.

◆ The purpose of Lean Six Sigma is to develop capabilities, making processes more efficient and effective.

◆ A call to action based on burning platforms, which generate support and buy-in for the Lean Six Sigma process, and foster true believers.

# Project Identification

Chapter 6 covers what's involved in identifying Lean Six Sigma projects, and we refer you there for important details. The key to know is that your ability to select the right Lean Six Sigma projects is one of the most important success factors. Therefore, in addition to the material in Chapter 6, Lean Six Sigma Champions and leaders should use the following 10 devices to pick good projects.

**Device #1. Strategy Flow Down.** This is a top-down approach whereby you identify improvement projects that align with your strategic objectives. To link projects, you first map your strategies from financial, customer, internal process, and learning standpoints (see the following diagram). For each strategic theme, you then establish measures and targets. Where you have performance gaps, when appropriate, you then convert those gaps into Lean Six Sigma projects.

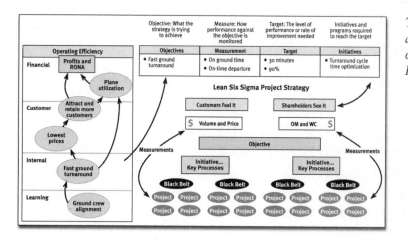

*This shows the general process of translating high-level organizational strategies into Lean Six Sigma projects.*

**Device #2. End-to-End Process Assessment.** The objective of this type of assessment is to identify projects that are associated with your different Value Streams. Major steps in completing this assessment are:

**Step 1.** Identify the Value Stream to improve.

**Step 2.** Characterize the current state of the chosen Value Stream.

**Step 3.** Develop the future state vision of the Value Stream.

**Step 4.** Complete a gap analysis between the current and future states.

**Step 5.** Complete a waste and financial analysis, and then convert gaps into actionable projects for further prioritization and scoping.

**Device #3. Financial Analysis.** This type of assessment evaluates detailed financial indicators within the business and identifies performance-improvement project themes. While the tendency is to choose projects on the basis of short-term financial health, it's advisable to look out to a 12- to 18-month period. Part of the financial assessment includes looking at assets and liabilities, and assessing how efficiently the company is managing scarce resources to achieve its objectives. Finally, you are well served to examine fixed and variable operational costs, inventory levels, product or service margins, and product or service mix—making comparisons with known industry benchmarks.

**Device #4. Performance Against Plan.** Here you are looking for variances in current performance against objectives, and the main way you do this is using Statistical Process Control Charts (see Chapter 21). Your main objective is to evaluate major budget deviations by studying performance metrics that are statistically in control but unacceptable (Common Causes), and performance metrics that are statistically out of control (Special Causes). Typically, high variation from budgeted performance is due to poor capability of the existing system, extraordinary circumstances, or incorrect forecasting.

**Device #5. Organic Projects.** This is the act of gathering project ideas from all levels of the organization. Some of these projects may not be strategic in nature but will have financial, customer satisfaction, or employee satisfaction impact. The process for this approach is to facilitate a brainstorming session with groups of employees at various levels, asking them for their ideas on broken processes and other pain points. Ideas are discussed as a group, and are clarified. They are then consolidated for further review and categorization.

**Device #6. Customer Process Projects.** This assessment involves identifying weaknesses in processes that interface with customers—with the objective of identifying waste and defects. This approach is especially relevant and important in service industries where customer satisfaction is directly correlated with the quality and speed of the customer-facing processes.

First, you identify the products and services for certain customers. Then map the processes that directly interact with those customers. Then identify the key performance measures that link to customer satisfaction. After this, measure your customers' satisfaction with the products and services, and identify reasons (waste/defects) for any dissatisfaction. This gives you a list of possible Lean Six Sigma projects.

**Device #7. Supply Chain Projects.** This type of assessment identifies key products and services provided by outside suppliers and documents their performance. When performing a supply chain assessment, you should examine your supply chain strategy, review supply chain processes for defects and waste, and identify gaps in supplier performance versus expectation. Such an assessment should lead to many opportunities for improvement that you can pursue via Lean Six Sigma in conjunction with your suppliers.

**Device #8. Innovation and Growth.** The majority of projects identified by assessing your innovation and growth processes will become candidates for Design for Six Sigma, or other innovation approaches. However, the Lean Six Sigma approach is the starting point for many of these projects, especially when they've already been designed but just aren't running as intended.

Your intent is to find areas where your products and services are falling short of competitors. This is your indication that something needs to change. If you can make enhancements to your processes without redesigning them, you can use Lean Six Sigma. If the needed changes require fundamental redesign, or invention, then you'll need to employ other means.

**Device #9. Customer and Product Data.** Databases of customer complaints and product warranty information can provide a wealth of information for project idea generation. Start your assessment by identifying various channels of customer feedback. These can include customer satisfaction surveys, customer service center information, call center databases, and warranty and repair center information. Your next step is to analyze the data from these sources and identify problems for improvements.

Your analysis techniques and approach depend on how data are collected, classified, and stored. For example, often call center data is stored in categories by type of information. In this case, as a first step, you would complete a Pareto analysis of the information to see if certain categories are more problematic than others. Your most problematic categories, of course, would become your candidates for Lean Six Sigma projects.

**Device #10. Compliance Processes.** Sarbanes Oxley and other compliance requirements are intended to make sure that certain processes are documented and monitored. Related audits determine the extent to which an organization complies with legislation and maintains control over these processes. Your related assessment approach is to evaluate your regulated processes and their key metrics, looking for weaknesses. These become your opportunities for Lean Six Sigma projects.

## Prioritize Projects

Once project ideas are identified using these 10 mechanisms, the next step is to prioritize these ideas using certain filters or criteria. Tools that aid in this process include the Cause-and-Effect Matrix (covered in Chapter 13), and the Benefit/Effort Matrix and the Prioritization Matrix (covered in Chapter 6). These tools provide a structured way for you to determine which project ideas promise the greatest return relative to the effort required.

## Assign Methodology

Once projects are prioritized as described, then you have to determine which methodology is needed. We covered what this entails in Chapter 9, and we provided a nice flow chart to assist in this. The key to remember if you are a Lean Six Sigma Champion is threefold. One, certain project ideas are "Just Do It" projects. The solution is known and you just have to implement it. Two, some projects require design or innovation. These are not Lean Six Sigma DMAIC projects. Three, all other projects having to do with operational improvement can become Lean Six Sigma projects, either implemented within a project framework over time, or through a shorter, more intensive Kaizen Event.

## Complete Project Charters

Your last Assess step is to create a Project Charter for each identified Lean Six Sigma project. Your job as a Lean Six Sigma Champion in this regard is to describe the project with a concise Problem and Objective statement. Also, as shown by the following example, you identify your process and its performance level, its planned time frame for completion, its expected savings, and other information.

It's important that the Lean Six Sigma Belt and Champion sign off on the Project Charter, as well as the finance representative who is confirming that the estimated financial benefits are valid. And it's not a bad idea for the Process Owner to sign off on this document as well. For more information on creating a Project Charter, see Chapter 9.

## Project Tracking Software

An enterprise project tracking solution should be developed or purchased as part of the infrastructure for Lean Six Sigma change. Such software, which we cover more in the next chapter, enables Lean Six Sigma leaders and practitioners to effectively manage their projects, review past projects, collaborate with team members, provide status updates to management, and replicate best practices across the organization.

Imagine a large company running about 2,000 Lean Six Sigma projects in a given year. A good project tracking system allows anyone (with the proper access permission) anywhere in the world to enter or retrieve real-time data by belt, region, project category, financial savings, and so on. In this sense, your project tracking system is a complete Lean Six Sigma dashboard and management tool.

| Lean Six Sigma Project Charter | | |
|---|---|---|
| **Date:** | 2/1/07 | Define Review |

| | | | |
|---|---|---|---|
| **Project** | **Project Title:** | New Customer Billing Errors | |
| | **Defect Definition:** | Error on a New Customer's First Bill. | |
| | **Problem Statement:** | From 1/1/06 to 12/31/06 25% of all new mobile phone customers had bills in error that required customer service center intervention. These errors generate NVA rework, slow cash flow and customers are often issued credits for their inconvenience. In contrast, the error rate for new residential phone customers is only 5%. | |
| | **Objective Statement:** | Reduce new mobile phone customer first bill error rate from 25% to 11% by 7/01/07. | |
| | **Process(es):** | Account Set-up, Customer Service. | |
| | **Baseline Sigma Level:** | 0.67 | 25% Error Rate |
| | **Entitlement Sigma Level:** | 1.64 | 5% Error Rate |
| | **Target Sigma Level:** | 1.23 | 11% Error Rate |
| | **Realized Sigma Level:** | | |
| | **Starting Date:** | 1/31/07 | |
| | **Expected Completion:** | 7/1/07 | |
| | **Actual Completion:** | | |

| | | |
|---|---|---|
| **Metrics** | **Primary Metric:** | Error Rate (Errors/New Mobile Customers) |
| | **Consequential Metric(s):** | Average Days to Issue First Bill |
| | **Financial Metric(s):** | Credits/Month, FTE/Month |
| | **Secondary Metric(s):** | Billing Calls/Week |

| | | | |
|---|---|---|---|
| **Financials** | **Benefits (Define):** | $324,000 | Credits and FTEs |
| | **Benefits (Measure):** | | |
| | **Benefits (Analyze):** | | |
| | **Benefits (Improve):** | | |
| | **Cost of Implementation:** | | |
| | **Realized Benefits (12 mos.):** | | |

| | | |
|---|---|---|
| **People** | **Black Belt:** | Beatrix Davies |
| | **Champion:** | Darren Kawolski |
| | **Process Owner:** | Roxanne Cervantes |
| | **SME:** | Pat Simons |
| | **Team Members:** | Eric Smith, Linda Jones, Fran Alber, Sean O'Keefe |
| | **Data Owners (Sources):** | Eric Smith (DataworX), Sally Ko (CusCare) |

| Black Belt | MBB | Champion | Finance |
|---|---|---|---|
| _____ | _____ | _____ | _____ |

*This is a sample Lean Six Sigma Project Charter. This is your guiding document as a Champion or Black Belt.*

## The Least You Need to Know

◆ Determine your burning platforms for change and use these to convince others you need Lean Six Sigma.

◆ Know for certain who is for the Lean Six Sigma initiative and who is against it. Turn your opponents into supporters if you can.

◆ Make sure your Lean Six Sigma initiative is well aligned with your organizational strategies. To do this, you have to assess those strategies.

◆ Use knowledge of your customers and their needs—and your competitive position in your industry—to help you identify opportunities for Lean Six Sigma.

◆ Assess how ready your people are for change, and equip them if necessary.

◆ The output of all your assessment activity is a list of prioritized Lean Six Sigma projects.

# 25

# Design Your Destiny

## In This Chapter

- ◆ Establish your big objectives
- ◆ Influencing people to get with the program
- ◆ Why you need an infrastructure for success
- ◆ You're only as good as you govern

After you assess your readiness for Lean Six Sigma and solidify your opportunities for improvement as a business, it's time to Design the rollout of your Lean Six Sigma initiative. Like any major undertaking, good planning (design) turns into good implementation, and good implementation turns into good results.

In this chapter, we outline and discuss each major step of the Design road map, which takes you through all the many activities required to plan for a successful Lean Six Sigma deployment. If you follow these steps as a Lean Six Sigma leadership team, you'll secure a great probability of success for your initiative.

# Design Road Map

Four activities are key for Lean Six Sigma leaders as they engage in the Design phase of deployment. First, you establish your deployment objectives. Second, you engage and leverage leadership support. Third, you align practitioner and project strategies. Fourth, you design a governance model for Lean Six Sigma deployment.

*Here are the steps you should follow in the Design phase of Lean Six Sigma deployment. Depending on your experience and unique situation, you may or may not follow these steps in set order.*

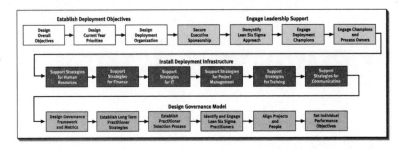

The complete Design activity is called deployment planning by many Lean Six Sigma companies. Deployment planning is the process of defining and documenting the executive vision and goals for a company's performance-improvement program, then turning those goals into a workable strategy and tactical plans for the desired Lean Six Sigma results.

# Establish Deployment Objectives

Three key activities comprise the road map for establishing your Lean Six Sigma deployment objectives. First, you design your overall program objectives. Second, you design your priorities for your first year of deployment. Third, you design your deployment organization, which will be responsible for driving and ensuring your Lean Six Sigma performance results.

## Design Overall Objectives

The first major step of deployment planning is to design the overall objectives for the Lean Six Sigma initiative. Depending on your unique organizational needs, and competitive situation, you might need to increase market share, improve customer satisfaction, cut costs, grow revenue, improve capacity, reduce defects, increase speed, improve capability, and/or change your working culture.

You might need any combination of these objectives in various parts of your company or organization, especially if it is truly global or large. Certain operational areas might need help in improving manufacturing capacity, while other areas might have customer satisfaction or defect issues. And so on, and so on.

The *Lean Six Sigma core team*, or *steering committee*, takes the outputs of its assessment activities (Chapter 24) into account to formulate the initiative's objectives. Care is taken to link those objectives to organizational strategies via such methods as *Hoshin Planning*.

> ### Lean Six Sigma Lingo
>
> **Lean Six Sigma core team/steering committee** is the team that configures, drives, reviews, and is responsible for the Lean Six Sigma initiative. Members include a company's primary executive sponsor, deployment leader, a hand-selected group of multidisciplinary leaders from critical organizational support functions, and others as determined or required.
>
> **Hoshin Planning** is the practice of cascading top-level organizational strategies into increasingly lower levels, with performance metrics attached. A sound Hoshin Planning system also provides a mechanism for regularly reviewing performance-to-plan at all levels, making necessary adjustments over time to ensure success.

## Current-Year Priorities

The key to remember in setting priorities for the first year is money. That's it. And incidentally, that's why for-profit companies exist: to make money (with zero negative consequence on the natural and social environments). So the most important criterion to keep in mind is the financial benefit of Lean Six Sigma to the organization (unless you're a nonprofit organization; but even if you are, you want to be as fiscally responsible as possible, and Lean Six Sigma helps you do this).

Primarily this means you look at the true, realized savings you can generate from your initiative as it removes waste, eradicates rework, and improves productivity with little or no capital investment. Secondarily, you should focus on balance-sheet impact through inventory improvements, accounts receivables, and the like. After this, you can identify projects and priorities that have strategic value for the future but cannot be tied to dollars saved now.

Chapter 8 provides more details about the different financial categories within which you can segment your Lean Six Sigma objectives and projects. The rule of thumb is that no more than 10 percent of your first year's priorities should be focused on soft savings or future savings. All other projects should yield hard dollars in the first year.

## Design the Organization

Any change initiative that involves a companywide deployment needs to be organized, and this includes Lean Six Sigma. Therefore, you will need to build a Lean Six Sigma organization before launching into the next major phase of Design (engage leadership support). The sample organization that follows should be a guide.

*Depending on your company and its approach to Lean Six Sigma, your organizational chart for the initiative may look something like this.*

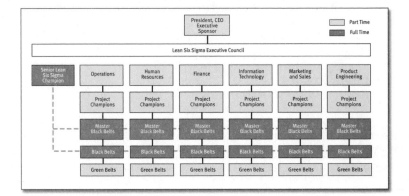

# Engage Leadership Support

If you've been involved in quality improvement or change initiatives in the past, you're well familiar with the party line about leadership commitment and support. If you have it, and it is tangible and real, then your initiative will succeed. If you don't have it, you're in trouble. And we might point out that leadership support means support at all levels of an organization, not just at the top.

Engaging leadership, therefore, means securing executive sponsorship at the top. It also means educating executives about the benefits and process of deploying Lean Six Sigma. Further, you have to educate and coach Champions, who oversee and lead Lean Six Sigma deployment in all your different areas, geographies, and functions. Finally, engaging leadership means equipping those who oversee work at the process level, the Process Owners.

## Secure Executive Sponsorship

Sustainable change initiatives are typically the result of a fully committed executive team and superior leadership. Unfortunately, large-scale change or paradigm shifts do not happen overnight and can take years. But results can be accelerated when you successfully gain wide support from your leadership team.

The Lean Six Sigma initiative must be driven from the top at the CEO level or very close to it. As with any change initiative, significant change usually starts with a small handful of visionaries in positions of influence and power. From there, as we covered in Chapter 24, those people begin to influence key stakeholders, and begin to orient the organization toward the desired change.

> **Lean Six Sigma Wisdom**
>
> Begin to generate support and buy-in for Lean Six Sigma to foster true believers, and leverage small victories to gain momentum. And remember: the power of influence lies in your ability to get people actively engaged in the process.

## Demystify the Approach

We are the first to admit that programs like Lean Six Sigma can seem daunting at first, even to very capable and educated managers. Yet once you get to know what Lean Six Sigma is and does, it all makes sense. Therefore, you'll want to schedule sessions and workshops with your business leaders, and Champions, to demystify the Lean Six Sigma approach.

Once key leaders understand that Lean Six Sigma really works, and makes the company stronger and more profitable, they buy in and help drive it. In some cases, your strongest naysayers in the beginning become your strongest supporters later—once you've done them the justice of proving that Lean Six Sigma is worth their time and effort.

At first, you can demystify Lean Six Sigma by clearly articulating and demonstrating the soundness of its principles and practices. You can also make sure to present the many success stories of companies that have achieved impressive results using Lean Six Sigma. (We covered some of these in Part 1.) Finally, after you implement your first successful pilot projects, you can use these to whip up support.

## Engage Deployment Champions

In large-scale initiatives, the Deployment Champion is a business leader who reports directly to a business unit President. The Deployment Champion is responsible for the planning and deployment of Lean Six Sigma within that particular division, region, or other large segment of a company.

Deployment Champions are engaged through education and working sessions that facilitate performance-improvement goal setting, initial project selection, Project

Champion selection, Black Belt selection in some cases, and other important planning and implementation activities.

Naturally, Deployment Champions have a great deal of rapport among their peers and have typically led other initiatives in their business units. They have established reputations, so you'll have to make them Lean Six Sigma believers before they will agree to lead and drive the initiative.

## Champions and Process Owners

At this stage of the game, you also want to select and engage your Project Champions and Process Owners. Project Champions are respected operational leaders and managers who help select Lean Six Sigma projects, define them, and make sure they are successfully completed. In this role, Project Champions clear organizational barriers for Black Belts and Green Belts (those actually leading process-improvement teams).

Project Champions also work with Process Owners after projects are completed to make sure the gains made are sustained over time. As well, Project Champions spread lessons learned from one project team to others, and to other parts of the organization. Finally, Project Champions (most of the time called just Champions) are coaches to Black Belts and Green Belts. In this sense they are friends, but also push Belts when they need to do better.

Process Owners have primary responsibility for the operation and output of a given process. In some cases, Process Owners are also Green Belts or Black Belts who drive the execution of a Lean Six Sigma project. In other cases, they work closely with Green Belts and Black Belts to achieve and sustain Six Sigma improvements. Additionally, Process Owners help Champions identify improvement project opportunities, since they know the most about their particular performance issues.

Due to their high level of influence and closeness to work processes, both Champions and Process Owners play a vital role in ensuring Lean Six Sigma success. Therefore, it pays big dividends to have them properly trained and equipped before making them accountable for the targeted results.

# Install Deployment Infrastructure

While hundreds of companies employ Lean Six Sigma practitioners (Black Belts) and realize continuous improvement, few companies take the time to install support systems that can drive true breakthrough performance. So let's be clear: you only achieve significant corporate breakthrough when you install a deployment infrastructure through the proper initialization of Lean Six Sigma.

Let's break it down. In the performance-improvement world, initialization is a term that refers to the many systems, people, structures, and procedures you must put in place at the corporate level to ensure widespread success. The resulting deployment infrastructure is your actual Lean Six Sigma foundation; it is the glue that holds everyone and all projects together and working in harmony toward the common goal of improvement sustainability.

Knowing this, your deployment infrastructure is installed in the following areas: human resources, finance, information technology, project management, training, and communications. We'll cover these one at a time so you get a feel and flavor for what's involved.

## Human Resources

Your HR infrastructure includes clear job roles and responsibilities for Champions, Black Belts, Green Belts, Master Black Belts, and others as defined by your company. (Some designate Yellow Belts, White Belts, and other job roles.) Your infrastructure also defines the policies and procedures by which you select Champions and Belts, hire new ones from the outside, develop them, promote them, evaluate their performance, and reward accomplishments.

## Finance

Your finance infrastructure focuses primarily on defining the many categories of project savings and results (hard savings, soft savings, revenue increases, cost avoidance, and so on). We define the classic financial categories in Chapter 8. What you need to know is that all Lean Six Sigma project savings and benefits must be quantified, categorized, and tracked. Usually, this is done with the aid of 1) a trained team or staff of Lean Six Sigma Finance representatives, and 2) enterprise project tracking software.

Additionally, you will have to train your group of finance reps to be involved in every Lean Six Sigma project from its beginning. At first, you have procedures for evaluating the potential savings of identified projects. This is done in the Define phase when deciding which projects to pursue and which to table. Later, often during the Measure or Analyze phases, a finance rep will reevaluate the project from a financial standpoint to ensure it is still worth pursuing.

Finally, after a project is completed, usually after about six months, the finance function becomes involved again to validate the actual savings from the project. No matter how well you do in making an improvement, or how much money you are certain to save, it only matters that you actually make the improvement, that it is sustained, and that it returns your investment in time, money, and effort many times over.

## Information Technology

Your information technology (IT) infrastructure will consist of enterprise and desktop software in the following areas: data collection and analysis; process definition, modeling, and simulation; project tracking and management; and e-learning. Don't underestimate the need for all the necessary technology tools, including this software as well as notebook computers for Black Belts, Champions, and others.

As with your other infrastructure planks, the IT plank requires that you form a special team of experts. Remember, you are deploying Lean Six Sigma to perhaps as many as 20 or more major divisions and hundreds or thousands of people spread all over the country or the world. You'll want to drive and manage all the technology aspects from one command center.

Despite the high level of technological competency shared by many practitioners today, proper data, network compatibility with possible outside vendors, security settings, and hardware and software guidelines should be established to enhance the initiative, limit confusion, and prevent any security threats from intruders.

## Project Management

The infrastructure for Project Management has two key components: technology and process. As for technology, you'll likely need an enterprise system that can keep track of all the many projects that are planned, underway, and completed. Some of the bigger-name systems are Power Steering, Microsoft Project, Instantis, and others.

These are professional performance-improvement software systems that enable you to engage in all the aspects of executing and managing projects. Check them out to see what they can do for you and your deployment. Their features are too many to list here. In general, however, these systems enable many people to view and manage thousands of projects in all areas of an organization. They are powerful and necessary tools for Lean Six Sigma leaders, executives, Champions, Belts, finance reps, and Process Owners.

Also, you'll need a process for regularly reviewing, or tollgating, Lean Six Sigma projects. The process entails assembling a review team (Champion, Master Black Belt, Process Owner, finance rep, other stakeholders) for every project. After each stage of DMAIC is completed, this team looks at the project activities and ensures they are on track. If they aren't, adjustments are made to ensure the project's success.

# Training

Any organization that would practice Lean Six Sigma first needs to train and educate its leaders and practitioners—and this is an ongoing rather than a one-time activity. At first, the services of an outside training/consulting firm are almost always necessary. When retaining a consulting firm, however, you should do so with the intention of learning to fish yourself.

Therefore, your training infrastructure should focus first on getting Champions and Belts trained and ready to execute their first projects. Then, while you are enacting your first round of projects, you should begin to train Master Black Belts. These are expert Lean Six Sigma practitioners and teachers who can train (and mentor/coach) subsequent rounds of Belts (Black, Green, Yellow, etc.).

Other aspects of your training infrastructure include:

**Curriculum development.** This can be a major undertaking, depending on your industry and needs. For instance, you may be a global company with several hundred thousand people, in dozens of countries, speaking multiple languages. If this is the case, you'll need curriculum for all the Lean Six Sigma roles in different languages, maybe even loaded with course content that is specific to your industry.

**Mentoring and support.** Using your consulting firm at first, you should develop and designate certain expert individuals to coach and mentor practitioners, and leaders. Part of this should include an instructor feedback system that evaluates the effectiveness of all your trainers.

**Online support.** In this day, you almost have to have an e-learning component to your Lean Six Sigma training. Such a component should provide Green Belt and even Black Belt training. It should also provide Champion training and awareness training for such others as Process Owners. In addition, many companies take advantage of chat and mentoring systems that provide real-time, online support to Belts.

## Communication

Your communication infrastructure should mirror the way you normally communicate in your company: e-mail, video broadcast, meetings, and so on. Every organization has its set communication vehicles, like the Monthly Reporter or the Message from the President. You get the idea.

It's a good idea sometimes to designate a new communication vehicle dedicated solely to the Lean Six Sigma initiative. This is often necessary at first as you are trying to get the initiative off the ground. Like a jumbo jet, it takes a lot of force to get liftoff; once you're flying you can turn down the engines.

Lean Six Sigma will fundamentally change the way your company thinks and operates. So your communication will have to address this, and will have to address a range of emotions—from fearful resistance to enthusiastic support. Here are some tips you can give to your communications team:

- Key messages need to focus on the "Why?" behind Lean Six Sigma. Cite the burning platforms.

- Messages need to be consistent and clear, and message repetition and frankness are key.

- Communication must occur in all directions and at all levels of the organization.

- Milestones and updates need to be provided as the process unfolds.

# Design Governance Model

You need to manage and govern your Lean Six Sigma initiative, just like you'd manage a company or oversee the construction of a jet engine. You need an organization. You need performance metrics. You need timelines for achieving program milestones. You need a charter that defines what your governance body is all about. And you need to engage in certain governance activities.

## Design Governance Metrics

You can't enjoy a car very well without a dashboard telling you how fast you're going, how far you've driven, when something malfunctions, and so on. Lean Six Sigma is the same: you need a robust dashboard of metrics to give you feedback on how well the program is progressing, and where and when you need to make adjustments.

Your dashboard metrics should include your Key Performance Indicators (KPIs), which stand as the performance targets for your initiative. These are business-level metrics like Cost Savings, Growth, Customer Satisfaction, Capacity, and Quality. Supporting these indicators are project indicators as follows:

◆ **Project pipeline**—The quantity and quality of projects.

◆ **Project volume**—The number of projects you have in process and completed at any given time.

◆ **Project cycle time**—Time from project initiation to completion (usually 6–8 months at first, 3–4 months later).

◆ **Project results**—How much money did the project(s) save or add to the top line?

The following is a stylized Lean Six Sigma dashboard, complete with business and enabling metrics, which include those related to projects, process, people, intellectual property, and culture.

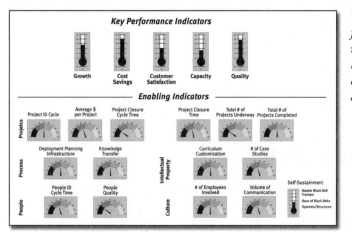

*This is a stylized dashboard for Lean Six Sigma deployment. Your dashboard may have some of these elements and other elements/metrics as well.*

# Long-Term Practitioner Strategies

The key is to decide whether your Belts will become the future leaders of the company, or whether you just need them to enact certain improvements, then go back to their normal jobs. Either scenario is valid, and it just depends on your needs and approach.

If you're going to use Lean Six Sigma as a springboard for future leaders, then you need to choose Belts that have demonstrated technical capability, as well as great interpersonal, communication, and influencing skills. Then you need to give many of these full-time Belts a promotion after their tour of duty for 18 to 24 months solving problems in different parts of the organization.

If on the other hand you aren't using Lean Six Sigma as a development platform, you need only to select those who are technically competent, and able to learn and apply the tools and DMAIC process.

## Establish Practitioner Selection Process

Everything is a process, so you'll need one for selecting your Lean Six Sigma practitioners. This is especially important because you really do need the right people involved in the initiative or it may fail. While your process will be different from the processes of others, you'll want to use the selection vehicles you currently have in place.

Whether you advertise on the outside for practitioners, or inside the organization, you'll need specific criteria and job descriptions. Best practices reveal that practitioners are usually selected by the deployment executive and/or deployment leader with input from HR and the career-development process.

## Identify Practitioners

You can use a Cause-and-Effect Matrix to systematically select practitioners in a team-based, disciplined environment. Instead of input variables, you're listing people as your causes, while your criteria are your effects. As the following sample shows, you select the best candidates for the job according to a rating scheme.

Here are the steps you follow to construct a Selection Matrix:

1. **Establish the selection criteria.** As a selection team, create individual lists of selection criteria that are based on prerequisites and expected roles.

2. **Set up the matrix.** Create the matrix on a flip chart with selection criteria as column heads and candidates as row heads. This is a good time to reaffirm the common understanding of and commitment to the criteria.

3. **Populate the matrix.** In each cell of the matrix, enter the appropriate rating by consensus or average of the team's input. Multiply the rating by the category weight to derive the weighted score.

4. **Evaluate the ratings.** Add the weighted scores to see which candidates stand out as the best for the job.

| Scoring Parameters | 9 | High | High | High | High | High | Low | High | | |
| | 3 | Med. | Med. | Med. | Med. | Med. | Med. | Med. | | |
| | 1 | Low | Low | Low | Low | Low | High | Low | | |
| | Criteria | | | | Evaluation Criteria | | | | | |
| | | Ability to Influence | Interest in Lean Six Sigma | Zeal to Learn | Problem Solving Skills | Ability to Train/ Mentor | Customer Orientation | Deep Process Knowledge | Total Project Score | Priority |
| Candidate Name | Category Weighting | 32% | 14% | 24% | 11% | 14% | 0% | 6% | | |
| Candidate A | Raw Score | 9 | 3 | 9 | 9 | 3 | 9 | 3 | 45.00 | 1 |
| | Weighted Score | 2.85 | 0.42 | 2.14 | 0.98 | 0.42 | 0.03 | 0.17 | 7.00 | |
| Candidate B | Raw Score | 9 | 3 | 3 | 3 | 3 | 1 | 1 | 23.00 | 3 |
| | Weighted Score | 2.85 | 0.42 | 0.71 | 0.33 | 0.42 | 0.00 | 0.06 | 4.78 | |
| Candidate C | Raw Score | 1 | 1 | 1 | 1 | 1 | 1 | 9 | 15.00 | 4 |
| | Weighted Score | 0.32 | 0.14 | 0.24 | 0.11 | 0.14 | 0.00 | 0.50 | 1.44 | |
| Candidate D | Raw Score | 9 | 3 | 3 | 9 | 1 | 3 | 3 | 31.00 | 2 |
| | Weighted Score | 2.85 | 0.42 | 0.71 | 0.98 | 0.14 | 0.01 | 0.17 | 5.28 | |

*A matrix like this enables you to make selections as objectively as possible. You can see that Candidate A is the number-one choice for selection among the four candidates considered.*

# Align Projects and People

To be successful, you have to assign the right Champions and Black Belts/Green Belts to the right projects. In the case of Champions, it's simple. If your Champions are full-time (which is rare), you can assign any projects in any areas to them—but it still makes sense to give certain Champions certain projects that fall within their area of experience and expertise.

If your Champions are devoted to Lean Six Sigma part-time, which is almost always the case, then you'll want to assign projects to them that fall within their organizational area. So a Champion in the accounting and finance area would oversee those types of projects. A Champion in manufacturing would oversee manufacturing projects, and so forth.

Belts are different, especially Black Belts. For them you can take one of two approaches. One approach is to assign them projects that fall only within their areas of immediate expertise. If you take this approach, projects are likely to get done faster. But there is some risk involved. Because the Black Belts are so close to the process, they may not be as likely to think out of the box and generate creative solutions.

The other approach is to purposefully assign projects to Black Belts that fall outside their immediate areas of expertise. This helps them broaden their knowledge of the organization and its processes, and grooms them to become future leaders. So if your intent as an organization is to use Lean Six Sigma as a leadership development mechanism, you'd probably adopt this approach.

## Set Performance Objectives

Just as the organization sets its Lean Six Sigma goals, so do the individual Champions and Belts. This only makes sense because, after all, you need a lot of people to make the big improvements your organization desires. They sure won't happen by themselves!

Therefore, a Champion might be accountable for reducing defects in a certain product within his or her area, or might be responsible for improving capacity in the Southwest region—that kind of thing. Black Belts, on the other hand, are responsible to complete about four projects per year saving close to $200,000 each, sometimes higher. For Green Belts that number is two, because they typically work on less complex projects part-time.

As with everything in the Lean Six Sigma world, you'll want to document the performance objectives for Champions and Black belts. Signed and agreed is the best way. Then you'll have a document for reference if needed.

## The Least You Need to Know

- Before you embark on your journey to performance excellence, make sure that you first establish the overall deployment objectives. This will be your lifeline during the deployment.

- You've committed a lot of money and time to this new initiative. Set your organization up for success by defining the right priorities to increase shareholder value.

- Only real and energetic leadership support will get you the results that you deserve. How do you do it? Lead and live by example, show them the *money*, and surround yourself with true believers.

- Communicate a simple and compelling message that not just echoes in the halls of your corporate office, but penetrates the hearts and minds of your people.

- Stay close and informed, and give your people what they need to get the job done.

# Chapter 26

# Enable Everyone Involved

## In This Chapter

- ◆ Modifying your intellectual property
- ◆ Cooperating with other initiatives
- ◆ What do Champions need to know?
- ◆ What do Black Belts need to know?

So the Chinese proverb goes: Give a man a fish and you feed him for a day; teach a man to fish and you feed him for a lifetime. This is what you have to do to make your Lean Six Sigma deployment successful. You have to Enable people—people in many different roles—to execute the initiative and sustain it over time. And the way you do this is to educate and train Lean Six Sigma leaders and practitioners.

Therefore, we'll cover the specifics of Lean Six Sigma knowledge transfer in this chapter. What is knowledge transfer? It's the act of getting the right knowledge to the right people at the right time to achieve your purpose. If your organization can do this, it will effectively transition itself from planning process change to making those changes—all to the benefit of your customers and your business.

# Enable Road Map

Three activities are key for Lean Six Sigma leaders as they engage in the Enable phase of deployment. First, you establish and adapt your intellectual property—the curricula and course content you'll need to train everyone. Second, you educate and build awareness amongst your managers and leaders. Third, you conduct all your initial orientation and training for your first wave of Lean Six Sigma practitioners.

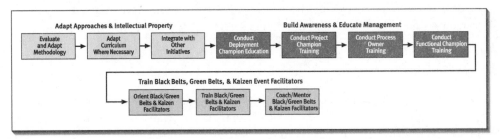

*Here are the steps you should follow in the Enable phase of Lean Six Sigma deployment. Depending on your experience and unique situation, you may or may not follow these steps in set order.*

# Adapt Approaches and Intellectual Property

If no one ever said it, we will. The key to survival is adaptation. Well, we just Googled this ("The key to survival is adaptation") and got 18 hits, so we know it's been said at least 18 times before! But back to the matter at hand. If you want your Lean Six Sigma initiative to be successful, you'll have to adapt, and adapt well.

First, you'll have to adapt certain aspects of the Lean Six Sigma method if necessary. Second, you'll have to adapt your curriculum to make it as relevant to your organization as possible. Third, you'll want to integrate your Lean Six Sigma program with other initiatives going on in your organization and company.

## Evaluate and Adapt Methodology

Lean Six Sigma is not a one-size-fits-all methodology, because its total set of tools and skills is very broad, especially when you include Design for Six Sigma (DFSS) tools and methods. Even in this book, we've only touched on the most widely used tools and concepts amongst a deep sea of options.

A major question to ask is whether you'll need more Lean-like skills, or more Six Sigma-like skills. If your business needs are more centered around cycle-time improvement, waste reduction, and value creation, then you'll focus more on the Lean tools within your deployment. If your needs are more in the areas of defect and variability reduction, or customer satisfaction, then you'll probably adopt more Six Sigma-oriented methods.

In other cases, your company may need to reinvent itself to catch up or outpace competitors. If this is true, you'll add an innovation twist to your Lean Six Sigma program—incorporating elements of other methods like TRIZ (Theory of Inventive Problem Solving). Or you'll include DFSS concepts and tools in your standard curricula.

In short, you'll adapt the standard Lean Six Sigma approach to address your specific needs and objectives. That's why we expect variability between one Lean Six Sigma initiative and another—variability in the road maps, tool sets, language, and approach you adopt.

## Adapt Curriculum

This is a very important success factor for your Lean Six Sigma program. In fact, it's critical. If you don't adapt your curricula and course content to fit your needs, you might run into significant difficulties.

It's true that a process is a process is a process, and that every organization has processes for what it does. Given this, you'd think anyone, anywhere, in any company could learn the trade of process improvement generically—then apply it to their specific process and circumstances.

If all your people were smart enough, and you had the best teachers, this would be true. But not everyone is good at abstract thinking, and at applying principles in any setting, regardless of how they're taught. This is why you want to consider adapting your Lean Six Sigma curricula to fit your environment and type of functions you perform.

For example, if you are a health-care organization, you don't want engineering-related curricula and course content. If you're a transactional company (like a bank or credit bureau), you need more concepts and tools related to helping you conduct reliable, high-volume transactions.

Terminology matters, too. One financial services company balked at the use of the word "customer" in its training materials, because it preferred the word "clients." The same company was uncomfortable with the concept of the "hidden factory." What's a factory got to do with us? they asked. Instead, they opted for using the language of the "hidden operation." That felt better and fit their industry and culture better.

## Integrate with Other Initiatives

Lean Six Sigma is not the only initiative in your organization's present or past, and it won't be the last. Because of this, you want to be aware of other initiatives underway and how Lean Six Sigma either complements or competes with these.

On the complementary side, your company might be implementing a Balanced Scorecard initiative, which systematically defines and distributes performance metrics throughout a company. Or you might use the Hoshin Planning methodology to translate your company's top strategies into lower-level performance objectives, along with plans for achieving those objectives.

Part of your Hoshin Plan surely might include using Lean Six Sigma to achieve certain objectives, especially those related to defect reduction or speed and efficiency improvement. Where your Balanced Scorecard and Hoshin Planning activities leave off, Lean Six Sigma picks up.

From the bottom up, you may have such initiatives as ISO 9000 and Sarbanes Oxley, both of which are concerned with establishing basic process management and documentation systems. This is a good foundation for implementing Lean Six Sigma, and the efforts should be coordinated.

Some initiatives that could compete with Lean Six Sigma are mergers and acquisitions, major technology deployments, or various electronic management systems like Customer Relationship Management, ERP, SAP, Oracle, or PeopleSoft. Such competition can create chaos and severely compromise the resources available for Lean Six Sigma, as well as its probability of success.

Therefore, dovetail Lean Six Sigma with these initiatives when possible, and adapt the approach when necessary to deal with these contingencies. Revisit your Stakeholder Analysis for more adaptation horsepower if you need it.

# Management Awareness and Education

We've said it before: you need leadership to be successful with Lean Six Sigma. But a good leader does not a good Lean Six Sigma leader make. Like anyone, executives and managers need education, and they need to know all about the programs they drive. For this reason, we'll cover some points about educating your Deployment Champions, Project Champions, Process Owners, and Functional Champions—your Lean Six Sigma leaders.

## Deployment Champion Education

We previously defined the role of a Deployment Champion (Chapter 25) as a leader who drives and oversees Lean Six Sigma deployment throughout a major business unit or division. Therefore, the education and training for this role should cover the knowledge and process involved in rolling the initiative out over a large organization.

Topics and material to cover include the basic tenets of Lean Six Sigma: why you do it, what it is, how it works. Then the sessions focus on specific duties, concepts, and knowledge required for Deployment Champions to drive Lean Six Sigma in their own business units. This includes ...

◆ Negotiating and committing to specific performance targets in set time frames.

◆ The development of a business unit Lean Six Sigma performance dashboard, including financial targets.

◆ The development of a resource plan that designates the number of Project Champions, Black Belts, and Green Belts required according to appropriate formulas.

◆ Guidance and coaching about how to work with Project and Functional Champions.

## Project Champion Training

Project Champions (often just called Champions) oversee all the aspects of project selection, definition, and completion. In this role, they need to understand the basic concepts of Lean Six Sigma, in addition to its tools and techniques. While they are not as proficient in the use of tools as Black Belts, they need to know what they are and generally how they're used.

Because they oversee Black and Green Belts, select projects, configure improvement plans, and interface with management, Champions also need to be trained in the principles and practices of change management. They really do function as their name implies: they are champions of change.

In addition, Champions need mentoring and coaching skills, so these should be part of their curriculum. They also need to understand the process of transitioning a project from the Belt to the Process Owner, and how to conduct DMAIC tollgate reviews.

Finally, Champions are responsible for achieving the grouped financial targets for all the Belts under their direction. This responsibility is also clarified during Champion training, and Champions sign up for achieving these targets.

## Process Owner Training

Process Owners play a critical role in Lean Six Sigma by providing information on the current state of a process, and helping to develop the future state. They also have primary responsibility for maintaining project results and sustaining the gains made by Lean Six Sigma project teams.

As such, Process Owners need to be well versed in the basic principles of Lean Six Sigma. In conjunction with the Champion, they need to know how to take a business problem and convert it into a Lean Six Sigma project. This requires an awareness of the different methodologies, and which one should be used for which type of problem. Process mapping tools are also a key component of their training.

Process owners need to understand the importance of data and how to acquire it to aid decision making. In addition, a thorough understanding of the Control phase, and its associated tools, is important in order to smoothly transition an improved process from the practitioner back to the Process Owner.

## Functional Champion Training

In Chapter 25, we talked about the different infrastructure areas needed to enable Lean Six Sigma. Remember human resources, finance, information technology, project management, training, and communication? Well, you need at least one Functional Champion in each of these areas to help drive your deployment. Some areas, such as finance, may have more than one Champion (or representative), as more involvement at the project level is required.

For these Champions, an overview of Lean Six Sigma goes without saying. More importantly, though, the Functional Champions need to understand the role their respective area plays in the big picture. In order to perform their functional responsibilities, customized training will be required for each type of Champion.

For example, the HR Champion is responsible for disseminating and supporting the policies and procedures developed during the Plan phase. As such, they may need some change leadership training. These Champions are also responsible for maintaining job descriptions and hiring practitioners, so they need a good understanding of the various Lean Six Sigma roles.

On the other hand, Finance Champions may undergo more technical training since they are typically more involved in Lean Six Sigma at the project level. They'll need to understand how to work with Champions to scope projects and how to help practitioners quantify project savings. They should also be trained to use the project tracking software, which they will use at key tollgate points throughout the DMAIC process.

# Black Belts, Green Belts, and Facilitators

Black Belts, Green Belts, and Kaizen Event Facilitators are the lynchpins of your success with Lean Six Sigma—and your investment in them will be its own reward. Belts and Facilitators are the leaders on the ground who make changes happen and solve difficult business problems for the last time. Typically, you develop these practitioners along three lines: orientation, training, and coaching/mentoring.

## Welcome to Your New Career

Orientation for Black Belts is recommended as they say goodbye to their old jobs and hello to their new Lean Six Sigma careers. Like any first day on the job, they will have questions, and you should strive to anticipate as many questions as possible. Here are a few of the more common topics covered in orientation:

◆ What is the role of a Black Belt in your organization? What is the difference between each role? (Black Belts are DMAIC experts. Green Belts are DMAIC proficient. Kaizen Event Facilitators are experts at moving teams through a compressed process of change.)

◆ What is expected of them as full-time practitioners? (See Chapter 25 for standard expectations.)

◆ What does it mean to be a team leader? (Driving change, passion, influence without authority.) How will they be expected to work with team members, Process Owners, Champions, and leadership?

◆ What can they expect in training? How long is it? Why are training sessions spread out over the course of two to four months, and what are they expected to do in between class weeks? (Work on and complete their first project!)

◆ What sort of project will they need to complete during training? What are some of the techniques for presenting a project summary to different groups?

 **Lean Six Sigma Wisdom**

More often than you think, Lean Six Sigma practitioners need guidance when it comes to dealing with people. Leadership (influencing without authority) is harder to learn for many than even statistics!

Orientation for Green Belts and Kaizen Event Facilitators is typically faster and less formal. Sometimes, you don't really need to conduct a formal orientation session for these roles; Green Belts and Kaizen Event Facilitators can get the orientation they need at the outset of their training.

# Training and Project Work

While Black Belts need in-depth knowledge of Lean Six Sigma concepts and tools, Green Belts are trained to a lesser extent. Kaizen Event Facilitators should have at least a Green Belt level of knowledge, plus additional experience related to getting a lot done in a short period of time in a team environment. All three types of practitioners are process-level leaders that need special training, as follows.

**Lean Six Sigma Black Belts.** Black Belt training takes longer and is more comprehensive than any other Lean Six Sigma role (except Master Black Belt). It makes sense, doesn't it, when you think about the myriad of tools and techniques they need to learn, not to mention the interpersonal and leadership skills required?

The training process for Black Belts typically consists of five weeks in the classroom, separated by periods of on-the-job application when they work on their chosen project with their teams. Usually the total cycle time for training is five months, and includes the completion of at least one DMAIC project and one Kaizen Event to be certified (and often more than one DMAIC project and Kaizen Event).

The Black Belt candidate is in the classroom for a week, then applies that learning for three weeks. In the best programs, curriculum is well balanced with both Lean and Six Sigma elements. Black Belts also receive such soft skills training as change leadership and the team process.

Here are just some curriculum elements for the Lean Six Sigma Black Belt:

| | |
|---|---|
| Value Stream Mapping | Mistake Proofing |
| The eight types of waste | Kanban calculations |
| Takt Time and cycle time | Workload Balancing |
| Data collection techniques | Queuing theory |
| Measurement System Analysis | Equipment Effectiveness |
| Hypothesis testing | Quick Changeover |
| Regression analysis | Control Charts |
| Design of Experiments | Standardized Work |
| Five S disciplines | Capability Analysis |

**Green Belts.** You'll recall (see Chapter 25) that Green Belts are part-time practitioners who complete fewer, less difficult projects than Black Belts. Therefore, Green Belt training is shorter than Black Belt training, and often occurs in one two-week-long consecutive program.

Green Belts should come out of training with some of the same know-how as Black Belts, but they will be more limited in their ability to solve difficult problems and performance issues. The idea is to equip Green Belts with enough knowledge of Lean Six Sigma to run small projects in their areas of expertise, very possibly with the assistance of Black Belts.

As with other practitioners, Green Belts should receive project reviews and other coaching as needed. Their mentors include Black Belts, Champions, and Master Black Belts. On the flip side, particularly talented Green Belts may be called upon to coach Yellow Belts and team members. (Yellow Belts have some Lean Six Sigma knowledge but less than Green Belts.)

**Lean Six Sigma Wisdom**

KISS (Keep It Simple Statistically). You don't have to use every tool in your Lean Six Sigma toolbox on every project. An important concept during training is learning which tool to use for which job.

**Kaizen Event Facilitators.** We recommend that all Kaizen Event Facilitators have at least been trained as Green Belts, even if they don't have experience in completing projects. In many cases, a Kaizen Event Facilitator will become certified only after completing at least one successful Kaizen Event (and often more than one).

Training for Lean Facilitators may not follow a set road map, but their training should cover the following concepts in depth:

- Lean Six Sigma in general, how and why it works, along with the Kaizen Event Facilitator's role in the initiative.

- The difference between Lean production and batch processing, and between push and Pull.

- How to identify and eliminate waste, increase efficiency, and increase Flow.

- The concept of value-added versus non-value-added activities—and how to set up a Value Stream Map.

- The concepts of cycle time and Takt Time.

- How and when to apply Lean techniques such as Mistake Proofing, Kanban, cellular layout, and Fast Changeover.

- The objective of a Kaizen Event and how to facilitate one, including all the work leading up to the event, as well as follow-up activities.

- An introduction to change management and/or leadership and, of course, facilitation skills.

## Coaching and Mentoring

Coaching and mentoring your Lean Six Sigma practitioners is an ongoing practice, not a one-time event. During training, instructors provide much of the coaching as the practitioners complete their first project or Kaizen Event.

As the Lean Six Sigma deployment takes root, the mentoring process transitions to the organization's Master Black Belts and Champions. Master Black Belts provide technical coaching and mentoring to Black Belts, while Champions provide business and organizational mentoring.

In general, Master Black Belts make sure that tools are applied correctly and road maps are followed. The Master Black Belt identifies areas where practitioners need assistance in applying the DMAIC process and tools, and provides corrective exercises and suggestions.

Champions, on the other hand, can assist the practitioners with leadership and change management issues, such as resolving team conflicts or garnering executive support. It is the Champion's role to remove obstacles and help the practitioners develop leadership skills.

## The Least You Need to Know

- The Enable phase of Lean Six Sigma deployment focuses primarily on the activities involved in knowledge transfer: curriculum integrity, course content, and training practitioners.

- It's best to tailor your curriculum to fit your organizational environment (health care versus financial services versus manufacturing, engineering, and so on).

- Lean Six Sigma is not the only initiative in your organization. Be aware of the others and either tap into the synergy or plan for how you'll meet resistance.

- Don't go light on training Champions and practitioners. The more prepared and ready they are, the more successful you'll be.

- Quick, what are the leadership roles for Lean Six Sigma? (Deployment Champion, Project Champion, Functional Champions for HR, IT, finance, training, communications, project management.)

- Quick again, what are the practitioner roles? (Master Black Belt, Black Belt, Green Belt, Kaizen Event Facilitator, Yellow Belt, team member.)

# Chapter 27

# Make It Happen

## In This Chapter

- ◆ Implementing all the changes
- ◆ Are you a Lean Six Sigma Master?
- ◆ Adapt your knowledge or die
- ◆ How healthy is your program?
- ◆ Refresh, renew, and reap rewards

There's a time in the life of every major initiative when it moves from planning and preparation to implementation. That's where we're at now in this chapter. You've assessed your organization's performance and diagnosed major performance gaps. You've carefully worked with business leaders to set the performance and financial objectives for every division of your company.

You've also built a strong infrastructure for Lean Six Sigma change, onboarded all your Champions and Belts, trained them, and have given them everything they need to be successful. Now you're ready to implement all your plans and projects. And you'll soon be conducting all the necessary activities to Sustain the momentum of the initiative over time.

We cover the main points of the Implement and Sustain phases of Lean Six Sigma deployment in this chapter: executing and managing projects, developing Lean Six Sigma trainers and mentors, checking and monitoring results and progress, adapting your deployment approach, and bringing fresh energy to the effort when needed. These are the points of concern. Pay attention to them and reap the rewards!

# Execute and Sustain Road Map

Five activities are key for Lean Six Sigma leaders as they engage in the Execute and Sustain phases of deployment. First, you roll out your first wave of projects and review progress along the way. Second, you develop your own internal Masters, or Master Black Belts, or Lean Six Sigma Masters, or whatever you want to call them. Third, you adapt your program based on learning and experience along the way. Fourth, you conduct an annual health check of the initiative. Fifth, you re-energize your program as needed to keep it alive.

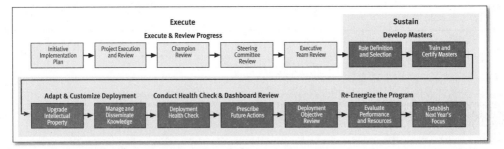

*Here are the steps you should follow in the Execute and Sustain phases of Lean Six Sigma deployment. Depending on your experience and unique situation, you may or may not follow these steps in set order.*

# Execute and Review Progress

When implementing Lean Six Sigma, you're essentially putting all your project and initiativewide plans into action. It's as simple as that. Some say success is 90 percent perspiration, and maybe this is true. But maybe success is 90 percent preparation. Maybe you need a lot of both to succeed. You've certainly prepared the organization for Lean Six Sigma, and now it's a matter of executing your plans.

## The Implementation Plan

Just like you have a plan for completing a Lean Six Sigma project, you also have a plan for executing the whole deployment initiative. Some elements of your plan should be ...

- Strategies and plans for integrating Lean Six Sigma with other initiatives, such as ISO 9000, Baldrige, Customer Relationship Management, ERP, SAP, and so on.

- A detailed Stakeholder Analysis.

- All the units and divisions within which Lean Six Sigma will be deployed (with the Deployment Champion for each unit noted).

- The specific business unit or division goals for Lean Six Sigma, including the amount of dollar savings targeted and by when.

- An infrastructure installation plan, including specifics for the various key functions of human resources, finance, training, information technology, project management, and communications. (All of these plans are large plans in and of themselves.)

- Timing for the initiative's rollout in all the business units, and as a whole, shown with a large Gantt Chart.

- A list of all the initially selected projects in each business unit.

- Plans for project tollgate reviews after each phase of DMAIC, and plans for reviewing the initiative as a whole with leadership at appropriate intervals.

- Provisions for transitioning the initiative from the expertise of the consultant to internal resources and control.

- An interconnected Lean Six Sigma performance dashboard that holds Key Performance Indicators (business indicators), as well as enabling indicators related to the initiative (e.g., number of projects completed, number of people trained, etc.).

 **Quotable Quote**

Have a bias toward action—let's see something happen now. You can break that big plan into small steps and take the first step right away.

—Indira Gandhi

## Execute and Review Projects

You should have a portfolio of projects entered in your tracking software and ready for execution. The queued projects selected and scoped by your Champions should have been reviewed by your Finance Champions to initially validate the proposed savings. Your Lean Six Sigma practitioners—Black Belts, Kaizen Event Facilitators, maybe even Green Belts—are poised on the starting line, trained and ready to go.

As the project work commences, finally everyone gets the chance to apply what they've learned. The practitioners collect data, look for waste, analyze, and experiment—according to the project execution process we laid out for you in Parts 2 and 3. If you're a Project Champion, the information in these parts is all you need to know when it comes to executing projects.

While we don't want to repeat ourselves, we will give you just a few reminders before launching into project execution mode. One, be sure you have selected the right and very best projects. They need to be aligned with your business objectives, they need to be properly defined and scoped, and they need to have a high probability of yielding significant, quantifiable financial benefits.

Two, make sure you have enterprisewide project management software that everyone can use. Various options exist, but all the good ones give you the ability to customize performance dashboards, slice and dice project data at will, manage people and tasks, and even include important prompts and tollgates that help you move smoothly through such popular road maps as DMAIC.

Three, you want to regularly review project progress at the process level after each stage of DMAIC. These are called tollgate reviews for a reason: if you haven't met the completion criteria for one stage, you cannot move on to the next. Develop your review criteria and process well; make sure reviews are attended by all pertinent stakeholders.

## Champion Review

As much as you review projects, you have to review the people who are responsible for project success—the Champions. Lean Six Sigma Champions should meet weekly, or at least monthly, to review two things: the status of the deployment and the progress of practitioners.

First, Champions must review the deployment initiative. Remember the dashboard we recommended you create in Chapter 25, the Enable phase? Make it visible and take a look at how your desired results compare to the real thing. Compare the number of projects, average savings, range of savings, project cycle time, Black Belt dropout rate, and anything else the dashboard shows.

Second, Champions need to remain acutely aware of how each of their practitioners is performing. Is Black Belt John on track? Are his results coming in as expected? Is his first project progressing as expected? Same for all the belts under your purvey, if you're a Champion.

Who needs coaching, and who needs a kick in the pants? Who is blazing trails, and who just can't cut it? The Champion is responsible to answer these questions, and to design plans for closing shortfalls and gaps. Don't be afraid to reallocate people if need be. The success of your deployment depends on it!

**Real-Life Story**

A national grocery store chain offered its senior executive Black Belt candidates the opportunity to become company officers in the future. Still, 30 percent of the executives who initially signed up dropped out later, going back to their old jobs. The lesson? Revisit Black Belt candidates during or after training to re-evaluate their interest and aptitude.

## Steering Committee Review

The Lean Six Sigma steering committee should meet monthly for a scorecard (dashboard) review. You guessed it. The purpose is to look at the planned improvements and all the dashboard indicators to see how they're performing. Look at the number of projects in progress, as well as how many have been completed and how many are in the pipeline.

In addition to quantity, examine the quality of your projects. Are you meeting the financial goals you predicted? Is project cycle time too slow, too fast (you wish!) or just right? Do you have the right number of Belts trained, and have their old positions been filled? How about the climate in general—are people getting on board with the new way of working, or do you still have some change management and communication work to do?

## Executive Team Review

Last but certainly not least, the organization's executive leadership team should meet at least quarterly to discuss the Lean Six Sigma deployment. The main question they need to ask is whether or not Lean Six Sigma is moving the business metrics in the right direction.

If you find that you're falling short, explore and implement corrective actions to keep the deployment on track. And this may entail more involvement from executives than just contacting their local Deployment Champion. Sometimes shortfalls in the Lean Six Sigma program are symptomatic of deeper business issues.

# Sustain the Initiative

If you've gotten this far, presumably you want to make Lean Six Sigma the way your organization does business, everywhere, all the time, with everyone involved. If you've achieved measurable gains throughout the company, why wouldn't you want to just keep on going and make improvement what it should be—continual and never ending?

To do this you have to make Lean Six Sigma second nature. You have to install additional mechanisms and supports to ensure a full transition to full self-sufficiency. As we've said, you'll need a consulting or training firm to get your leadership team on board, your deployment infrastructure installed, and your people trained. After this, however, shame on you if you don't figure out how to do it yourself.

# Master Development

The reason you have to develop Masters, or Master Black Belts, is because they become your Lean Six Sigma experts after the consultants are gone. Your Deployment and Project Champions already know enough to keep growing with the initiative and performing their leadership functions. But it's the technicalities of Lean Six Sigma that can drag you down.

The devil is in the details, and you don't want your initiative to stall later for lack of knowledge and deep Lean Six Sigma expertise. Therefore, make sure you invest in developing Master Black Belts by first defining their role and, second, training them, coaching them, and certifying their skills.

## Role Definition and Selection

Master Black Belts are more than just tool masters and technical experts. They're also a strong force for change as they work with management to configure improvement opportunities. Almost always full-time in their roles, Master Black Belts develop curricula and course content, train Belts, and mentor Belts. They also get called upon to lead large or complex projects, and to advise management on business governance issues.

You may decide that certain Master Black Belts will specialize in the Six Sigma skill set, while others will specialize more in Lean. In true Lean Six Sigma spirit, it might be wise to integrate this expertise at the Master Black Belt level. This way their intellectual leadership will serve to bring the two methodologies as close together as possible for reasons we've certainly articulated in this book.

Typically, Master candidates are selected from amongst your highest-performing Black Belts. However, if your organization employs highly educated, statistically minded people who also have a demonstrated teaching ability, you may have yourself a built-in Master Black Belt.

Again, the size of your organization and the complexity of the Master role will determine how many you need. Once you've chosen your candidates, you need to review their qualifications against some set of criteria using a tool like a Pugh Matrix (there's an example in Chapter 25).

## Train and Certify Masters

In addition to a customized training track for your Master teachers and technical leaders, you should follow a certification road map that ensures they are willing and able to meet the higher expectations of the job. Becoming a certified Master Black Belt means more than just high scores on Black Belt exams. The typical requirements are listed here (your certification program may vary, of course):

- **Classroom training**—A mixture of hard and soft skills training is recommended, keeping in mind the specific role the Master will fulfill.

- **Black Belt equivalent exams**—Typically a high score (90 percent or above) is required on all exams.

- **Project submissions**—As many as three projects may be required to show competency. At least one project should be a larger, more complex project. Preferably, even more project experience is a big plus.

- **Demonstrated teaching ability**—Candidates must have previous teaching experience or co-teach a set number of hours to gain proficiency in this area.

The bottom line is to establish your Master criteria based on the needs of your organization, then make it enterprisewide and stick to it (at least for the first couple of years). Nothing is more demoralizing than requiring a stringent certification path for some, while others squeak by due to inconsistent enforcement.

# Adapt and Customize Deployment

After your first deployment cycle, you want to take a huge step forward and evolve your program. From a knowledge standpoint, this entails upgrading your intellectual property and disseminating the many lessons you learned. Just remember that it's not enough to do well; you have to do even better and use past experience to fuel future success.

## Mine for Gold in Your Own Backyard

After your deployment has been running at least six or eight months, and many projects have been completed, you've accrued a whole lot of learning. And people are a lot smarter about your organization, its customers, its weaknesses, and its processes than ever before. So what will you do?

The right answer is that you'll make sure all that learning and knowledge gets out of the heads of a few and into the heads of many. You have to go and find it, organize it, publish it, distribute it, reward it, manage it, and incorporate it back into your training and curriculum.

Mine for the gold nuggets. Talk to practitioners, team members, and Champions. Search the project tracking system. Review project reports and tollgate presentations. Take these nuggets—examples and success stories—from your own program and sprinkle them throughout your intellectual property and your curriculum. Your next round of students will be the better for it, as will those on the periphery who still don't quite "get it."

By the way, case studies are a terrific way to illustrate the results of Lean Six Sigma, especially for anyone not intimately involved with the processes or areas of current focus. You can publish your success stories in trade magazines, or simply make them available internally to generate buy-in and encourage others to join the effort.

## Manage and Disseminate Knowledge

Take some time to think about how you manage and disseminate the knowledge gained from your Lean Six Sigma deployment. Where do you store all the updated documentation to ensure that process changes stay intact? What about lessons learned? If someone has already solved the problem, how do you disseminate that knowledge so that someone else doesn't have to reinvent the wheel? And how do you encourage best practices or project replication? After all, a successful outcome in one area of the business may spark a project idea in another area.

 **Quotable Quote**

Those who cannot remember the past are condemned to repeat it.

—George Santayana

There is no one-size-fits-all solution (although you can bet Microsoft is trying). You can share project information informally (e.g., case studies, company newsletters, and word of mouth), or you can take a more rigorous approach. Many organizations use their project tracking system as their knowledge management and dissemination vehicle. Not a bad idea, but you can use other methods, too, such as your existing document management system or network.

One good idea is to set up a Lean Six Sigma web page on your company's intranet (if you have one). Such a portal can provide one-stop shopping for everything related to your initiative—general information and announcements, case studies, project highlights, training schedules, and employment opportunities. Plus your portal could have e-learning programs for practitioners, chat rooms or bulletin boards, policies and guidelines, possibly even a log-on to the project tracking system or other relevant applications.

# Health Check and Dashboard Review

Similar to the shorter-cycle Champion and steering committee reviews mentioned earlier in this chapter, you should plan on conducting an annual checkup of your deployment. How well has the initiative lived up to expectations? Are any adjustments or changes needed? Just like anything, if you don't check up on it from time to time, it tends to go awry.

## Deployment Health Check

Even if you've weaned your deployment off of consultants by now, this is one time you might want to bring someone in from outside the organization. For one thing, an outside opinion will keep you from having the same discussions you may have been rehashing in all your other reviews. For another, you may encounter issues that you're not sure how to get past, especially if you're fairly new to Lean Six Sigma.

Whether or not you involve an objective outsider, your health reviews should occur at the business-unit level—the organization over which each of your Deployment Champions presides. Your reviews should include the Deployment Champion, various Master Black Belts, certain Functional Champions, Project Champions, Black Belts, Green Belts, team members, and executives.

View the health checkup as a state-of-the-union meeting for Lean Six Sigma in the particular deployment division. But it's not a place people go to hear a speech, although that may happen. Your health checkups are a time and place to ask difficult questions, make adjustments, and do whatever you have to do to keep your initiative on track.

Here's a rundown of what you'll want to look at during your checkup. Just as a physician evaluates your health on several levels, you'll want to assess all the different dimensions of your deployment:

◆ **Strategy:** Evaluate the objectives/goals of your deployment.

◆ **Focus:** Evaluate the focus of current projects.

- ◆ **Methods:** Evaluate your current approaches to performance improvement and how well they're integrated.

- ◆ **Project Selection:** Evaluate your current approaches to project selection and how they're linked to business strategy, operations, and customer processes.

- ◆ **Engagement:** Evaluate how well key leaders and Process Owners are aligned and linked to performance improvement strategies.

- ◆ **Execution of Projects:** Evaluate the extent of project achievement and financial benefit.

- ◆ **Process Management:** Measure the process management maturity of your organization and the degree to which Lean Six Sigma enables that path.

- ◆ **Knowledge Transfer:** Measure the degree to which performance improvement knowledge has been transferred and customized to your organization's needs and culture.

- ◆ **People/Leadership Development:** Evaluate talent attraction, development, and retention regarding your Lean Six Sigma deployment.

- ◆ **Communication:** Evaluate existing internal and external communication approaches.

- ◆ **Culture:** Discuss how Lean Six Sigma is viewed by your entire organization, and to what degree it enables the desired cultural shift.

- ◆ **Metrics:** Evaluate the metrics and measures used to drive your business.

**Real-Life Story**

During a recent checkup at a financial services company, participants discussed the fact that the only road map they had ever employed was the DMAIC methodology. Given the transactional nature of their business, they realized that using a Kaizen Event approach, they could improve certain processes better and faster. This became an action item resulting from the annual review.

## Doctor, Doctor, Give Me the News

After such a complete examination, you'll undoubtedly walk away with some healthy recommendations for improving your Lean Six Sigma initiative, and for guaranteeing it a long life. In other words, you should come out of the checkup with a prescription—a list of action items. Delegate the work appropriately, but make sure to follow up to see that the changes are actually implemented (and do this before the next annual checkup!).

After your health diagnosis is a great time for communicating an update to everyone about your Lean

Six Sigma initiative. You can convey as many details as makes sense for each audience. But one message should be consistent: Lean Six Sigma works. We're tweaking it to make it better, but it works and it's here to stay. It will become the way we do business.

# Re-energize the Program

So you've reached the end of the Lean Six Sigma road, and there's nothing more to do. Right? Wait a minute. Wrong! After coming this far, we certainly hope we don't have to remind you again that improvement is a never-ending journey. Therefore, Lean Six Sigma never ends either, because the world changes, your customers' needs change, and, therefore, your processes change.

Take these last few actions to make sure your initiative stays alive: regularly review your deployment objectives, evaluate your performance and resources, and establish your focus for the upcoming year—every year, year after year!

## Deployment Objective Review

Just when you thought there couldn't possibly be anything else to discuss, assess, or review, we come to the annual objective evaluation. As with the quarterly executive reviews mentioned earlier, you gather the leadership team together to recall the business reasons for deploying Lean Six Sigma in the first place.

While you should definitely assess how well your deployment met the past year's goals, the other reason for meeting is to decide on next year's goals. Will you continue to focus on customer satisfaction, or will you shift focus slightly to encompass a new product line? Can you expand the money-saving processes from one business unit to another? What performance indicators need your attention now?

 **Real-Life Story**

For the first two years of its deployment, DuPont Corporation focused on cost reduction and productivity. In its third year, the company shifted its focus to growth, while maintaining healthy activities in the domains of cost reduction and productivity.

## Evaluate Performance and Resources

Remember, you can't do everything, or at least not all at once. As part of the annual objective review, go back to your business needs assessment. At the organizational level, measure your current performance against your entitlement. Now that you've been taught to fish, are you fishing to your ultimate capability?

This is also a time to review your personnel placement. Do you need to hire more resources, or reallocate existing resources to do better? How engaged is management, at all levels? Are your Champions still taking an active role in project selection? Are your Process Owners taking improvements to the bank, or have they reverted to business as usual?

## Establish Focus for Next Year

It's a funny thing. After healthy and visible success, when an organization establishes its Lean Six Sigma focus for the following year, those themes tend to become a key input into strategic planning for the corporation. Now the initiative is viewed not only as a way of sweeping the organization clean of waste and defects, but it's also determined to be a strategic weapon.

Many famous CEOs have commented about the space between strategy and execution, using such rhetoric as:

> "Strategy is all about execution."—IBM's Louis Gerstner

> "Unless you translate big thoughts into concrete steps for action, they're pointless."—AlliedSignal's Larry Bossidy

Well, ask anyone from any company that's deployed Lean Six Sigma with a fervor, and they'll tell you this: Lean Six Sigma is what lives between strategy and execution. It may not be easy, but it's the real thing.

## The Least You Need to Know

- ◆ The key to successful execution is having a good plan and having everyone lined up to make it happen. Aside from this, you have to review, review, review your progress along the way.

- ◆ Master Black Belts are the technical Lean Six Sigma leaders. Their skill and strength will determine the skill and strength of all your practitioners.

- ◆ You should capture your learning and get it to everyone and anyone who can use it, and by all means, upgrade your training materials when you can.

- ◆ Make sure the Lean Six Sigma initiative becomes fully integrated into the strategic planning process after its first cycle (12 to 18 months).

# Glossary

**accuracy**   The extent to which measurement system values compare with the truth.

**Affinity Diagram**   A tool used to group items into logical categories, and naming the categories with a title that characterizes the group.

**Alternate Hypothesis**   *(H$_A$)* Relative to hypothesis testing, a statement of difference or dependence (e.g., changes in $x$ do affect $Y$).

**Analysis of Variance (ANOVA)**   Statistical method used to test the hypotheses that changes in levels for each $x$ factor cause changes in the response variable $Y$.

**ask why five times**   The act of questioning until you get the root cause of a problem.

**attribute data**   Discrete data gathered into categories, such as Large, Small, On, Off, Red, Blue, Pass, Fail, and so on.

**Autonomous Maintenance**   A subset of Total Productive Maintenance (TPM) which makes the worker the first line of maintenance.

**average**   See "mean."

**average Flow Time**   Actual amount of time it takes to complete process steps, including waiting and rework.

**Balanced Scorecard**   A system of metrics that measures and displays all the different aspects of organizational performance.

**baseline performance**    Snapshot of process performance before Lean Six Sigma project improvements.

**benchmarking**    Comparing your organization or process to those who are world-class at what you do.

**Benefit/Effort Matrix**    Sometimes called an Impact/Effort Matrix, enables you to determine which project ideas have the most value and which don't.

**Black Belt**    An expert problem solver who is trained in Lean Six Sigma methods and statistical tools.

**bottlenecks**    Disruptions in Flow when processing time exceeds Takt Time; or process steps that are rate limiting.

**Box Plot**    Graph commonly used to display differences between categorical *x*s.

**Box-Behnken Design**    A type of response surface design used to identify quadratic and interaction effects of input factors.

**brainstorming**    Group sessions used to elicit a wide range of ideas. In Lean Six Sigma, often used to generate a list of potential *x*s.

**burning platform**    A known need or emergency in an organization that can be used to promote and sustain change.

**Cause-and-Effect Matrix**    Brainstorming tool that estimates the strength of relationship between a list of *x*s and *Y*s.

**cellular operations**    Method of designing the physical layout of a process in a way that minimizes space, time, equipment, and inventory. Also called cellular manufacturing or cellular layout.

**Champion**    Manager or business leader who spearheads the selection, implementation, and completion of Lean Six Sigma projects.

**changeover**    A non-value-added activity necessary to continue production but causing downtime of equipment or resources.

**checksheet**    Data collection tool designed to collect categorical (attribute) data with minimal effort but high visibility. Tally sheets are one example.

**clean data**    Data that is accurate and free of correlation between input factors.

**Common Cause variation**    Variation you get by virtue of nature, or by virtue of the way you design your product or process.

**concurrent engineering**   The practice of simultaneously engineering a product and the processes that make it.

**confidence**   Likelihood of not making a Type I error, symbolized by $(1-\alpha)$. (See "Type I error").

**consequential metrics**   Negative side effects that could happen as a result of Lean Six Sigma improvements.

**Control Chart**   Used to monitor process performance using Control Limits (see "Control Limits").

**control freak**   A person who refuses to believe the gains he or she has made will be maintained by others in his or her absence.

**Control Limits (UCL and LCL)**   The extremes of expected variability of a stable process based on the control metric (e.g. individuals, means, proportions, defect per unit).

**Control Plan**   Institutionalizes a new process by documenting exactly how critical inputs and outputs will be kept in control.

**core team/steering committee**   Team that configures, drives, reviews, and is responsible for the Lean Six Sigma initiative.

**correlation**   Strength of the relationship between two variables (but doesn't imply causation).

**correlation coefficient**   $(r)$ Used to quantify the linear relationship between two variables.

**critical success factors**   Factors that are necessary to the success of a Lean Six Sigma deployment.

**Critical $X$ Worksheet**   Sorts significant $x$s from those that don't impact the process or $Y$ of concern.

**Critical-To characteristic (CT)**   Any feature of a product or process that is important to the customer or the business.

**CT Flowdown**   The cause-and-effect chain of critical factors related to any process or product.

**customer outcomes**   Answering the question "What human need does the product or service fulfill?"

**cycle time**   The time it takes to complete one process step.

**data collection sheet**   Used to collect detailed information on potential $x$s and supply specific $x$-$Y$ data for analysis.

**defect**   Any output of any process or business task that does not meet its intended performance target within some extent of acceptable variation. Also known as error.

**deployment**   The act of spreading, coordinating, and driving many improvements throughout an organization.

**Deployment Champion**   A leader who drives and oversees Lean Six Sigma deployment throughout a major business unit or division.

**deployment infrastructure**   Systems, supports, functions, and software required to proliferate Lean Six Sigma throughout an organization.

**deployment planning**   Process of defining and documenting how an organization will deploy Lean Six Sigma or some other initiative.

**Design for Six Sigma (DFSS)**   The branch of Six Sigma that enables you to prevent defects from occurring in the first place through superior design based on the Voice of the Customer (VOC).

**Design of Experiments**   Uses specific design combinations (arrays) of changes (levels) of input factors (independent variables) to observe changes in output responses (dependent variables).

**Discrete Process Simulation**   Model that shows the visual flow of materials through the process to help identify bottlenecks and resource utilization.

**DMAIC project**   Performance improvement project that progresses through Define-Measure-Analyze-Improve-Control phases. Colloquially known as the "breakthrough strategy."

**DPMO**   Defects per Million Opportunities.

**Ease/Impact Matrix**   A grid that compares the impact and ease of potential solutions.

**eight wastes**   Lean concepts of Waiting, Overproduction, Rework, Motion, Processing, Inventory, Transportation, and Intellect.

**80/20 rule**   Frequently related to Pareto Charts, this rule states that, often, 80 percent of any effect is caused by 20 percent of the input variables. Also known as the "vital few" versus the "trivial many."

**Entitlement**   Best performance possible based on your process design, disregarding variation you can't control.

**EPIC Solution Matrix**   Method of rating possible solutions according to the dimensions of Ease, Permanence, Impact, and Cost.

**External Changeover Steps**   Changeover activities that can be done while the process is running.

**external customer**   Person who purchases the final product or service.

**Failure Mode and Effects Analysis (FMEA)**   Tool used to identify and rank potential possibilities of failure.

**final report**   Project report including storyboard visuals as well as additional information. Written in a narrative fashion so anyone can understand it.

**first-time yield**   Extent to which a process produces its intended outcome right the first time.

**Fishbone Diagram**   Also called Cause-and-Effect Diagram, this is used to brainstorm possible causes of the output *(Y)* variable.

**Five Ss**   Five disciplines that can transform a messy, cluttered, and inefficient process into one that is clean and streamlined (*seiri, seiton, seiso, seiketsu,* and *shitsuke* in Japanese; Sort, Store, Shine, Standardize, and Sustain in English).

**flow**   Lean principle to make sure your workloads are even and humming along at full utilization in a steady way.

**Flow Kaizen**   A type of Kaizen Event that looks at improving the entire value stream.

**Force Field Analysis**   Technique for weighing the enabling versus opposing forces relative to any desired outcome.

**Gantt Chart**   Classic project management tool used to keep track of tasks, people, deadlines, and costs.

**Genba**   The "actual place" where the work is performed.

**Green Belt**   Part-time Lean Six Sigma practitioner who completes fewer, less difficult projects than a Black Belt.

**hard savings**   Quantifiable financial savings that result directly from a Lean Six Sigma project.

**hidden factory**   Rework built into a process as a "necessary" step (called "editing" or "correction" or "revision"). Prevents doing it right the first time.

**Histogram**   A bar chart that displays numerical data by frequency of occurrence within defined intervals.

**Hoshin Planning**    Practice of cascading top-level organizational strategies into increasingly lower levels, with performance metrics attached, and plans for improvement.

**hybridization**    Theory that certain functions of products and systems become melded together over time (Lean Six Sigma is a hybridized solution).

**hypothesis testing**    Using samples to challenge assumptions about population parameters to standards or other populations, and making statements of statistical significance about the populations.

**Ideal Final Result (IFR)**    A perfect solution with no trade-offs or negative consequences used as a starting point to generate solutions using TRIZ (see "Theory of Inventive Problem Solving").

**Ideal Manning Levels**    Determined by dividing the sum of your manual cycle times (time required to perform a job) by your Takt Time (rate of customer demand).

**Implementation Plan**    Documents all the actions required to implement project changes, as well as when the changes are to be done and by whom.

**initialization**    The process by which an organization readies itself to deploy Lean Six Sigma.

**input**    What flows into the process. This can include personnel, material, equipment, information, etc. … the "$x$" in $Y = f(x)$.

**interaction effect**    When $x$s interact with each other to produce some measured outcome.

**internal changeover steps**    Activities that must be done while a process is idle. Should be avoided or minimized whenever possible.

**internal customer**    Someone who needs the output of the previous process step to do one's job.

**inventive benchmarking**    Convergent brainstorming technique where participants work their way to a specific solution through the use of established inventive principles and thinking by analogy.

**Just Do It project**    A project for solving a problem when the solution is known and you just have to implement it.

**Kaizen Blitz**    "Change for the better." Planned and structured process improvement effort that enables a small group of people to improve some aspect of their business in a quick, focused manner. Also called a Kaizen Event.

**Kaizen Event**   See "Kaizen Blitz."

**Kaizen Event Facilitator**   A Lean Six Sigma practitioner who is trained to lead Kaizen Events.

**Kanban**   Lean Pull systems are called "Kanban" systems in Japanese. Kanban means "card" or "sign." Kanban systems are inventory replenishment systems that function on the basis of demand.

**Kano Model**   Asserts that, for some customer requirements, satisfaction is proportional to the extent that the product or service is fully functional. Others are disproportional.

**Key Performance Indicators**   Leverage variables contributing to business success. Entire set of KPIs is also known as "system of indicators."

**knowledge transfer**   Getting the right knowledge to the right people at the right time to achieve your purpose.

**lead time**   Sum of all the cycle times and wait times for a particular process; or the length of time it takes a good or service to go through the entire process.

**Lean**   Body of knowledge and tools organizations use to remove all non-value-added time and activity from their processes. Based on the Toyota Production System.

**Lean Six Sigma**   The blend of two root methodologies into one approach that optimizes the quality, speed, and cost of doing business.

**Little's Law**   Formula that shows the relationship between lead time, work in process, and completion rate.

**log sheet**   Data collection tool for recording process information compiled by those most closely associated with particular tasks.

**logbook**   Data collection tool for communicating process problems and actions taken.

**Master Black Belt**   Teaches Black Belts (and Green Belts) to become proficient in executing Lean Six Sigma projects. Also coaches, mentors, and advises management.

**mean**   Also known as "arithmetic mean" or "average," a measure of central tendency determined by adding all data points in a population, then dividing the total by the number of points.

**Measurement Systems Analysis (MSA)**   Validating the amount of error in a measurement system.

**Median**   The middlemost value of a data set after the numbers have been arranged in ascending order.

**Mindmapping**   Brainstorming technique for diagramming concepts and relationships that stem from an original problem statement.

**Mistake Proofing**   "Poke-yoke." Term coined by Shigeo Shingo to describe the technique of changing a process to prevent mistakes from occurring.

**Mistake Proofing Kaizen**   A Kaizen Event focused on eliminating a specific defect from occurring in the process.

**Monte Carlo Simulation**   Uses mathematical models, probability, decision rules, and induced variability in inputs to simulate real-life scenarios and identify variability in outputs.

*muda*   The Japanese word for "waste." Eliminating *muda* is a key component of a Lean process.

**Multiple Skills Matrix**   Tool used by managers to plan and track employee training to help sustain Standard Work and process performance improvements.

**multivoting**   Technique used to gain concensus from a group.

*mura*   Unevenness in operations (poor flow) contributing to *muda*.

*muri*   Overburden of people or machines contributing to *muda*.

**non-value-added**   Any work the organization performs that does not add value to itself or the customer (e.g., waiting time).

**Null Hypothesis**   *(H₀)* Relative to hypothesis testing, a statement of no difference or independence (e.g., *x* does not affect *Y*).

**optimization routine**   Linear algebra or complex search methods used to determine the best settings of factor levels to meet performance criteria.

**outliers**   Data points that appear far removed from the main body of data.

**output**   The finished product or service from each process step; the "*Y*" in $Y = f(x)$.

**Overall Equipment Effectiveness**   A clearly defined measure of actual process/asset performance relative to its maximum capability.

**p-Value**   Common method for determining if one population is different from another. Typically, a p-Value of less than 0.05 indicates statistically different populations.

**Pareto Chart**   A bar chart that displays categorical data by descending frequency of occurrence.

**performance dashboard**  Group of hierarchically linked performance metrics monitored on a regular basis.

**pilot**  Small-scale test of a proposed change applied to the real process, not a hypothetical or simulated process.

**Point Kaizen**  A type of Kaizen Event that works to improve a specific point in the Value Stream. Led by a front-line associate. Sometimes called a "Genba Kaizen."

**population**  The entire set of items under study. Populations may be finite or infinite (extending into the future).

**Power Influence Map**  Used to identify who can influence, positively or negatively, the outcomes of your projects or initiative.

**precision**  The degree to which measurements are closely grouped together using the same system.

**primary metric**  The key outcome ($Y$) of concern.

**Prioritization Matrix**  Used to narrow down a list of potential projects or options to the best ones.

**Probability Plot**  Graph that shows frequency of sample data compared to a specific mathematical distribution (e.g., normal distribution).

**process capability**  Extent to which process outputs meet customer specifications. Commonly expressed as yield or sigma level.

**Process Owners**  Lean Six Sigma participants who have primary responsibility for the operation and output of a given process.

**productivity**  Figuring out how to do more with the same or fewer resources.

**Project Charter**  The guiding document for a Lean Six Sigma project.

**Project Transition Action Plan (PTAP)**  List of what needs to be done to transfer the control responsibility from the Belt to the Process Owner.

**Pugh Matrix**  Tool for comparing competing solutions against a reference (usually the current situation).

**Pull**  Lean dynamic by which you store, use, and produce only what you need when you need it, in real time ideally, or as close to this as possible.

**quality**  Products, processes, or services that meet their specified performance standards.

**Quality Function Deployment (QFD)**  Method for collecting and organizing customer requirements and mapping them to functional requirements.

**Quality Rate**   The percentage of time you meet performance standards the first time. Also known as "first-time yield."

**queue models**   Statistical models used to evaluate waiting lines and their impact on flow rates and inventory levels.

**Queuing Theory**   Mathematical science of organizing the flow of people, material, information, data, supplies, and other items through a process to create balance and harmony.

**random word**   Brainstorming technique that incorporates a random word into the thinking pattern to generate new thought patterns.

**Rapid Changeover**   Lean practice of quickly changing over from one mode of production (or service) to another. Also called "Single Minute Exchange of Die."

**red-tag event**   The process of removing unneeded items in order to complete the Sorting step of the Five Ss.

**regression analysis**   Used to provide equations that estimate input-output ($x$-$Y$) or other predictor-response relationships.

**repeatability**   A desirable trait that occurs when the same person can get the same measurement result more than once.

**reproducibility**   A desirable trait that occurs when different people can get the same measurement result at different times.

**Response Surface Methods**   Specific experimental design combinations used to develop mathematical models with linear, quadratic, and interaction terms to seek optimum performance from a given set of factors and response variables.

**Risk Priority Number (RPN)**   In a FMEA, the product of a potential failure mode's Severity, Occurrence, and Detect ratings.

**Rolled Throughput Yield (RTY)**   The final yield of a process after exposure to the cross-multiplied probabilities of failure along the chain of all process steps and activities.

**root cause**   The $x$ (cause) that possesses the most leverage in determining the state of the desired outcome (effect).

**Run Chart**   Visually plots data in time sequence order as the process "runs."

**Sample**   A selection of items from a population used to make some inference about the population.

**Scatterplot**   Graph used to display pairs of continuous $x$ and $Y$ data.

**scientific management**   Born in the 1920s, the science of how an organization quantifies and optimizes the way it creates value, or does business.

**secondary metrics**   Desirable performance side effects that may result from Lean Six Sigma improvements.

**Shewhart cycle**   The cycle of Plan/Do/Study/Act developed by statistician Walter Shewhart. Also known as the Plan/Do/Check/Act cycle.

**shift**   A dramatic change in the mean of a process metric.

**Shift and Drift**   Tendency for process variation to shift 1.5 sigma from the short to the long run. Also called the 1.5 sigma shift.

**sigma capability**   See "sigma level."

**Sigma Kaizen**   Kaizen Event that moves rapidly through the five phases of the breakthrough strategy (Define-Measure-Analyze-Improve-Control).

**sigma level**   The common Six Sigma metric for the capability of a process, calculated by translating the frequency of defects into a Z-score based on a normal distribution.

**simulation**   Experimentation used to manipulate critical $x$s to see how they impact the overall process.

**Single Minute Exchange of Die (SMED)**   See "Rapid Changeover."

**SIPOC Map**   Short for Suppliers-Inputs-Process-Outputs-Customers. A high-level process map.

**Six Thinking Hats**   Brainstorming technique used to view a problem from six disctinctly different perspectives (Analytical, Emotional, Critical, Positive, Creative, Managed).

**soft savings**   Future savings, or avoided costs (as opposed to current-year "hard" savings); or, intangible benefits like "employee satisfaction."

**Spaghetti Diagram**   Map of how people, information, paper, materials, etc., travel in a process.

**Special Cause variation**   Variation caused by something going wrong with the process, producing a faulty output, the root cause of which can be determined and rectified.

**specifications**   Exacting requirements for CTs (Critical-To characteristics) expressed mathematically so they can be constantly measured and monitored.

**Stakeholder Action Plan**   Tool for planning actions for moving stakeholders into stronger positions of support.

**Stakeholder Analysis**   Tool used to identify your project's stakeholders and figure out who is for and who may resist you.

**standard deviation**   *(α)*. Measure of the average distance of the data values from their mean. Not the same as sigma level.

**standard operating procedures (SOPs)**   Work procedures for all to follow. Otherwise just called "procedures," or "policies and procedures."

**Standard Work analysis**   Breaks down process steps in small increments and compares performance to the Takt Time.

**statistic**   A calculated value derived from a set of sample data used to describe a characteristic of a population.

**Statistical Process Control (SPC)**   Use of Control Charts to monitor process performance and make decisions on how and when to adjust the process.

**Storyboard**   Visual depiction of a Lean Six Sigma project used to bring all stakeholders up to speed on what has changed, why, and the results.

**supplier**   Person or organization that provides inputs into the process.

**Swim Lane Flow Chart**   Displays the steps of a process and shows functional ownership for each one.

***t*-test**   Most common test to challenge assumptions about population means when populations are normally distributed.

**Takt Time**   Means "keep in step" or "keep time" (from German). Available amount of work time divided by customer demand for a specific time period.

**theoretical flow time**   The average amount of time needed to perform process steps with no waiting or rework.

**Theory of Constraints**   Only a few barriers stand in the way of success for any person, process, or organization.

**Theory of Inventive Problem Solving (TRIZ)**   An innovation methodology that uses a proven matrix of generic solutions to solve specific problems.

**tollgating**   Process for regularly reviewing Lean Six Sigma projects at the end of each successive phase of DMAIC. Also called "tollgate review."

**Total Productive Maintenance (TPM)**   To make all equipment downtime 100 percent predictable and minimized.

**Total Quality Control (TQC)**   From its Japanese roots, the application of quality improvement throughout all the functions and processes of a company.

**Total Quality Management (TQM)**   The act of managing for organizationwide quality improvement according to the Malcolm Baldrige Award criteria.

**transfer function**   The mathematical relationship between a set of process inputs and a specific output feature.

**trend**   Six consecutive points on a control chart, each higher or lower than the previous point, which may indicate Special Cause variation.

**Type I error**   Detecting a false difference, or declaring that the $x$ influences $Y$ when it's only random variation. Also known as "alpha ($\alpha$) risk."

**Type II error**   Not having enough evidence to detect that $x$ really does influence $Y$. Also known as "beta ($\beta$) risk."

**value creation**   Act of transforming a set of inputs into a set of outputs that bring in revenue greater than the costs incurred.

**Value Stream**   The total set of activities, both value-added and non-value-added, that occur as a process unfolds.

**Value Stream Map (VSM)**   Depicts how a process operates, with the added dimensions of documenting the people involved, inventory counts, queue times, process cycle times, and lead times.

**value-added**   A necessary function, activity, or step in a process.

**variable data**   Data gathered according to a scale, such as Time, Weight, Length, etc. Also known as "continuous data."

**variation**   Extent to which performance varies around the average. Range of difference between the statistical mean and all data points used to calculate the mean.

**Voice of the Customer (VOC)**   The collective needs, wants, and desires of your customers.

**work-in-process inventory**   Any materials or needed inputs that reside, virtually or physically, at different points in the process.

**Workload Balance**   Distribution of total work cycle time, and the pacing of that work content to the customer demand rate.

**$Y = f(x)$**   $Y$ is the outcome. The $x$s are the causal factors, or inputs, that produce the outcome. $f$ is the function performed on the inputs to produce the outputs.

**Yellow Belt**   A less informed and trained Belt who collects data, characterizes process performance, and assists Black and Green Belts with project execution.

**Z-score**   Statistical measure that quantifies the distance a point is from the mean in terms of standard deviations.

# Road Maps and Blueprint

We want to give you the whole Lean Six Sigma project execution process in a nutshell. So here it goes .... Look at the first two road maps that follow; they give you the big picture of the Lean Six Sigma Define-Measure-Analyze-Improve-Control approach. Then study the third diagram, Blueprint for Breakthrough. It gives you the main tasks you need to accomplish for each phase of DMAIC, along with the key tools and techniques to use.

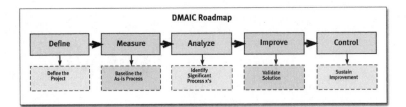

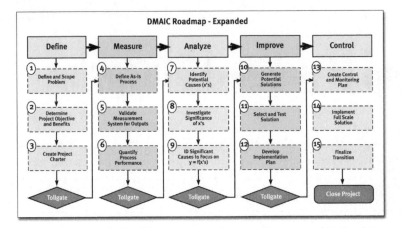

## DMAIC Blueprint for Breakthrough

| | Define | Measure | Analyze | Improve | Control |
|---|---|---|---|---|---|
| **Deliverables** | 1. Define and Scope Problem<br>2. Determine Project Objective and Benefits<br>Create Project Charter | 4. Define As-Is Process<br>5. Validate Measurement Systems for Outputs<br>6. Quantify Process Performance | 7. Identify Potential Causes (x's)<br>8. Investigate Significance of x's<br>9. ID Significant Causes to Focus on y = f(x's) | 10. Generate Potential Solutions<br>11. Select and Test Solution<br>12. Develop Implementation Plan | 13. Create Control and Monitoring Plan<br>14. Implement Full Scale Solution<br>15. Finalize Transition |
| **Tasks** | • ID the Business Gap<br>• Document the Process<br>• Collect and Translate the VOC<br>• Define Metrics and Defects<br>• Establish Preliminary Baseline & Entitlement<br>• Develop Problem and Objective Statements<br>• Estimate Financial Benefit<br>• Confirm Improvement Methodology<br>• Define Project Roles and Responsibilities<br>• ID Project Risks<br>• Create Communication Plan | • Create Value Stream Map<br>• Create Process Flow Diagram<br>• Expose Simplification Opportunities<br>• Run a SCORE Event<br>• Analyze Measurement Systems<br>• Improve Measurement Systems (if needed)<br>• Collect Data (Y's)<br>• Examine Process Stability<br>• Perform Capability Analysis | • Develop List of Potential Causes<br>• Narrow Down List of Potential Causes (x's)<br>• Collect Data on x's<br>• Perform Graphical Analysis<br>• Perform Statistical Analysis<br>• Conduct Waste Analysis<br>• Evaluate the Impact of the x's on Y<br>• State Preliminary Y = f(x's) | • Generate Potential Solutions<br>• Create Future State VSM<br>• Evaluate Potential Solution<br>• State y = f(x's)<br>• Run a SCORE Event<br>• Develop Implementation Plan | • Mistake Proof the Process<br>• Determine the x's to Control and Methods<br>• Complete MSA on Critical x's<br>• Determine Y's to Monitor and Report<br>• Revise/Develop Process Documentation<br>• Implement Solution<br>• Evaluate Implementation<br>• Develop Transition Plan<br>• Handoff to Process Owner<br>• Capture Lessons Learned<br>• Write Final Report/ Presentation<br>• Celebrate! |
| **Tools & Techniques** | • Project Definition Worksheet<br>• SIPOC<br>• Surveys & Interviews<br>• Affinity Diagrams<br>• Brainstorming<br>• In/Out of Frame<br>• Pareto Charts<br>• CT Trees<br>• Cost Benefit Analysis<br>• Benchmarking<br>• Metric Charts<br>• Project Charter<br>• Stakeholder Analysis<br>• Communication Plan | • Data Collection Plan<br>• Process Flow Diagram<br>• Value Stream Map<br>• Spaghetti Diagram<br>• SCORE™<br>• Measurement System Analysis<br>• Check Sheets<br>• SPC<br>• Capability Analysis<br>• Run Chart<br>• Graphical Analysis<br>• Elements of Waste<br>• 5s | • Fishbone<br>• Process Flow Diagram<br>• Value Stream Map<br>• FMEA<br>• Cause & Effect (C & E) Matrix<br>• Data Collection Plan<br>• Graphical Analysis Selection Matrix<br>• Statistical Analysis Selection Matrix (Hypothesis Testing and Regression)<br>• Takt Time<br>• Workload Balancing<br>• Work Combination Chart | • Future State Value Stream Map<br>• Random Word<br>• TRIZ<br>• Six Thinking Hats<br>• Cellular Layout<br>• SCORE™<br>• Kanban<br>• Visual Workplace<br>• DOE<br>• Solution Selection Matrix<br>• Implementation Plan<br>• SMED<br>• TPM<br>• Mistake Proofing | • SPC<br>• Control Plan<br>• MSA<br>• Mistake Proofing<br>• Dashboard<br>• Project Transition Action Plan (PTAP)<br>• Capability Analysis<br>• Communication Plan |

# Sigma Conversion Chart

Use this chart to convert capability percentages into sigma levels, and vice versa. Remember, especially at the higher sigma levels (4.5 and above), that the sigma score (or Z-score) enables you to differentiate performance more easily than using only straight capability percentages.

| Yield % | Sigma | Defects per Million Opportunities |
|---------|-------|-----------------------------------|
| 99.9997 | 6.00 | 3–4 |
| 99.9995 | 5.92 | 5 |
| 99.9992 | 5.81 | 8 |
| 99.9990 | 5.76 | 10 |
| 99.9980 | 5.61 | 20 |
| 99.9970 | 5.51 | 30 |
| 99.9960 | 5.44 | 40 |
| 99.9930 | 5.31 | 70 |
| 99.9900 | 5.22 | 100 |
| 99.9850 | 5.12 | 150 |
| 99.9770 | 5.00 | 230 |
| 99.9670 | 4.91 | 330 |
| 99.9520 | 4.80 | 480 |
| 99.9320 | 4.70 | 680 |

*continues*

*continued*

| Yield % | Sigma | Defects per Million Opportunities |
|---------|-------|-----------------------------------|
| 99.9040 | 4.60 | 960 |
| 99.8650 | 4.50 | 1,350 |
| 99.8140 | 4.40 | 1,860 |
| 99.7450 | 4.30 | 2,550 |
| 99.6540 | 4.20 | 3,460 |
| 99.5340 | 4.10 | 4,660 |
| 99.3790 | 4.00 | 6,210 |
| 99.1810 | 3.90 | 8,190 |
| 98.9300 | 3.80 | 10,700 |
| 98.6100 | 3.70 | 13,900 |
| 98.2200 | 3.60 | 17,800 |
| 97.7300 | 3.50 | 22,700 |
| 97.1300 | 3.40 | 28,700 |
| 96.4100 | 3.30 | 35,900 |
| 95.5400 | 3.20 | 44,600 |
| 94.5200 | 3.10 | 54,800 |
| 93.3200 | 3.00 | 66,800 |
| 91.9200 | 2.90 | 80,800 |
| 90.3200 | 2.80 | 96,800 |
| 88.5000 | 2.70 | 115,000 |
| 86.5000 | 2.60 | 135,000 |
| 84.2000 | 2.50 | 158,000 |
| 81.6000 | 2.40 | 184,000 |
| 78.8000 | 2.30 | 212,000 |
| 75.8000 | 2.20 | 242,000 |
| 72.6000 | 2.10 | 274,000 |
| 69.2000 | 2.00 | 308,000 |
| 65.6000 | 1.90 | 344,000 |
| 61.8000 | 1.80 | 382,000 |
| 58.0000 | 1.70 | 420,000 |
| 54.0000 | 1.60 | 460,000 |

| Yield % | Sigma | Defects per Million Opportunities |
|---|---|---|
| 50.0000 | 1.50 | 500,000 |
| 46.0000 | 1.40 | 540,000 |
| 43.0000 | 1.32 | 570,000 |
| 39.0000 | 1.22 | 610,000 |
| 35.0000 | 1.11 | 650,000 |
| 31.0000 | 1.00 | 690,000 |
| 28.0000 | 0.92 | 720,000 |
| 25.0000 | 0.83 | 750,000 |
| 22.0000 | 0.73 | 780,000 |
| 19.0000 | 0.62 | 810,000 |
| 16.0000 | 0.51 | 840,000 |
| 14.0000 | 0.42 | 860,000 |
| 12.0000 | 0.33 | 880,000 |
| 10.0000 | 0.22 | 900,000 |
| 8.0000 | 0.09 | 920,000 |

# Resources

There's a veritable plethora of books related to Lean Six Sigma. (Of course, we'd like to think that you're holding one of the best.) The ones listed below we also recommend, as well as the websites. Enjoy!

## Books

Womack, James P., and Daniel T. Jones. *Lean Thinking: Banish Waste and Create Wealth in Your Corporation, Revised and Updated.* New York: Free Press, 2003.

Originally released in 1996, the book was ahead of its time and ended up on the *Business Week* bestseller list—five years later. Expounding on the Lean production concept introduced in Womack's previously bestselling groundbreaker, *The Machine That Changed the World, Lean Thinking* translates the concept into principles that can be applied in any industry (although the examples included are largely based in manufacturing).

Gygi, Craig, Neil DeCarlo, and Bruce Williams. *Six Sigma for Dummies.* New Jersey: Wiley Publishing, Inc., 2005.

Co-authored by yours truly, this Six Sigma primer is designed for beginners and presented in a fun and easygoing manner. If you can't get enough of Six Sigma tools and statistics, this book's for you.

Pyzdek, Thomas. *The Six Sigma Handbook: The Complete Guide for Green Belts, Black Belts, and Managers at All Levels, Revised and Expanded Edition.* New York: McGraw-Hill, 2003.

This well-respected volume includes coverage on the science of Six Sigma, but focuses especially on the management and implementation of Six Sigma. Deployment leaders, Champions, and Master Black Belts will find the discussions especially helpful when selecting practitioners and aligning projects with the voice of the customer. The revised edition includes expanded coverage of DMAIC, Lean, and DFSS.

Henderson, Bruce A., Jorge L. Larco, and Stephen H. Martin. *Lean Transformation: How to Change Your Business into a Lean Enterprise.* Virginia: Oaklea Press, 1999.

Known in Lean manufacturing circles as the "yellow book," this widely used reference guide helps managers integrate Lean principles into their processes. The authors offer real-world examples, best practices, and advice, as well as charts, diagrams, and step-by-step instructions. Also available is a companion workbook *(A Workbook for Assessing Your Lean Transformation)* geared toward enabling readers to rate their progress compared to other Lean organizations.

George, Michael L., John Maxey, David T. Rowlands, and Michael George. *The Lean Six Sigma Pocket Toolbook: A Quick Reference Guide to 100 Tools for Improving Quality and Speed.* New York: McGraw-Hill, 2005.

A must have for the serious Lean Six Sigma practitioner, this handy guide contains detailed explanations of nearly 100 tools to help you understand when and why to use a tool, as well as how to use it and how to interpret the results.

Waldo, William Wes, and Tom Jones. *A Team Leader's Guide to Lean Kaizen Events.* Colorado: Breakthrough Performance Press, 2006.

This guide is written for Kaizen Event team leaders who have already been trained in the principles and tools of Lean, but are looking for a step-by-step process for conducting a successful Lean Kaizen Event. It includes templates and matrices (hard and electronic copies) to assist team leaders with each phase of the event, and a CD-ROM with Lean workplace posters.

Harry, Mikel, Ph.D., and Don R. Linsenmann. *The Six Sigma Fieldbook: How DuPont Successfully Implemented the Six Sigma Breakthrough Management Strategy.* New York: Doubleday, 2006.

A comprehensive case study of how DuPont Corporation implemented Six Sigma throughout its many divisions worldwide, reshaping its business model and saving billions of dollars in the process. The lessons learned by DuPont's managers can be applied to any large Lean Six Sigma deployment. It's co-authored by Mikel Harry, Ph.D., the father of Six Sigma, and Don R. Linsenmann, DuPont's Six Sigma Champion.

# Websites

**www.isixsigma.com.** This site offers free information for Six Sigma followers, including articles, tutorials, discussion forums, a glossary of terms, and industry-specific case studies. Also has a bookstore and job postings.

**www.sixsigmazone.com.** A clearinghouse for Six Sigma news, events, and training opportunities. Includes articles, free presentations, and a glossary of terms.

**www.lean.org.** Presented by the Lean Enterprise Institute, this site is an online outlet for Lean information, training, and advice a la Lean guru James P. Womack, the institute's CEO.

**www.superfactory.com.** A well-organized site focused on Lean for manufacturing. Includes Lean concepts, articles, and presentations (available for a small fee). Home of the "Evolving Excellence" blog.

**www.productivitypress.com.** An extensive portfolio of Lean publications largely translated from Japanese. Also features a list of related links, and the "Lean Insider" blog.

**www.isssp.com.** Primarily serving members of ISSSP (International Society of Six Sigma Professionals), this site includes articles, white papers, training, and event information. It even lets members build their own Six Sigma "professional portfolio."

**www.asq.org.** Official website of the American Society for Quality and its members. Dedicated to knowledge transfer of quality tools and concepts across many disciplines. Includes sections geared toward specific industries (e.g., education, health-care, government, etc.).

**www.onesixsigma.com**. A Six Sigma information portal for practitioners in Europe. Primarily focused on jobs, training, consultants, and products. Also features white papers, interviews, news, and events.

**www.minitab.com**. What can we say? If you're a Lean Six Sigma practitioner, you'll need Minitab software. Get it here, along with support, training, macros, and other helpful resources.

# Index

## Numbers

8.5-by-11 Syndrome, 120

## A

adaptation, 318-320
   deployment, 333-335
Affinity Diagrams, 90, 156-157, 223
alignment, business metrics, verifying, 92-94
AlliedSignal
   Lean Six Sigma, contributions to, 57-58
   Six Sigma, development of, 28
Alternate Hypothesis, 189-190
Analysis of Variance (ANOVA), 199
Analyze phase, 153-156, 161-163, 179, 193
   Affinity Diagrams, 156-157
   ask why five times, 159
   bottlenecks, identifying, 177-178
   brainstorming sessions, 156
   C&E (Cause-and-Effect) Analysis, 194
   C&E (Cause-and-Effect) Matrix, 162-163, 195
   correlation, 195-197
      ANOVA (Analysis of Variance), 199
      DOE (Design of Experiments), 197-199
      Monte Carlo Simulation, 197, 200-201

Critical X Worksheet, 194-195
   effect analysis, 159-161
   failure mode, 160-161
   Fishbone Diagrams, 157-159
   FMEA, 159-161
   graphical analysis, 186-188
   hypothesis testing, 189-190
   inventory levels, 168-172
      Kanban systems, 171-172
      Little's Law, 169-170
      Queuing Theory, 168-169
      Takt Time Analysis, 170-171
   multivoting, 162
   OEE (Overall Equipment Effectiveness), 175-177
      Quick Changeover opportunities, 176
      TPM (Total Productive Maintenance), 177
   p-Values, 190
   Process Maps, 156
   resource usage, 172-174
      Ideal Manning Levels, 173
      Spaghetti Diagrams, 174
      Standard Work Analysis, 174
      Workload Balance, 173-174
   sample size calculations, 184-186
   special studies, 183
   statistical analysis, 189
      methods, 190-192
   tollgate reviews, conducting, 205-206
   VSM (Value Stream Map), 167

   waste, 166-167
   $x$s
      data collection, 180-183
      prioritizing, 194-195
   $Y = f(x)$ equation, stating, 201-205
ANOVA (Analysis of Variance), 199
Appraiser Scores, system performance, 130
ask why five times, 159
assessment, Needs Assessment, 290
   opportunity assessment, 295-301
   organizational readiness, 290-291
   organizational strategies, 293-295
   stakeholder assessment, 291-292
attribute data, MSA (Measurement System Analysis), 129-131
attribute Gage R&R, 130
averages, 36
   comparing, 185
   testing for, 191-192

## B

background noise, overcoming, 190
Balanced Scorecard, 68
balancing workloads, 20
Baldridge Award, creation of, 28
baseline performance, establishing, 94-95
benchmarking, 96
Benefit/Effort Matrix, 72-74

Bennett, Bo, 330
Black Belts (Sigma Six), 17, 322
  coaching and mentoring, 326
  Master Black Belt, 332
    certification, 333
    role definition, 332-333
    selecting, 332-333
    training, 333
  orientation, 323
  training, 324-325
Bossidy, Larry, 29
bottlenecks, identifying,
  177-178
Box Plots (graphs), 188
Box-Behnken Design (experimental trials), 225
brainstorming, 221
brainstorming sessions, Analyze
  phase (DMAIC), 156
burning platforms, looking for,
  290
business focus, Lean Six Sigma,
  49
business metrics, verifying
  alignment, 92-94
business owner views, projects,
  65-66

## C

C&E (Cause-and-Effect)
  Analysis, 194
C&E (Cause-and-Effect)
  Matrix, 162-163, 195
calculations
  Flow Time Efficiency, 18-19
  OEE (Overall Equipment
    Effectiveness), 175-177
  sample size calculations,
    184-186
  Standard Deviation, 95-96
candidates, selecting Master
  Black Belt, 332-333
capability analysis, processes,
  146-149

Cause-and-Effect (C&E)
  Matrix, 162-163
Cause-and-Effect Diagrams, 90,
  157-159
celebrating projects, 273
cellular layout, 215
  developing, 20-21
  equipment rebalancing,
    215-216
  Kaizen Events, 217-218
  quick changeover, 216
  TPM (Total Productive
    Maintenance), 216-217
certification, Master Black Belt,
  333
Champion Review, 330-331
Champions (Six Sigma), 17
  Champion Review, 330-331
  Deployment Champions,
    307-308
    education, 320
  Functional Champions,
    training, 322
  Process Champions, 308
  Project Champions, 308
    training, 321
  projects, 308
changeover
  OEE (Overall Equipment
    Effectiveness), quick
    changeover opportunities,
    176
  quick changeover, cellular
    layout, 216
  rapid changeover, practicing,
    17-18
charters, creating Project
  Charters, 107-109
charts
  Control Charts, 144-145,
    182, 254-255
    Common Cause, 261
    creating, 255-256
    cycles, 260-261
    I & MR Control Charts,
      257

    Individuals Control
      Chart, 256-257
    interpreting, 258-262
    outliers, 259
    $p$-Charts, 257
    shifts, 259, 260
    Special Cause, 259-261
    trends, 260
    $u$-Charts, 257
    $x$-bar & R Control
      Charts, 257
    $x$-bar & S Control Charts,
      257
  flow charts, 110
  Flow Charts, creating,
    117-121
  Pareto Charts, 188
  Run Charts, 143-144
  Swim Lane Map, 118-120
  VSM (Value Stream Map),
    121-124
check sheets, data collection,
  182
clustering processes, 144
coaching Black Belts, 326
Common Cause, Control
  Charts, 261
Common Cause variation, 40
communication
  deployment infrastructure,
    installing, 312
  projects, importance of, 111
comparing
  averages, 185
  percentages, 186
composing problem statement,
  78-80
contour plots, 227
Control Charts, 254-255
  Common Cause, 261
  creating, 255-256
  cycles, 260-261
  data collection, 182
  I & MR Control Charts, 257
  Individuals Control Chart,
    256-257
  interpreting, 258-262

outliers, 259
*p*-Charts, 257
processes, stability examinations, 144-145
shifts, 259-260
Special Cause, 259-261
trends, 260
*u*-Charts, 257
*x*-bar & R Control Charts, 257
*x*-bar & S Control Charts, 257
Control phase, 241-247, 253, 263
   Control Charts, 254-255
      Common Cause, 261
      creating, 255-256
      cycles, 260-261
      I & MR Control Charts, 257
      Individuals Control Chart, 256-257
      interpreting, 258-262
      outliers, 259
      *p*-Charts, 257
      shifts, 259-260
      Special Cause, 259-261
      trends, 260
      *u*-Charts, 257
      *x*-bar & R Control Charts, 257
      *x*-bar & S Control Charts, 257
   FMEA (Failure Mode and Effects Analysis), 247
   Mistake Proofing, 244-245
   planning, 249-251
   SOPs (standard operating procedures), 247-249
correlation, 195-197
   ANOVA (Analysis of Variance), 199
   DOE (Design of Experiments), 197-199
   Monte Carlo Simulation, 197-201
cost avoidance, projects, 98-99

countermeasures, risks, 236-237
critical success factors, Lean Sigma Six, 285-287
Critical X Worksheet, 194-195
Critical-To (CT) characteristics. *See* CT (Critical-To) characteristics
criticality, projects
   identifying, 64, 74-76
   methodically determined elements, 74
   Prioritization Matrix, 75-76
   strategically critical elements, 74
   tactically necessary elements, 74
Crosby, Philip, 27
CT (Critical-To) characteristics, 36-39
   processes, 41-42
   projects
      breaking down, 66-67
      CT Flow Down, 66-67
      Prioritization Matrix, 75-76
   specifications, 37
CT (Critical-To) Flow Down, 66-67
cultural readiness, establishing, 291
customer views, projects, 64-65
customers
   external, 115
   internal, 115
   requirements, validating, 136-138
cycle time, 5
cycles, Control Charts, 260-261

**D**

Dashboard Reviews, deployment, 335
data collection, 140
   planning for, 140-143
   statistical sampling, 141-143

*x*s, 180-183
   check sheets, 182
   computer databases, 180-181
   Control Charts, 182
   forms, 181
   independent observation, 182
   logs, 181
data points, statistical populations, 37
databases, data collection, 180-181
defect-based requirements, customers, 136-137
defects, 37
   errors, compared, 38
   primary performance metric 8.5-by-11 Syndrome, 120
   determining, 117-124
   Process Flow diagrams, 117-118
   Swim Lane Map, 118-120
   VSM (Value Stream Map), 121-124
Defects per Million Opportunities (DPMO), 42
Define phase
   communication, importance of, 111
   methodologies, choosing, 109-110
   processes, 78, 89, 101
      baseline performance, 94-95
      benchmarking, 96
      business metrics, 92-94
      Entitlement performance, 94-95
      financial benefit estimates, 97-99
      high-level process definition, 80
      Kano Model, 86-88
      non-value-added processes, 83-84

objective statements, 96-97

problem statements, 78-80

process documentation, 82-83

project metrics, 91-92

SIPOC (Suppliers-Inputs-Process-Outputs-Customers) Map, 81-82

Spaghetti Diagrams, 84-85

Standard Deviation, 95-96

value-added processes, 83-84

VOC (Voice of the Customer), 85-86

Project Charters, creating, 107-109

project teams, identifying, 102-103

project timelines, establishing, 107

risks, identifying, 105-106

stakeholders, identifying, 103-105

tollgate reviews, conducting, 111-112

Define-Measure-Analyze-Improve-Control (DMAIC). *See* DMAIC (Define-Measure-Analyze-Imrove-Control)

defining high-level processes, 80-85

Deming, W. Edwards, 27, 55, 117

deployment
adaptation, 333-335
Dashboard Reviews, 335
Deployment Champions, 307-308
education, 320
Design phase, 304
Enable phase, 318
health checks, 335-337

Implement and Sustain phase, 328-332
Champion Review, 330-331
Executive Team Review, 331
implementation plans, 328-329
Steering Committee Review, 331
Lean Six Sigma, 277-278
critical success factors, 285-287
product/service life cycles, 279
structured methodologies, 279-282
TPE (Total Performance Excellence), 282-285
Objective Review, 337-338

Deployment Champions, 307-308
education, 320

deployment infrastructures, installing, 308-312

deployment objectives, establishing Design road maps, 304-306

Design for Six Sigma (DFSS), 40

design governance models, 312-316

Design of Experiments (DOE), 183

Design phase, deployment, 304

Design road maps
creating, 304
deployment infrastructure, 308-312
deployment objectives, establishing, 304-306
design governance model, 312-316
leadership support, 306-308

DFSS (Design for Six Sigma), 40

diagrams
Affinity Diagrams, 156-157, 223
Cause-and-Effect Diagrams, 157-159
Fishbone Diagrams, 136, 157-159
Histograms, 145-146
Process Flow diagrams, 117-118
Spaghetti Diagrams, 174

Disney, Walt, 111

disseminating knowledge, 334-335

DMAIC (Define-Measure-Analyze-Improve-Control), 9, 23, 33-34
Analyze phase, 153-156, 161-163, 179, 193
Affinity Diagrams, 156-157
ANOVA (Analysis of Variance), 199
ask why five times, 159
bottleneck identification, 177-178
brainstorming sessions, 156
C&E (Cause-and-Effect) Analysis, 194
C&E (Cause-and-Effect) Matrix, 162-163, 195
correlation, 195-201
Critical X Worksheet, 194-195
data collection, 180-183
DOE (Design of Experiments), 197-199
effect analysis, 159-161
failure mode, 159-161
Fishbone Diagrams, 157-159
FMEA, 159-161
graphical analysis, 186-188

hypothesis testing, 189-190
Ideal Manning Levels, 173
inventory levels, 168-172
Kanban systems, 171-172
Little's Law, 169-170
Monte Carlo Simulation, 200-201
multivoting, 162
OEE (Overall Equipment Effectiveness), 175-177
p-Value, 190
Process Maps, 156
Queuing Theory, 168-169
Quick Changeover opportunities, 176
resource usage, 172-174
sample size calculations, 184-186
Spaghetti Diagrams, 174
special studies, 183
Standard Work Analysis, 174
statistical analysis, 189-192
Takt Time Analysis, 170-171
tollgate reviews, 205-206
TPM (Total Productive Maintenance), 177
VSM (Value Stream Map), 167
waste, 166-167
Workload Balance, 173-174
x prioritization, 194-195
Y = f(x) equation, 201-205
Control phase, 241-247, 253, 263
  Control Charts, 254-262
  FMEA (Failure Mode and Effects Analysis), 247
  Mistake Proofing, 244-245
  planning, 249-251

SOPs (standard operating procedures), 247-249
Define phase
  communication, importance of, 111
  methodologies, choosing, 109-110
  processes, 78, 89, 101
  Project Charters, creating, 107-109
  project teams, identifying, 102-103
  project timelines, establishing, 107
  risks, identifying, 105-106
  stakeholders, identifying, 103-105
  tollgate reviews, conducting, 111-112
Improve phase, 207-208, 219, 231
Kaizen Events, 59-60
Measure phase, 113-114, 126
DMAIC projects, 24
documenting processes, 82, 83
DOE (Design of Experiments), 183
  correlation, 197-199
  origins of, 197
DPMO (Defects per Million Opportunities), 42, 46

**E**

Ease/Impact Matrix, 223-224
effect analysis, 159-161
Effects Plots (graphs), 188
empirical data, collecting, 116
Enable phase, deployment, 318
Entitlement performance, 32-33
  projects, establishing, 94, 95
equations, Y = f(x), stating, 30-31, 201-205
equipment, rebalancing, 215-216

Erlang, A.K., 27
errors and defects, compared, 38
Executive Team Review, 331
experimental trials, conducting, 224-226
external customers, 115

**F**

F-tests, variance, 203
Facilitators (Kaizen Event), 322
  orientation, 323
  training, 325
failure mode, processes, 159-161
Failure Mode and Effects Analysis (FMEA). See FMEA (Failure Mode and Effects Analysis)
Final Reports, 266-270
finances, installing deployment infrastructure, 309-310
financial benefits, estimating, 97-99
Fishbone Diagrams, 136, 157-159
Fisher, Ronald, 197
Five S disciplines, 21, 210
  Shine (Seiso), 211
  Sort (Seiri), 210
  Standardize (Seiketsu), 211-212
  Store (Seiton), 211
  Sustain (Shitsuke), 212
Fleming, J.H., 295
flow, 166
  importance of, 8
  Lean Flow, maintaining, 18-19
  mura, 166
flow charts, creating, 110, 117-121
Flow Kaizen, 9
Flow Time Efficiency, calculating, 18-19

FMEA (Failure Mode and Effects Analysis), 106, 159-161
   Control phase, 247
   origins of, 160
Force Field Analysis, 106
Ford, Henry, 5-6, 55
forms, data collection, 181
formulas
   standard deviation, 95-96
   statistical sampling, 142-143
Franklin, Benjamin, 5
Functional Champions, training, 322
future state, creating, 209-210

## G

Galvin, Bob, 29
Gandhi, Indira, 329
Gantt, Henry, 5
Gantt charts, origins of, 5
Genba Kaizens, 9
General Electric, implementation of Six Sigma, 28
Gilbreth, Frank, 5
Gosset, W.S., 27
graphical analysis, 186-188
graphs
   Box Plots, 188
   Dot Plots, 187
   Effects Plots, 188
   graphical analysis, 186-188
   Histograms, 187
   Matrix Plots, 188
   Probability Plots, 188
   Scatter Plots, 188
Green Belts (Six Sigma), 17, 322
   orientation, 323
   training, 324-325

## H

Harry, Mikel, 28-32
health checks, deployment, 335-337

hidden processes, identifying, 25-26
high-level processes
   defining, 80-85
   documenting, 82-83
   Kano Model, 86-88
   non-value-added processes, 83-84
   Process Flow Maps, 82
   Product Family Matrix, 82
   SIPOC (Suppliers-Inputs-Process-Outputs-Customers) Map, 81-82
   Spaghetti Diagrams, 84-85
   value-added processes, 83-84
   VOC (Voice of the Customer), collecting, 85-86
Histograms, stability examinations, 145-146
Honeywell (AlliedSignal)
   Lean Six Sigma, contributions to, 57-58
   Six Sigma, development of, 28
Hoshin Planning methodology, 305, 320
human resources, installing deployment infrastructure, 309
hybridization, 56-57
   risks, 56
hypothesis testing, 189-190

## I

I & MR Control Charts, 257
idea trigger sessions, 221
Ideal Final Result (IFR), 221
Ideal Manning Levels, determining, 173
idiot-proof systems, creating, 21-22
IFR (Ideal Final Result), 221
iGrafix, Flow Charts, creating with, 121

Impact/Effort Matrix. *See* Benefit/Effort Matrix
Implement and Sustain phase, 328-332
   Champion Review, 330-331
   Executive Team Review, 331
   implementation plans, 328-329
   Steering Committee Review, 331
implementation plans, developing, 237-239
implementing Lean Six Sigma, 277-278
   critical success factors, 285-287
   product/service life cycles, 279
   structured methodologies, 279-282
   TPE (Total Performance Excellence), 282-285
Improve phase, 207-208, 219, 231
   Affinity Diagram, 223
   cellular layout, 215
      Kaizen Events, 217-218
      quick changeover, 216
      rebalancing equipment, 215-216
      TPM (Total Productive Maintenance), 216-217
   countermeasures, 236-237
   Ease/Impact Matrix, 223-224
   experimental trials, conducting, 224-226
   Five S disciplines, 210
      Shine (*Seiso*), 211
      Sort (*Seiri*), 210
      Standardize (*Seiketsu*), 211-212
      Store (*Seiton*), 211
      Sustain (*Shitsuke*), 212
   future state, creating, 209-210
   implementation plans, developing, 237-239

risks, identifying, 236-237
solutions
  evaluating, 222-224
  generating, 220-222
  piloting, 234-236
  selecting, 232-234
Standard Work operations,
  212-213
  managing, 213-214
  Multiple Skills Matrix,
    214-215
tollgate reviews, 239-240
$Y = f(x)$
  contour plots, 227
  optimization routines,
    227-228
  stating, 226-229
improvements, identifying,
  114-116
inadvertent mistakes, avoiding,
  21-22
Individuals Control Chart, creating, 256-257
intellect, waste of, 16-17
intellectual property, modifying,
  318-320
Interaction Plot, 198
internal customers, 115
interpreting, Control Charts,
  258-262
inventory
  waste of, 16
  work-in-progress, 168
inventory levels
  examining, 168-172
    Kanban systems, 171-172
    Little's Law, 169-170
    Queuing Theory, 168-169
    Takt Time Analysis,
      170-171
Ishikawa, Kaoru, 157
IT (information technology),
  deployment infrastructure,
  installing, 310

## J–K

Jones, Daniel, 8
Jones, Tom, 217
Juran, Joseph, 27

Kaizen Event Facilitators, 322
  orientation, 323
  training, 325
Kaizen Events, 3, 9-10
  cellular layout, 217-218
  DMAIC, compared, 59-60
  guidelines, 9-10
  Sigma Kaizens, 9
Kanban systems, 19-20
  analyzing inventory levels,
    171-172
Kano, Noriaki, 86-88
Kano Model, 86-88
Kaplan, Robert, 68
Key Performance Indicators
  (KPIs), 128
KISS (Keep it Simple
  Statistically), 325
knowledge, managing and dis-
  seminating, 334-335
KPIs (Key Performance
  Indicators), 128

## L

layouts, developing cellular layouts, 20-21
LCL (lower control limits),
  data, 144
leadership support, Design road
  maps, 306-308
Lean, 3-5, 17
  benefits of, 4
  cellular layout, developing,
    20-21
  cycle time, 5
  Five Ss, 21

Lean Flow, maintaining,
  18-19
Lean Pull, 19-20
  origins of, 5-9
  principles of, 8
  Rapid Changeover, practic-
    ing, 17-18
  Standardized Work, 22
  striving for perfection, 5
  TPS (Toyota Production
    System), 4
  workloads, balancing, 20
Lean Flow, maintaining, 18-19
Lean Pull, 19-20
Lean Six Sigma, 47-48
  business focus, 49
  deploying, 277-278
    critical success factors,
      285-287
    product/service life cycles,
      279
    structured methodologies,
      279-282
    TPE (Total Performance
      Excellence), 282-285
  hybridization, 56-57
    risks, 56
  origins of, 54-59
  processes, 77
    Define stage, 78
  Six Sigma, compared, 48-53
  statistical focus, 50-51
  Value Creation, 53-54
    mutual exchange of value,
      53-54
Lean Six Sigma core teams, 305
Lean Thinking, 8
Learmonth, Arthur B., 58
Little's Law, inventory levels,
  analyzing, 169-170
logs, data collection, $xs$, 181
lower control limits (LCL),
  data, 144
Luce, Clare Booth, 92

# M

*Machine That Changed the World, The*, 8
Main Effects Plot, 198
management system (Six Sigma), 25
Master Black Belt (Six Sigma), 17, 332
  certification, 333
  role definition, 332-333
  selecting, 332-333
  training, 333
Matrix Plots, 188
Maytag, contributions to Lean Six Sigma, 58-59
means, statistical populations, 37
Measure phase, 113-114, 126
  8.5-by-11 Syndrome, 120
  customer requirements, validating, 136-138
  improvements, identifying, 114-116
  measurement systems
    identifying, 128
    improving, 134-136
  MSA (Measurement System Analysis), 128-129
    attribute data, 129-131
    variable data, 131-134
  primary performance metric, determining, 117-124
  Process Flow diagrams, 117-118
  quick-hit opportunities, 125-126
  simplification opportunities, exposing, 124-126
  Swim Lane Map, 118-120
  VSM (Value Stream Map), 121-124
measurement, importance of, 31-32

measurement systems
  existing measurement systems, identifying, 128
  improving, 134-136
  MSA (Measurement System Analysis), 128-129
    attribute data, 129-131
    variable data, 131-134
  repeatability, 129-130
  reproducibility, 129-130
mentoring, Black Belts, 326
methodically determined elements, identifying, 74
methodologies
  adaptation, 318-320
  Hoshin Planning methodology, 305, 320
  projects, choosing, 109-110
  statistical analysis, 190-192
  structured methodologies, deploying, 279-282
metrics
  business metrics, defining, 92-94
  projects, defining, 91-92
mindmapping, 221
Minitabs, capability analysis, 147
Mistake Proofing, 244-245
mistakes, avoiding inadvertent mistakes, 21, 22
mixtures, processes, 144
Monte Carlo Simulation, 197, 200-201, 224
motion, waste of, 14
Mototrola, creation of Six Sigma, 28
MSA (Measurement System Analysis), 128-129
  attribute data, 129-131
  variable data, 131-134
*muda*, 11, 166
Multiple Skills Matrix, 214-215
multivoting consensus technique, 162
mutual exchange of value, 53-54

# N

Needs Assessment, 290
  opportunity assessment, 295-301
  organizational readiness, 290-291
  organizational strategies, evaluating, 293-295
  stakeholder assessment, 291-292
Needs Assessment, looking for burning platforms, 290
neural network software, 188
non-value-added labels, processes, 124
non-value-added processes, value-added processes, compared, 83-84
Norton, David, 68
Null Hypothesis, 189-190

# O

Objective Review, deployment, 337-338
objective statements, developing, 96-97
OEE (Overall Equipment Effectiveness)
  calculating, 175-177
  Quick Changeover opportunities, 176
  TPM (Total Productive Maintenance), 177
Ohno, Taiichi, 6-8, 12
one output feature ($Y$), 91
opportunity assessments, conducting, 295-301
optimization routines, 227-228
organizational readiness, assessing, 290-291
organizational strategies, evaluating, 293-295

orientations
    Black Belts, 323
    Green Belts, 323
    Kaizen Event Facilitators, 323
oscillation, processes, 144
outliers, Control Charts, 259
overproduction, 13

# P

p-Charts, 257
p-Value, 190
Pareto Charts, 90, 188
percentages
    comparing, 186
    testing for, 192
performance metric, primary
    8.5-by-11 Syndrome, 120
    determining, 117-124
    Process Flow diagrams, 117-118
    Swim Lane Map, 118-120
    VSM (Value Stream Map), 121-124
phases
    Analyze phase, 153-156, 161-163, 179, 193
        Affinity Diagrams, 156-157
        ANOVA (Analysis of Variance), 199
        ask why five times, 159
        bottleneck identification, 177-178
        brainstorming sessions, 156
        C&E (Cause-and-Effect) Analysis, 194
        C&E (Cause-and-Effect) Matrix, 162-163, 195
        correlation, 195-201
        Critical X Worksheet, 194-195
        data collection, 180-183

DOE (Design of Experiments), 197-199
        effect analysis, 159-161
        failure mode, 159-161
        Fishbone Diagrams, 157-159
        FMEA, 159-161
        graphical analysis, 186-188
        hypothesis testing, 189-190
        Ideal Manning Levels, 173
        inventory levels, 168-172
        Kanban systems, 171-172
        Little's Law, 169-170
        Monte Carlo Simulation, 200-201
        multivoting, 162
        OEE (Overall Equipment Effectiveness), 175-177
        p-Value, 190
        Process Maps, 156
        Queuing Theory, 168-169
        Quick Changeover opportunities, 176
        resource usage, 172-174
        sample size calculations, 184-186
        Spaghetti Diagrams, 174
        special studies, 183
        Standard Work Analysis, 174
        statistical analysis, 189-192
        Takt Time Analysis, 170-171
        tollgate reviews, 205-206
        TPM (Total Productive Maintenance), 177
        VSM (Value Stream Map), 167
        waste, 166-167
        Workload Balance, 173-174
        $x$ prioritization, 194-195
        $Y = f(x)$ equation, 201-205

Control phase, 241-247, 253, 263
        Control Charts, 254-262
        FMEA (Failure Mode and Effects Analysis), 247
        Mistake Proofing, 244-245
        planning, 249-251
        SOPs (standard operating procedures), 247-249
    deployment
        Design phase, 304
        Enable phase, 318
        Implement and Sustain phase, 328-332
    Improve phase, 207-208, 219, 231
        Affinity Diagram, 223
        cellular layout, 215-218
        countermeasures, 236-237
        Ease/Impact Matrix, 223-224
        experimental trials, 224-226
        Five S disciplines, 210-212
        future state creation, 209-210
        implementation plans, 237-239
        optimization routines, 227-228
        risk identification, 236-237
        solution piloting, 234-236
        solution selection, 232-234
        solutions, 220-224
        Standard Work operations, 212-215
        tollgate reviews, 239-240
        $Y = f(x)$ statement, 226-229
    Measure phase, 113-114, 126
        8.5-by-11 Syndrome, 120
        customer requirement validation, 136-138

improvement identification, 114-116

measurement system identification, 128

measurement system improvements, 134-136

MSA (Measurement System Analysis), 128-134

primary performance metric, 117-124

Process Flow diagrams, 117-118

quick-hit opportunities, 125-126

simplification opportunities, 124-126

Swim Lane Map, 118-120

VSM (Value Stream Map), 121-124

philosophy (Six Sigma), 25

Plan-Do-Check-Act cycle, 27

Plan-Do-Study-Act cycle, Standard Work, 213-214

planning data collection, 140-143

Point Kaizens, 9

poke-yoke, 21-22, 244-245

potential savings, 98

Power Influence Maps, 104

PowerPoint, creating Flow Charts with, 121

primary performance metric
8.5-by-11 Syndrome, 120

determining, 117-124

Process Flow diagrams, 117-118

Swim Lane Map, 118-120

VSM (Value Stream Map), 121-124

Prioritization Matrix, projects, 75-76

prioritizing *x*s, 194-195

C&E (Cause-and-Effect) Matrix, 195

Critical X Worksheet, 194-195

Probability Plots (graphs), 188

problem statements, writing, 78-80

Process Champions, 308

processes, 77
Analyze phase, 153-156, 161-163, 179, 193

Affinity Diagrams, 156-157

ANOVA (Analysis of Variance), 199

ask why five times, 159

bottleneck identification, 177-178

brainstorming sessions, 156

C&E (Cause-and-Effect) Analysis, 194

C&E (Cause-and-Effect) Matrix, 162-163, 195

correlation, 195-201

Critical X Worksheet, 194-195

data collection, 180-183

DOE (Design of Experiments), 197-199

effect analysis, 159-161

failure mode, 159-161

Fishbone Diagrams, 157-159

FMEA, 159-161

graphical analysis, 186-188

hypothesis testing, 189-190

Ideal Manning Levels, 173

inventory levels, 168-172

Kanban systems, 171-172

Little's Law, 169-170

Monte Carlo Simulation, 200-201

multivoting, 162

OEE (Overall Equipment Effectiveness), 175-177

p-Values, 190

Process Maps, 156

Queuing Theory, 168-169

Quick Changeover opportunities, 176

resource usage, 172-174

sample size calculations, 184-186

Spaghetti Diagrams, 174

special studies, 183

Standard Work Analysis, 174

statistical analysis, 189-192

Takt Time Analysis, 170-171

tollgate reviews, 205-206

TPM (Total Productive Maintenance), 177

VSM (Value Stream Map), 167

waste, 166-167

Workload Balance, 173-174

*x* prioritization, 194-195

$Y = f(x)$ equation, 201-205

bottlenecks, identifying, 177-178

capability analysis, 146-149

clustering, 144

Control phase, 241-247, 253, 263

Control charts, 254-262

FMEA (Failure Mode and Effects Analysis), 247

Mistake Proofing, 244-245

planning, 249-251

SOPs (standard operating procedures), 247-249

CT (Critical-To) characteristics, 37-42

specifications, 37

data collection, 140

planning for, 140-143

statistical sampling, 141-143

defects, 37

Define stage, 78, 89, 101
  baseline performance,
    94-95
  benchmarking, 96
  business metrics, 92-94
  communication, 111
  Entitlement performance,
    94-95
  financial benefit estimates,
    97-99
  high-level process defini-
    tion, 80
  Kano Model, 86-88
  methodology selection,
    109-110
  non-value-added pro-
    cesses, 83-84
  objective statements,
    96-97
  problem statements,
    78-80
  process documentation,
    82-83
  Project Charters, 107-109
  project metrics, 91-92
  project teams, 102-103
  project timelines, 107
  risk identification,
    105-106
  SIPOC (Suppliers-Inputs-
    Process-Outputs-
    Customers) Map, 81-82
  Spaghetti Diagrams,
    84-85
  stakeholder identification,
    103-105
  Standard Deviation, 95-96
  tollgate reviews, 111-112
  value-added processes,
    83-84
  VOC (Voice of the
    Customer), 85-86
deployment
  adaptation, 333-335
  Dashboard Reviews, 335
  health checks, 335-337
  Objective Review,
    337-338

Design road maps
  creating, 304
  deployment infrastruc-
    ture, 308-312
  deployment objectives,
    304-306
  design governance model,
    312-316
  leadership support,
    306-308
  documenting, 82-83
DPMO (Defects per Million
  Opportunities), 46
hidden processes, identifying, 25-26
high-level processes, defining, 80-85
implementing, 328-332
  Champion Review,
    330-331
  Executive Team Review,
    331
  implementation plans,
    328-329
  Steering Committee
    Review, 331
Improve phase, 207-208,
  219, 231
  Affinity Diagram, 223
  cellular layout, 215-218
  contour plots, 227
  countermeasures, 236-237
  Ease/Impact Matrix,
    223-224
  experimental trials,
    224-226
  Five S disciplines,
    210-212
  future state creation,
    209-210
  implementation plans,
    237-239
  optimization routines,
    227-228
  risk identification,
    236-237
  solution piloting, 234-236

  solution selection,
    232-234
  solutions, 220-224
  Standard Work opera-
    tions, 212-215
  tollgate reviews, 239-240
  $Y = f(x)$ statement,
    226-229
Kano Model, 86-88
Lean Flow, maintaining,
  18-19
Measure phase, 113-114, 126
  8.5-by-11 Syndrome, 120
  customer requirement
    validation, 136-138
  improvement identifica-
    tion, 114-116
  measurement system
    identification, 128
  measurement system
    improvements, 134-136
  MSA (Measurement
    System Analysis),
    128-134
  primary performance
    metric, 117-124
  Process Flow diagrams,
    117-118
  quick-hit opportunities,
    125-126
  simplification opportuni-
    ties, 124-126
  Swim Lane Map,
    118-120
  VSM (Value Stream
    Map), 121-124
mixtures, 144
non-value-added labels, 124
non-value-added processes,
  83-84
oscillation, 144
problem statements, writing,
  78-80
Process Flow Maps, 82
Process Owners, 308
  training, 321-322
Product Family Matrix, 82

RTY (Rolled Throughput Yield), 42-43
SIPOC (Suppliers-Inputs-Process-Outputs-Customers) Map, 81-82
Spaghetti Diagrams, 84-85
stability
    Control Charts, 144-145
    examining, 143
    Histograms, 145-146
    problems, 144
    Run Charts, 143-144
Standardized Work, 22
sustaining, 332
tollgate reviews, conducting, 149-150
trends, 144
twenty-percent rule, 135
upstream activities, 37
value-added labels, 124
value-added processes, 83-84
value-enabling labels, 125
variation, shift and drift, 43-46
VOC (Voice of the Customer), collecting, 85-86
wasteful processes, 15-16
Process Flow diagrams, 117-118
Process Flow Maps, 82
Process Maps, 156
Process Model, creating Flow charts with, 121
Process Owners, 308
product/service life cycles, 279
Product Family Matrix, 82
products, CT (Critical-To) characteristics, 37-39
Project Champions, 308
    training, 321
Project Charters
    completing, 300
    creating, 107-109
project management, installing deployment infrastructure, 310-311
Project Owners, training, 321-322

Project Storyboards, 266-270
Project Summaries, 264-265
project teams, identifying, 102-103
project timelines, establishing, 107
projects, 63, 71
    Balanced Scorecard, 68
    baseline performance, establishing, 94-95
    benchmarking, 96
    Benefit/Effort Matrix, 72-74
    business metrics, defining, 92-94
    business owner views, 65-66
    celebrating, 273
    Champions, 308
    communication, importance of, 111
    cost avoidance, 98-99
    criticality
        identifying, 64, 74-76
        methodically determined elements, 74
        Prioritization Matrix, 75-76
        strategically critical elements, 74
        tactically necessary elements, 74
    CT (Critical-To) characteristics
        breaking down, 66-67
        CT Flow Down, 66-67
    customer views, 64-65
    deployment
        adaptation, 333-335
        Dashboard Reviews, 335
        health checks, 335-337
        Objective Review, 337-338
    Design road maps
        creating, 304
        deployment infrastructure, 308-312
        deployment objectives, 304-306

    design governance model, 312-316
    leadership support, 306-308
    Entitlement performance, establishing, 94-95
    Final Reports, 266-270
    financial benefit estimates, 97-99
    Functional Champions, training, 322
    implementing, 328-332
        Champion Review, 330-331
        Executive Team Review, 331
        implementation plans, 328-329
        Steering Committee Review, 331
    improvements, identifying, 114-116
    methodologies, choosing, 109-110
    needs
        identifying, 297-299
        prioritization, 300
    objective statements, developing, 96-97
    primary performance metric, determining, 117-124
    Process Champions, 308
    Project Champions, 308
        training, 321
    Project Charters
        completing, 300
        creating, 107-109
    project metrics, defining, 91-92
    Project Storyboards, 266-270
    Project Summaries, 264-265
    project teams, identifying, 102-103
    project timelines, establishing, 107
    revenue growth, 98-99
    risks, identifying, 105-106

savings, 98-99
scope, 90
simplification opportunities, exposing, 124-126
SOPs (standard operating procedures), 267-269
stakeholders, identifying, 103-105
Standard Deviation, calculating, 95-96
sustaining, 332
tollgate reviews, conducting, 111-112, 272-273
transitions, 270-272
VOC (Voice of the Customer), 68-70
VSM (Value Stream Map), 70-71
proportions
comparing, 186
testing for, 192
Pugh Matrix, 233
Pull, 8, 166
Lean Pull, 19-20

## Q

QFD (Quality Function Deployment), 86
Queuing Theory, analyzing inventory levels, 168-169
quick-hit opportunities, executing, 125-126
Quick changeover, 7
quick changeover, cellular layout, 216

## R

random words, brainstorming, 221
RapAnalyst neural network software, 188
Rapid Changeover, 7
practicing, 17-18

Rapid Improvement Events. *See* Kaizen Events
rebalancing equipment, 215-216
repeatability, measurement systems, 129-130
reproducibility, measurement systems, 129-130
resource usage, analyzing, 172-174
Ideal Manning Levels, 173
Spaghetti Diagrams, 174
Standard Work Analysis, 174
Workload Balance, 173-174
Response Surface Methods (experimental trials), 225
revenue growth, projects, 98-99
rework as waste, 13-14
risks
countermeasures, 236-237
FMEA (Failure Mode and Effects Analysis), 106
Force Field Analysis, 106
hybridization, 56
identifying, Improve phase, 236-237
projects, identifying, 105-106
RPN (Risk Priority Number), 160-161
role definition, Master Black Belt, 332-333
RPN (Risk Priority Number), 160-161
RTY (Rolled Throughput Yield), processes, 42-43
Run Charts, stability examinations, 143-144

## S

S*O*D Ratings, 160-161
sample size calculations, 184-186
Santayana, George, 334
savings
potential savings, 98
projects, 98-99
soft savings, 98

Scatter Plots (graphs), 188
scientific methodology (Six Sigma), 25
scope, projects, 90
Score vs. Attribute, system performance, 130
Screen Effective Scores, system performance, 130
Screen Effective Scores vs. Attribute, system performance, 130
*Seiketsu* (Standardize) discipline, 211-212
*Seiri* (Sort) discipline, 210
*Seiso* (Shine) discipline, 211
*Seiton* (Store) discipline, 211
Shewhart, Walter, 27, 55
shift and drift, processes, 43-46
shifts, Control charts, 259-260
Shine (*Seiso*) discipline, 211
Shingo, Shigeo, 7, 244
*Shitsuke* (Sustain) discipline, 212
sigma, 36
SigmaFlow, creating Flow charts with, 121
Sigma Kaizens, 9
sigma level, 36
sigma scores, capability analysis, 147-148
simplification opportunities, exposing, 124-126
simulation, Monte Carlo Simulation, 197-201
Single Minute Exchange of Die (SMED), 7
SIPOC (Suppliers-Inputs-Process-Outputs-Customers) Map, 81-82
Six Sigma, 23-25, 29
benefits of, 25
Black Belts, 17
Champions, 17
Green Belts, 17
Lean Six Sigma, 47-48
compared, 48-53
origins of, 54-59

management system, 25
Master Black Belt, 17
origins of, 27-29
philosophy, 25
purpose of, 5
scientific methodology, 25
toolbox, 25
vision, 24
$Y = f(x)$, 30-31
SMED (Single Minute
Exchange of Die), 7
Smith, Bill, 29
soft savings, 98
solutions
evaluating, Improve phase,
222-224
generating, Improve phase,
220-222
piloting, Improve phase,
234-236
selecting, Improve phase,
232-234
SOPs (standard operating procedures), 267-269
Control phase, 247-249
Sort (*Seiri*) discipline, 210
Southwest Airlines, success of, 9
Spaghetti Diagrams, 84-85
resource usage, analyzing,
174
Special Cause, Control Charts,
259-261
Special Cause variation, 40
special studies, 183
specifications
CT (Critical-To) characteristics, 37
limitations, 36
SQC (statistical quality control),
55
stability, processes
capability analysis, 146-149
Control Charts, 144-145
examining, 143
Histograms, 145-146
problems, 144

Run Charts, 143-144
tollgate reviews, 149-150
Stakeholder Action Plans, 105
Stakeholder Analysis, conducting, 103
stakeholders
identifying, 103-105
Needs Assessment, conducting, 291-292
Power Influence Maps, 104
Stakeholder Action Plans,
105
Stakeholder Analysis, conducting, 103
Standard Deviation, calculating,
95-96
standard deviations, 36-39
overcoming, 190
Standard Work Analysis, 174
Standard Work operations,
212-213
managing, 213-214
Multiple Skills Matrix,
214-215
Standardize (*Seiketsu*) discipline,
211-212
Standardized Work, 22
statistical analysis
conducting, 189
methods, 190-192
statistical focus, Lean Six
Sigma, 50-51
statistical means, 36
statistical populations, 37
statistical quality control (SQC),
55
statistical sampling, data collection, 141-143
steering committees, 305
Steering Committee Review,
331
Store (*Seiton*) discipline, 211
storyboards, Project
Storyboards, 266-270
strategically critical elements,
projects, identifying, 74
striving for perfection, 5, 8

structured methodologies,
deploying, 279-282
Suppliers-Inputs-Process-
Outputs-Customers (SIPOC)
Maps. *See* SIPOC (Suppliers-
Inputs-Process-Outputs-
Customers) Map
Sustain (*Shitsuke*) discipline, 212
sustaining projects, 332
Swim Lane Map, 118-120
Swim Lanes, 82

**T**

tactically necessary elements,
projects, identifying, 74
Takt Time, 137-138
capability analysis, 148-149
inventory levels, analyzing,
170-171
Taylor, Fredrick, 5
*Team Leader's Guide to Lean
Kaizen Events, A*, 125
teams, identifying project teams,
102-103
testing
for averages, 191-192
for proportions, 192
Theory of Inventive Problem
Solving (TRIZ), 221
time
cycle time, 5
primary performance metric
8.5-by-11 Syndrome, 120
determining, 117-124
Process Flow diagrams,
117-118
Swim Lane Map,
118-120
VSM (Value Stream
Map), 121-124
Takt Time, 137-138
time-based requirements, customers, 137-138
timelines, establishing, 107

tollgate reviews
   conducting, 111-112,
      205-206, 272-273
      Improve phase, 239-240
   processes, conducting,
      149-150
toolbox (Six Sigma), 25
TPE (Total Performance
   Excellence), 282-285
TPM (Total Productive
   Maintenance), 28
   cellular layout, 216, 217
   OEE (Overall Equipment
      Effectiveness), 177
TPS (Toyota Production
   System), 55
   Lean, 4
   origins of, 6-8
TQC (Total Quality Control),
   27
TQM (Total Quality
   Management), 28
training
   Black Belts, 324-325
   deployment infrastructure,
      installing, 311
   Functional Champions, 322
   Green Belts, 324-325
   Kaizen Event Facilitators,
      325
   Master Black Belt, 333
   Process Owners, 321-322
   Project Champions, 321
transitions, projects, 270-272
transportation, waste of, 14-15
trends
   Control Charts, 260
   processes, 144
TRIZ (Theory of Inventive
   Problem Solving), 221
twenty-percent rule, 135
Type I errors, 190
Type II errors, 190

## U–V

*u*-Charts, 257
UCL (upper control limits),
   data, 144
upstream activities, processes,
   37

value
   importance of, 8
   VSM (Value Stream Map),
      70-71
value-added labels, processes,
   124
value-added processes and non-
   value-added processes, compared, 83, 84
value-enabling labels, processes,
   125
Value Creation, 53-54
values, p-Values, 190
Value Stream Map (VSM). *See*
   VSM (Value Stream Map)
value streams, importance of, 8
variable data, MSA
   (Measurement System
   Analysis), 131-134
variance
   ANOVA (Analysis of
      Variance), 199
   F-tests, 203
variation, 36, 40
   Common Cause variation, 40
   processes
      shift and drift, 43-46
      twenty-percent rule, 135
   Special Cause variation, 40
Visio, creating flow charts with,
   121
vision (Six Sigma), 24
VOC (Voice of the Customer)
   collecting, 85-86
   projects, 68-70
VSM (Value Stream Map), 82,
   121-124, 167
   projects, 70, 71

## W

waiting as waste, 12
Waldo, Wes, 125, 217
waste, 11-12
   identifying, 166-167
   intellect, 16-17
   inventory, 16
   motion, 14
   *muda*, 166
   *mura*, 166
   overproduction, 13
   processing, 15-16
   rework, 13-14
   transportation, 14-15
   waiting, 12
Welch, Jack, 29
Whirlpool, contributions to
   Lean Six Sigma, 58-59
Will, George, 92
Womack, James, 8-9
work, Standardized Work, 22
work-in-progress inventory, 168
Workload Balance, determining,
   173-174
workloads, balancing, 20
writing problem statements,
   78-80

## X

*x*-bar & R Control Charts, 257
*x*-bar & S Control Charts, 257
*x*s
   data collection, 180-183
      check sheets, 182
      computer databases,
         180-181
      Control Charts, 182
      forms, 181
      independent observation,
         182
      logs, 181

prioritizing, 194-195
    C&E (Cause-and-Effect)
    Matrix, 195
    Critical X Worksheet,
    194-195

# Y–Z

*Y* (one output feature), 91
*Y*-related project metrics, defining, 91-92
$Y = f(x)$ equation, 30-31
  stating, 201-205, 226-229
yields, processes, RTY (Rolled
  Throughput Yield), 42, 43
*Y*s
  correlation, 195-197
    ANOVA (Analysis of
    Variance), 199
    DOE (Design of
    Experiments), 197-199
    Monte Carlo Simulation,
    197-201

Z-score, 36